China and its Regions

NEW HORIZONS IN INTERNATIONAL BUSINESS

Series Editor: Peter J. Buckley
Centre for International Business,
University of Leeds (CIBUL), UK

The New Horizons in International Business series has established itself as the world's leading forum for the presentation of new ideas in international business research. It offers pre-eminent contributions in the areas of multinational enterprise – including foreign direct investment, business strategy and corporate alliances, global competitive strategies, and entrepreneurship. In short, this series constitutes essential reading for academics, business strategists and policy makers alike.

Titles in the series include:

Corporate Governance and Globalization
Long Range Planning Issues
Edited by Stephen S. Cohen and Gavin Boyd

The European Union and Globalisation
Towards Global Democratic Governance
Brigid Gavin

Globalization and the Small Open Economy
Edited by Daniel Van Den Bulcke and Alain Verbeke

Entrepreneurship and the Internationalisation of Asian Firms
An Institutional Perspective
Henry Wai-chung Yeung

The World Trade Organization in the New Global Economy
Trade and Investment Issues in the Millennium Round
Edited by Alan M. Rugman and Gavin Boyd

Japanese Subsidiaries in the New Global Economy
Edited by Paul W. Beamish, Andrew Delios and Shige Makino

Globalizing Europe
Deepening Integration, Alliance Capitalism and Structural Statecraft
Edited by Thomas L. Brewer, Paul A. Brenton and Gavin Boyd

China and its Regions
Economic Growth and Reform in Chinese Provinces
Edited by Mary-Françoise Renard

Emerging Issues in International Business Research
Edited by Masaaki Kotabe and Preet S. Aulakh

Network Knowledge in International Business
Edited by Sarianna M. Lundan

Learning in the Internationalisation Process of Firms
Edited by Anders Blomstermo and D. Deo Sharma

Alliance Capitalism and Corporate Management
Entrepreneurial Cooperation in Knowledge Based Economies
Edited by John H. Dunning and Gavin Boyd

China and its Regions

Economic Growth and Reform in Chinese Provinces

Edited by
Mary-Françoise Renard
University of Auvergne,
CERDI-IDREC, CNRS

NEW HORIZONS IN INTERNATIONAL BUSINESS

Edward Elgar
Cheltenham, UK • Northampton, MA, USA

Published by
Edward Elgar Publishing Limited
Glensanda House
Montpellier Parade
Cheltenham
Glos GL50 1UA
UK

Edward Elgar Publishing, Inc.
136 West Street
Suite 202
Northampton
Massachusetts 01060
USA

A catalogue record for this book
is available from the British Library

Library of Congress Cataloguing in Publication Data
China and its regions : economic growth and reform in Chinese provinces / edited by Mary-Françoise Renard.
p. cm. — (New horizons in international business)
Papers presented at a symposium held on Oct. 22–23, 1998 at the Center for Studies and Research on International Development in France.
Includes index.
1. China—Economic conditions—1976- —Congresses. 2. China—Economic policy—1976- —Congresses. I. Renard, Mary-Françoise. II. Series.

HC427.92 .C45145268 2002
338.951—dc21 2001051254

ISBN 1 84064 581 4
Printed and bound in Great Britain by MPG Books Ltd, Bodmin, Cornwall

Contents

List of Figures

List of Tables

List of Contributors

Martine Audibert is a Research Director, CNRS, CERDI, France.

Jean-François Brun is a Senior Lecturer, University Blaise Pascal and CERDI-IDREC, France.

Fang Cai is a Professor at the Chinese Academy of Social Science, China.

Ningshan Chen is an Associate Professor at Weifang Medical College and Beijing Medical University, China.

Jean-Louis Combes is a Professor at the University of Auvergne, CERDI, France.

Sylvianne Guillaumont Jeanneney is a Professor at the University of Auvergne, CERDI.

Patrick Guillaumont is a Professor at the University of Auvergne, and President of CERDI, France.

Ping Hua is a Research Economist, CERDI-IDREC, France.

Olivier Jammes is a PhD Student, CERDI-IDREC, France.

Aart Kraay is an Economist at The World Bank, United States.

Shantong Li is a Senior Research Fellow, Development Research Centre, The State Council, China.

Shi Li is a Professor at the Chinese Academy of Social Sciences, China.

Zhou Li is a Professor at the Chinese Academy of Social Science, China.

Justin Yifu Lin is a Professor at Beijing University and Hong Kong University of Science and Technology, China.

Jacky Mathonat is a Professor at the University of Auvergne, CERDI, France.

Barry Naughton is a Professor at the University of California, San Diego, Graduate School of International Relations and Pacific Studies, United States.

Sandra Poncet is a PhD Student at CERDI-IDREC, France.

Mary-Françoise Renard is a Professor at the University of Auvergne, and Head of IDREC at CERDI-IDREC.

Qiumei Yang is an Economist at the OECD Development Centre, France.

Wing Thye Woo is a Professor, in the Economics Department, University of California, Davis, United States.

Yanrui Wu is a Lecturer at the Department of Economics, University of Western Australia, Australia.

Fan Zhai is a Senior Associate Research Fellow, Development Research Centre, The State Council, China.

Preface

The economic openness of China and the implementation of the reforms were accompanied by profound changes in economic organization, notably in its spatial dimension. The size of the country, the importance given to regional policies and the role of decentralization have provoked great interest in regional disparities, their causes and their implications. The object of this work is to analyze the impact of Chinese openness, through various contributions, on its spatial dynamics and the resulting inequalities.

The question of Chinese openness has often been discussed and leaves no doubt. Nonetheless, it is a complex notion which is difficult to measure, especially when we wish to apply the same criteria as those used for western countries. It is thus essential that we keep in mind the size of China and consider not only its global openness, but also that of each of the regions which make up the country.

Several authors observe an increase in inequalities with respect to both growth and income, resulting from the different aptitudes of the regions to seize the new opportunities presented by the development of the markets. It is important to place this in a historical context in order to analyze the spatial disparities, as regional policy has had an important role for a long time, whether concerning redistribution, before 1978, or the valorization of comparative advantages since then. The results are, therefore, different according to whether or not the region benefited from significant subsidies from the state before the implementation of the reforms. There is, thus, an increase in inter-regional disparities.

International openness can affect these disparities via regional specialization. Indeed, the pursuit of economies of scale and the valorization of their comparative advantage leads the regions to increase their specialization, the evolution of which presents a link with their degree of openness.

Observing regional disparities leads us to think that, in the future, the development of Chinese competitiveness will be accompanied by a polarization of its industrial activity in certain privileged regions. We should, then, hope that a diffusion to other regions will limit the damaging effects of this process. We also observe an increase in productivity in the country as a whole. Similarly, Chinese membership of the WTO will probably lead to an increase in the inequalities of income, especially between rural and urban zones. An appropriate fiscal system could compensate for losses due to a reduction in customs duties. Regional inequalities also result from the localization of direct foreign investment, the distribution of which shows a positive relation with the level of development of human capital. It has also been observed that this investment does not only have a short-term effect in promoting Chinese growth, but also has a more long-term effect through externalities, thanks to the incorporation of new know-how and the existence of a diffusion process for these effects.

In general, the institutional changes which accompanied international openness and the development of a market economy led to an increase in the disparities between different groups, – qualified and non-qualified workers, the urban and rural populations, or even the respective inhabitants of the three groups of regions: eastern, western and central. In each of these cases, there is a marked increase in the inequalities between each group and sometimes an even more marked increase within each group. Breaking down incomes according to source also leads to the conclusion that there is an increase in inequalities greatly due to localization.

However, these disparities must not hide the fact that the increase in incomes has an effect on several domains, notably in the field of health. In this case, the effects of openness are only indirect, as is shown by the study on infant mortality. Here too, we can again note an increase in the disparities between the coastal provinces and the others. The inequalities are also perceptible if we consider them at company level, as we note a certain delay for rural firms in the non-coastal regions. The differences are also a result of the existence of learning effects. Indeed, exports are all the more accompanied by improved performances if we are dealing with long-standing exporters.

Observing these facts since the implementation of the reforms leads to the conclusion that, although it has been accompanied by an improvement in performances, Chinese international openness has also been the source of an increase in inter-regional inequalities. This is not in contradiction with the development of a context of competition: however, this phenomenon implies an additional constraint for the government with respect to redistribution.

These chapters were presented as draft versions during a symposium organized by the Chinese Economy Research Institute (IDREC) at the Center for Studies and Research on International Development (CERDI), 22–23 October 1998. Some of them have been published in the *Revue d'Economie du Développement* under the auspices of P. Guillaumont and S. Démurger.

This symposium was organized with the support of the French Ministry for Foreign Affairs and the Regional Council of the Auvergne.

I would like to thank all the authors for their participation in this work, and also Sylvette Prévost for having typed part of the manuscript. I wish to extend my thanks to J.F. Brun for his help, to Patrick Guillaumont, President of CERDI and Patrick Plane, Director of CERDI for their support.

1. On the measurement of the openness of the Chinese economy

Jean-Louis Combes, Patrick Guillaumont and Sandra Poncet*

1 INTRODUCTION

Once again this year we will not be at leisure to dress in silk;
Tomorrow we will go and sell it at the west gate.
Fan Tch'eng-ta (1126–1193)

Nobody denies that the Chinese economy has opened up to the exterior over the past 20 years. However, everyone knows that the idea of economic openness is very complex and difficult to measure in most economies, even more so in China. In this chapter, we endeavour to find a way to represent Chinese openness, a way that is quantitative, simple and at the same time capable of reflecting different aspects thereof.

We cannot forget the long history of China's foreign relations or its geographical situation. Gentelle (1994) thus maintains that for the Chinese government, 'openness is the opportunity of having access to the world without the world being able to enter China. Openness', he writes, 'is a palliative, a defence mechanism which should leave the time to save itself. That is why openness can only be progressive' (p. 98). With respect to the geographic orientation of openness, the same author quoting Creyssey (1934), recalls the intentions according to which 'formerly, China faced the north and west and turned its back on the Pacific. The Jade Gate in the Great Wall of China, which opens on Kansou (Gansu), was the main entry to China… Henceforth, it looks towards the Pacific' (Creyssey, 1934). In brief, voluntary and progressive openness takes the place of an openness brutally imposed in the past.

* CERDI (Centre for Study and Research in International Development), Université d'Auvergne and CNRS, 65, bd François Mitterrand, 63000 Clermont-Ferrand.

Facts demonstrate that internal trade within China is more liberal today than it was 20 years ago, and that this liberalization has been accompanied by a spectacular increase in trade. However, the picture becomes less clear when we attempt to situate China and its development with respect to other developing countries by applying comparable criteria, aimed at capturing political openness to the exterior and the development thereof.

Indeed, the fact that China is the most populous country in the world brings with it two consequences for measuring openness. The first is that we must take the population figure into account when we endeavour to compare not only the relative significance of foreign trade, but also the extent to which it is a result of the policy implemented. The demographic dimension is essential in distinguishing between observed openness and openness policy.

The second consequence of the size of China is that its 31 provinces can be considered as countries of medium or large importance. Openness to the exterior for each province – outside China and to the other Chinese provinces – can be observed statistically as for any other country. Moreover, as the provinces have progressively acquired a certain autonomy in their economic affairs, it is legitimate to consider the more or less open nature of the policy followed by each of the provinces and to examine whether or not the indicators serving as a comparison of openness policies between various countries of the world can be transposed to a comparison between the Chinese provinces.

This chapter is thus divided into three parts: the definition of the basic concepts, used later, with respect to openness; the analysis of Chinese openness compared to that of other countries; and the analysis of the relative openness of the different Chinese provinces with respect to each other.

2 AMBIGUITIES OF OPENNESS: OBSERVED OPENNESS AND OPENNESS POLICY

As the observed openness of economies depends on both structural factors and economic policy, it is logical to distinguish it from openness policy.

Observed Openness, Trade and Financial

The openness of an economy can be seen from different perspectives. Let us briefly recall the main indicators employed in this domain, both with respect to foreign trade and the movement of capital, with a view to applying them to the case of China.

Trade openness is generally calculated by the ratio of the sum of exports and imports to GDP, or $(X + M)/GDP$. We prefer to retain the trade of goods *and* services (not factors) rather than goods alone, if the statistics relative to services are available. It is often the case that the ratio of exports only to GDP is preferred: indeed, the ratio of imports to GDP is less sure in the interpretation as it can be reduced by protectionist policy as well as by increased competitiveness.[1] It is true that the rate of exports itself is of uncertain significance in that it is the ratio of a turnover to value added (which explains why it can be higher than 100% in certain countries, such as Singapore): the significant ratio would be the ratio of GDP to the value added included in the exports. Lacking this, we use the gross rate of exports, or better still, the ratio of exports to the total of available resources $[X/(GDP + M)]$.[2]

Observed financial openness can be defined in many ways. The most comparable to the indicators of commercial openness is the ratio of capital *flows* to GDP, either using only the entries, that is, gross flows (in a similar way to the rate of exports), or the sum of entries and outgoings (similar to the sum of the rates of exports and imports), but naturally not the net flows which mean nothing with respect to openness. Here, as an indicator of financial openness for all countries, we retain the ratio of the sum of annual flows (both assets and liabilities) of capital as direct investments and portfolio investments to GDP. With regards to the Chinese provinces, the only data available concerns direct investments.[3]

Whichever indicator is used, the question remains as to what extent the observed rates and their evolution result from economic policy rather than from factors independent of this.

Openness Policy: Can It Be Measured?

It is known that in China, as elsewhere, the policy of openness is infinitely complex, that it is first and foremost a state of mind of the governors, an attitude, a desire, which is then translated by multiple measures, directly affecting trade, but also the exchange rate, the regulation of activities and infrastructures, and that in the final accounts it is shown through more intense foreign trade and capital movements. We understand, then, that various methods have been used to appreciate the more or less outward-looking nature of economic policies, and that the expression 'outward-looking policies' can be understood in several different ways. Opinions differ as to whether or not these indicators are equivalent in the end. Edwards (1998) maintained that they are roughly the same (by virtue of their power to predict growth); on the contrary, Pritchett (1996) demonstrated that the rank correlations established between several of the indicators are very weak.

Certain indicators relate to the main instruments of policy likely to affect trade (average level of tariffs, percentage of liberalized imports, level of export taxes, appropriateness of exchange rates and so on, see, for example Sachs and Warner (1995)). The information supplied by these indicators for a country over time is naturally instructive. However, as it is a matter of comparing the openness of different countries, the choice made between these different aspects of the policy, and their possible weighting, is necessarily arbitrary.

Other indicators, on the contrary, attempt to capture the effect of multiple policy measures on observed trade, by comparing the value of the latter with a normal or expected value according to structural factors only. This is the method we developed in the past (compare Guillaumont 1985, 1989, 1994) and which we retain here in order to express openness in China by applying it, as was done recently (Combes et al. 2000), to the movements of capital and no longer specifically to trade, and also over several periods. The basic idea is to estimate, for a number of countries (and over a number of periods) the expected value of an observed openness indicator, by including in the function all the structural factors, independent of economic policy, capable of influencing it, and these only; the residual is thus an indicator of 'revealed' openness policy, as long as the function is suitably specified and that the structural factors particular to each country do not influence the residual. Let us underline the fact that the indicator of obtained openness policy is an indicator of openness relative to the other countries in the sample. If we consider a panel model over several periods (Combes et al. 2000), the indicator can also permit the monitoring of an evolution. However, in any case, the average of the residuals being zero, the indicator of openness is relative to the other countries as well as, in a panel case, to the different periods covered.

In dealing with the policy of openness, a further ambiguity should be noted. Revealed openness is, by definition, *a result indicator, not an instrument indicator*. It is thus influenced by any measure which converges on that result. Openness in the literature is often assimilated to the absence of distortions (Balassa, 1985, stated the absence of bias against exports) or to competitiveness. However, the promotion of exports can be guaranteed both by competitiveness of activities – by the market – or by an interventionist policy of encouraging exports or even of authoritarian allocation of a part of production to exports. In the case of China, as soon as a relatively long period is covered, this ambiguity in the revealed openness indicator – controlled or competitive openness – must be kept in mind. More generally, it leads us to distinguish between the *openness of borders*, which corresponds to the promotion of trade, and the *openness of markets*, which implies free competition of activities: *The Economist* (1998) maintained that the Asian crisis was due not to an excess openness towards foreign capital, but rather to insufficient openness towards competition between foreign banks and local banks.

3 OPENNESS IN CHINA COMPARED TO THAT OF OTHER COUNTRIES: IS IT SPECIFIC?

The stages, during which China seemed to open up to the outside have been described and analysed many times (for example Cabrillac, 1997; Fukasuku and Solignac Lecomte, 1996; Hua, 1996; Lemoine, 1994; Pin, 1994; Schmiedel, 1998). An idea often put forward is that China's rapid growth in foreign trade since the beginning of the reforms (1978) until the present day has moved China from a relatively low level of openness to a normal situation (compare, for example, World Bank, 1997, pp. 84–5).

Observed Openness: Rapid Growth, but Sensitive to the Method of Measurement

The evolution of observed commercial openness can be traced with the help of Figures 1.1–1.3.

Figure 1.1 describes the evolution of various indicators of observed openness, measured using Chinese statistical data: the ratio of exports to product (X/GDP), the rate of commercial openness $(X + M)/GDP$, the ratio of exports to supply ($X/(GDP + M)$), and finally the ratio of the rate of openness to supply $(X + M)/(GDP + M)$. The observed growth is spectacular, since the rate of exports compared to the GDP increases from 5% in 1978 to 20% in 1997, and the rate of openness from 10% to 36%. Let us note that the increase in the rate of openness is obviously smaller if the ratio $X/(GDP + M)$ or $(X + M)/(GDP + M)$ is used, that is, openness compared to total supply or demand: it increases then from 4% to 18% and from 9% to 32%, respectively. Another way of relativizing the usual rate of openness $(X + M)/GDP$ consists in specifying that about half of Chinese trade (according to Chinese statistics) is trade based on the assembly industry, that is, products imported with a view to re-exporting including little value added.

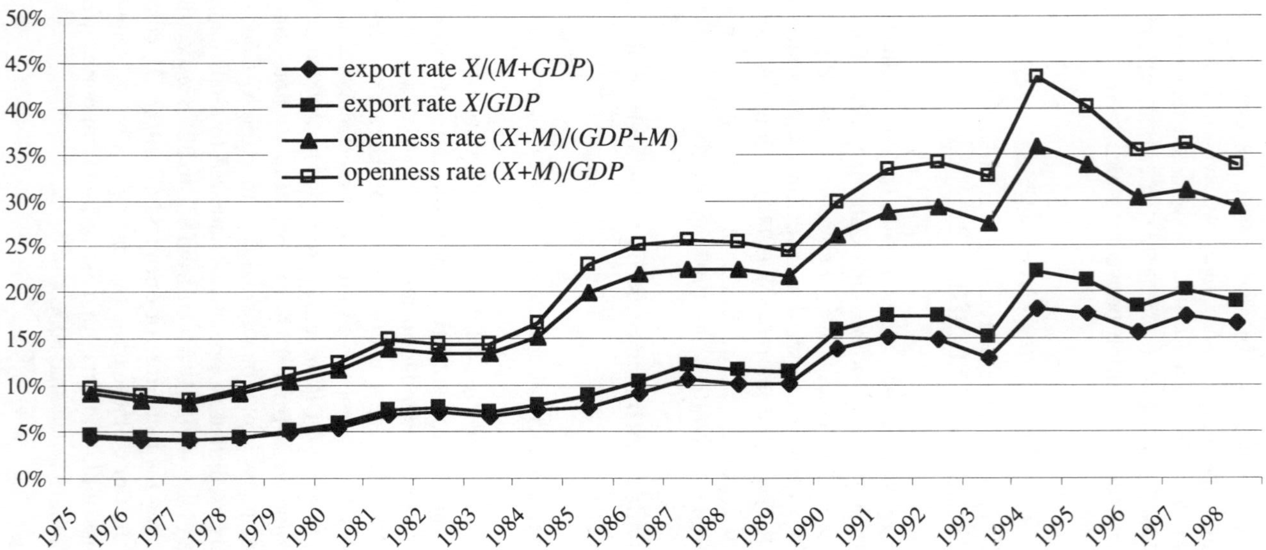

Figure 1.1 Comparison of Chinese trade openness according to different definitions (Chinese Statistical Yearbook)

The apparently cyclical nature of the rate of openness, common to the various indicators, can be explained mainly by the mechanical impact of the evolution of the real exchange rate, the depreciation increasing the internal relative price of exports and imports. The combined reaction of imports and exports also translates the fact that Chinese imports are largely destined for transformation into exported products (compare, World Bank 1997, p. 85).[4]

Does the observed evolution depend on the sources used? Figure 1.2 shows that the evolution traced using Chinese data and data provided by the World Bank (*World Development Indicators,* 1998) hardly differs in its general tendency (although the last data relate to the trade of goods and services).

The evolution of the rates of trade openness taken from Summers and Heston (Penn Tables, 1991, 1997) – only available from 1978 to 1992 – is itself little different from that obtained using Chinese statistics: the departure point of 1978 is a little higher [$(X + M)$/GDP = 12.5%] because, we imagine, of a re-estimation of the initial level of Chinese GDP.

In any case, the rates of openness of Summers and Heston do not relate to the GDP estimation in purchasing power parity (PPP). We know that the estimations of Chinese GDP made in PPP lead to a considerable revaluation of the latter (compare notably the works of Ren Ruon, 1997). If we compare, for example, the estimation of Chinese GDP in 1997 in PPP to that given in current dollars, according to the *World Development Report* by the World Bank (1998), the ratio is 1 to 4: the rate of openness estimated in ratio to the GDP in PPP would then be divided by 4 (it would no longer be equal to 36% but 9% … or if we estimate it in ratio to total supply it would no longer be 32% but 8 % …). This rate translates the sum of the real contribution of imports to the global supply and the real share of resources or global expenditure allocated to exports.

In fact, resorting to estimations in PPP in order to measure openness, and especially its evolution has, in the case of China, rather surprising results. The bottom line on Figure 1.2 shows the evolution of the rate of openness calculated using the GDP estimation in PPP at current international prices (data from Summers and Heston) and the available data for Chinese foreign trade expressed in current dollars (CHELEM data in this case).[5] The rate of openness seems to rise from 2.3% in 1970 to 4.4% in 1978 and 7.4% in 1992. Normally, the relative deviation between GDP measured at the country's prices and GDP measured in international prices (PPP) is comparatively larger the smaller the per capita income of the country becomes, (Balsassa theorem and works of the international comparison programme, compare Balassa, 1994; Baneth, 1994); as a result, as growth has been very strong in

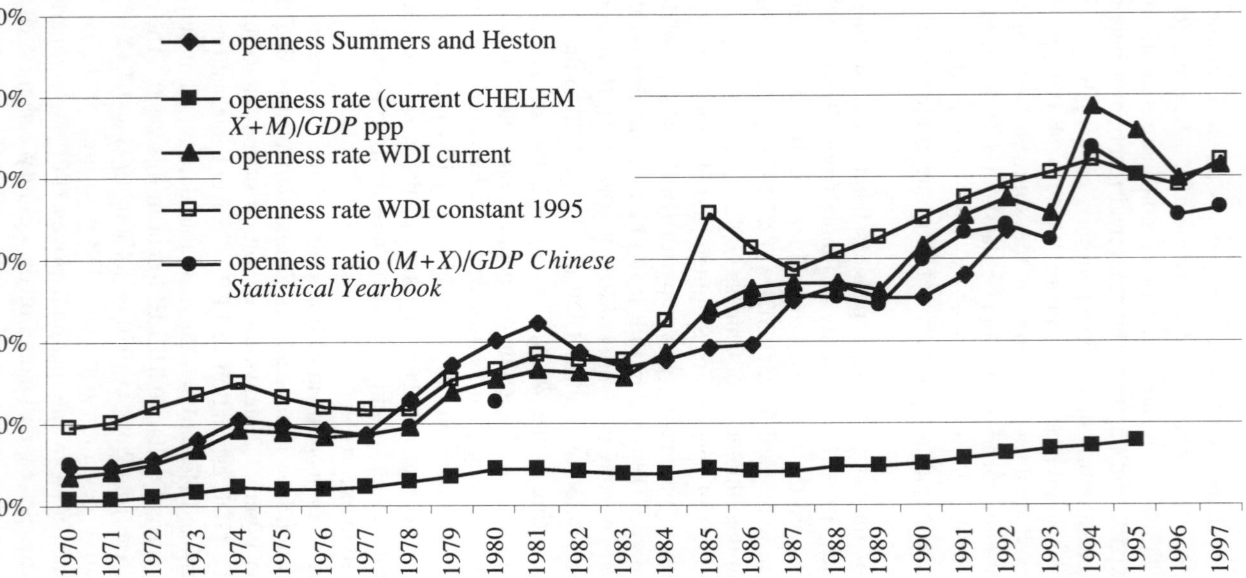

*Figure 1.2 Comparison of Chinese trade openness according to different definitions (*Chinese Statistical Yearbook*)*

China over the past 20 years, the rate of openness as a ratio to GDP at international prices should have increased more quickly than the ratio to GDP at local prices, which was not the case.[6]

Figure 1.3 concerns financial openness. It is measured here by the ratio of direct and portfolio investments (therefore only the gross long-term investments made in China, without taking into account the very weak flows in the opposite direction) to GDP. Here once again, and more markedly, its growth which is in the main ascribable to direct investment, is very rapid and recent: the ratio, which is 1% from 1985 to 1991, increases rapidly in 1992 and 1993, reaching about 7% in 1993–1994 only to drop to 5% again in 1996 (percentages with respect to GDP expressed in current dollars).

Comparison to Other Countries

Despite their strong increase, the rates of openness of the Chinese economy seem to remain greatly inferior to those of other countries.

Tables 1.1 and 1.2 allow us to situate the rates of commercial openness and financial openness of China per large period (see in Appendix the exhaustive list of countries by geographical zone).

*Table 1.1 Rate of trade openness (*X + M*)/*GDP *(simple averages in percentages)*

Low and intermediate revenue economies					High revenue economies	All countries
	China	Asia	Latin America	Sub-Saharan Africa		
1971–75	7	44	59	64	70	62
1976–86	17	67	76	70	83	74
1987–95	27	70	70	67	85	73

Although China remains a relatively closed country compared to the rest of the world, and even compared to other Asian countries, we note nonetheless a very clear tendency towards openness from the end of the Maoist period.

The main conclusion to be drawn from Table 1.2 is a strong increase in the financial openness of China since 1987, which pushes the ratio of long-term capital inflows as a percentage of GDP to a slightly higher level than the average for Asian countries.

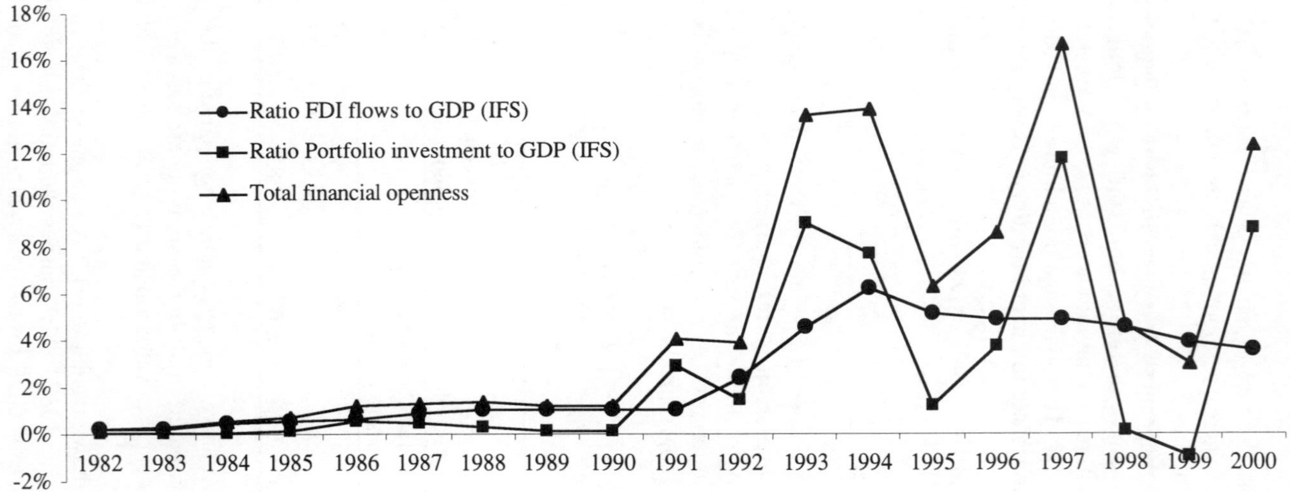

Figure 1.3 Evolution of Chinese financial openness (IFS data)

Table 1.2 Rate of financial openness (simple averages in percentages)

Low and intermediate revenue economies					High revenue economies	All countries
	China	Asia	Latin America	Sub-Saharan Africa		
1971–75	*na*	4	2	4	3	3
1976–86	1	1	2	1	4	2
1987–95	3.5	3	5	2	8	4

Na: no available.

China's Policy of Openness: Short of or Beyond the Asian Norm?

The evolution that we have just observed certainly reflects a more open policy than in the past. However, is this policy more open or less open than that of other developing countries? As shown earlier, it is very difficult to construct an indicator of openness policy which can be used to compare a large number of countries based on the observation of measures taken with respect to foreign trade and the control of exchange. Here, we resort to the indicator of openness policy presented above, according to which the more or less open nature of economic policy is measured by the share of observed commercial openness, which on a transversal basis, cannot be explained by structural factors. In other words, it is a matter of openness revealed by these results and which therefore takes into account the combined effect of the multiple measures of economic policy, without resorting to subjective weightings.

The indicators of openness policy thus established, not only for commercial but also for financial openness, are calculated as the residuals of normalization equations (compare Combes et al., 2000). Openness policy is measured by the deviation between the effective or observed value of the rate of openness of a variable and its value, estimated using a combination of exogenous explicative factors, such as the size of the economy or the localization of the country. The effective value of the rates of openness is an average over three periods. The rate of trade openness is ratio to GDP of the sum of annual export receipts and import expenditure for goods and services.[7] The rate of financial openness is the ratio of GDP to the sum of annual flows (both assets and liabilities) of capital as direct and portfolio investments.[8] These variables are retained as logarithms. The residual of the estimated equation can therefore be interpreted as an indicator of the openness policy of the country, more precisely the more or less open nature of the policy of a country relative to the average of the sample. Of course, using a normalization equation presupposes that a certain number of conditions be fulfilled: the exogenous factors must have been clearly identified;[9] moreover, the residual must not result from random factors independent of the country's will.

The structural factors retained are very close for both commercial and financial openness. The first is country size, measured by the population napierian logarithm for the beginning of the period (lnpop_{it}), which is a factor of less commercial and financial openness. Indeed, the larger a country is, the less it is specialized. Furthermore, the larger dimension generally brings with it higher savings rates and lower foreign capital inflows.

Moreover, it would seem normal that the existence of mining and petroleum resources in a country increases its export rate. As the mining and petroleum sectors of a country are highly capital intensive, it is possible that they also generate significant capital inflows. This variable is measured by a logarithm of the rate of mining and petroleum exports: Ln$mining_{it}$.

It is also plausible that the greater the level of development, the greater a country's capacity to specialize and be competitive with respect to a wide range of products. Moreover, with the increase in per capita product (expressed as a logarithm lny_{it}, we witness a differentiation in demand which is favourable to commercial openness. With regard to financial openness, we might think that the more a country is developed, the more the rate of savings increases, which would certainly reduce the need for foreign financing, but would also increase the capacity to lend to foreign countries. Furthermore, the economy is increasing in complexity and along with this, there is a greater differentiated demand for capital.

The most landlocked countries are logically the least commercially open as a result of transport costs, but these costs have few reasons to affect financial openness. A dummy variable (*landlocked*$_i$) is thus introduced in the commercial openness equation.

Finally, transport costs also depend on the average distance (orthodromic) of each country from the principal world markets: ln$dist_i$. These are defined as the ten foremost world economic powers according to the criterion of GDP.

The normalization equations are estimated by the ordinary least squares for a sample of 148 countries at every level of development. For each country, three observation points are available, corresponding to the periods 1971–75, 1976–86 and 1987–95. The Student *t* are corrected for heteroskedasticity by White's method. The results of the normalization equations are shown in Table 1.3 and correspond to the proposed hypotheses.

Table 1.3 The normalization equations for the rates of openness

Explained variable	Ln (rate of commercial openness)	Ln (rate of financial openness)
Number of observations	331	249
Constant	5.27	-6.97
	(5.44)***	(6.26)***
Ln$pop_{i,t}$	-0.24	-0.19
	(18.39)***	(2.48)**
Ln$mining_{i,t}$	0.05	0.32
	(5.76)***	(4.37)***
Ln$y_{i,t}$	0.11	0.96
	(4.26)***	(7.18)***
$Landlocked_i$	-0.07	
	(1.30)	
Ln$dist_i$	-0.18	
	(1.88)*	
R^2 adjusted	0.56	0.29

Note: The Student *t* are shown in brackets. Significant at *** 1%, *** 5%, * 10%.

We use Chow tests to check, on the one hand, the stability of the coefficients in the normalization equations according to the level of development and, on the other hand, the fact that China is not an outlier in that its omission from the sample does not significantly alter the coefficients.

The residuals of the normalization equations which are assimilated to indicators of commercial and financial openness policy are shown in Tables 1.4 and 1.5 per period and category of country. Let us recall that these purely relative indicators simply situate the policy of one country compared to the others. That is to say that a zero residual does not mean that a country has not adopted an openness policy, but simply that its choices are no different from those of the average in the sample. Panel estimation allows us to obtain an average of non-zero residuals for each period of the estimation and thus to locate not only the deviations in residuals from one country to the next, but also the variations in residuals through time, thus giving a progression of openness policy.

Table 1.4 Indicators of relative trade openness policies (as percentage of GDP)

Low and intermediate revenue economies					High revenue economies	All countries
	China	Asia	Latin America	Sub-Saharan Africa		
1971–75	-6	4	-12	-3	7	-1
1976–86	3	13	-9	4	19	6
1987–95	13	24	-8	8	20	9

Table 1.5 Indicators of relative financial openness policies (as percentage of GDP)

Low or intermediate revenue economies					High revenue economies	All countries
	China	Asia	Latin America	Sub-Saharan Africa		
1971–75	*na*	1	0	3	0	1
1976–86	1	1	0	1	0	0
1987–95	3	3	2	1	3	2

Na: no available.

We thus observe, for all countries, an orientation of trade policies towards a greater openness. This evolution is particularly notable for China. Unsurprisingly, we note a relatively closed position of China for the first period. However, it is notable that openness is already to be witnessed as of the second period. This position from the beginning of the reforms can be explained not only by the level of factors having acted as normalizers (large dimension, low per capita product), but also by the fact that China practised a planned openness policy, which only progressively became a policy of market openness. When we arrive at the third period, the level reached by the openness policy indicator rises above the average level for all the countries on the planet. It is significantly higher than that of Africa. However it remains clearly below the level reached by the Asian countries as a whole. Figure 1.4 allows us to visualize this evolution of China's commercial openness policy, which has probably favoured rapid growth.

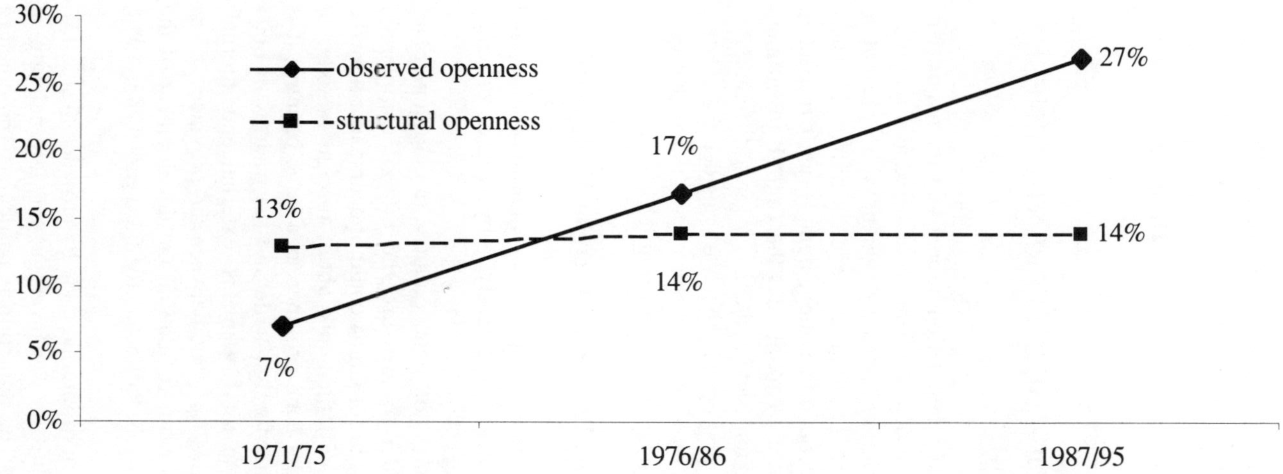

Figure 1.4 Comparison of Chinese rates of openness: observed and structural

With respect to financial openness, we can observe in China policies which are more and more favourable and becoming even as favourable, during the third period, as those of the rest of Asia as a whole. This position is thus, in essence, due to direct foreign investment of which China is one of the most important beneficiaries.

4 RELATIVE OPENNESS OF THE DIFFERENT CHINESE PROVINCES

The considerable dimension – be it by population or area – of the majority of the Chinese provinces itself justifies each one being considered as a relatively large country and that their observed rates of openness be presented. However, it is noted more and more often that each province is partly autonomous with regards to its economic policy, notably with respect to foreign trade (Lee, 1998) and foreign capital, and the central government even deliberately endeavours to favour trade and activities in a differentiated way for each province. It is thus appropriate that we consider the relative 'openness policy' of the provinces by applying the same method as that used to situate the openness of China compared to other countries.

Observed Openness in the Different Provinces: Diverging Evolutions

Tables 1.6, 1.7 and 1.8 present the rates of openness – interior, exterior and total (sum of the two previous rates) respectively – by type of province (landlocked, coastal or neighbouring coastal).

In dealing with the provinces of one country, a supplementary specification is necessary in order to measure the rate of commercial openness: the trade taken into account for China could of course be solely the trade vis-à-vis the exterior (we will then talk about foreign or external openness). However, if we consider each province as a large country, it is preferable to retain the sum of this foreign trade and the trade with other provinces (we will thus talk about total openness, external and internal: Table 1.8). In any case, the statistics for trade between the provinces, taken from the World Bank (1994) report on regulation and development of the internal Chinese market, could only be collected for the years 1985, 1988, 1990, 1991 and 1992.

Let us first consider the evolution of internal trade by province (Table 1.6) between 1985 and 1992. We note that, on average, the internal rate of openness ($X + M$/GDP) has fallen. The reduction is particularly pronounced before 1990 and then slows down. While inter-provincial trade progresses in value, it falls when compared to provincial GDP. The reduction in the rate of domestic openness is in contrast with the strong progression of foreign trade in the provinces both in value and relative to the GDP (the rates of average annual growth of exports and imports with the exterior are 28% and 20% respectively). Virtually all the provinces saw their rate of external openness, calculated in yuans, more than double between 1985 and 1992 (Table 1.7). In this way, trade in general developed more easily with the exterior than between the Chinese provinces. The World Bank (1994) notes that 'there was an increasing tendency for the provinces, taken individually, to behave as independent countries intensifying their links with the external world and, in relative terms, reducing their links with other provinces in the country' (p. 40).

Table 1.6 Average interior openness by province subgroups according to geographical position (per cent)

	1985	1988	1990	1991	1992
Coastal provinces	27.8	24.4	19.1	17.3	15.1
Neighbouring coastal provinces	23.8	25.6	21.9	20.6	20.1
Landlocked provinces	23.1	22.2	16.7	16.5	14.4
Total	24.8	23.9	18.9	17.8	16.1

Table 1.7 Average exterior openness by province subgroups according to geographical position (per cent)

	1985	1988	1990	1991	1992
Coastal provinces	16.26	19.47	25.10	28.37	30.58
Neighbouring coastal provinces	5.15	7.49	8.91	10.48	11.96
Landlocked provinces	3.74	5.10	5.58	6.90	8.53
Total	9.8	11.9	14.2	16.4	18.2

Behaviour, with respect to internal trade, certainly differs greatly from one province to the next. The internal rate of openness of the coastal provinces suffered a much more sudden fall than that of the other provinces, whereas on average their rate of openness to the exterior (Table 1.7) increased from 19.5% in 1988 to 30.6% in 1992. As for the provinces neighbouring the coastal provinces (neither landlocked nor coastal), they resisted strongly with respect to internal commercial openness and also experienced an expansion in their foreign trade. On the other hand, according to World Bank (1994), the rates of openness in the three town states (Beijing, Tianjin et Shanghai), which were (at the end of the 1980s) far superior to those in the other provinces, diminished over the years. The author of this remark suggests that 'these towns under the direct control of the central government have become more autarkic over time, notably in comparison to the other provinces' (p. 40).

Table 1.8 Average total openness by province subgroups according to geographical position (per cent)

	1985	1988	1990	1991	1992
Coastal provinces	46.2	48.2	46.6	45.7	47.2
Neighbouring coastal provinces	28.3	33.5	31.0	31.1	31.7
Landlocked provinces	27.4	27.9	22.9	24.2	24.0
Total	33.7	36.4	33.8	34.9	35.6

With regard to financial openness, we restrict our analysis to direct investments, which are the only movements of capital available at the level of the provinces. Figure 1.5 shows the evolution over time from 1983 to 1996 of the rate of direct foreign investment. The gap between the coastal and landlocked provinces (and to a lesser extent between the landlocked provinces bordering the coastal provinces and the others) is, according to the ratio of direct investment to GDP, very marked.[10] Whereas the level of the ratio was still negligible for each category in 1983, it reached a level, after a peak in 1994, common to the three categories of province but surely a result of the accounting effect of the depreciation of the renminbi, of a little more than 7% in 1995 in the coastal provinces, 2% in the neighbouring provinces and 1% in the other landlocked provinces.

Relevance of 'Provincial' Indicators of Openness Policy

The considerable dimension, in terms of population and area, of the different Chinese provinces, as well as their increasing autonomy, justifies the analysis of each province as a country. An indicator which expresses the commercial openness policy pertaining to each of the Chinese provinces can thus be calculated using the same method employed to situate China compared to the rest of the world. The indicator of openness policy is thus calculated as the residual of the normalization of the rate of total observed openness (inter-

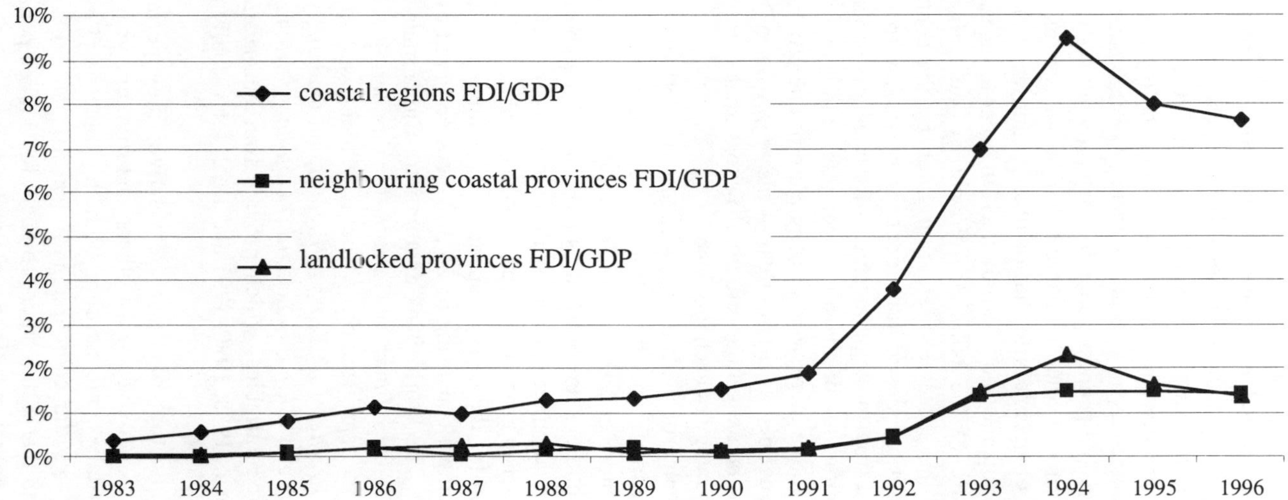

Figure 1.5 Evolution of FDI by Chinese group of regions

provincial and international) estimated as a function of its structural factors. The residual is supposed to express the relative will for openness of the different provinces considered, in a way, as autonomous entities. It is obvious that the provinces are not independent countries, but central policy can be considered vis-à-vis each province as an exogenous factor. We thus attempt to capture the autonomous share of openness policy for each province.

We are thus led to examine whether or not the indicators, serving to compare the Chinese policy of openness to that of other countries, can be used equally well to study the openness of the provinces, in order to measure the more or less open nature of the policies followed by the Chinese provinces, independently of the strategic orientation given by the central authorities. The relative political desire for openness particular to the provinces is thus distinguished from strategic incentives for openness decided by the central power. The indicator of the total openness policy of each province (which corresponds to the more or less open nature of one province compared to another) is thus defined as the residual of the regression of the rate of observed openness on the exogenous structural factors, that is to say independent of the particular strategy of each province.

Comparing the observed value of the rates of openness of a province to their expected value, as a function of only their structural factors, provides an indicator of policy which is more or less favourable to trade depending on each province if the same conditions are fulfilled as those used to elaborate an indicator of this type on an international scale: non-omission of an important structural factor, either in general or specific to the observed entity.

The normalization equation for the rates of openness is estimated by the ordinary least squares on a sample consisting of 26 provinces observed over four years from 1988 to 1992. The World Bank data on intra-China trade do not, indeed, include Hainan, Tibet, Hunan or Guizhou for this period. The other explicative variables of the regression come from the Chinese statistics: *China Regional Economy: A Profile of 17 Years of Reform and Opening-up*, *China Statistical Yearbooks* and *China Industrial Economic Statistical Yearbooks* for energy resource variables, which provide four observation points corresponding to the years 1988, 1990, 1991 and 1992, for virtually all the other provinces.

Let us recall that the indicators obtained are relative; they permit, therefore, the comparison of one province to the others, and from one year to the next. The model, which takes into account both the transversal and temporal dimensions, facilitates the comparison of 'specific strategy of openness' of one province with that of the other provinces for a given period and the evolution of the trade policy specific to a particular province in time, as the sum of the residuals is not zero for each period.

The Estimation of the Indicators

The rate of observed total trade openness of each province *i* at time *t* (*t* covering the four years 1988, 1990, 1991 and 1992) was calculated as a ratio to GDP (in current yuans) of the sum:

a) of annual inter-provincial export revenues and import expenditure for goods,
b) of international exports and imports converted into yuans at the official national exchange rate.

This rate of openness was estimated according to the same structural determinants as those used in the first part (population, initial per capita GDP, landlocked position, existence of mining resources) in order to compare the degree of voluntary openness in China to that of the other countries, and also according to other structural variables capable of influencing the openness of the Chinese provinces, such as area, the state of infrastructure and coastal position. The supplementary variables are introduced on the basis of the following hypotheses: we suppose that the greater the area, the greater the possibility for the province to diversify its economy and the greater the transport costs, subsequently the less incentive there is for the province to trade with the outside. Transport costs, which negatively influence trade, are also supposed to be just as high as the level of the infrastructure is low, which would justify the introduction of a variable representing the length of the transport infrastructures (motorways, railways, navigable waterways).

The estimation by the OLS focuses on 95 observations covering 26 provinces and four selected years. The Student *t* are corrected for heteroskedasticity by White's method. After having introduced three dummy variables to capture the possible specificity of one observation year, it would appear that only the dummy for 1988 is significant and positive.

The Ramsey test for functional form, carried out by calculating the *F*-statistics of the Ramsey Reset test, allows us to accept the hypothesis of good specification of the model.

The results are given in Table 1.9. The determination coefficient shows that 80.6% of the total variance is explained by the nine explanatory variables chosen.

Table 1.9 Normalization equation for the rates of total trade openness of the Chinese provinces 1988-1992

Explained variable	Ln (rate of commercial openness)	
Constant	-6.26	(-7.73)***
Ln$pop_{i,t-1}$	-0.268	(-4.78)***
Ln$y_{i,t-1}$	0.56	(8.09)***
$Mining_{i,t}$	-7.07	(-5.14)***
$Mining_{i,t}$*$Ress10_{i,t}$	4.02	(3.60)***
Ln$area_i$	-0.057	(-1.85)*
Ln$infra_{i,t-1}$	0.41	(4.66)***
A88	0.33	(6.29)***
$Landlocked_i$	-0.17	(-2.21)**
$Coastal_i$	0.21	(3.26)***
R^2 adjusted	0.86	

Note: The Student *t* are shown in brackets.
*** significant at 1%; ** significant at 5%; * significant at 10%.

The coefficients obtained are, for the most part, significant at the 1% level and correspond to the proposed hypotheses. This is notably the case for the variables common to the 'international' estimation of the rate of openness presented in the first part. The per capita product, which approximates the level of development of the provinces, is here delayed (Ln$y_{i,t-1}$) in order to avoid simultaneity bias. The positive relation obtained with the rate of total openness is particularly significant and incidentally logical.

On the other hand, we obtain a negative sign for the two variables which express the dimensions of a province, that is, the area napierian logarithm (Ln$area_i$) and the delayed population logarithm (Ln$pop_{i,t-1}$): the larger the province, the larger its internal market, so the greater the diversity of its production and the less significant its trade openness.

However, seemingly paradoxically, the sign obtained for the coefficient – significant – of the variable representing the existence of mining and energy resources ($Mining_{i,t}$), calculated here as the ratio of the total production (in value) of coal, oil, gas and metallic minerals to total production (agricultural and industrial), is not positive, as in the international transversal study, but negative. At the level of the Chinese provinces, the link between mineral resources and openness proves to be of a different nature than at the international level: the reason for this may be that the wealth of a province in hydrocarbons and coal encourages a process of industrialization geared to the substitution of imports. It is interesting to note that virtually all the provinces produce coal (with the exception of Tianjin and Shanghai) and more than half of them produce oil, even though it may be in risible quantities. Doubtless, the provinces have been led to exploit the resources available to them whatever the cost or the yield, thus conserving the extracted quantities for their own use.

To better capture this relation, surprising at first, we wanted to test the hypothesis that the relation between the share of mining and energy production in total production and total commercial openness of the province is not linear. For this, we used a multiplicative dummy variable, $Ress10_{i,t}$, which takes the value 1 when the value of $Mining_{i,t}$ is higher than 10% and 0 when it is not. The few provinces (notably Heilongjiang, Xinjiang, Ningxia, Shanxi, Gansu and Shandong) for which the share of mineral, coal and oil production is above 10% of total production ($Ress10_{i,t} = 1$), fulfil the purpose of supplying the rest of the country with these goods. Thus we expect the coefficient of $Mining_{i,t} * Ress10_{i,t}$ to be positive, which is the case at the 1% level. The wealth of the earth, and what is underneath it, is to a certain level a factor of diminished trade, although when it is very significant, it implies an increased total openness (inter-provincial and international).

In order to capture the influence of geographical position, which is an important structural determinant for commercial openness on the international level, we not only isolated the landlocked provinces, but also the coastal provinces by means of two dummy variables: $Coastal_i$ (value of 1 for the coastal provinces and 0 for the others), and $Landlocked_i$ (value of 1 for the landlocked provinces with no coastline or no border with a coastal province, and 0 for the others): the two variables appear to be correlated with observed commercial openness (positively and negatively respectively).

It is suitable to note that in China, the landlocked factor incorporates a larger idea than the simple notion of transport costs and a physical obstacle to trade. The localization of the Chinese provinces (landlocked or coastal position) is not only a structural factor; it is also associated with a strategy of commercial openness determined by the central power. Indeed, the Chinese authorities clearly encouraged the commercial openness (international and national) of the coast by granting advantages to the coastal provinces (higher rate of currency retention, creation of special economic zones, tax advantages, favourable price system). As we are attempting here to express the will for openness specific to each province, the measures undertaken by the central power to encourage or favour the internal and external commercial openness of the coastal provinces can be considered as an exogenous factor, justifying the introduction of these dummy variables in the regression. A landlocked or coastal position thus proves, either because of the consequences on transport conditions, or because of the decisions taken by the central power, to be a factor independent of the political will of the provinces for openness. It is thus normal, if we want the residual of the function to express the will for openness specific to each province, that the corresponding variables be introduced as an explicative factor of the rate of openness.

Let us finally note that the infrastructure variable Ln*infra*$_{i,t}$, which is delayed to ensure its exogeneity, is significant and positive. It should be specified that much of the trade between the Chinese provinces goes by water, thus the length of the internal navigable waterways has been integrated into the infrastructure variable.

Some Results According to Localization

Table 1.10 below shows the non-weighted average of the residuals for each year, on the one hand for all the provinces, on the other hand for the landlocked and coastal provinces separately.

Table 1.10 Average residuals by group of provinces

Period	Coastal provinces	Landlocked provinces	All provinces
1988	-0.006	0.026	-6.4^{E}-14
1990	0.101	-0.011	0.034
1991	0.032	0.015	0.097
1992	0.049	-0.03	-0.041
Average for 1988–92	0.036	-1.2^{E}-14	-3.2^{E}-14

We can note that on average (similarly using the median) trade policy seems to be systematically less open for the provinces considered to be landlocked than for the rest of China between 1990 and 1992. On average, the coastal provinces thus prove to have a more open commercial strategy, even after controlling for their coastal position in the regression. The results for the year 1988 can, doubtless, be explained by the paroxysm experienced that year in the commercial wars between provinces (both coastal and interior). Indeed, the strong economic growth between 1985 and 1988 led to an increase in commercial conflicts between provinces with a virtually identical industrial structure. Numerous provinces (both on the coast and in the interior) struggled to ensure their supply of inputs of production. Various famous wars over agricultural products were waged in 1988 and saw producer and consumer provinces (mainly coastal) confronting one another. The silk wars saw the producer province of Sichuan in opposition to the consumer provinces of Guangdong, Jiangsu and Zhejiang. Similarly, Hunan and Fujian refused to supply several provinces, such as Guangdong, Zhejiang and Jiangxi with rice and cereals respectively. With the cooling of the economy at the end of 1989, export restrictions on agricultural inputs turned into limitations imposed by the interior provinces on imports of manufactured goods produced in the coastal regions.

When we consider the residuals for the provinces for the four years, it is clear that, among the provinces with the lowest rates of openness, notably in 1990 and 1991, we find those provinces which have been shown in the literature to have resorted most to protectionism. In this way, Xinjiang and Qinghai, the two provinces of Western China with a strong minority and traditionally in opposition to the centre, are included in the five provinces with the smallest residuals during these two years. For 1990, the year of the recession, the five provinces considered to be the least open according to our indicator are Hubei, Qinghai, Xinjiang, Anhui and Shaanxi. The province of Hubei systematically appears among the least open for each observation year: it is an agricultural province, producing much cereal, but was keen to develop its industry and is recognized for its automobile sector. The fact that it resorted to internal protectionism (notably during the cereal wars which took place between 1987 and 1989) has been highlighted in the literature. The residual for the province of Shaanxi was also one of the weakest between 1988 and 1990 (it was the weakest in 1988), although it increased in 1991 and 1992, placing the province around the median mark for the sample in 1992. Shaanxi is the cradle of Chinese civilization. Its resources are very limited, its soil infertile. It is the holy place of the Chinese revolution. This province conveys an image of a hard-working, rural land, faithful to the ideology of Mao where in people's minds it has been difficult to accept the market economy. It would seem quite logical that these landlocked provinces had a tendency to resort to protectionist measures, aiming at self-sufficiency and the development of their own industries, sheltered from competition from the privileged coastal regions, which is seen as unjust.

Seemingly, certain provinces, traditionally considered to be closed, such as Gansu, Sichuan and Yunnan, have not practised the least open strategies, once we have controlled for their immense size, their poorly developed transport infrastructure and their landlocked position. These three provinces in fact are to be found among the five most open provinces, notably during the first three years.

The provinces which prove to be the most open are, logically, Guangdong and Shanghai. Guangdong saw its indicator for openness strategy increase between 1988 and 1992 to become the most open province in 1992, ahead of Fujian and Jiangxi (their common neighbour). Zhejiang is the least open coastal province, its residuals for 1991 and 1992 placing it among the least open provinces in the sample. Similarly, Tianjin saw its indicator for openness strategy fall between 1990 and 1992, going from one of the highest residuals in 1990 to a position below the median in 1992. This town, which has an old industrial base, must face serious problems of re-conversion and suffers from an unfavourable northern position. The city-state of Beijing shows one of the least open commercial policies in the whole sample, surely due to its smaller level of autonomy with respect to the central state and thus to its reduced capacity to implement its own strategy of openness. Furthermore, its residual, which is a relative indicator, is declining due to the effort towards openness undertaken by the other provinces, notably in the interior of the country.

At the beginning of the 1990s, it seems that the protectionist specificity of the landlocked provinces (pursuit of self-sufficiency, imports substitution and internal trade wars) diminished to such an extent that the provinces that were noticeable at the start of the period for their protectionist practices no longer show the lowest residuals, even if they remain below average. These results seem to be coherent with the political evolution in China during the 1990s, even if the absence of data for inter-provincial trade prevents us from pursuing the analysis for the end of the decade. Indeed, the deepening of the reforms (especially as regards tax), the greater degree of autonomy granted to the landlocked provinces in managing their resources and becoming involved in international trade, as well as the reduction of price distortions necessary for the abandoning of internal protectionist measures have certainly eased the prime motivation for resorting to protectionism and encouraged the provinces, especially the least outward-looking, to open up.

5 CONCLUSION

This chapter aimed to present certain quantitative indicators allowing us, on the one hand, to situate the openness of China to the exterior compared to that of other countries of the world and especially the largest countries in Asia, and on the other hand, to situate the openness of the different Chinese provinces with respect to each other.

It is obvious that since the reforms implemented at the end of the 1970s, China has rapidly opened itself to the exterior, progressively on a commercial level, more brutally on a financial level. However, this multi-faceted openness proves very difficult to measure. The rates of openness –commercial or financial– as a ratio to GDP depend crucially on the method of measurement, an issue that is highly controversial in the case of China. Resorting to estimations in terms of purchasing power parity obviously reduces the rates of openness considerably. Does this necessarily mean that policy in China has not really been 'open'?

This is not our conclusion. Indeed, the degree of openness cannot be appreciated independently of the structural characteristics specific to each country, and the indicators of openness policy must be corrected for the influence of these characteristics. It would, then, appear, that although China seemed to remain closed during the period 1971–1975 in comparison to other countries of the world, given its size and per capita product, as early as the period 1976–1986, it had ceased to be closed, and during the period 1987–1995, it seemed, on the contrary, to be relatively 'open', commercially as well as financially. The indicator of trade openness policy for China thus seemed to converge with the level of that for the most advanced Asian countries. The indicator for financial openness policy even surpasses these countries, but with a radically different content, as it is essentially linked to direct investment.

The counterpart of openness is vulnerability. This has recently become a fashionable concept, both with regard to the identification of the least developed countries and after the financial crisis of some emerging economies. Vulnerability can itself be defined in several ways. Let us consider it as the risk of being destabilized by exogenous shocks, either natural or external (Guillaumont, 2000). Like openness, it has two components: one structural and another policy-related. In becoming more open, has China become more vulnerable? According to available indicators of structural vulnerability, China appears to be the least vulnerable among low (and lower middle) income countries (United Nations, 2000). This result is not paradoxical. It is mainly linked to the large population size of the country, which simultaneously is a factor of a weak structural openness. Moreover, as shown elsewhere (Combes et al., 2000), whereas structural openness is a factor of income growth volatility, the policy component of openness (the outward-looking nature of the policy) is a reduction factor of this volatility[11] because it corresponds to a higher competitiveness, resulting in a stronger resilience.

NOTES

1. The OECD also uses an indicator 'of exposure to foreign competition' which is the ratio

$$\frac{X}{GDP} + \frac{M}{GDP}\left(\frac{GDP - X}{GDP - X + M}\right)$$

that is, the sum of the rate of exports and the product of the rate of imports multiplied by the rate of absorption satisfied by internal production.

2. A better approximate indicator, using the hypothesis that the content of imports and exports in percentage is the same as total expenditure or employment (absorption D and exports), would indeed be to weight the rate of exports by the percentage of expenditure satisfied by internal production, which leads us to calculate the ratio of exports to total employment (or resources). This gives:

$$\frac{X}{GDP}\left(\frac{GDP}{D + X}\right) = \frac{X}{GDP + M}$$

As for the rate of openness taking into account both exports and imports, it could be defined by the ratio:

$$\left(\frac{X + M}{GDP + M}\right)$$

3. Financial openness, contrary to trade openness, can also be measured in terms of stock by the value of foreign commitments in the country, that is, by the rate of debt (ratio of outstanding debt to GDP) and/or by the ratio of the stock of direct foreign investment to GDP and/or by the sum of the two (depending on the object of the study, we can also consider the commitments of the country abroad).
4. The evolution and the levels obtained are relatively similar if we use a different source, probably derived from the first, such as the World Bank statistics (compare Figure 1.1).
5. Calculations made on the basis of other sources for foreign trade provide in neighbouring results.
6. Nonetheless, the estimations of Ren Ruon, curiously, provide a smaller increase in the degree of openness (considered since 1985), but only for the period 1985–1994 (p. 138). The reason for this is probably because the estimation of the GDP in Chinese prices is based on the current exchange rate which was overvalued at the beginning of this period.
7. Source: World Bank (1995).
8. Source: International Monetary Fund (1998), *Balance of Payment Statistics Yearbook*. The direct investments cover the initial transactions and all subsequent transactions, as well as transactions between similar firms in the form, or not, of companies between direct investors and the direct investment firms. The portfolio investments cover the transactions focusing on stocks and bonds (bonds and other proofs of loan), instruments of the monetary market and financial products derived when these instruments give rise to debts and commitments.
9. The fact that, in the normalization equation, we take into account variables which are measured at the beginning of the period aims to eliminate the simultaneity bias.
10. In fact more marked than for commercial openness.
11. Moreover, it should be noted that the policy factor of a higher level of financial openness may not have the same results (Combes et al., 2000).

REFERENCES

Aubert, C., J.-P. Cabestan and F. Lemoine (eds) (1996), 'La Chine après Deng', *Revue Tiers Monde*, no. 147.

Balassa, B. (1985), 'Export Policy Choice and Economic Growth in Developing Countries after the 1973 Oil Shock', *Journal of Development Economics*, 18, pp. 22–35.

Balassa, B. (1994), 'La théorie de la parité des pouvoirs d'achat: un reexamen', *Revue d'Economie du Développement*, no. 1, pp. 17–34.

Baneth, J. (1994), 'La théorie de la parité des pouvoirs d'achat: un nouveau réexamen', *Revue d'Economie du Développement*, no. 1, pp. 35–72.

Cabrillac, B. (1997), *Economie de la Chine*, collection Que Sais-Je?, Paris: PUF.

Combes, J.-L., P. Guillaumont, S. Guillaumont Jeanneney and P. Motel-Combes (2000), 'Ouverture sur l'extérieur et instabilité des taux de croissance', *Revue Française d'Economie*, 15(1), pp. 3–33.

Creyssey, G.B. (1934), *The Geography of China*.

Edwards, S. (1998), 'Openness, Productivity and Growth: What Do We Really Know?', *Economic Journal*, 108(447), pp. 383–98.

Fukasaku, K.N. and H.B. Solignac-Lecomte (1996), 'Transition économique et réforme de la politique commerciale en Chine', *Revue d'Economie du Développement*, 1-2, pp. 120–85.

Gentelle, P. (1994), *Economie de la Chine*, Paris: Armand Colin.

Guillaumont, P. (1985), 'Protectionnisme, substitution à l'importation et développement tourné vers l'intérieur: quelques équivoques illustrées par le cas des pays africains de la zone franc', in M. Lassudrie-Duchêne and J.L. Reiffers, *Le protectionnisme*, Paris: Economica, pp. 203–29.

Guillaumont, P. (1989), 'Stratégie de développement et ouverture sur l'extérieur', *Revue africaine de développement*, Banque africaine de développement, 1(1), June, pp. 40–57.

Guillaumont, P. (1994), 'Politique d'ouverture et croissance économique: les effets de la croissance et de l'instabilité des exportations'. *Revue d'Economie du Développement*, 1, pp. 91–114.

Guillaumont, P. (2000), 'Ouverture, vulnérabilité et développement', *Etudes et Documents*, CERDI, July.

Guillaumont, P. and S. Guillaumont Jeanneney (eds.) (1988), *Stratégies de Développement Comparées, Zone Franc et hors Zone Franc*, Paris: Economica.

Hua, P. (1996), 'Les déterminants du commerce extérieur', *Revue d'Economie du Développement*, 1-2, pp. 207–31.

International Monetary Fund (1998), *Balance of Payment Statistics Yearbook*, Washington DC: IMF.

Jianqi, W. (1993), 'On the "Block Economy": Its Birth, Consequences, and Cure', *Chinese Economic Studies*, 26(5), pp. 9–22.

Kumar, A. (1994), 'China's Reform, Internal Trade and Marketing', *The Pacific Review*, 7(3), pp. 323–39.

Kumar, A. (1994), 'Economic Reform and the Internal Division of Labour in China: Production, Trade and Marketing', in D.S. Goodman and G. Segal (eds), *China Deconstructs: Politics, Trade and Regionalism*, London: Routledge.

Krugman, P. (1998), *What Happened to Asia?*, Web, mit.edu/krugman/www/ January.

Leamer, E. (1988), 'Measures of openness', in R. Baldwin (ed.), *Trade Policy and Empirical Analysis*, Chicago: University of Chicago Press.

Lee, P.K. (1998), 'Local Economy Protectionnism in China's Economic Reform', *Development Policy Review*, 16(3), September, pp. 281–305.

Lemoine, F. (1994), *La Nouvelle Économie Chinoise*, Paris: La Découverte.

Peoples's Republic of China (1995), *China Regional Economy: A Profile of 17 Years of Reform and Opening-up*, National Bureau of Statistics, China Statistics Press.

Peoples's Republic of China (1985, 1988, 1989, 1990, 1991, 1992), *China Statistical Yearbooks*, National Bureau of Statistics, China Statistics Press.

Peoples's Republic of China (1998), *China Industrial Economic Statistical Yearbooks*, National Bureau of Statistics, China Statistics Press.

Pin, J.-L. (1994), *L'ouverture extérieure de la Chine depuis 1978*, PhD dissertation, Grenoble II.

Pritchett, L. (1996). 'Measuring Outward Orientation in LDCs: Can It Be Done?', *Journal of Development Economics*, 49(2), pp. 307–35.

Raiser, M. (1998), 'Subsidising Inequality: Economic Reforms, Fiscal Transfers and Convergence Across Chinese Provinces', *The Journal of Development Studies*, 34(3), February, pp. 1–26.

Ruon, R. (1997), *Les Performances Economiques de la Chine dans le Contexte International*, OECD, Development Center.

Sachs, J.D. and A.M. Warner (1995), 'Economic Reform and the Process of Global Integration', *Brookings Papers on Economic Activity*, 1, pp. 1–118.

Schmiedel F. (1998), *L'orientation géographique des échanges commerciaux de la Chine: analyse de ses déterminants et de la position européenne à partir des modèles de gravité*, PhD dissertation, Clermont I.

Sicular, T. (1996), 'Redefining State, Plan and Markets: China's Reforms in Agricultural Commerce', in Andrew G. Walder (ed.), *China's Transitional Economy. Studies on Contemporary China*, Oxford and New York: Oxford University Press, pp. 58–84.

Sicular, T. (1988), 'Plan and Market in China's Agricultural Commerce', *Journal of Political Economy*, 96(2), pp. 283–307.

Shihua, L. (1993), 'Anatomy of Local Protectionism', *Chinese Economic Studies*, 26(5), pp. 51–8.

Summers, R. and A. Heston (1991), 'The Penn World Table, Mark 5: An Expanded Set of International Comparisons, 1950–1988', *Quarterly Journal of Economics*, vol.106, 2, pp. 327–68.

Summers, R. and A. Heston (1997), *The Penn World Table*, NBER, Cambridge, MA.

United Nations (2000), *Poverty Amidst Riches: the Need for Change*, Report of the Committee for Development Policy on the 2nd Session, Department of Economic and Social Affairs, April.

Wedeman, A.H. (1993), 'Editor's Introduction', *Chinese Economic Studies*, 26(5), pp. 3–7.

Wenyi, L. (1993), 'On Local Protectionism in China's Market Development', *Chinese Economic Studies*, 26(5), pp. 59–78.

Womack, B. and G. Zhao (1994), 'The many worlds of China's Agricultural Commerce', in D.S. Goodman and G Segal (eds), *China Deconstructs: Politics, Trade and Regionalism*, London: Routledge, pp. 131–76.

World Bank (1998), *World Development Report*, Washington, DC: World Bank.

World Bank (1998), *World Development Indicators*, Washington, DC: World Bank.

World Bank (1997), *World Development Report*, Washington, DC: World Bank.
World Bank (1995), *World Tables*, Washington, DC: World Bank.
World Bank (1994), *China: Internal Market Development and Regulation*, Washington, DC: World Bank.
World Bank (1993), *China: The Achievement and Challenge of Price Reform*, Washington, DC: World Bank.
World Bank (1992), *Price Reform in China*, A World Bank Country Study, Washington, DC: World Bank.
World Bank (1990), *China: Between Plan and Market*, Washington, DC: World Bank.
World Bank (1987), *World Development Report*, Washington, DC: World Bank.
Youpeng, L. (1993), 'Current Regional Blockades and Suggested Solutions', *Chinese Economic Studies*, 26(5), pp. 37–50.
Yuk-Shing, C. and T. Shu-Ki (1994), 'The Changing Grain Marketing System in China', *The China Quaterly*, 140, pp. 1081–104.
Zhengyi, L. (1993), 'In-Depth Exploration of the Question of Regional Blockades', *Chinese Economic Studies*, 26(5), pp. 23–36.

APPENDIX: EXHAUSTIVE LIST OF COUNTRIES BY GEOGRAPHICAL ZONE

Sub-Saharan Africa: 45

Angola Congo Equatorial Guinea Mozambique Somalia
Benin Côte d'Ivoire Kenya Niger Sudan
Botswana Djibouti Lesotho Nigeria Swaziland
Burkina Faso Ethiopia Liberia Uganda Tanzania
Burundi Gabon Madagascar Rwanda Chad
Cameroon The Gambia Malawi Sao Tomé Togo
Cape Verde Ghana Mali Senegal Zaire
Central Africa Guinea Mauritius Seychelles Zambia
Comoros Guinea Bissau Mauritania Sierra Leone Zimbabwe

Other countries: 20

Algeria Turkey Yugoslavia Oman Yemen
Saudi Arabia Iraq Lebanon Qatar South Africa
Bahrain Iran Libya Syria Cyprus
Egypt Jordan Morocco Tunisia Greece

Asia: 24

Afghanistan India Nepal Samoa Bangladesh
Indonesia Pakistan Sri Lanka Bhutan Macao
Papua N.G. Taiwan Myanmar Malaysia Philippines
Thailand China Maldives Korea Tonga

Fiji Mongolia Solomon Islands Vanuatu

Latin America: 34

Antigua and Barbados Chile Grenada Nicaragua St Lucia
Argentina Colombia Guatemala Panama St Vincent
Bahamas Costa Rica Guyana Paraguay Surinam
Barbados Cuba Haiti Peru Trinidad and Tobago
Belize San Domingo Honduras Puerto Rico Uruguay
Bolivia El Salvador Jamaica Dominican Republic Venezuela
Brazil Ecuador Mexico St Christopher

High-income economies: 25

Germany United Arab Emirates Ireland Norway Singapore
Australia Spain Israel Netherlands Austria
United States Italy Portugal Belgium Finland
Japan United Kingdom Canada France Kuwait
Sweden Denmark Hong Kong New Zealand Switzerland.

2. Social Consequences of economic reform in China: an analysis of regional disparity in the transition period*

Justin Yifu Lin, Fang Cai and Zhou Li

1 INTRODUCTION

The relationship between economic growth and the income distribution in a country or region is an important subject in economics, articulated strongly by Adelman and Morris (1973), along with studies on the distinctions and interactions between growth and development. Kuznets (1955) first analysed the common trend between the growth of national income and its distribution. He found that, as per capita income level went up, the disparity of personal income distribution became bigger until such a point where it began to narrow again. Williamson (1965) investigated the changing regional disparities of income distribution in the US by economic zones and states during 1840–1961. The results of his study showed that regional disparity of income distribution followed the same inverted-U pattern, growing bigger first and then narrowing. By comparing the disparities of salary and labour productivity of French farmers, Williamson concluded that regional income distribution is positively related to the disparity of regional GDP level. He further inferred that within a nation, the regional income disparities will also evolve along the inverted-U pattern as times (GDP levels) change.

It is worth pointing out, though, that the inverted-U pattern of income distribution does not represent an inevitable trend and thus should by no means be taken as a general law. In fact, economies that do follow the inverted-U pattern are often characterized by 'growth first, distribution next'. In some cases, excessive disparity of income distribution can lead to social unrest. There are plenty of examples in this world, either at earlier or recent times, of growth with improving income distribution. In other words, in addition to the 'growth first, distribution next' model, there is a more

* This chapter has been published in a special issue of Revue d'Economie du Développement, no. 1-2, 1999.

successful model of 'growth with equity'. Successful examples in the latter case include Sweden, which became a developed economy at a fairly early stage; Japan, which later joined the developed world; and the 'four little dragons' of Asia that created the East Asian miracle (UNDP, 1996).

Movement along the inverted-U pattern with unequal income distribution or along a better path that takes care of both income distribution and regional disparities during the development process, depends not only on the government's economic development strategy but also on its social policies. For a developing economy, the inverted-U shape of income distribution of Kuznets (1955) and Williamson (1965) can be avoided by following a development strategy that taps the maximum potential of its comparative advantage – its abundant labour resources – and by adopting social policies which focus on income distribution (Fei et al., 1979).

China began her transition from a planned to a market economy towards the end of the 1970s. By first improving incentives and microeconomic efficiency and then focusing on the allocation of newly created resources to more productive sectors, economic reform in China followed a gradualist approach with the Pareto-improvement characteristic (Lin et al., 1996). The success of China's reform approach in terms of stimulating economic growth has been widely acknowledged and attracted much attention. Meanwhile, the social consequences of the reforms have also become a topic of great interest to researchers. When the economy grows at a miraculously high speed, what is the situation of income distribution, particularly that among regions, likely to be and what is going to be its trend? Answers to these questions have become subjects of persistent research efforts in the academic community. To date, a lot of research has been carried out, both inside and outside China, in an attempt to discover the trend of disparities in income distribution and GDP level before and after the reforms.

The latest research efforts on regional disparity in China are characterized by more in-depth analysis. Some remarkable progress can be summarized as follows. First, researchers have generally applied a wide range of statistical indicators of regional disparity. Tsui, for example, studied the provincial disparities of net material product and national income during 1952–1985 and concluded that the provincial disparities were not narrowed before reform in spite of the existence of a powerful fiscal income transfer mechanism (Tsui, 1991). Second, as more and more applicable data has become available, research efforts have not only concentrated on the study of the trend of overall regional disparities, but also attempted to decompose it. Rozelle (1993) tried to find out the structural causes of regional disparities of rural GDP level by breaking down total rural social output into five sectors (agriculture, industries, transportation, construction and commerce and services). Tsui (1993) based his research on data at the county level and decomposed regional disparities into intra-province disparity, inter-province disparity, internal disparity of the rural areas, internal disparity of the urban areas and rural–urban disparity. He found that the rural–urban disparity had the strongest impact on regional disparities. Third, research on regional disparities is no longer confined to comparisons of per capita income and output, but has started to include comparisons of per capita consumption and other social indicators. For instance, comparisons of infant mortality rate and illiteracy rate were made in Tsui's decomposing analysis. The World Bank (1995) divided China into seven regions and made comparisons not only in terms of output, income and consumption indicators of each region versus the national average, but also in terms of demographic distribution, infant mortality rate, education and health care. Fourth, more and more researchers have come to conclude that the fundamental cause of regional disparities in China is the economic development strategy. Yang (1990), for example, labelled the development strategy concerning regional development before the reform of the 1970 as the 'Maoist development strategy' which was characterized by high dependency on redistribution measures to narrow regional disparities. The development strategy after reform was called by him the 'uneven development strategy'. However, Tsui's empirical studies showed that redistribution efforts of the central government before the 1980s did not contribute much to narrowing the regional gap (Tsui, 1991).

Based on existing research results, this chapter aims to provide a more accurate description of the trend of regional disparities in China since the reform in 1979 and to reveal the economic causes affecting the trend by more careful analysis.

2 TREND OF REGIONAL DISPARITIES SINCE REFORM: A GENERAL PICTURE

Statistical measurements are widely used in the literature related to disparity research. Many of them describe the extent to which a certain object is distributed unequally. Therefore, the higher the value of the inequality index goes, the more unequal the distribution is. Generally speaking, the inequalities reflected by the major indicators share similar patterns. In this chapter, we will use one or several of these indicators, according to the needs, to describe the situation of disparities. In addition, the statistical indicators serve different purposes when we try to decompose the indicators to find out the cause of regional disparities.

In this section, our analysis is based on the observations from the 30 provinces, municipalities under central administration, and autonomous regions (hereafter referred to as 'provinces') in mainland China. First, the disparity indexes of per capita GDP show that during 1978–1995 when national per capita GDP grew several times, there was no dramatic increase in regional disparities. The disparity indexes, except for the coefficient of variation which had a declining trend, all showed common trends of GDP level. The Gini coefficient, for example, went down gradually from 0.24 to 0.23 during 1978–1982, began to rise in 1985 and reached 0.27 in 1995. The coefficients of variation that initially dropped more drastically underwent a more gradual decline in the late 1980s and 1990s with slight rises in 1995 (see the first two columns of Table 2.1).

Table 2.1 Regional disparities of per capita GDP and per capita income

	Per capita GDP	Gini coefficient	Per capita income	Gini coefficient
1978	359	0.2438	164	0.1261
1979	386	0.2394	197	0.1174
1980	414	0.2394	217	0.1119
1981	431	0.2391	248	0.0998
1982	465	0.2335	279	0.1003
1983	517	0.2404	311	0.1057
1984	580	0.2323	357	0.1123
1985	660	0.2324	376	0.1106
1986	700	0.2355	409	0.1198
1987	762	0.2467	423	0.1271
1988	847	0.2463	420	0.1326
1989	870	0.2419	408	0.1394
1990	892	0.2414	443	0.1452
1991	975	0.2436	464	0.1407
1992	1135	0.2538	509	0.1484
1993	1331	0.2613	551	0.1629
1994	1523	0.2695	607	0.1685
1995	1715	0.2747	656	0.1670

Sources: The Statistical Yearbook of China (various issues).

The last two columns of Table 2.1 show per capita income weighted by the ratio between urban and rural population and its Gini coefficient. Similar to changes of the Gini coefficient of per capita GDP, the level of disparities of per capita income was on the decline from 0.13 to 0.10 during 1978–1982 and began to rise thereafter. It reached 0.13 in 1987, the level of 1978, and went up further to hit 0.17 in 1995.

3 REGIONAL DEVELOPMENT DISPARITIES: A STUDY OF PER CAPITA GDP

In order to attain a better understanding of the changes of per capita GDP across the provinces, we started by decomposing the Gini coefficient of per capita GDP so as to find out which industry contributed most to the changes. GDP is thereby divided into the gross products of the primary industry, the secondary industry and the tertiary industry and the Gini coefficient, Gini proportion and Gini elasticity of each industry are calculated.[1] The Gini proportion indicates the contribution of each of the individual industry's Gini coefficient to the overall Gini coefficient. The Gini elasticity represents the impact of an industry's output growth on the increase of the overall Gini coefficient.

As shown in Table 2.2, while the Gini coefficient and the Gini proportion of the primary industry may be low, they tend to increase gradually. With the Gini coefficient rising from 0.135 in 1978 to 0.189 in 1995 and the Gini proportion from 0.001 to 0.016, the impact of the primary industry on the overall Gini coefficient and its changes has been growing stronger from a negligible level. The Gini coefficient of the tertiary industry has dropped slightly from 0.369 in 1978 to 0.354 in 1995, but its Gini proportion has the same rising trend as that of the primary industry and went up from 0.204 to 0.286. Consequently, the two industries are playing an increasingly important role in widening the regional disparities of per capita GDP.

Meanwhile, the Gini coefficient and Gini proportion of the secondary industry, though higher than those of other industries, have been declining since 1978 from 0.496 to 0.427 and from 0.795 to 0.698, respectively. Therefore, the impact of the secondary industry on overall regional disparities can partially offset the impacts of the primary and the tertiary industries. It can be concluded from Table 2.2 that the rising Gini coefficients and Gini proportions of the primary and the tertiary industries were the main reason for the rising Gini coefficient of per capita GDP during 1978–1995, particularly since the mid-1980s. However, as a result of the downward trend of the Gini coefficient of the secondary industry which remains the leading sector of the economy, the overall Gini coefficient has increased only slowly. The Gini elasticities of both industries are found to be negative, -0.098 and -0.010 respectively in 1995. In other words, growing output of these two

Table 2.2 The Gini coefficients of per capita GDP and the individual industry

		Gini coefficient			Gini proportion			Gini elasticity		
	GDP	Primary	Secondary	Tertiary	Primary	Secondary	Tertiary	Primary	Secondary	Tertiary
1978	0.350	0.135	0.496	0.369	0.001	0.795	0.204	-0.225	0.221	0.004
1979	0.346	0.157	0.492	0.357	0.004	0.795	0.201	-0.218	0.219	0.001
1980	0.351	0.167	0.490	0.363	0.011	0.782	0.207	-0.200	0.204	-0.004
1981	0.346	0.181	0.498	0.357	0.020	0.763	0.217	-0.203	0.209	-0.006
1982	0.334	0.166	0.483	0.355	0.015	0.751	0.233	-0.214	0.212	0.002
1983	0.377	0.157	0.535	0.352	0.008	0.808	0.184	-0.195	0.225	-0.030
1984	0.337	0.147	0.476	0.362	0.028	0.723	0.249	-0.190	0.189	0.001
1985	0.329	0.162	0.466	0.340	0.015	0.742	0.243	-0.182	0.194	-0.012
1986	0.328	0.161	0.461	0.342	0.012	0.728	0.260	-0.177	0.187	-0.010
1987	0.336	0.165	0.477	0.335	0.005	0.739	0.257	-0.177	0.201	-0.024
1988	0.331	0.171	0.450	0.328	0.012	0.724	0.264	-0.156	0.174	-0.018
1989	0.326	0.159	0.445	0.325	0.003	0.724	0.272	-0.160	0.177	-0.016
1990	0.327	0.164	0.444	0.336	0.013	0.700	0.288	-0.156	0.164	-0.008
1991	0.326	0.166	0.436	0.331	0.014	0.693	0.293	-0.146	0.153	-0.008
1992	0.335	0.173	0.435	0.338	0.017	0.689	0.294	-0.127	0.137	-0.010
1993	0.337	0.175	0.425	0.340	0.015	0.698	0.287	-0.116	0.128	-0.012
1994	0.344	0.186	0.426	0.345	0.016	0.705	0.280	-0.106	0.121	-0.015
1995	0.349	0.189	0.427	0.354	0.016	0.698	0.286	-0.098	0.108	-0.010

Source: As Table 2.1.

industries can result in less overall disparity, while the secondary industry has been developing in the opposite direction.

For the purpose of measuring more accurately the contributions to the overall regional per capita GDP disparities from the inter- and intra-regional disparities of eastern, central and western regions, we apply the Theil entropy method to decompose the overall disparities into intra-regional disparities of eastern, central and western regions and the interregional disparities of these three regions.[2] The overall disparities are set to 100 so as to facilitate the measurement of each of the four components' contribution to the overall disparities. As shown in Table 2.3, the interregional component always had the largest impact on the overall regional disparities, with its share moving around 50%. The eastern region's internal disparities always had the second largest impact, contributing about 25% to the overall disparities. The effects of the internal disparities of central region and western region ranged between 12% and 13%.

From the changes of individual components, we can see that the contribution of eastern region's intra-regional disparities to the overall disparities dropped from 26.84% in 1978 to 22.86% in 1995, that of the central region from 13.06% to 12.53%, and that of the western region from 13.15% to 12.88%, while the contribution of interregional disparities increased from 46.95% to 51.72%. Furthermore, we can see that, although the contributions from the central region's and western region's intra-regional disparities are declining, the changes are very small. Comparatively, the eastern region's intra-regional disparities' contribution changes quite substantially. The interregional disparities' contribution has similar change in magnitude but in an opposite direction. This indicates that the eastern region achieves a substantial growth with a decline of internal disparities. In other words, the eastern region's growth in the past 17 years proceeded in a balanced manner among the provinces in the region.

To present the picture from another perspective, during 1978–1995, disparities among the eastern provinces have become smaller as a result of the catching up of more backward provinces while the internal disparities of central and western regions narrowed because of the decline of economic ranking of the more advanced provinces in these two regions. The consequences are: (1) As the eastern region continues its growth and the central and western regions lag further behind the national average, regional disparities among the three regions become increasingly noticeable. The World Bank has reached the same conclusion in its analysis of the seven regions (World Bank, 1995). (2) The internal disparities of each of these three regions are invariantly narrowing during this period. As a result, in spite of the widening of gaps between the three regions, the Gini coefficient of per capita GDP for the nation as a whole with individual provinces as observations did not have significant changes.

Table 2.3 The contribution of intra- and interregional disparities to the overall regional disparities: the per capita GDP of eastern, central and western regions (%)

	Intra-east disparities	Intra-central disparities	Intra-west disparities	Interregional disparities
1978	26.84	13.06	13.15	46.95
1979	26.97	13.00	13.07	46.96
1980	26.79	12.93	13.09	47.19
1981	26.32	12.97	13.47	47.24
1982	25.85	13.18	13.44	47.53
1983	26.09	13.09	13.06	47.76
1984	26.31	12.97	13.06	47.66
1985	25.99	12.95	13.16	47.89
1986	25.88	12.88	13.09	48.16
1987	25.37	13.37	12.90	48.36
1988	25.51	12.89	13.09	48.51
1989	25.48	12.96	13.04	48.52
1990	25.37	12.97	13.04	48.62
1991	24.79	12.96	13.09	49.16
1992	24.14	12.79	13.02	50.06
1993	23.25	12.72	13.02	51.02
1994	22.89	12.63	12.95	51.52
1995	22.86	12.53	12.88	51.72

Source: As Table 2.1.

4 CHANGES IN REGIONAL INCOME DIFFERENCES

The per capita income of a region is both result and indicator of its level of economic development. Therefore, the trends of per capita income and per capita GDP, generally speaking, will move in the same direction, or alternatively, are highly correlated. However, on cursory examination, we see that the correlation between the two trends is hardly perceivable. If we observe more closely, we find that changes of regional disparities in terms of per capita GDP and per capita income carry the following features. First, the disparity of per capita GDP was growing in a gradual manner instead of making as drastic a turn as that of per capita income in the mid-1980s. In contrast, the difference of per capita income hit its turning point in the mid-1980s and grew larger rapidly henceforth. Second, in terms of the changes of per capita GDP differences, the eastern, central and western regions shared a similar trend. However, in the case of per capita income, the more developed a region is, the larger the margin becomes, and the backward regions lag even further behind the national average. Third, as a consequence of the first two features, inter-provincial disparities of per capita GDP have not changed much and the increase in disparities came mainly from the increase in the disparities among the three regions. The increase in the per capita income disparities, however, are found to come not only from the increase in the disparities among the three regions, but also from the increase among the provinces within the regions. The above analysis shows that differences of regional GDP level can only give a partial explanation of regional disparities of per capita income. To find out the other part of the explanation, we have broken down urban and rural income by their sources.

Per capita income of farm households is analysed first. Under the people's commune system prior to the 1979 reform, the income of farmers came from one single source – allocation by the production brigades. There might have been differences in the economic conditions as a historical legacy in the rural areas, which resulted in regional differences of farmers' income. However, the differences were not significant because of similar agricultural production patterns and fixed prices of agricultural products. Since the adoption of the household responsibility system and, particularly, with the diversification of the rural industrial structure and the rapid growth of township and village enterprises, the sources of farmers' income began to diversify. According to Chinese statistics, the income of farm households now comes from four sources: (1) labour; (2) family farming activities; (3) transfers; and (4) properties. Among them, income from labour and family farming activities forms the basic income of the farm households, the former referring to income from non-agricultural employment in the rural areas and the latter being income from farming on the land. They contribute to 93% of the total income of the farmers at the national level, therefore, determining the situation of regional distribution of farmers' income.

Table 2.4 shows that the Gini proportions of labour income and income from family farming activities are rather high, 58% and 35% respectively in 1995, which means that these two components contribute to more than 90% of the regional disparity of farmers' income. However, the weight that these two sources carry in the total income of farm households varies drastically among the rural areas. At the lower end of the spectrum, we find the ratio between labour income and household income to be as low as 4.1% (Hainan) whereas, at the other end of the spectrum, the ratio can be as high as 231% (Shanghai). Since land is distributed according to the number of family members and active labour in each farm household under the household responsibility system, there is no significant difference in the land area for each family and thus relatively small regional differences in income from family farming activities. However, there is much greater regional disparity in labour income because non-agricultural employment opportunities depend more on the GDP level of each region. Consequently, the difference in the ratio between the two sources of income is mainly caused by differences of labour income. As Table 2.4 shows, the interregional Gini coefficient of labour income runs much higher than that of income from family farming, the former being 0.54 and the latter only 0.13 in 1995. It is easy to conclude that the main cause of growing regional disparity of farmers' income is unequal access to non-agricultural employment opportunities of different regions. While the regional difference of income from transfers and properties may be large, the Gini proportion and the Gini elasticity of the two sources of income are too insignificant to be considered. Therefore, it is irrelevant to policy making to include them in the analysis.

We now turn our attention to the income of urban residents. Before the reforms were initiated, the wage system was one of the components that formed the traditional planned economy. Urban residents enjoyed relatively stable incomes as a result of the full employment policy. However, urban income back then had two features: (1) There had been little change in the wage income of employees over a long period of time; (2) The main sources of urban income were wages distributed by state-owned and collective sectors, determined solely by the planning agencies of the government, with little difference between regions, industries and ranks. The two features are no longer true since reform started. First, the overall level of urban income in all regions is growing rapidly. Second, the structure of urban income has changed and sources of income have diversified. The latter development had a stronger impact on regional income disparities.

Currently the state-owned sector has maintained, to a large extent, the traditional wage system, with insignificant differences in the average wage income among provinces. The Gini coefficient is from 0.10 to 0.13 (Table 2.5). However, the average wage of the collective economy is characterized by larger disparities among provinces, with the Gini coefficient from 0.27 to 0.33. The most remarkable income difference among provinces is found in the wages of 'other forms of business entities' including the joint ventures, stockholding enterprises and enterprises with foreign investment or investment from Hong Kong, Macao and Taiwan. The Gini coefficient runs as high as more than 0.7.

Table 2.4 The decomposition of regional disparities of farmers' per capita income

		1993	1994	1995
Farm household per capita income	Gini coefficient	0.1992	0.2233	0.2297
Labor income				
	Gini coefficient	0.4911	0.5517	0.5449
	Gini proportion	0.4825	0.5791	0.5797
	Gini elasticity	0.2546	0.3219	0.3152
Household farming income				
	Gini coefficient	0.1399	0.1342	0.1331
	Gini proportion	0.4556	0.3589	0.3464
	Gini elasticity	-0.2636	-0.3205	-0.3231
Transfer income				
	Gini coefficient	0.3347	0.3597	0.3514
	Gini proportion	0.0451	0.0375	0.0403
	Gini elasticity	0.0019	-0.0006	0.0043
Property income				
	Gini coefficient	0.4824	0.3790	0.4078
	Gini proportion	0.0167	0.0245	0.0336
	Gini elasticity	0.0070	-0.0008	0.0037

Source: As Table 2.1.

As a result of the provincial differences of wage income and employment ratio between the state and non-state sectors, the income disparities among provinces are mainly subject to two factors. First, the state-owned sector has contributed to reducing income differences because of its higher Gini proportion (> 50%) and larger negative Gini elasticity. Second, other sectors, though with less than 50% of Gini proportion, are working towards greater income disparity (Tables 2.5). In other words, the growing urban income disparity among provinces witnessed in recent years came about largely as a result of a stronger effect of the non-state sectors in the provision of employment and as a source of urban income.

When studying the trends of per capita urban and rural income of each province, we find that the trends develop in the same direction. However, in provinces with the rank of income rising, the increase of farmer's income is especially conspicuous, whereas in provinces with the rank of income dropping, the declining of farmer's income is equally significant. The end

Table 2.5 Decomposition of regional disparities of urban annual per capita household income

		1991	1992	1993	1994	1995
State-owned sector	Gini coefficient	0.1086	0.0947	0.1077	0.1259	0.1154
Wage income	Gini proportion	0.5565	0.5485	0.5685	0.5580	0.5343
	Gini elasticity	-0.1045	-0.1173	-0.9242	-0.1059	-0.1348
Collective sector	Gini coefficient	0.2716	0.2840	0.2989	0.3324	0.3134
Wage income	Gini proportion	0.1132	0.1094	0.1318	0.1020	0.0959
	Gini elasticity	0.0154	0.1486	0.0416	0.0280	0.2212
Other sectors	Gini coefficient	0.7464	0.7548	0.7391	0.7420	0.7635
Wage income	Gini proportion	0.0231	0.0346	0.0411	0.0552	0.0739
	Gini elasticity	0.1973	0.0294	0.0337	0.0433	0.0595
Other income	Gini coefficient	0.1962	0.1885	0.2209	0.2263	0.2512
	Gini proportion	0.1056	0.0830	0.1045	0.0799	0.0791
	Gini elasticity	0.3291	0.1525	0.0300	0.1032	0.0238
Transfer	Gini coefficient	0.2512	0.2087	0.1675	0.2248	0.1930
	Gini proportion	0.2014	0.2245	0.1540	0.2049	0.2168
	Gini elasticity	0.0364	0.0578	-0.0129	0.2428	0.0293

Source: As Table 2.1.

result is that per capita income disparity among farmers grows faster than that of urban residents. When these two effects are reflected in the trend of income disparity between urban residents and farmers, we find that the income levels of farmers have remained lower than those of urban residents ever since 1978 and the urban–rural income difference has been growing larger.

To date, family farming income remains the main source of income for farmers. In 1995, it contributed to 79.1% of farmers' basic income, of which a larger share (68.8%) comes from agricultural production than other operations. Therefore, the more dependent a region is on agriculture, the more closely farmers' income is related to the price of agricultural products. Before 1984, rural system reform (that is, the adoption of the family responsibility system) and market development (that is, raising the prices of agricultural products) contributed to drastic increases in farmer's income (Lin, 1992). By the end of 1984 the effect of the farming institutional reform had been exhausted. Grain prices, which had been on the rise, dropped because of adjustments of the grain procurement and marketing system in 1985. The income of farmers began to stagger. Thereafter, the increase of farmer's income depended on the development of the non-agricultural sector and the up and down of prices of agricultural products, particularly of grain, led to the fluctuation of farmer's income. It was not until the 1990s when grain prices began to climb that the income of farmers started to grow faster again. In addition, the rapid development of township and village enterprises in the late 1980s was mainly concentrated in the east coastal region. The regional comparative advantages in the central and western regions were grain and other primary products. However, the prices of grain and major primary products were controlled and depressed. As a result, the GDP levels in the central and western regions lagged behind and the regional disparity of farmers' income increased. The expanding of regional disparity of farmers' income in the mid-1980s and thereafter was due to the differences of regional comparative advantages and the price structure.

We have once again used the Theil entropy decomposition method to study the impact of regional factors on the trend of per capita income disparity. We have first decomposed the regional disparities of the weighted average of urban and rural per capita income. Like the decomposition analysis of per capita GDP, we broke up the overall regional difference into the intra-regional disparity of each of the east, central and western regions and the interregional disparities among the three regions. As the last three columns of Table 2.6 show, among the factors contributing to the overall regional disparity of per capita income, the interregional disparities among the east, central and western regions have the strongest impact, contributing

Table 2.6 The contribution of intra- and interregional disparities to the overall regional disparity: the per capita income of eastern, central and western regions vs. urban area and rural area (%)

	Intra-east	Intra-central	Intra-west	Interregional disparities	Intra-rural	Intra-urban	Urban–rural disparities
1978	21.52	14.95	14.57	48.95	23.82	22.82	53.36
1979	21.21	14.78	14.67	49.34	24.16	23.21	52.63
1980	21.12	14.72	14.76	49.40	24.45	23.63	51.92
1981	20.79	14.75	14.87	49.59	24.72	23.95	51.33
1982	20.67	14.77	14.91	49.66	25.04	24.2	50.76
1983	20.61	14.81	14.95	49.64	25.33	24.43	50.24
1984	20.71	14.74	14.95	49.60	25.73	24.37	49.89
1985	20.74	14.73	14.92	49.62	25.17	24.36	50.47
1986	20.76	14.69	14.91	49.64	25.06	23.93	51.01
1987	20.73	14.66	14.85	49.76	25.23	23.98	50.79
1988	20.74	14.65	14.87	49.75	25.36	24.05	50.58
1989	20.84	14.62	14.81	49.73	25.38	23.77	50.85
1990	20.78	14.70	14.78	49.74	26.12	23.86	50.02
1991	20.77	14.61	14.66	49.96	26.27	23.65	50.08
1992	20.80	14.57	14.67	49.96	26.15	23.56	50.29
1993	20.99	14.43	14.61	49.96	26.10	23.4	50.50
1994	21.09	14.36	14.68	49.87	26.42	23.37	50.21
1995	20.88	14.39	14.58	50.15	27.02	23.47	49.51

Source: As Table 2.1.

to 50% of the overall disparity. The next major factor is internal disparity of the east region, contributing to more than 20% of the overall disparity, followed by internal differences of the central and western regions with each contributing about 15%. The impact of the internal disparity of the east and central regions are on the decline, though not significantly, while that of the western region is increasing slightly. As a result, the impact of interregional disparity among the three regions as the major factor determining the level of overall disparity, though not as obvious as in the case of per capita GDP, rose from 48.95% in 1978 to 50.15% in 1995.

By following the same methodology, we can observe the impact of internal disparities of per capita income in the rural and urban areas and that of urban–rural income disparity on the overall regional income disparity. From the figures on the right of Table 2.6, we can conclude that urban–rural disparity had the strongest impact on overall income disparity, contributing to more than 50% of the disparity on a continuous basis. The rest of the overall disparity resulted from internal disparities of the urban and rural areas, with the internal rural disparity contributing more than the urban disparity. In terms of the trend, the contribution of internal rural disparity is rising substantially, from 23.82% in 1978 to 27.02% in 1995. The contribution of internal urban disparity increased by a small margin only from 22.82% to 23.47%. An interesting phenomenon is that the contribution of urban–rural disparity to overall income disparity, important as it is, is actually on the decline, going down from 53.36% to 49.51%. This trend of decline began in 1979 and gained further momentum in the mid-1980s before the family contract responsibility system was extended to the whole country. While the expansion of the urban–rural income gap since reform easily attracted our attention, the fact that this gap is having a diminishing impact on the overall level of income disparity is often ignored.

To take another step further, we have broken down the regional disparity of per capita income into seven parts, that is, internal rural disparity of each of the three regions, internal urban disparity of each of the same regions and urban–rural disparity. Table 2.7 shows the results of our calculations. We can see that urban–rural income disparity, with a contribution rate of around 50%, is of predominant importance in determining the level of overall income disparity. The second major factor is the internal disparity of the east region, contributing to about 10%. The central and western regions share a similar rate ranging between 6% and 7%. In terms of the trend of change, the contribution rate of the internal rural disparity of the east region has gone up to 0.112 from 1978 to 1995 while that of internal urban disparity grew only 0.03 in the same period of time. The contribution rates of internal rural and urban disparities of the central and western regions remained relatively

Table 2.7 The contribution of intra- and interregional disparities to the overall regional disparity: the per capita income in the urban and rural area of eastern, central, and western regions (%)

	Internal rural disparity			Internal urban disparity			Urban–rural disparity
	Eastern rural	Central rural	Western rural	Eastern urban	Central urban	Western urban	Interregional
1978	9.66	6.97	6.80	9.17	6.75	6.78	53.87
1979	9.75	6.96	6.90	9.28	6.85	6.94	53.32
1980	9.85	7.04	7.07	9.41	6.97	7.08	52.60
1981	9.89	7.16	7.17	9.54	7.09	7.15	52.00
1982	10.05	7.23	7.25	9.62	7.16	7.23	51.46
1983	10.13	7.33	7.32	9.71	7.22	7.33	50.96
1984	10.42	7.23	7.30	9.70	7.17	7.27	50.90
1985	10.15	7.14	7.24	9.72	7.14	7.27	51.34
1986	10.07	7.05	7.14	9.55	7.05	7.07	52.07
1987	10.07	7.03	7.12	9.55	7.05	7.08	52.10
1988	10.09	7.06	7.16	9.59	7.08	7.06	51.96
1989	10.13	6.95	7.04	9.47	6.99	6.96	52.47
1990	10.54	7.06	7.11	9.44	7.02	6.99	51.84
1991	10.47	6.97	6.98	9.33	6.93	6.92	52.41
1992	10.33	6.86	6.89	9.28	6.86	6.84	52.94
1993	10.26	6.71	6.74	9.18	6.75	6.73	53.62
1994	10.41	6.70	6.68	9.17	6.70	6.67	53.67
1995	10.38	6.72	6.74	9.20	6.71	6.69	53.57

Source: As Table 2.1.

Table 2.8 Province-level and county-level Gini coefficients for the nation and county-level Gini coefficients for each province, 1992

	Per capita income	Rural per capita income	Urban per capita income
Nation (province-level)	0.1484	0.1437	0.0910
Nation (county-level)	0.3519	0.2003	0.1448
Beijing	0.0446	0.1330	
Tianjin	0.1434	0.0251	
Hebei	0.2996	0.1741	0.0616
Shanxi	0.3158	0.1460	0.0951
Neimenggu	0.2331	0.1328	0.0691
Liaoning	0.2408	0.1475	0.0631
Jilin	0.1991	0.0491	0.0505
Heilongjiang	0.2142	0.1240	0.0991
Shanghai	0.1171	0.0893	
Jiangsu	0.2991	0.1575	0.0813
Zhejiang	0.3134	0.2258	0.0498
Anhui	0.2593	0.1258	0.0533
Fujian	0.2375	0.1006	0.1229
Jiangxi	0.2154	0.1578	0.0289
Shandong	0.3118	0.1336	0.0586
Henan	0.2470	0.1301	0.0798
Hubei	0.3122	0.1554	0.0572
Hunan	0.2272	0.1181	0.0700
Guangdong	0.3969	0.1239	0.1194
Guangxi	0.2455	0.1710	0.0475
Hainan	0.2949	0.0818	
Sichuan	0.3038	0.1752	0.0445
Guizhou	0.3385	0.1770	0.0386
Yunnan	0.3886	0.2515	0.0499
Tibet	0.1644	0.1644	
Shaanxi	0.2954	0.1320	0.0652
Gansu	0.3803	0.2362	0.0706
Qinghai	0.3069	0.1510	
Ningxia	0.4259	0.3026	
Xinjiang	0.3141	0.1524	0.1048

Note: For the province, which is less than three samples, the Gini coefficient of urban per capita income is not calculated.

Source: As Table 2.1.

stable, with only minimal decline. The contribution rate of urban–rural disparity has also been creeping down. The situation described here correlates positively to situations mentioned in previous paragraphs.

The provincial data basically reflects the overall situation in each province. Nevertheless, it covers the intra-provincial differences. To overcome this shortcoming, we use the 1992 county-level data to estimate the income disparities in the nation as a whole and in each province. The results are reported in Table 2.8. First, comparing the results in the first and second rows, we see that, as expected, in the national level all three Gini coefficients – per capita income, per capita income in rural areas, and per capita income in urban areas – which are based on the county-level data are larger than the Gini coefficients which are based on provincial-level data. Second, whether the estimates are based on provincial data or county data and whether for each province or for the nation as a while, the Gini coefficient of per capita income is larger than the Gini coefficients of per capita income in rural areas and in urban areas. The results indicate that the urban–rural disparities are the major source of regional disparities in China. Third, for most provinces, the county-level Gini coefficients of per capita income are smaller than the county-level Gini coefficient of per capita income for the nation as a whole. This means the regional disparities in most provinces are smaller than the regional disparities for the national as a whole. However, Guangdong, Yunnan, Gansu and Ningxia are exceptions. In these four provinces, the intra-province regional disparities are larger than the regional disparities for the nation as a whole. Lastly, Beijing, Tianjin and Shanghai – the three largest metropolitan areas in China – the internal income disparities are the smallest among all the provinces.

5 REGIONAL DEVELOPMENT STRATEGY AND THE CHANGING PATTERN OF DISPARITIES

The GDP level of a country and the disparity of its per capita income are, in general, subject to the influence of two factors. First, the uneven regional distribution of conditions for economic growth. Second, the economic and social policies of the government related to regional development. The choice of economic development strategy will, in the final analysis, determine the effects of these two factors. One option is, a comparative advantage development strategy that focuses on the creation of an integrated national market system to facilitate the exploitation of the nation's comparative advantage. If interregional trade is transaction cost free, with integrated national markets, the interregional commodity trade alone will lead to the equalization of returns to factors of production across regions. In reality, commodity trade relies on a series of market facilities including transportation and storage. It is impossible to completely ease out regional differences of returns on production factors by interregional trade alone. An additional facilitator for narrowing the gap of returns on factors is the development of factor markets for the flow of production factors across regional borders. Under this development strategy, regional disparities may still be a fact of life because of historical, geographical and resource endowment reasons, but will tend to decline.

Contrary to the comparative advantage development strategy is the anti-comparative advantage development strategy, or the 'leap forward development strategy', which aims at accelerating the development of certain industries which are inconsistent with the comparative advantage of the economy. As it chooses to ignore the comparative advantage of a country or region, the prices of products and factors are, more often than not, distorted and the unified domestic market is suppressed. Therefore, the role of the product market and factor market in closing the regional gap is undermined, leading to unbalanced regional development. This development strategy can entrench some regions in a state of underdevelopment by impairing their basic conditions for economic growth (Lin et al., 1996).

Prior to the economic reform, China pursued a leap-forward development strategy with heavy industry as the first priority. As capital was scarce, resource allocation by the market was substituted by a central planning allocation system. With the absence of an integrated domestic market, the trade of products among the regions was suppressed. The industrial structure in a region did not correspond to the region's comparative advantage. Therefore, the function of market mechanisms in mitigating regional disparities was also suppressed. As such, the investment policy of the planned economy assumed a vital role in the economy. Under the traditional system, the regional development gap grew bigger as a result of denying the regional comparative advantages, but the tendency to grow was checked to a certain extent by the investment policies of central government, which somewhat favoured the underdeveloped central and western areas.

However, the traditional development strategy is by no means a strategy for balanced regional development. Despite investment policies biased towards the central and western regions, there were problems with the investment structure. First, most investment projects were heavy industry and military industry undertakings that did not conform with the comparative advantages of the regions. Consequently, the enterprises established with strong investment support from the state never attained self-sustainability and always depended upon protection by the government. After the initiation of reform, most heavy industrial enterprises have been struggling for survival except for those that shifted from military to civilian production at an earlier stage than others. Second, the investment was unevenly distributed within the central and western regions, concentrating in a few areas of a few provinces. It contributed to growing internal disparities in the central and western regions and thus to a larger development gap among regions. Third, as the investment was made regardless of local comparative advantages, it was not cost effective in that it neither brought about the development of related industrial sectors, nor promoted services and employment for the local population. Studies by Tsui (1991) fully explored the actual effects of the policy. He concluded that the redistribution and industrial structure policies of the central government before reform failed to achieve either efficiency or balanced economic development as Yang (1990) perceived. Therefore, the state-dominated development strategy practised before reform was more a leap-forward strategy as pointed out by Lin et al. (1996) than a distribution-oriented one as perceived by Yang.

From the perspective of patterns of regional development, it is not appropriate to conclude that the development strategy adopted since 1978 is an unbalanced development strategy (Yang, 1990). In general, the market-oriented reform measures since the late 1970s created better possibilities for the utilization of local comparative advantages by developing the product and factor markets. Development opportunities were made available to regions at different levels of development. A regional development strategy as such is more a comparative advantage strategy than those of the past. This is partially proved by the fact that there is no drastic change in the provincial disparity of per capita GDP. Meanwhile, we have also observed that the internal disparities of the three regions and their contribution to overall disparity is getting smaller while, on the other hand, the development gap among the three regions and its contribution to overall regional disparity is getting bigger. The situation shows that in the transition from an anti-comparative advantage development strategy to a comparative advantage strategy, provinces within a region shared a similar trend of change when utilizing market mechanism and development opportunities because of similar features and historical conditions. However, disparities among the regions begin to grow as a result of differences of features and historical conditions of the regions.

Compared with the central and western regions, the eastern region is in a much better position to make use of market opportunities, particularly those provided by the international market. First, transportation facilities as part of the market conditions make a great difference. Historically, China's population has always been concentrated in the coastal areas of southeast

China. Population density in the east far exceeds that of the central and western regions, which is also related to the intensity of economic activities. As a physical condition for market development, transportation capacity is not only a result of the intensity of economic activities, but also a contributor to the regional differences in the intensity of economic activity. There has always been a disparity among the three regions in terms of transportation capacity and, thus, the tremendous differences in their capacity in utilizing market opportunities. In fact, the intensity of transportation reflects, to a certain extent, the intensity of the market. Whatever the circumstances, the differences of physical conditions related to the market are undoubtedly an important factor leading to the disparities of development among the regions.

Second, the eastern region enjoys a higher level of social development and, therefore, better accumulation of human resources. The different levels of nutrition, health and education which affect the quality of the labour force are translated into differences of human resources of the regions. The new economic growth theory has showed that progress of education, health care and R&D has positive externality on productivity (UNDP, 1996). Differences in such progress are brought about by the differences of economic development of the regions and will, in turn, lead to larger regional disparities.

Third, the eastern region is closer to the international market in both human and geographical terms and in terms of its pattern of economic growth. China's opening to the outside world is characterized by an increasing influx of foreign capital and growing exports and imports. The southeast coastal region enjoys overwhelming advantages in attracting overseas investment because it is a close neighbour of Hong Kong, Macao and Taiwan, and home to most overseas Chinese. It is also endowed with favourable transportation and port facilities and a good position to benefit from entrepôt trade via Hong Kong. Export-oriented growth and the exploitation of the region's comparative advantage in labour-intensive production have facilitated various industries to locate in or to relocate to the region and to upgrade their production in accordance with the changes in the region's comparative advantages. It is also important that the eastern region is home to China's earliest special economic zones and development zones. Since the mid-1980s, the well-developed township and village enterprises of the eastern region have gained an important position in China's economic development. Moreover, the government's coastal development strategy in the mid-1980s granted many special policies to this region. Once conditions were laid down for utilizing market opportunities, economic growth of the east region began its benign cycles.

6 CONCLUSIONS AND RECOMMENDATIONS

The study of regional growth and income disparities shows that regional disparities in China since 1978 are mainly reflected by the differences among the eastern, central and western regions. Income disparity is found to be more remarkable than the growth disparity. In summary, when market mechanisms assume a greater role in guiding the economic development of the regions, the fundamental cause of regional income and growth disparities will increasingly be the disparity of their capacities to capitalize on market and development opportunities. This conclusion may lead to the following policy recommendations.

First, investment by direct government redistribution of resources is no longer applicable in the transition from an anti-comparative advantage, government-dominated development strategy to a comparative advantage, market-oriented development strategy. As pointed out in previous sections, the regional development policy based on the government's distribution of investment has failed to narrow regional gaps even at the expense of the incentive mechanisms and efficiency of economic growth. As the central and western regions are disadvantaged in their ability to make use of market opportunities, the social and economic policies of the government that aim at narrowing regional gaps should focus on the improvement of transportation and other infrastructure, education and health care of the residents and the labour force and capacity-building for capitalizing on market opportunities.

Second, it is still necessary to have an industrial policy that aims at reducing the regional development gap, but government support should be granted in accordance with the realities of the central and western regions. In the income disparity analysis, regional income disparity of farmers has experienced the most dramatic increase and is a major contributor to overall regional disparity. As regional income disparity of farmers is mainly a result of uneven employment in non-agricultural sectors, policies aimed at promoting the development of non-agricultural sectors in the central and western regions are to be commended. However, the effectiveness of the policies will depend on the sectors that they choose to promote. In the early 1990s, the central government gave great importance, in terms of credit and loans, to the development of township and village enterprises in the central and western regions. The policy did not turn out to be effective. When the government gave its support to township and village enterprises, it was, in fact, trying to boost rural industry. It is very costly to create and sustain industrial production capacity in the absence of necessary infrastructure and market conditions. The township and village enterprises set up with direct government support and interference are, more often than not, short-lived and can result in serious waste of capital resources. Trade has the potential function of reducing regional disparities. In the central and western regions, it is more pertinent and easier to achieve sustainable development of tertiary industry than industrial production. In line with the conclusions of this chapter, the growth of tertiary industry that facilitates interregional trade will contribute to narrowing the regional development gap. Therefore, trade-facilitating tertiary industry should be the focus of development efforts of the central and western regions in order to cut down regional disparities. In addition, the government should give a high priority to the development of market infrastructure in the central and western regions, including transportation, communication, and so on.

Third, for the purpose of reducing rural–urban disparities, the reform of price and distribution systems of agricultural products should be furthered. In the analysis of rural–urban income disparity, we see that both the rural–urban income disparity and its contribution to overall regional disparity are related to changes in the relative prices of agricultural products. By the end of 1994, the prices of more than 79% of agricultural products were determined by the market. However, the prices and distribution of grain remain under the control of the government. The incomes of farmers are, therefore, subject to the influence of both policy adjustments and market price fluctuations. While China as a whole is gradually losing its comparative advantage in agricultural production, the central and western regions (the central region in particular) still enjoy this comparative advantage. The policy of grain self-sufficiency in each province has not only wasted the resources of the developed regions, but also deprived the central and western regions of their comparative advantage in grain production. A market-oriented grain distribution and price system is highly desirable to promote specialization among regions, so that the central and western regions can make full use of their comparative advantages in grain production and the farmers can gain higher incomes from agricultural development.

NOTES

1. The calculations have not been weighted because of statistical constraints and are, therefore, different from those in the first section. However, the trends of change share similar patterns.
2. We have used the categorization of the State Statistics Bureau. The eastern region includes 12 provinces: Beijing, Tianjin, Hebei, Liaoning, Shanghai, Jiangsu, Zhejiang, Fujian, Shandong, Guangdong, Guangxi and Hainan. The western region includes nine provinces in south-west and north-west China: Sichuan (sometimes categorized as a central province), Guizhou, Yunnan, Tibet, Shaanxi, Gansu, Qinghai, Ningxia and Xinjiang. The central region includes all other provinces in China: Shanxi, Inner Mongolia, Jilin, Heilongjiang, Anhui, Jiangxi, Henan, Hubei.

REFERENCES

Adelman, I. and C.T. Morris (1973), *Economic Growth and Social Equity in Developing Countries*, Stanford: Stanford University Press.

Fei, J., G. Ranis and S. Kuo (1979), *Growth with Equity: the Taiwan Case*, New York: Oxford University Press.

Jiang, Z. (1995), 'Appropriately Dealing with Several Important Relations in the Construction of Socialist Modernization', *Documents of the CPC's Fifth Plenary Meeting of the Fourteenth Central Committee*, Beijing: People's Press.

Kuznets, S. (1955), 'Economic Growth and Income Inequality', *American Economic Review*, 45, pp. 1–28.

Lin, J.Y. (1992), 'Rural Reforms and Agricultural Growth in China', *American Economic Review*, 82(1), March, pp. 34–51.

Lin, J.Y., F. Cai, and Z. Li (1996), *The China Miracle: Development Strategy and Economic Reform*, Hong Kong: Chinese University Press.

Rozelle, S. (1993), 'Rural Inequality in China', Food Research Institute, Stanford University (mimeo).

Tsui, K.Y. (1991), 'China's Regional Inequality, 1952–1985', *Journal of Comparative Economics*, 15, pp. 1–21.

Tsui, K.Y. (1993), 'Decomposition of China's Regional Inequalities', *Journal of Comparative Economics*, 17, pp. 600–27.

UNDP (1996), *Human Development Report 1996*, New York: Oxford University Press.

Williamson, J. (1965), 'Regional Inequality and the Process of National Development', *Economic Development and Culture Change*, 13, p. 25

World Bank (1995), 'China Regional Disparities', *Report No. 14496-CHA*, Country Operations Division, China and Mongolia Department, East Asia and Pacific Regional Office.

Yang, D. (1990), 'Patterns of China's Regional Development Strategy', *China Quarterly*, June, pp. 230–57.

3. Provincial economic growth in China: causes and consequences of regional differentiation*

Barry Naughton

1 INTRODUCTION: PROGRESS AND PARADOX

There has been in recent years an outpouring of literature on provincial growth in China and on the economic disparities among Chinese provinces.[1] The large volume of literature is due to the confluence of two streams of scholarly interest. The first stream is China-specific: within China, and within the China research community, there has long been an interest in problems of regional equity and regional patterns of industrialization. This dates back to the critique during the 1920s–1940s of the 'unbalanced' pattern of early industrialization, which began in the foreign-dominated Treaty Ports along the coast. After 1949, the Chinese government announced that it would correct this pattern and it used central planning to redistribute investment inland and create a more 'balanced' distribution of industry. This strategy was later abandoned, and the subsequent adoption of a Coastal Development Strategy after 1987 has been accompanied by continuous discussion and debate over the distributional consequences of different development strategies.

The second stream consists of the new economic growth theories that have achieved prominence among the international community of economists recently, and that have stimulated interest in 'convergence' of economies initially at different developmental stages. Beginning with the innovative paper by Barro and Sala-I-Martin (1991), the convergence literature asks whether there is a general trend toward equalization in the return to different productive factors – and especially labour – as development proceeds in various areas. If convergence exists, the literature generally interprets this as

* This chapter has been published in a special issue of Revue d'Economie du Développement, no. 1-2, 1999.

a 'natural' outcome of the spread of information, technologies, and infrastructure that permits markets to spread and impose the 'law of one price'. Convergence may be 'conditional', applying only to economies with similar policy regimes and/or trading relationships, or 'absolute'. If there is no convergence, the literature invites us to ask if identifiable obstacles or barriers prevent convergence, or whether externalities and agglomeration economies reinforce regional differences. The convergence literature is interesting precisely because it explores what ought to be a fundamental characteristic of markets – that they lead to the equalization of factor returns – in a world characterized in fact by extreme differences in factor incomes.

China, with 30 provincial-level units publishing data, is a convenient source of data. Change in China has been rapid, so there is a great deal of activity to explain. Moreover, China should be an ideal case for testing propositions about economic growth. China is big, rugged and diverse, so that, within a common government and policy regime, there is wide scope for barriers imposed by geography, or by local policies or development levels. Market forces have increased enormously in China over the past two decades, so provincial growth paths might be expected to reveal something about the working of the market in China and perhaps about market processes in general. Thus, China could be a crucial source of empirical observations to prove or disprove general hypotheses relating to market forces, economic geography, and growth.

In spite of this intellectually promising situation, it is hard to resist the conclusion that recent progress in analysing regional development in China has been disappointing. Essentially this is because the initial empirical studies that make up the basic building blocks of contemporary analysis produced findings that were surprising, and sometimes contradictory or paradoxical. Subsequent analyses have not yet been able to integrate the most important findings into a persuasive interpretive framework. Existing empirical results can be grouped into three areas: convergence, rank order reversals, and sensitivity of results to deflation.

1.1 Convergence

The most important empirical result is a finding of regional convergence, first reported by David Denny (1991). Provincial GDP (or net material product) per capita, measured at current prices, converged through the 1980s. Inter-provincial inequality declined significantly through 1990; subsequently there was a tendency toward renewed widening of inequality, but the trend is not sufficient to reverse the previous result. This result is quite robust: related findings have been reported by, among others, Chen and Fleisher (1996), Guillaumont and Debray (1996), and Jian et al. (1996). Figure 3.1 shows my own version of the (updated) Denny result, based on current price GDP per capita of 29 province-level units (Tibet has been discarded; Hainan has been retroactively separated from the rest of Guangdong). The figure shows the coefficient of variation (COV), which is the standard deviation divided by the mean, a measure of divergence. This measure declined by 39% through 1990, before rebounding slightly for a total decline of 34% by 1997.

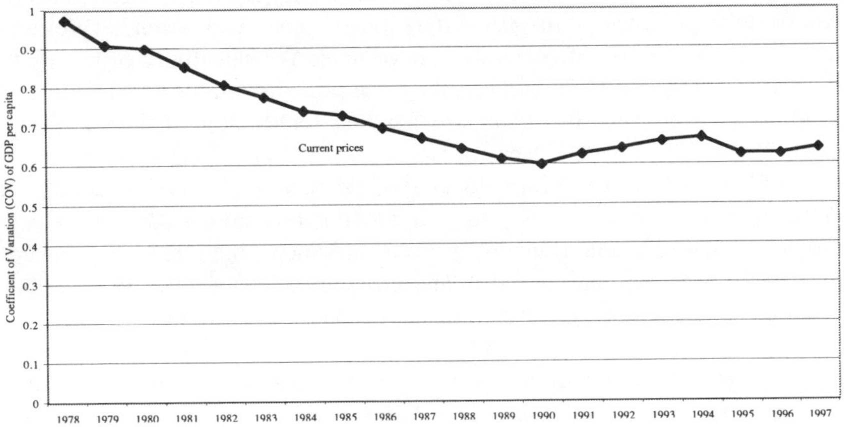

Figure 3.1 Provincial disparities: GDP per capita COV

Since 1990, there has been a trend toward increased divergence, but the magnitude is not large. The year-to-year pattern in the 1990s is not particularly meaningful, but the multi-year trend is strongly supported. The drop in the COV in 1995 is partially due to an adjustment of provincial population figures after a special census in that year. The adjusted figures reflect rural to urban migration more accurately, and thus pick up population shifts of significant magnitude beginning around 1992. The overall pattern of strong convergence through the 1980s, followed by modest divergence in the 1990s is thus well founded (cf. Fan, 1995; Lyons, 1991).

These results are surprising to many. Casual observers of China have believed that coastal provinces are experiencing accelerating growth, and that the gap between the rich coastal provinces and the poor inland provinces has been increasing. Big differences in geographical and human capital endowment that favour coastal provinces have been reinforced by preferential government policies for open coastal regions. Moreover, in the popular mind, economic reforms are associated with a general trend away from egalitarian but inefficient socialism, towards a more efficient, but inevitably less 'fair' market economy. As a result, there is a widespread received wisdom that regional disparities in China are widening. How can we reconcile those impressions with the robust finding of convergence?

Thus far, the major efforts to reconcile empirical research with casual observation have been through examining the relationship between interprovincial change and interregional change. The aggregate of provinces can display certain statistical characteristics even while 'regions' – aggregates of two or more provinces – display different, even contrasting trends (Wei and Ma, 1996). A number of researchers have noted the sensitivity of results to the way in which the three outliers, the three province-level municipalities of Beijing, Tianjin, and Shanghai, are handled (especially Shanghai) (Tsui, 1991; Yang, 1997). One clever attempt to incorporate all these trends into a single framework was put forward in a World Bank report (1997: 20–21). It argued that there is a tendency toward convergence among the (12) coastal provinces, and also among the (17) inland provinces, but a tendency toward divergence between coastal and inland provinces. This accurately describes what the numbers show, given a particular decomposition of the data.

Nonetheless, there are a number of problems with this literature as it stands. First, it's not entirely clear what the conclusions are: is regional inequality in China increasing or not? Is there really an evident trend toward convergence? Second, if there are processes of partial or contingent convergence, why is this so? What factors might prevent convergence on a broader geographic scale, while facilitating convergence on a more limited scale? Instead of addressing these questions, analysts tend to *ad hoc* arguments about economic growth. One popular explanation is that regional trends reflect early success in rural reforms. For example, Jian et al. (1996: 14–15) argue that:

> China exhibited strong regional income convergence after the onset of market reforms in 1978 ... convergence occurred during the first phase [1978–85] of reform because rural areas started out below average in per-capita income and then benefited disproportionately from the reforms and thus grew faster ... convergence occurred during the second phase of reform for two reasons: poorer rural areas continued to grow fast; but rural areas near open coastal cities grew especially fast.

This statement is plausible, but doesn't explain what it means when it declares that rural areas benefited disproportionately. It implies that agriculture grew more rapidly than other sectors, and that differential agricultural growth can explain regional growth differentials, both of which are demonstrably false. There is no discussion of relative price changes, and the question of what the specific mechanism of differential growth could be is left open.

1.2 Rank Order Reversals

The second striking empirical fact is that economic change since 1978 has brought enormous changes in the rank order of provincial GDP per capita (Table 3.1). It is worth noting how unusual this is. In studies of US regional

Table 3.1 Change in provincial GDP per capita rankings

	Rank in 1978	Rank in 1995	Change in Rank
Fujian	24	9	15
Guangdong	16	5	11
Hainan	17	6	11
Zhejiang	14	4	10
Guangxi	29	19	10
Shandong	19	10	9
Xinjiang	18	12	6
Anhui	26	21	5
Inner Mongolia	20	16	4
Henan	27	23	4
Yunnan	28	25	3
Hunan	22	20	2
Sichuan	25	24	1
Shanghai	1	1	0
Beijing	2	2	0
Tianjin	3	3	0
Jiangsu	7	7	0
Hubei	15	15	0
Guizhou	30	30	0
Hebei	11	13	-2
Jilin	12	14	-2
Jiangxi	23	26	-3
Liaoning	4	8	-4
Heilongjiang	5	11	-6
Shaanxi	21	27	-6
Shanxi	9	18	-9
Qinghai	6	17	-11
Ningxia	10	22	-12
Gansu	13	29	-16
Tibet	8	28	-20

Note: Current price provincial GDP per capita.

growth, it has been shown that the relative positions of US states changes very little over long periods of time. The rank order of state GDP per capita has changed very little in 100 years, with states moving up two or three places in rank order at most. By contrast, in China provinces have moved up – and down – 10 places in a rank order of 28 provinces. The pace of relative change in China is enormous, and is not easily explained with reference to theories of convergence, or lack of convergence.

1.3 Sensitivity of Results to Deflation

The results on convergence are sensitive to proper deflation. When province-specific GDP deflators are used, much of the convergence result disappears. Figure 3.2 shows changes in the GDP per capita COV for real GDP. It emerges that the main reason predominantly rural provinces appear to grow more rapidly is that systematic changes in relative prices favour the agricultural sector. Relative price changes are as important an explanation for observed trends as are differences in real growth rates, such as the more rapid growth of rural-based industry than urban industry. Province-specific GDP deflators have only been available for the last year or two. Thus, earlier studies were unable to use GDP deflators, and instead used, for example, provincial retail price indices to deflate data. Unfortunately, these surrogates are practically and theoretically inadequate to reflect real differences in inter-provincial price trends.

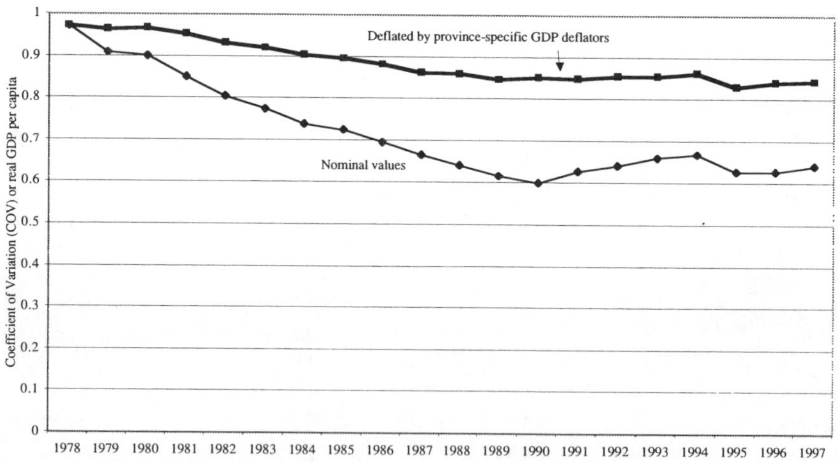

Figure 3.2 Provincial disparities: COV of real GDP (per cent)

This chapter argues that these striking empirical facts cannot be well explained by the standard approaches to growth and convergence that have been applied to the data thus far. Instead, I argue that regional growth can only be understood by placing it in the context of the system of interregional redistribution that prevailed under the planned economy. Observed trends can largely be explained as the outcome of the gradual erosion of the system of redistribution, and the slow reassertion of tendencies that were suppressed during the period of the planned economy. Conversely, I argue that neglecting these factors leads to a misunderstanding of regional growth trends.

At the outset, we can differentiate between three different regional effects of the redistributive system. First, and most obviously, the redistributive system provides resources differentially to different provinces, primarily through the mechanism of industrial investment. Planners concentrate resources in government hands, and distribute them to provinces according to their own preferences, politics, and development strategies. Conversely, as the redistributive system declines in relative importance, provinces that previously benefited from redistributive investment policies will experience a relative decline in economic standing. Second, the redistributive system depended on a particular price system to accumulate resources in the hands of planners in the first place. The price system substituted for an explicit taxation system, and relied primarily on keeping prices of agricultural products low. By keeping farmers' incomes and workers' food costs low, those low prices concentrated profits in the hands of urban state-owned factories. This price system affected provinces differently, placing a higher tax burden on provinces with large numbers of farmers. Conversely, as the redistributive price system erodes, provinces previously disadvantaged by confiscatory agricultural pricing will experience a relative improvement in economic standing. Third, and finally, while the preceding two changes will have an immediate impact on the distribution of resources and income across provinces, they will also have a delayed long-term effect on growth, as resources invested in new production gradually come on stream. How changes in resource distribute affect long-run growth depends ultimately on the differences in productivity across provinces. If there are sustained differences in factor returns, high productivity provinces will both attract more investment and use it more efficiently as market forces spread.

The gradual erosion of the redistributive system during economic reform can be expected to produce all the effects described in the previous paragraph, but at an uneven pace. I will argue below that changes in the extent of redistribution actually began before economic reforms, but continued and accelerated after reform began. Changes in relative prices had the most important impact during the early 1980s: the main effect was an increase in farm prices. This had an immediate impact in increasing regional equity, since farmers are by far the lowest income group of Chinese. But while the erosion of the redistributive system had a progressive impact on income distribution in the short run, it had a very different impact on long-run growth processes. Real growth quickly accelerated in provinces with superior endowments. When the singular institutional changes of the reform period are fully integrated into our perspective on regional growth, we are left with strong contemporary trends that are tending to cause divergence at the present and into the foreseeable future. Surprisingly, one of the most significant trends is the relative decline of the north, and the rise of the south. Despite the conclusion that regional disparities are increasing, there are reasons for optimism. Already, we can discern a pattern in which the benefits of economic growth may be beginning to spillover from the most advanced coastal provinces into some nearby provinces that are large, populous and relatively poor.

2 THE REDISTRIBUTIVE SYSTEM

On the eve of reform, in 1978, patterns of provincial output were significantly influenced by central government policy, which had been broadly redistributive for 30 years. As a result, the analysis of regional growth in China in subsequent years largely reflects the legacy of the institutions and allocative choices made under the planned economy. The reform process must be understood both as the unravelling of the planned economy, and as the gradual formation of a market economy. It is of course widely recognized that the Chinese government made extensive efforts to redistribute industrial development inland during the entire period of planned industrialization. First the northeast, then several central region cities, and finally the inland 'Third Front' regions were given priority (Lardy, 1980; Naughton, 1988). However, the impact that this programme had on the measured provincial income on the eve of reform it is not often appreciated. Before reform, industrial location and provincial income were substantially determined by planners' redistributive policies.

Figure 3.3 shows the 'top third' richest provinces in 1978.[2] It is quite an odd assortment: three municipalities, three northeast provinces dominated by heavy industry, the advanced lower Yangtze province of Jiangsu, and two far inland provinces, Qinghai and Ningxia. With the exception of Jiangsu, these provinces are all clear beneficiaries of the redistributive system, though in different ways. The northeast enjoyed investment priority for many years, and the three municipalities benefited from the socialist price system and the large number of state-owned factories they possessed. Most striking are the cases of Qinghai and Ningxia. They show up as rich essentially because the central government moved substantial numbers of 'urban' workers into these relatively remote locales. Because these provinces had modest agricultural populations to begin with, a high proportion of their labour force was engaged in modern-sector activities, in this case activities that were sponsored and subsidized by the central government. It makes sense to think of these provinces as 'precociously' urbanized far beyond their 'natural' potential.

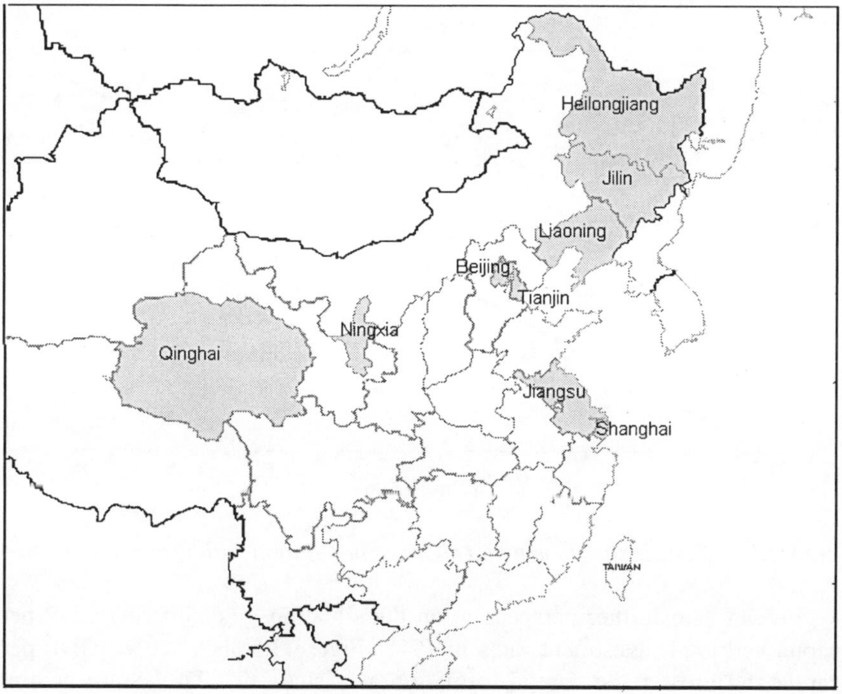

Figure 3.3 'Top Third' richest provinces, 1978 (nine provinces with highest GDP per capita in 1978)

Provincial income was largely explained by the share of urban dwellers in the province's population. Figure 3.4 shows 1978 GDP per capita for each province, along with the share of provincial population with urban resident status.[3] The top nine per capita GDPs are also the top nine in the share of urban residents (with one exception, Jiangsu). Moreover, the relationship between share of urban residents and GDP per capita is robust throughout the range of income levels, as Figure 3.4 shows. Share of urban residents is so dominant in explaining provincial per capita GDP, that there is not much scope for additional factors. Yet share of urban residents significantly reflects government redistributive policies, since the central government could and did assign state workers to development projects in different regions. At the other extreme, seven of the poorest nine provinces in 1978 were also in the bottom third in terms of share of urban residents. This group contains large populations that are predominantly agricultural. They are also predominantly southern.

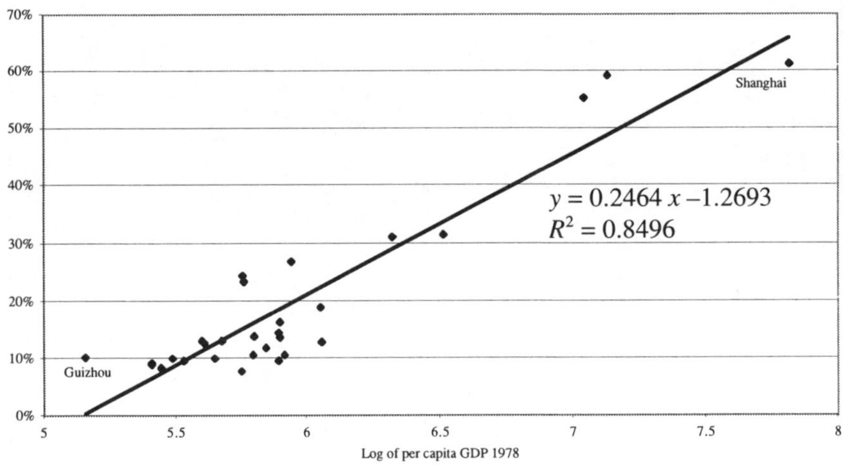

Figure 3.4 Per capita income and share of population with urban status

We can gain further perspective on the situation by comparing GDP per capita and total investment rates in 1978. Figure 3.5 shows 1978 GDP per capita and gross fixed capital formation as a share of GDP.[4] Since central government policy was broadly redistributive, and investment was primarily decided by government planners in 1978, most provinces fall into the northwest or southeast quadrants, reflecting either high investment in low-income provinces, or low investment in high-income provinces. Shanghai, always the outlier, is far to the southeast, with the lowest investment rate and by far the highest income. But the provinces in the northeast and southwest quadrants are also of great interest. The provinces in the northeast, which I label 'beneficiaries', are those provinces that received so much investment that it boosted them into the ranks of provinces with per capita GDP above the median. These provinces have very high investment rates, above 50% in the cases of Ningxia and Qinghai. There are only five provinces in this quadrant. In the southwest quadrant there are four provinces which have investment rates below the median, despite the fact that their per capita GDPs are also below the median. Two are coastal–Zhejiang and Fujian–but two are inland–Henan and Anhui. I label these four provinces 'orphans', because of their relative neglect despite obvious poverty.

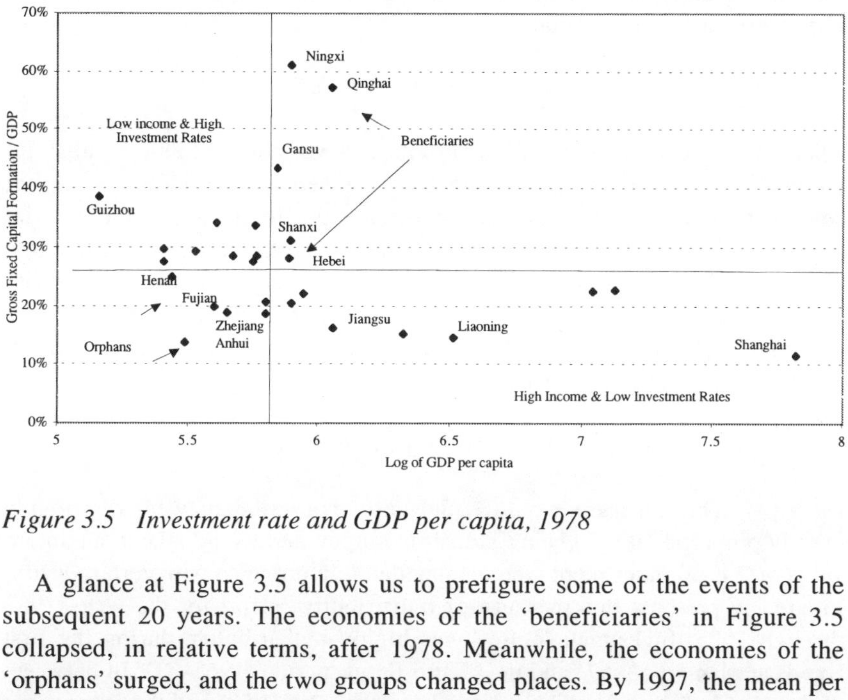

Figure 3.5 Investment rate and GDP per capita, 1978

A glance at Figure 3.5 allows us to prefigure some of the events of the subsequent 20 years. The economies of the 'beneficiaries' in Figure 3.5 collapsed, in relative terms, after 1978. Meanwhile, the economies of the 'orphans' surged, and the two groups changed places. By 1997, the mean per capita GDP of the four orphans was two-thirds *higher* than that of the five beneficiaries. Moreover, not all the 'orphans' are coastal provinces. The fact that these two groups first converge, then switch places, and then diverge obviously contributes to the empirical patterns discussed in the first section of this chapter.

3 THE END OF REDISTRIBUTION

3.1 Changes in the Regional Distribution of Investment

3.1.1 In the mid-1970s, before the beginning of economic reforms, planners substantially scaled back the intensity of the redistributive effort

A few simple statistics make it possible to describe changes in government redistributive activity over time. One approach would be to compute, for each province and each year, the difference between the respective shares of that province in national industrial investment and in national industrial output. That is, for each province compute

$$R_p = Inv_p \,/\, Inv - Ind_p /Ind$$

where a p subscript indicates a province, a variable without a subscript indicates the national total, and *Inv* represents state industry capital construction investment, and *Ind* represents the total value of industrial output.[5] This measure will be positive if the province is a relative beneficiary of government investment policies, receiving a larger share of industrial investment than its share in output, and negative in the reverse case.

A national measure of redistributive effort can then be calculated by summing the absolute values of all R_p. That is,

$$R = \Sigma \left| Inv_p \,/\, Inv - Ind_p /Ind \right|$$

for all p. This measure would equal zero if investment were distributed exactly proportional to existing industrial output, and would take a maximum value of 2 if all investment were channelled to a province with zero industry. Figure 3.6 presents this measure of redistributive effort for the years 1953 through 1995. Investment policy was highly redistributive during the first five-year plan (1953–57) and the 'Third Front' period (1965–71). In between, during the period of the 'Great Leap Forward' (1958–60) and the subsequent economic recovery period (1961–64), the redistributive effort was moderated. Most striking, though, is the fall-off in redistributive effort after 1971. From 1973 onward, R falls sharply, and during the 1980s the redistributive effort is only half what it was in previous periods. The end of large-scale central government redistribution in China basically came in 1973–75.

It is striking that this change came during the mid-1970s, before the initiation of major economic reforms. The planners themselves began to perceive the high costs and limited results of the redistributive programme, particularly that which directed investment to remote Third Front locations. From the mid-1970s, central planners attempted to direct investment resources towards locations that would enable them to increase economic growth, that is, back toward the existing industrial bases, which had relatively favourable endowments. The ability to redistribute resources geographically is one of the major *raisons d'être* for central planning. If central planning is not being used to redistribute resources, there is one less argument for retaining central planning. This shift in planners' philosophy may have been one of the contributing factors leading to China's reform policies.

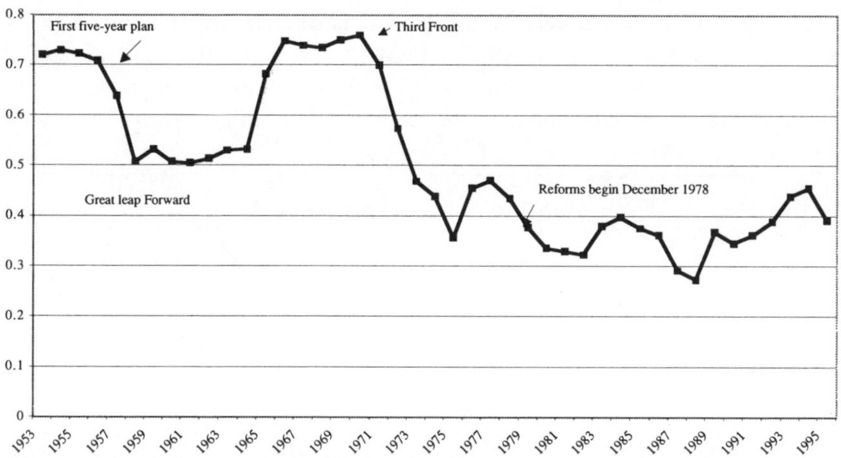

Figure 3.6 Industrial investment policy: degree of regional redistribution

3.1.2 With the onset of reform, the remaining redistribution became much less progressive (favoured low income provinces less)

Changes in government redistributive policy were not limited to changes in redistributive effort. Generally speaking, Chinese government redistribution has been progressive, in the sense that relative beneficiaries of industrial investment policy (in the sense defined above) have generally had lower incomes, as measured by GDP per capita. However, the degree of progressivity has also varied substantially over time. One measure of progressivity would be the simple correlation coefficient between R_p, the measure of investment redistribution defined above, and provincial per capita GDP in any given year. Figure 3.7 shows this measure for each year from 1953 through 1995, and the changes are striking. During the first five-year plan (1953–57), progressivity was moderate, with a correlation coefficient around –0.4. Although the redistributive effort was large, much of its was focused on industry in the relatively well-endowed northeast, as well as some central provinces. From 1958 through 1980, redistribution was highly progressive, with a correlation coefficient around –0.8. While redistributive effort fluctuated during those years, what redistribution there was consistently went to provinces that had relatively low per capita GDPs.

After 1980, however, government policy ceased to systematically redistribute industrial investment toward poorer provinces. Correlation coefficients fluctuate between zero and –0.3. Many past beneficiaries have been cut off, and forced to restructure. While mild progressivity persists, it is barely significant. Moreover, the scale of redistributive effort having already been reduced after the mid-1970s, there is, after 1980, little in central government investment policy that could be expected to systematically offset whatever regional trends would be created by market forces.

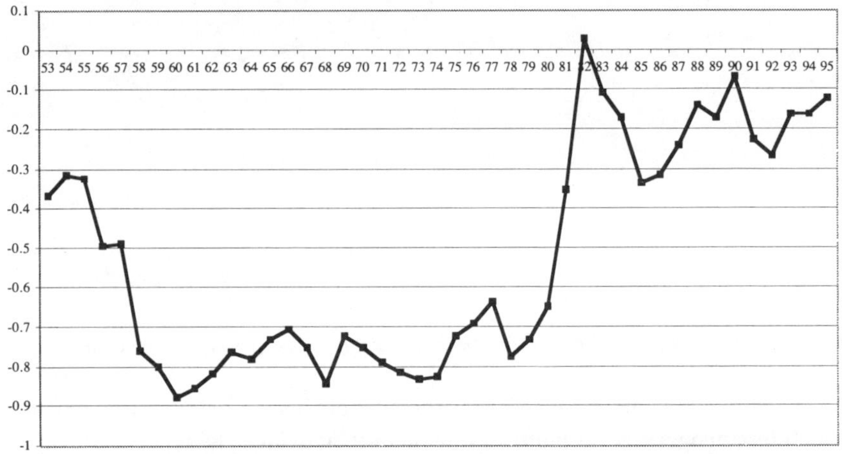

Figure 3.7 Correlation between redistributive flows and per capita GDP

To be sure, Figure 3.7 summarizes a complex reality. Investment policy has at various times favoured or discriminated against key industrial provinces such as Shanghai, Guangdong, Sichuan and the three northeastern provinces. It has consistently discriminated against coastal provinces such as Shandong, Jiangsu, and Zhejiang. These three provinces, with their large non-state industrial sectors, have never received state industrial investment proportional to their output, even though they were below the national average GDP per capita through the 1970s. Equally consistently, at least since the mid-1950s, policy has favoured the western provinces, in an arc from Yunnan through Xinjiang. Seven provinces in the West – not including Sichuan – consistently received investment greater than their share of output over the last 40 years, continuing up to the present. However, as the relative magnitude of these transfers has changed, the overall impact of government redistribution has also shifted.

After 1980, redistribution was no longer the predominant force in changes in regional development, except insofar as the legacy of past redistribution influenced how we see contemporary developments. Nevertheless, that legacy remains important in explaining observed trends. Discussion of convergence, or of trends in regional inequality, inevitably refers to movement from some designated starting point. In China, though, that starting point cannot be naively considered a state of 'underdevelopment', but rather must be seen as the outcome of years of intrusive state-directed development strategies.

3.1.3 Total investment became strongly regressive after the late 1980s

During the 1980s, the relationship between total investment and provincial development levels changed even more fundamentally than that between state capital construction and provincial GDP per capita. With economic reform and decentralization, a larger share of state enterprise revenues were left retained within the firm, so local investment increased rapidly as a share of total state investment. The distribution of this kind of state investment naturally tended to replicate the existing distribution of provincial industry and income. After 1982, total state investment was thus positively correlated with provincial GDP per capita. Non-state investment was initially small, but became increasingly important after the mid-1980s. At first, nearly all of this non-state investment went to rural township and village enterprises. Rural enterprises were of course located in the countryside, so there was a strong correlation between non-state investment and the agricultural share of the population through the mid-1980s. Since more rural provinces are poorer, non-state investment was 'progressive', going to lower income provinces at this time. However, during the 1990s, non-state investment – now swelled by private and foreign investment – also shifted to a positive correlation with GDP per capita.

These changes are shown for the single year 1995 in Figure 3.8, which replicates the format of Figure 3.5. By the mid-1990s, total investment has become strongly positively correlated with provincial per capita income. As investment pours into the richer provinces from both state and non-state funding sources, the growth processes that contribute to regional divergence are accelerating. The two richest municipalities –Shanghai and Beijing– actually have the highest total investment rates. Investment flows on this scale contribute to inequality today, but more crucially will fuel increasing divergence in the future.

3.2 The Redistributive Price System

Thus far, we have discussed geographical redistribution as if it could be treated in isolation from the price system. In fact, the only way to make sense of these results is to investigate them in the context of the changing government role in the price system. Government redistribution was intimately related to the price system. The socialist price system overvalued manufactured products – creating high profitability, while 'squeezing' agriculture through the 'price scissors'. The government then tapped into this profitability by drawing state-owned industrial enterprise profits directly into the state budget. Inevitably, this meant that measured income was particularly high in urban and manufacturing provinces, and these provinces made net financial contributions to the central government budget that were used to fund transfers to poorer provinces.

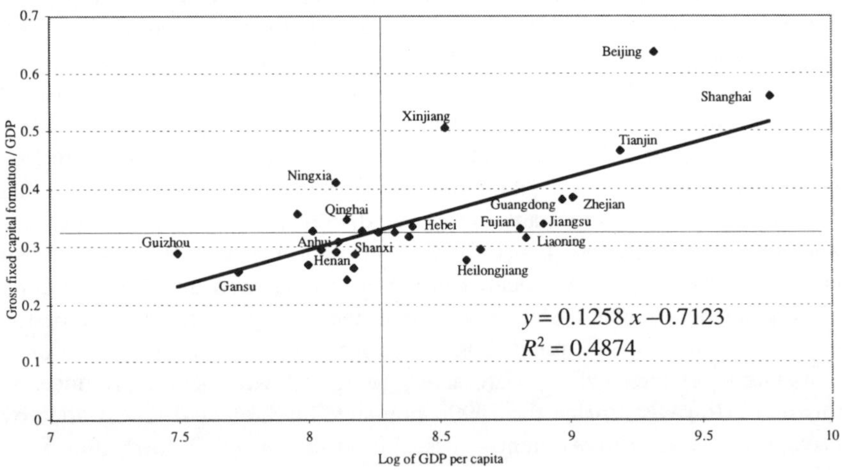

Figure 3.8 Investment rate and GDP per capita, 1995

It is important to keep this perspective in mind when discussing trends in regional inequality. Even apparent beneficiaries were sometimes penalized by the system. The central government (through the price system) artificially concentrated revenues in urban centres, then collected them and transferred them to areas of new investment. Some revenues were transferred to rural areas which had been disadvantaged by the price system in the first place. Who really benefited from this system? It is not easy to make a simple judgement. Most important for our purposes, though, is to recognize and properly account for the large changes in relative prices that were caused by the beginning of reform. Generally speaking, the monopoly system that privileged industry with high mark-ups has gradually eroded and disappeared (Naughton, 1992). All else held constant, such a change in relative prices will cause urban centres to diverge less from the rest of the (predominantly rural) economy; that is, they will stand out less obviously as high-income outliers. Yet if this change in relative prices is also accompanied by a reduction in transfers away from those high-income outliers, there may be relatively little change in productivity or welfare (this point is made very well in Garbaccio and La Croix, 1997). Of course, it will never be the case that all else could be held constant: changing prices and redistributive relationships will also be accompanied by changes in growth patterns, and also changes in the pattern of net beneficiaries. However, in principle it is important to control for the offsetting effects of changing price relations.

This general point can be illustrated by focusing on the case of Shanghai. A discussion of the particular experience of Shanghai is justified by its importance, its extreme value in all the data we have been examining, and the dramatic changes in policy that have affected its position. All of China's big cities were net contributors to the government budget. But Shanghai was the biggest, most productive city, and by 1978, it was contributing by far the most to the central budget. Yet Shanghai's relation to the national economy, both before and after 1978, has been deeply paradoxical. Consider first trends up through 1978. Throughout the 1952–78 period, national investment policy discriminated against Shanghai, and resources were redistributed away to other regions. Shanghai's share of Chinese industrial output declined from 19% in 1952, with some bumps, to 12% in 1978. But paradoxically, Shanghai's share of national income (measured here by net material product (NMP)) increased substantially from below 6% to 8%, and NMP per capita compared to the national average actually doubled! In 1952, Shanghai's NMP per capita was 3.7 times the China average; and by 1978 was 7.1 times that average.[6]

The increase in Shanghai's share of national income reflected the increasing profitability of Shanghai's industries (profit is part of value added, and thus part of national income and GDP). By 1978, the average total rate of return (profit and tax) on capital in Shanghai industry was 75%, compared to 24% nationally. Already astonishing, the rate of return actually increased to 80% in 1980, before beginning a long secular decline (Ho and Tsui, 1996: 161). Planners, of course, took away virtually all the super-normal profits that Shanghai earned. By 1978, the government budget was drawing a net sum of money out of Shanghai equal to 60% of its total GDP (Ho and Tsui, 1996; Garbaccio and La Croix, 1997). This can be seen as an unfair exaction on Shanghai (White, 1989). But it should also be recognized that planners were tapping into revenues that they themselves had created, by keeping industrial prices high and by keeping traditional industries 'penned up' within Shanghai.

Moreover, from the beginning of the reform process, Shanghai was restricted and limited by the enormous attention paid to it by the more conservative factions in the national government, and especially by Chen Yun and his group. Precisely because of Shanghai's enormous financial and technological importance to the national economy, conservatives led by Chen kept a close eye on the city.[7] Chen Yun made sure that Shanghai did not establish any Special Economic Zones, or grant special privileges to foreign investors. He maintained his own protégés in leadership positions in Shanghai, especially in the person of Chen Guodong, Party Secretary between 1980 and 1985.[8] It was not until 1987–88 that policy really shifted. At that time Jiang Zemin became Party Secretary and Zhu Rongji became Mayor. Perhaps more crucial than the change of personnel, though, is that at the same time, Zhao Ziyang introduced the Coastal Development Strategy and a new programme of fiscal decentralization. This meant for the first time that Shanghai had access to its incremental foreign exchange earnings, and that its fiscal burden was capped at a predictable level. At this point, Shanghai's position in the national economy began to change. Resources to carry out industrial restructuring began to be available. Subsequently, the entire national leadership endorsed a new more dynamic role for Shanghai, with the approval of the Pudong New Zone in April 1990. Investment in Shanghai began to take off, and it assumed its position as the highest investing province, shown in Figure 3.8.

Shanghai shows that the changes set in motion by the erosion of the redistributive system do not occur at a uniform pace in different localities. In Shanghai, the price changes occurred *first,* so Shanghai was squeezed by shifts in relative prices *before* it had a chance to benefit from changes in the direction of redistributive investment. As a result, the 1980s were a very difficult period for the city, but the 1990s have seen a kind of renaissance. In other provinces, of course, the sequence of changes was quite different.

Putting together the result of changes in the price system in all provinces, we get the result seen most clearly by comparing Figure 3.1 and Figure 3.2. Most of the convergence of GDP per capita in the 1980s disappears when properly deflated provincial data are used. Alternately stated, most of the convergence of current price income is due to changes in relative prices. Using current price province-level data, there is an apparent convergence of provincial GDP per capita equivalent to a 34% decline in the COV. Of this reduction of 34%, though, relative price changes account for a reduction of 23%. This shows that systematic shifts in prices that favoured low-income (and predominantly agricultural) provinces were the single most important cause of the convergence of nominal incomes during the 1980s. Jian et al. (1996) are correct to say that rural areas 'benefited disproportionately' from the reforms, but wrong to say that they 'thus grew faster'. In fact, the benefit came predominantly through a shift in relative prices. Changing relative prices, in turn, reflect the collapse of the socialist price system, and the impact of prices closer to those dictated by the market. Erosion of monopoly protection for manufacturing will slow the apparent growth rate of industrialized provinces. Or, saying the same thing from the other side, more rapid increases in agricultural than industrial prices will benefit predominantly agricultural (and predominantly poor) provinces, making them appear to 'catch up' if we use current price data. If we are concerned solely with equity, we might wish to continue using current price relationships, since current prices, after all reflect what provincial actors actually receive for their productive activity.[9] However, if we are concerned with real growth patterns, we will wish to remove the effects of relative price changes.

4 MEASURED TRENDS: RELATIVE CHANGES AND SHIFTING COMPETITIVENESS

Table 3.2 shows real provincial per capita GDP growth, over the entire 1978–1995 period. Growth is deflated by province-specific GDP deflators, so the data correspond to the trends plotted in Figure 3.2 (rather than Figure 3.1). Omitting Tibet from consideration, note that the three slowest growing provinces include three from the list of the wealthiest provinces in 1978, Ningxia, Heilongjiang, and Qinghai. In essence, what happened in these provinces is that expensive central government programmes of industrialization collapsed after the introduction of market forces. Part of the apparent convergence is the phenomenon of artificially rich provinces returning toward a more normal ranking. Indeed, provinces like Ningxia and

Qinghai are clearly headed from the top third to the bottom third; for these provinces, 'convergence' will be only temporary, as they pass through the middle on their way to the bottom. Conversely other provinces – notably Fujian – were in a position to exploit fundamental locational and human capital advantages, once they were released from the constraints of the centrally planned system. It is not surprising to find Fujian near the top in growth rates, shown in Table 3.2.

Thus, part of what we observe in China post-1978 is not convergence so much as reversion. That is, 'outliers' return to a position more in line with their underlying economic fundamentals, once the impact of government redistributive policies is relaxed. Given the fact that provinces like Qinghai and Fujian were such extreme outliers in 1978, reversion looks like convergence in its early stages. However, reversion needs to be distinguished from convergence. This is partially, but not primarily, because reversion will only temporarily look like convergence – once provinces return to a ranking more in accord with their fundamentals, the apparent convergence will disappear. More important is what the phenomenon means for the analysis of growth. Reversion does not imply that a process of equalization of returns to factors (like labour or capital) is underway, except in the most mechanical way. It is entirely consistent with a long-run pattern of widening regional inequality.

Table 3.2 Real per capita GDP growth (1978-95)

Zhejiang	12.8%	Inner Mongolia	8.3%
Guangdong	12.2%	Yunnan	8.2%
Fujian	12.1%	Guangxi	8.0%
Jiangsu	11.5%	Shanghai	8.0%
Shandong	10.6%	Liaoning	7.7%
Hainan	10.2%	Shaanxi	7.6%
Henan	9.2%	Tianjin	7.5%
Xinjiang	9.2%	Beijing	7.5%
Anhui	9.1%	Guizhou	7.5%
Hubei	9.0%	Hunan	7.4%
Jiangxi	8.8%	Gansu	6.9%
Shanxi	8.7%	Ningxia	6.6%
Hebei	8.7%	Tibet	6.5%
Sichuan	8.5%	Heilongjiang	6.1%
Jilin	8.4%	Qinghai	5.1%

4.1 Patterns of Shifting Competitiveness

As market forces have become more important, regions have experienced shifts in competitiveness and have faced unprecedented pressures to restructure their industries. To analyse competitiveness and structural change, I use the method known as shift-share analysis to decompose provincial growth, first for growth by GDP components and then for industrial sectors. This enables us to uncover the mechanics of differential growth rates. This exercise demonstrates clearly that differences in the pace of industrialization dominate all other factors in explaining provincial differences in growth rates.

Shift-share analysis is based on the idea that provincial growth can be analysed as the sum of three factors. Provincial growth equals the national average growth rate, plus differences in expected growth due to provincial output structure in the initial period, plus changes in competitiveness (or market share) in each of the major components of output. 'Competitiveness' here is simply derived as a residual: it includes any change in national output share for the particular sector. It could be low because economies are shedding activities as part of upgrading, or high because economies are benefiting from restructuring in neighbouring locations. Subtracting average national growth from both sides yields the equation that the difference between provincial and national growth is accounted for by initial structure plus changes in competitiveness.

This is not the place to present the full shift-share decomposition. However, the most striking result is that changes in the competitiveness of manufacturing industry explain nearly all of the difference in growth performance among provinces. In 20 out of a total of 29 province-level units, more than half of the differential between provincial growth and national average growth is explained by gain or loss of competitiveness of industry (including mining, manufacturing, utilities, and construction). These 20 include all of the provinces with large changes in relative position. In two provinces, more than half the differential between provincial and national growth is explained by shifts in the competitiveness of agriculture, but since the two provinces, Xinjiang and Hainan, have very distinctive agricultural sectors, this is not too surprising. In the remaining seven cases, varying combinations of relatively small shifts offset each other and yield small net divergences from national average growth rates. Among this latter group, the three adjacent northern provinces of Beijing, Hebei, and Shanxi are interesting, in that industrial competitiveness declines in all three, but this is offset either by favorable initial structure, or by rapid services (tertiary sector) growth. Overall, differences in provincial growth rates are overwhelmingly explained by changes in industrial competitiveness.

In this result, there is a strong regional trend. Figure 3.9 uses the GDP shift-share analysis to show the provinces that lost industrial share across the board. The entire northern tier of China lost competitiveness in industry. While planners talk incessantly about coast and inland, the strongest pattern that emerges from a more detailed breakdown is actually a north–south division. The north is losing out across the board in industrial competitiveness. The reasons for this are as of yet unclear, but may turn out to be related to the predominance of older, energy-intensive and inefficient forms of heavy industry, which might simply be doomed to obsolescence. Thus, northern China might bear some more similarities to the former Soviet Union than does the south. Even here, though, we should be cautious. Overall, heavy industry has not become less important in China. Rapid industrialization requires heavy as well as light industry, and both have grown substantially.

We can gain further insight by pushing the shift-share decomposition a step further to look at shares of manufacturing output.[10] Once again, we turn to Shanghai for an important example. By 1995, Shanghai industrial output was 36% below what it would have been if each of Shanghai's industrial sectors had maintained national average growth rates from 1980 (the following discussion maintains these two years as the basis for comparison). This was despite a 10% benefit from being specialized in 1980 in sectors that were poised to grow quickly over the succeeding 15 year period. The decline in competitiveness was visible in nearly every manufacturing sector, but was concentrated in two areas: 13.5% of total output forgone was due to the textile sector (including garments and synthetic fibres), and 11% due to electronics (including computers and communication equipment). Only in transportation equipment was there a small gain. Of course, Shanghai restructuring has accelerated dramatically since 1995. For example, the textile industry had grown slowly up until 1995, but since 1995 it has virtually disappeared. The massive impact of foreign investment in Shanghai had only begun to show up in the industrial structure through 1995.

In Jiangsu, the pattern of structural change in neighbouring Shanghai was partially reversed. Output was 71% above what it would have been if each sector had maintained national average growth rates, including 7% due to advantageous initial positioning. Of the 71% above trend output, 20.5% of total output was due to textiles, and 17% to machinery (including industrial machinery, metal products and transport equipment). It is reasonable to interpret the fit between the textile numbers as reflecting the restructuring of Shanghai's textile industry, and its relocation to Jiangsu.[11]

Figure 3.9 Loss of industrial competitiveness (provinces with 1995 GDP more than 9% below expected value due to loss of industry share)

The change in manufacturing structure in Shanghai, and its relationship to neighbouring Jiangsu, should be seen in the same context as rural industrial growth. It is well known that rural industry has been the most dynamic sector in Chinese growth in the reform era, and is responsible for much of the changing position of individual provinces. But rural industry should also be seen in the context of urban restructuring. The most important processes of regional growth are taking place within Skinnerian 'macro-regions' as cities push out from their peripheries. Peri-urban regions grow most rapidly as a result of their favourable location. Rapid growth in Jiangsu and Zhejiang is inseparable from industrial restructuring in Shanghai.

However, not all macro-regions are the same. For example, Beijing's industry has also lost 38% of output, compared to expected 1995 value, despite an expected gain of 15% due to favourable positioning. Like Shanghai, loss of market share has been across the board (except in petroleum refining). Sectors responsible for the biggest losses were chemicals (12%), electronics (10%) and textiles (9%). But in this case, we see little evidence of surrounding regions picking up the benefits of restructuring. Neighbouring Hebei province experienced a loss of 15% of expected industrial output, although most of this was due to unfavourable initial position (9%). Thus, there is little evidence of regional restructuring in the north China region.[12] Perhaps there is some reason why the process of rural industrialization is less closely related to urban restructuring in north China than in south China. If this is so, it might explain part of the reason for the across the board loss in competitiveness of the northern industrial sectors, shown in Figure 3.9. However, at this point, this explanation must remain in the realm of conjecture.

5 CONCLUSION: DIVERGENCE AND SPILLOVER EFFECTS IN THE 1990s

The divergent trends in provincial development are clearly evident in Figure 3.10, which shows the richest and poorest provinces in 1995. By 1995, all the richest provinces are coastal; while the poorest provinces are now all inland regions. Moreover, the process of coastal differentiation is now consolidating and accelerating. Already high income, the coastal provinces now have the highest investment rates and the highest growth rates. Clearly, future trends point to substantial divergence. In this sense, the World Bank (1997) clearly has accurately described a pattern of divergence between coastal and inland regions.

However, we are now in a better position to understand how this most recent diverging trend fits into broader processes of change since 1978. In essence, two trends relating to the dissolution of the redistributive system contributed to across the board convergence. The first of these was the end of the redistributive price system, which led to new relative prices that favoured agricultural provinces and reduced regional inequality. The second was the *reversion* of artificial economies that had been sustained by central government investment. As these artificially high income provinces reverted to levels of development more consistent with their underlying fundamentals, the first result was an apparent convergence across the board. Both these trends, however, now appear to be at an end. Agricultural terms of trade could still improve, but given world price trends and the possibility that China will begin importing more food as part of a World Trade Organization entry agreement, it seems unlikely that agricultural price increases will be part of increasing regional equality in the future. It is even more unlikely that state investment will ever again prop up regional economies on a significant scale. Thus, the two aspects of reform that contributed to convergence have now been played out.

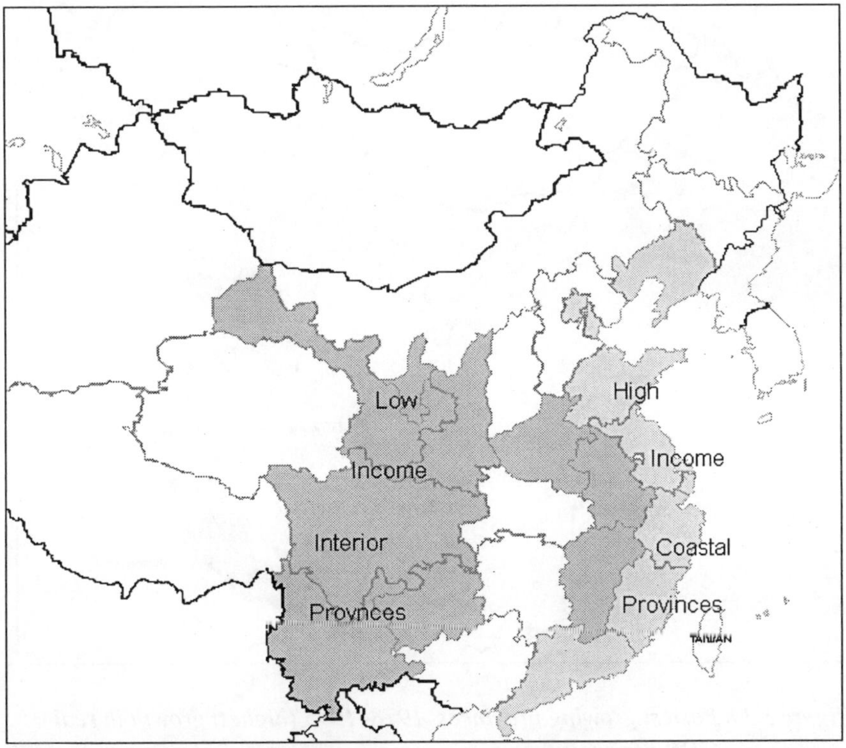

Figure 3.10 Richest and poorest provinces in 1995

That leaves only the long-run growth effects that are created when investment begins to flow back to areas where rates of return are higher. All indications are that those regional differentials are still significant in China. In this sense, it appears that China is in a phase of her economic development in which 'growth poles' take shape, and increasingly differentiate themselves from the remainder of the economic landscape. China's contribution to the theory of economic growth may come out of the study of the emergence of these growth poles, and the opportunities their rapid formation may provide to assess the importance of local agglomeration economies in a dynamic context. It is hard to envisage other forces leading back toward convergence in the near future.

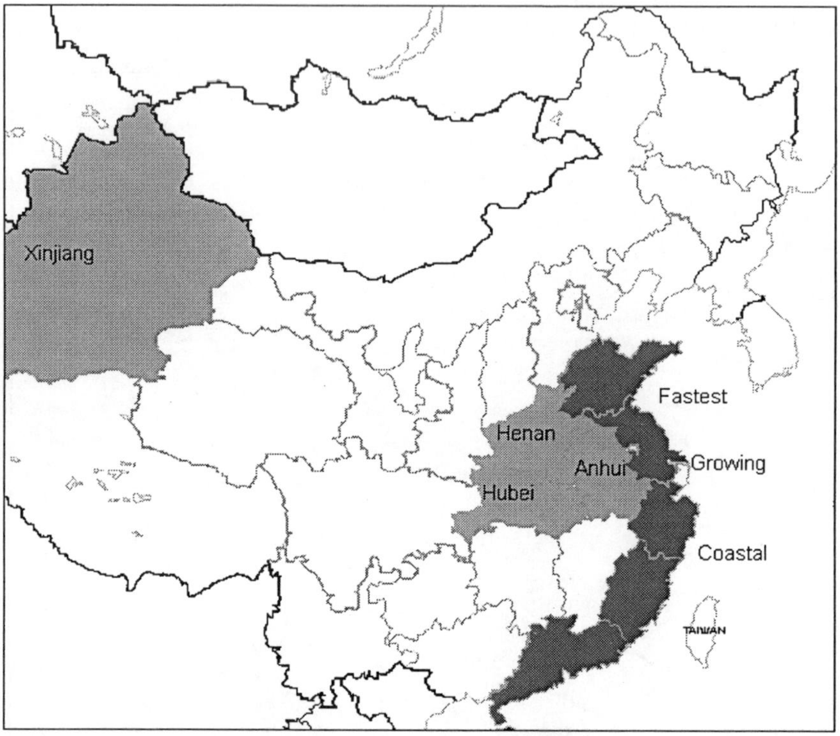

Figure 3.11 Fastest growing provinces, 1978–1995 (highest growth in real GDP per capita)

However, this is not necessarily an entirely negative phenomenon. In the first place, it is possible that this is an inescapable concomitant of economic growth. More importantly, though, we can anticipate that the spread of economic growth output, where these 'growth poles' are, will begin to bring broader areas into the accelerated growth process. Initially, the phenomenon of metropolitan spread initially was of benefit primarily to relatively developed provinces like Jiangsu. However, the process is continuing.

Particularly notable is the recent rise of the provinces just to the north of the Yangtze (Figure 3.11, based on Table 3.2). The provinces of Anhui, Henan, Hubei and Shandong have all grown more rapidly than the national average. These provinces traditionally make up a huge belt of poverty, one of the largest and most populous in China. Anhui, Henan, and Shandong were among the ten poorest in China during the 1950s and 1960s (as measured by NMP per capita). More significantly, Anhui and Henan were two of the four 'orphans' tracked in Figure 3.5. Shandong grew rapidly through the 1970s and 1980s, and is now one of the ten most developed provinces in China; but Anhui and Henan are still among the bottom ten, despite their above average growth. These three provinces had a population of 238 million in 1995. Compare the total of 274 million in the nine western provinces, including the 112 million in Sichuan. Indeed, since Sichuan has been split into two provinces, Henan is now the single most populous province in China, with enormous numbers of poor households. Yet this province is beginning to experience significant spillover growth from the booming coastal regions.

This is a hopeful development that has significant policy implications. Policy makers should recognize that growth in this region is the most promising in terms of moving large numbers of people out of absolute poverty. The central government can foster some infrastructure creation in this region, even though parts of its are coastal, and they are not the poorest parts of the country. Lacking a major urban centre of their own, these regions are nonetheless gradually being brought within the orbit of expanding metropolitan economies along the coast. It is most likely that this kind of gradual spread is the spatial process that will bring most of China into the scope of a modern economy. In the meantime, the biggest spatial problem facing the Chinese economy is probably not the coastal–inland split which has dominated discussions of regional equity in China. Rather, the biggest problem is the failure of the northern tier to restructure and bring its industrial potential to bear. The competitiveness analysis clearly shows that southern China is rising. So far, however, northern China has suffered from the collapse of the old system of state-supported industrialization, and in a relative sense has so far failed to take advantage of a new set of opportunities opened up by marketization.

NOTES

1. I have made an effort to cite some of the most important papers in English, but have undoubtedly missed many. I have made no effort to cite the literally thousands of papers in Chinese addressing this topic. The statistical analysis in this chapter is drawn from official Chinese sources. Data on provincial GDP and GDP deflators are drawn from State

Statistical Bureau, National Accounts Division (1997). Data on investment are from Fixed Investment Statistics (Annual). Industrial data by sector are derived from 1995 PRC Industrial Census and 1985 PRC Industrial Census. These data have been check and supplemented with data from Development Research Center (1992), Provincial Historical Materials (1990), and State Statistical Bureau (1996).

2. For the following analysis, Hainan is included with Guangdong, since some data are not available for separate consideration of Hainan before its establishment as a province (unlike the GDP data). Thus, I have separated 28 province-level units into a top nine, a middle ten, and a bottom nine.
3. In the Chinese system, these households were classified as 'non-agricultural'. The category corresponds reasonably well to members of households containing state and urban collective workers.
4. This is a broader measure of investment than state capital construction, used previously. It includes state investment in existing facilities (technical transformation) and non-state investment. In 1978, however, state capital construction was still the most important component.
5. State capital construction is over 80% of total investment in early years, and the data are most reliable for this component of investment. Most important, capital construction accounts for essentially all the large *de novo* projects that have the potential to significantly alter the regional distribution of industry. It is the primary source of flexibility for planners. Other channels of state investment become important in the 1980s, but these typically fund smaller-scale projects extremely unlikely to be associated with regional redistribution. In addition, non-state investment becomes significant after the mid-1980s as well.
6. Similar trends are visible in Beijing which went from 137% in 1952 to 386% in 1978.
7. Chen Yun was also a native of Jiangsu, and spent every winter in Shanghai.
8. Cheung, 1996: 68–70; Gao and He, 1993: 86; Zhu, 1994.
9. Although to the extent that we were concerned solely with equity, it would seem more reasonable to conduct an analysis using household or personal incomes, since these are presumably the levels of analysis at which equity is most meaningful.
10. The following results are part of a larger analysis of changing industrial structure in China. Only a few selected results are presented here. The analysis is based on *PRC Industrial Census* (1985, 1995).
11. By contrast, Shanghai's lost electronics industry did not relocate to Jiangsu. Instead, Shanghai's loss of competitiveness in electronics reflects the rise of a competing region; the electronics industry in Guangdong has grown and taken market share away from Shanghai.
12. What about Guangdong? Guangdong is the province whose total economy has grown the most rapidly of all. Some of this is immigration: Zhejiang has actually grown slightly faster in per capita terms. Guangdong's industrial outut in 1995 was actually 180% *above* expected based on national trends – almost three times as big – notwithstanding zero impact from initial positioning. Of this increment, 60% comes from electronics (explaining much of the missing electronics sectors in Beijing and Shanghai); 25% in textiles and garments; 19% in the omnibus group of leather, sports, and plastics items; 18% in machinery and 11% food and beverages. Surely this performance is simply exceptional even by Chinese standards. But while it is true that Guangdong's performance is outstanding, it is also true that it reflects the same trends as other rapidly growing Chinese provinces. Many will recognize that the sectors in which Guangdong growth is concentrated are precisely those sectors in which the industry of Hong Kong achieved predominance during the 1960s and 1970s. Output in those sectors has dropped dramatically in Hong Kong as production has been relocated to Guangdong. Thus in the 'Lingnan' macro-region as well, metropolitan expansion can explain much of the overall growth experience.

REFERENCES

Barro, R. and X. Sala-I-Martin (1991), 'Convergence across States and Regions', *Brookings Papers on Economic Activity*, (1), pp. 107–82.

Chen, J. and B. Fleisher (1996), 'Regional Income Inequality and Economic Growth in China,' *Journal of Comparative Economics* 22(2), pp. 141–64.

Cheung, P.T.Y. (1996), 'The Political Context of Shanghai's Economic Development', in Y.M. Yeung and Yun-wing Sung (eds), *Shanghai: Transformation and Modernization Under China's Open Policy*, Hong Kong: The Chinese University Press, pp. 49–92.

Denny, D. (1991), 'Regional Economic Differences During the Decade of Reform', in US Congress Joint Economic Committee, *China's Economic Dilemmas in the 1990s*, Washington, DC: Government Printing Office, pp. 186–208.

Development Research Center (ed.) (1992), *Zhongguo Diqu Fazhan Shuju Shouce* [*Handbook of China Regional Development Statistics*], Beijing: Zhongguo Caizheng Jingji.

Fan, C.C. (1995), 'Of Belts and Ladders: State Policy and Uneven Regional Development in Post-Mao China', *Annals of the Association of American Geographers*, 85 (3), pp. 421–49.

Fixed Investment Statistics, *Zhongguo Guding Zichan Touzi Tongji Ziliao (Nianjian)*, (Annual), Beijing: Zhongguo Tongji.

Gao, X. and B. He (1993), *Zhu Rongji Zhuan (A Biography of Zhu Rongji)*, Taipei: Xin Xinwen Wenhua.

Garbaccio, R.F. and S.J. La Croix (1997), 'Regional Convergence in Output and Consumption in China: Evidence from the Maoist and Reform Periods', Honolulu, Hawaii: East-West Center. Unpublished discussion paper.

Guillaumont, P. and G. Boyreau Debray (1996), 'La Chine et la convergence,' *Revue d'economie du developpement*, 1–2, pp. 33–67.

Ho L-S. and Tsui K-Y. (1996), 'Fiscal Relations Between Shanghai and the Central Government', in Y.M. Yeung and Yun-wing Sung (eds.), *Shanghai: Transformation and Modernization Under China's Open Policy*, Hong Kong: The Chinese University Press, pp. 153–70.

Industrial Economy Statistical Materials (1949–1984, and 1986), Beijing: Zhongguo Tongji.

Jian, T., J. Sachs and A. Warner (1996), 'Trends in Regional Inequality in China', *China Economic Review*, 7(1), pp. 1–22.

Lardy, N. (1980), 'Regional Growth and Income Distribution in China,' in R.F. Dernberger (ed.), *China's Development Experience in Comparative Perspective*, Cambridge, Mass: Harvard University Press, pp. 153–90.

Lyons, T. (1991), 'Interprovincial Disparities in China: Output and Consumption', *Economic Development and Cultural Change*, 39, pp. 471–506.

Naughton, B. (1988), 'The Third Front: Defense Industrialisation in the Chinese Interior', *The China Quarterly*, 115, pp. 351–86.

Naughton, B. (1992), 'Implications of the State Monopoly Over Industry and Its Relaxation', *Modern China*, 18(1) (January), pp. 14–41.

PRC Industrial Census (1995), Regional volume; Summary volume, esp. pp. 131–3 and 164–5.

PRC Industrial Census (1985), Vol. 4: 29 Provinces.

Provincial Historical Materials (1990), *Quanguo Gesheng, Zizhiqu, Zhixiashi Lishi Tongji Ziliao Huibian (1949–1989)*, Beijing: Zhongguo Tongji.

State Statistical Bureau (1996), *Gaige Kaifang Shiqinian de Zhongguo Diqu Jingji* [*China Regional Economy: A Profile of 17 Years of Reform and Opening-up*], Beijing: Zhongguo Tongji.

State Statistical Bureau, National Accounts Division (1997), *Zhongguo Guonei Shengchan Zongzhi Hesuan Lishi Ziliao [The Gross Domestic Product of China, Historical Materials] 1952–1995*, Dalian: Dongbei Caijing Daxue.

Tsui, K-Y. (1991), 'China's Regional Inequality, 1952–1985', *Journal of Comparative Economics*, 15(1), pp. 1–21.

Wei, Y. and L.J.C. Ma (1996), 'Changing Patterns of Spatial Inequality in China, 1952–1990', *Third World Planning Review*, 18(2), pp. 177–91.

White, L.T., III (1989), *Shanghai Shanghaied? Uneven Taxes in Reform China*, Hong Kong, University of Hong Kong Centre for Asian Studies.

World Bank (1997), *Sharing Rising Incomes: Disparities in China*, Washington, DC: The World Bank.

Xin Shanghai Gongye Tongji Ziliao (1949–1990) (1992), Shanghai Statistical Bureau.

Yang, D. (1997), *Beyond Beijing: Liberalization and the Regions in China*, New York: Routledge.

Zhu J. (1994), *Shanghai Jingji 15 Nian*, Shanghai: Shanghai Shehui Kexueyuan.

4. International trade and regional specialization in China

Jean-François Brun and Mary-Françoise Renard

1 INTRODUCTION

More than 20 years of reform have greatly altered economic organization in China. The successive transformations adopted in agriculture (system of responsibility of households) and in the running of firms (harder budget constraint) have permitted the development of a competitive logic that has oriented China towards a market economy. Furthermore, the strategy of growth is largely founded on industry, which represents more than half of the GDP. The aim of policies attracting foreign investments was to obtain not only capital but also new technologies. The priority is no longer simply heavy industry, but also the development of equipment and consumer industries, in part thanks to transfers of technology. The openness to trade and to foreign investment is thus fundamental and the efforts of China to join the World Trade Organization reflect these priorities.

The research carried out on international integration has shown its direct link to the location of industries. The analyses proposed, for instance, by Krugman (1991c and 1996) and by Venables (1996) have aroused new interest in the spatial organization of industry. More specifically, this literature is interested in the changes in industrial location provoked by an increasing openness to foreign trade. The starting point for this is to recognize the fact that specializations can diverge, even in the absence of initial advantages or disadvantages.

Two sectors of production are considered: agriculture, where there are constant returns to scale and where the geographical distribution of activity is largely determined by the distribution of the land; and industry, where there are increasing returns, which lead to a location of production on a limited number of sites. All things being equal, the preferred sites are those with a high local demand. Two important points must be underlined: the existence of returns to scale and the existence of transport costs in industry.

In these models, there are two favourable effects on concentration: the effect of the market size and the evolution of wages, which can result in the mobility of labour. There is also one unfavourable effect: that of the weight of immobile agriculture.

This analysis can be extended by considering transaction costs in general, that is, not only transport costs, but also the evolution of customs duties. Thus, the reduction in protectionism in the form of tariffs could lead to an increasing geographical concentration of activities (Venables, 1996). It could incite firms to localize their production on a single site, or a limited number of sites, if they can reduce their costs by exploiting economies of scale while still supplying the national (or regional) and foreign markets. We could thus expect to see more marked regional disparities.

The aim of this chapter is to test the hypothesis of the relation between international openness and geographical specialization of activities in the case of China. Indeed, in recent years the country has experienced very significant economic reforms notably in the liberalization of its international trade.

In the first section, we analyse the evolution of regional specializations. The second section is devoted to an econometric analysis, in panel data for the Chinese regions, of the relation between openness and regional specializations.

2 SPATIAL DYNAMICS OF INDUSTRY IN CHINA

2.1 The Evolution of Political Strategies on Industrial Location

The size of China and the strategic stakes, which were the source of numerous conflicts, explain the continuous interest shown over the centuries in the regional question.

At the time of the establishment of the communist regime in 1949, most industry was concentrated in the coastal regions, notably Shanghai, Jiangsu and Liaoning, and essentially in their urban centres. The rest of the country was, for the most part, agricultural. The policy led by Mao was inspired by both the Soviet experience and by a concern for military security. The existing imbalances were thus considered as inefficient on an economic level and dangerous on a military level. Indeed, on the one hand the natural resources of the inland regions were poorly exploited and their use by distant industries was costly; reducing transport costs would have required a relatively well-developed transport system, which was not in existence. On the other hand, the location of industry in the coastal regions, and especially close to the harbours, made it vulnerable in the case of military attack.

The strategy of Mao's government therefore consisted in implementing a balanced regional development and encouraging the construction of a relative regional autonomy. This resolution appeared as of the very first five-year plan covering the period 1953–57. Almost two-thirds of the projects, the main part of which were built with aid from the Soviet Union, were localized in the inland regions (Yang, 1997). No project benefiting from Soviet aid was implemented in the coastal regions. For example, over the period 1953–1957, 59.4% of investment by state firms was effected in the inland regions, the remaining 40.6% going to the coastal provinces. The framework of the first five-year plan can be considered as generally coherent – firms were built either near to the sources of raw materials or close to towns – although the aim of 'rebalancing' was less successful and significant inequalities persisted. Although this policy was aimed at re-balancing, significant inequalities persisted (Jian et al., 1996).

The following period was that of the 'Great Leap Forward', which with respect to industrial growth, was centred on heavy industry, especially steel and aluminium. However, as the main preoccupation was still that of military security, it was in the armaments sector that most of the investment was made. This policy has been called the Third Front, each front corresponding to a regional group: coastal, central and western.

The Third Front policy consisted of strong investments in the western regions (Naughton, 1988). These investments were made in two periods. The first, running from 1964 to 1966, concerned Sichuan, Hubei and Gansu. During the second period, running from 1969 to 1972, the investments were localized in Sichuan, Hubei, Shaanxi, Henan and Guizhou.

Naturally, these policies led to a lack of regional specialization and little effort to exploit economies of scale, each region being encouraged to have the widest possible scope of production. Generaly, investment during this period was made on a regional basis, with no real national coherence. This policy was first relaxed during the 1970s with the renewal of relations between China and the United States. The Third Front programme was slowed down perceptibly and openness was seen in the development of imports, notably of equipment, from western countries. This new programme resulted in regional imbalances, half of the imports being attributed to investments localized in the coastal regions. The second change came in 1978 when the reforms introducing elements of a market economy were implemented.

One of the fundamental features of the strategy with respect to regional policy was the exploitation of comparative advantage. The sixth and seventh five-year plans stipulated the priority of the development of the coastal regions which were already the most highly industrialized. They were to develop consumer goods, industries with high value added, improve the technological content of traditional industries, and transfer high energy-consuming or pollutant industries to the less-industrialized regions. The central regions were to produce energy, raw materials and agricultural products, while the western regions were to concentrate on agriculture, forestry, transport, certain raw materials and transformation industries. The objective was clearly a complementarity of regional productions, rather than self-sufficiency (Yang, 1997).

This new policy took the form of a strategy to attract foreign investment (the first law on joint ventures was promulgated in 1979). Four Special Economic Zones were created: Shenzen, Zhuhai and Shantou in the region of Guandong, and Xiamen in the region of Fujian. They offered special incentives to foreign investors. These first measures were followed by the establishment first of 14 coastal towns as towns open to foreign investment, and then of a certain number of development zones. Even if these Special Economic Zones were subsequently created in other regions, the coastal regions clearly benefited from preferential treatment.

The authorities have moved towards rebalancing investments between the regions and have suppressed the legal and taxation privileges of the coastal regions with respect to international investment. In the five-year plan 2001–2005, the authorities' efforts are more concentrated on the western regions. The regional dimension is thus very important in Chinese economic policy which, even with centralized planning, has always relied on regional components (compare, for example, Qian and Xu, 1995).

From 1979, one of the first measures reflecting the desire to evolve towards a market economy was the increase in economic decentralization. The use of resources was thus handed over to the different lower levels of the hierarchy, the central government hoping in this way to approach a market economy more quickly and reduce the part of the economy relying on planning. In that year, reforms in agriculture and collective firms greatly changed the development possibilities, both in agriculture and industry, by increasing productivity in the first sector and by permitting a certain spatial diffusion in the second, notably thanks to migrations. Rural industrial development was significant and was at the source of an increase in regional disparities (Sun and Dutta, 1997).

2.2 Regional Protectionism

Nevertheless, these evolutions cannot be understood without reference to a Chinese particularity: the existence of regional protectionism. This is a result of the trade wars which were to be seen between the regions during the 1980s for certain products, such as wool. In order to satisfy local demand by local production, the authorities controlled imports by establishing and implementing quotas. In certain regions, such as Xinjiang, 48 different products were subject to quantitative restrictions at the beginning of the nineties (Lee, 1998). Many other examples lead us to think that, from this point of view, the local governments did not always act in order to liberalize trade and to establish a greater degree of integration. In this context, local protectionism seemed to the inland provinces to be the only mean of developing a productive system. Indeed, in view of the development strategy of the coastal regions, the inland regions, if they opened up to the products of the coastal regions, would suffer from too high a level of competition and would be unable to remain competitive. They were thus incited to develop their own industries and to practise protectionism.

This phenomenon of local protectionism should have resulted in a strong diversification in the productive structure of each region, but in fact, the coastal regions, the most open and which experienced the strongest growth, suffered more from the protectionism of the other regions, and they also practised it the least.

The successive reforms have had implications for the decentralization process and there have been changes in the responsibility of local governments who have taken an increasing role in determining industrial policy. Two parallel movements can be observed: an evolution in economic organization by the market and a shift in economic decision making from central government towards local government.

3 OPENNESS AND THE EVOLUTION OF DISPARITIES

Numerous authors studied the evolution of the disparities between the Chinese regions. Most often, they retained the criterion of income and frequently came to the conclusion that there had been a certain interregional convergence since the start of the reforms (compare, for example, Boyreau Debray and Guillaumont, 1996; Chen and Fleisher, 1996; Jian et al., 1996). However, this convergence is in general weak, it depends on the level of division, and the reduction in the inequality between the regions taken as a whole goes hand in hand with an increase in the disparity of incomes between coastal and non-coastal regions (Chen and Fleisher, 1996). Certain works (for example Yao, 1997) underline the increase in the disparities observed if we limit the analysis to rural China. It is very interesting to note that, although there is a visible convergence until 1990, followed by a slight divergence since then, a more in-depth analysis reveals that the economic changes following from the reforms resulted in the reclassification of the different provinces (Naughton, chapter 3, this volume). From this the author concludes that these results are difficult to interpret based on the convergence theory and that it is necessary to refer to the regional policies implemented.

3.1 Measuring the Disparities

This specialization can be measured by several coefficients (Jayet, 1993). We chose the Isard coefficient, which has been the basis of numerous works (see for example Kim, 1995 and Krugman, 1991c). We thus rely on a reasoning in relative terms, specialization being considered in comparison to a national norm.

An indicator of specialization was calculated for each region over the period 1988–1994, in the following way:

$$I = \frac{1}{2}\sum_j \left| \frac{VA_{jR}}{VA_R} - \frac{VA_{jN}}{VA_N} \right|$$

where:

VA: value added
R: region
j: sector
N: nation.

This indicator measures the difference between the weight of a sector in regional value added and its weight in national value added. The higher it is, the greater is the degree of specialization of the region.

The results (Appendix 2) show an opposition on the basis of the geographical position of the regions, which allows us to distinguish three levels of specialization for 1994:

1. regions with little specialization: $I < 25$
2. regions with medium specialization: $25 \leq I \leq 30$
3. regions with very high specialization: $I > 30$.

We observe a geographic proximity within each type of specialization, as the map below (Figure 4.1) shows. There is an increase in specialization after 1993, except for Henan and Hubei.

The regions with a medium level of specialization (indicator between 25 and 30) are the southern coastal regions and the central regions, which have a very diversified production. The western and northern regions are the most specialized.

Apart from Tibet, the region with the greatest degree of specialization is Yunnan, where more than 60% of the industrial value added comes from tobacco. Next in line are Heilongjiang, with 36% of the value added coming from the exploitation of petroleum; Hainan, with 22% of the value added in the food industry; and Xinjiang where 27% of the value added comes from the extraction of petroleum and 21% from textiles.

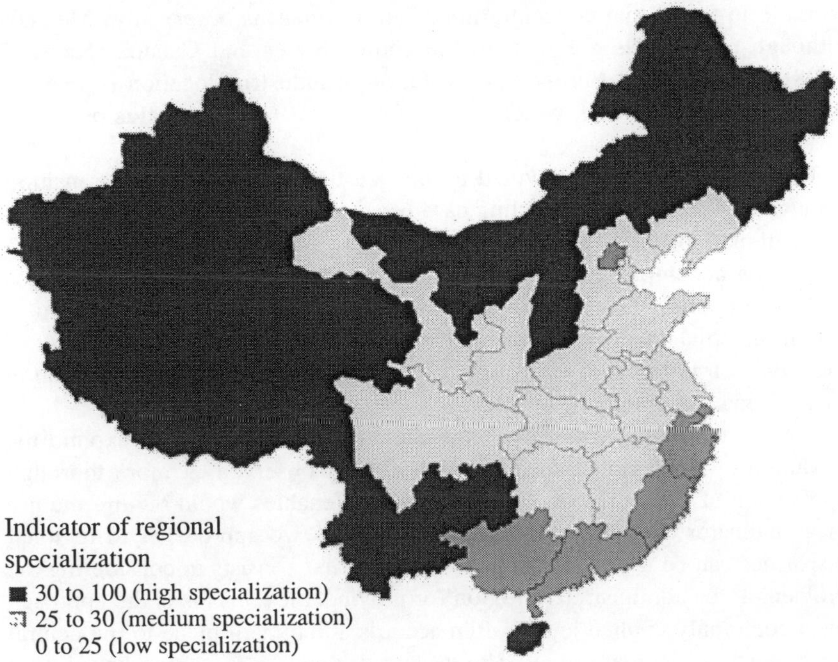

Source: UMR Regards – UNESCO, *Dynamique spatiale de l'industrialisation Chine, Inde, Thaïlande*, based on authors' calculations.

Figure 4.1 The industrial specialization of Chinese provinces – 1994

In this category of highly specialized regions with an indicator above 30, we find a group with a location coefficient between 30 and 40. The production is concentrated in three or four main sectors. This is the case, for instance, of Shanxi, where 22% of the value added comes from the treatment of ferrous metals, 12% from the chemical industry, and 12% from mechanical construction. In a similar position is the province of Ningxia, with 17% of value added in mechanical construction, 17% in the chemical industry and 11% in food production, as well as the provinces of Qianghai, Jilin and Inner Mongolia.

3.2 Has Chinese Openness Increased Regional Specialization?

The empirical works on the spatial consequences of integration increased with the construction of NAFTA (North American Free Trade Association) and with the European Union integration process. In the first case, an increase in the spatial concentration of employment is observed in Mexico, although few effects are seen in the United States and Canada (Hanson, 1998). In the case of Europe, the evolution of industrial location is also the topic of several studies which most often come to the conclusion of an increase in specialization.

Few studies have been devoted to this question in developing or transition economies. China is an interesting case because of the reforms resulting in an international openness. Moreover, the imminent entry of China into the WTO should be accompanied by further tariff reductions which will doubtless increase imports, but will also permit the strengthening of export dynamics. To this external openness can be added an internal integration as the result of the reduction in regional protectionism. Consequently, there is a reduction in transaction costs within the country.

We want to know whether or not international openness can explain the evolution of the regional specialization already observed. A more thorough application of the works of Krugman and of Venables would require the use of an indicator of spatial concentration. Indeed, two approaches to regional disparities can be used (Johnston, 1999). The first consists in considering the problem at the administrative region (or province) level. This is the approach most commonly applied and it often accords a dominant place to the central government's regional policy. The second demands a reasoning based on a system of industrial zones in order to explain the spatial concentration of industry. It better fits the analysis logic presented by Krugman (1991c). In this approach, spatial dynamics is considered without necessarily thinking about regional divisions.

However, in order to obtain empirical validation of the relations between openness and location using the second approach, it would have been necessary to have data with the same classification for the different sectors, for production and for exports, which is not currently the case. So, we use the first approach in terms of specialization which has been retained by other authors, such as Sapir (1996) or Kim (1995).

Moreover, it seems to us consistent with the specificity of China since Chinese industrial diversity was built on a regional basis. We thus try to estimate the link between the evolution of specialization and openness to international trade, and thus we retain the regions as the level of our analysis.

The techniques of panel data are used so as to allow us to capture unobserved regional specificities. The estimation is carried out on 29 regions and covers the period 1988–1994. The data set is constructed using the *China Regional Economy* and the *China Industrial Economic Statistical Yearbook*.

The variables retained are as follows:

- the explained variable is the indicator of regional specialization (*I*);
- the explicative variables are:

  - the rate of regional exportation measured by the ratio of exports to value added, which represents international openness (*OPEN*).
  - economies of scale by sector, estimated by the ratio of value added in a particular sector to the total value added of the whole region. (It is a method used for example by Amiti, 1998.) However, in order to avoid the bias introduced by the very weak representation of certain sectors in certain regions, only the five most important sectors in terms of value added are retained. As the value added seemed to us to be insufficient to measure these economies of scale correctly, we control them by considering the significance of employment. Thus, for each region, we calculate the ratio of the value added (and employment) in the five main sectors to the regional value added (and total regional employment) for the initial year: 1988. Furthermore, the permanence of a certain level of planning is taken into account by separating the sectors according to whether they obey competitive rules (*EM*) or whether they are, in part, subject to planning (*EP*). This information was provided by the State Council Research Centre. It should be noted that this distinction does not necessarily cover a division in terms of types of property as state enterprises can function according to a market logic. Here, it is more specifically a case of distinguishing the sectors according to whether or not the prices are market prices.

- Regional per capita gross domestic product, in order to take into account the size of the regions (*GDPP*).
- Regional per capita consumption; this variable can represent the role of the local market in the firms' choice of location (*CONSP*).
- Foreign direct investment, measured by the ratio of employment in firms using foreign capital to total employment in the region (*FDI*).
- The landlocked regions, captured by a dummy variable which takes the value of 1 for regions with no access to the sea and 0 otherwise (*LANDLOCK*).

As has already been highlighted, a two-way model was retained in order to capture an unobserved heterogeneity, proper to each region (spatial effect) and to each year (time effect). The time effects also capture the administrative and judicial changes which, as we have already seen, tend to free trade within China and can also have an impact on spatial organization. In this way, it is the effects of international trade which are captured by the openness variable and not those of domestic integration.

The estimated equation can be represented in the following way:

$$I_{it}=f(OPEN_{it},VAM_{it},VAP_{it},EM_{it},EP_{it},GDPP_{it},FDI_{it},\\ CONSP_{it},LANDLOCK_{it},u_i,v_t,\varepsilon_{it})$$

u_i = regional effect
v_t = time effect
$_{it}$ = term of errors

The results (see Table 4.1) indicate that, in accordance with the theoretical model, the international openness of China, measured by its exports, increases the specialization of the regions. This leads us to believe that with international openness, the regions were encouraged to exploit economies of scale and are thus incited to specialize.

The relation between the exploitation of economies of scale, measured by value added, and regional specialization does not indicate any difference whether it is a planned sector or a market-based sector. The coefficients are positive and not significantly different; nevertheless, the coefficient for the market economy sectors is more significant than that corresponding to the sectors where prices are still, for the most part, planned. The variables controlling for employment show a different result according to the type of sector; in the market economy sectors, the effect is negative, whereas it is positive for the other sectors.

Economic activity, captured by per capita GDP, is linked negatively to specialization. This means that regions with a high per capita GDP will be less likely to specialize. On the other hand, foreign direct investment does not have a significant influence on regional specialization. With regard to this, we should recall that this investment is, for the most part, localized in the coastal regions, mainly because of the advantages given to the Special Economic Zones. It is not the result of the exploitation of economies of scale, but rather the result of deliberate policy from the central government.

Table 4.1 Explained variable: indicator of specialization

Explicative variables	
OPEN	0.075
	(1.68)*
VAM	0.38
	(3.37)***
VAP	0.37
	(1.55)*
EM	-2.90
	(3.25)***
EP	0.80
	(3.62)***
GDPP	-0.0015
	(2.18)**
FDI	-0.014
	(1.40)
CONSP	0.0032
	(1.78)*
LANDLOCK	6.36
	(1.68)*
Numberof observations	203
R^2 adjusted	0.96
F statistic (regional effects)	139.13***
Hausman test	0.10

Notes:
t-tests are in parentheses.
*** significant at a level of 1%; ** significant at a level of 5%; * significant at a level of 10%.
The *F* statistic detects the presence of regional effects; the Hausman test leads us to retain a effects model.

As for consumption, it is positively linked to regional specialization. The increase in internal market size is an incentive to increase specialization. This could lead us to believe that firms are concentrated in space in order to profit from the effects of market size. Finally, landlockness is a factor of specialization.

4 CONCLUSION

The statistical analysis of industry in the Chinese regions allowed us to reveal a tendency towards the accentuation of regional specialization. We attempted to link these observations to the evolution of exports by the Chinese regions. Using econometric analysis, we were thus able to show a positive effect of openness on the degree of industrial specialization in the regions, as predicted in the theoretical models. However, although openness has a favourable effect on specialization, the latter is, of course, subject to other effects, such as the extent of economic activity, which can, on the contrary, encourage a certain diversification.

The evolution towards a competitive economy and the encouragement of the government to exploit regional competitive advantage will doubtless serve only to reinforce these tendencies.

These results lead us to believe that Chinese industry has still used only a part of its opportunities for spatial specialization and for economies of scale, and that a significant evolution could result from the liberalization of migratory movements.

REFERENCES

Amiti, M. (1998), 'New Trade Theories and Industrial Location in the EU – a Survey Evidence', *Oxford Review of Economic Policy*, 14(2), pp. 45–53.

Boyreau Debray, G. and P. Guillaumont (1996), 'La Chine et la convergence', *Revue d'Economie du Développement*, 1-2, pp. 33–67.

Cadène. Ph., B. Chaudhuri, L. Kennedy, D. Kermel-Torrès, M.F. Renard and Ph. Schar (2002), *Dynamique spatiale de l'industrialisation Chine, Inde, Thaïlande*. Editions de l'UNESCO.

Chen, J. and B.M. Fleisher (1996), 'Regional Income Inequality and Economic Growth in China', *Journal of Comparative Economics*, 22(2), pp. 141–64.

Hanson, G.H. (1998), 'North American Economic Integration and Industrial Location', *Oxford Review of Economic Policy*, 14(2), pp. 30–44.

Jayet, H. (1993), *Analyse spatiale quantitative*, Economica, Bibliothèque de Science Régionale, Paris.

Jian, T., J.D. Sachs and A.M. Warner (1996), 'Trends in Regional Inequality in China', *China Economic Review*, 7(1), pp. 1–21.
Johnston, M.F. (1999), 'Beyond Regional Analysis: Manufacturing Zones, Urban Employment and Spatial Inequality in China', *China Quarterly*, March, pp. 1–21.
Kim, S. (1995), 'Expansion of Markets and the Geographic Distribution of Economic Activities: The Trends in U.S. Regional Manufacturing Structure, 1860–1987', *Quarterly Journal of Economics*, 60(4), pp. 881–908.
Krugman, P. (1991a), 'Increasing Returns and Economic Geography', *Journal of Political Economy*, 99(3), pp. 483–99.
Krugman, P. (1991b), 'History and Industry Location: The Case of the Manufacturing Belt', *American Economic Review*, 82(2), pp. 80–3.
Krugman, P. (1991c), *Geography and Trade*, Cambridge, Mass.: MIT Press.
Krugman, P. (1996), *Development, Geography, and Economic Theory*, Cambridge, Mass.: MIT Press.
Krugman, P. (1998), 'What's New about the New Economic Geography?', *Oxford Review of Economic Policy*, 14(2), pp. 7–17.
Krugman, P. and A. Venables (1995), 'Globalization and the Inequality of Nations', *Quarterly Journal of Economics*, 60(4), pp. 857–80.
Lee, P.K. (1998), 'Local Economy Protectionism in China's Economic Reform', *Development Policy Review*, 16(3), pp. 281–303.
Liu, X., H. Song and P. Romilly (1997), 'An Empirical Investigation of the Causal Relationship between Openness and Economic Growth in China', *Applied Economics*, 29(12), pp. 1679–86.
Naughton, B. (1988), 'The Third Front: Defense Industrialization in the Chinese Interior', *The China Quarterly*, September, pp. 351–86.
Qian, Y. and C. Xu (1993), 'The M-form Hierarchy and China's Economic Reform', *European Economic Review*, 37(2-3), pp. 541–8.
Sapir, A. (1996), 'The Effects of Europe's Internal Market Program on Production and Trade: A First Assessment', *Weltwirtschaftliches Archiv*, 132(3), pp. 457–75.
Sun, H. and D. Dutta (1997), 'China's Economic Growth During 1984–93: A Case of Regional Dualism', *Third World Quarterly*, 18(5), pp. 843–64.
Venables, A.J. (1996), 'Localization of Industry and Trade Performance', *Oxford Review of Economic Policy*, 12(3), pp. 52–60.
Yang, D.L. (1997), *Beyond Beijing, Liberalization and the Regions in China*, London: Routledge.
Yao, S. (1997), 'Industrialization and Spatial Income Inequality in Rural China, 1986–92', *Economics of Transition*, 5(1), pp. 97–112.

APPENDIX 4.1. LIST OF SECTORS

1. Beverage manufacturing industry
2. Chemical fibres
3. Chemical materials and products manufacturing industry
4. Clothing and other chemical fibre products manufacturing
5. Coal mining and preparation
6. Cultural, educational and sports articles manufacturing industry

7. Electric equipment and machinery manufacturing industry
8. Electronic and telecommunications equipment manufacturing industry
9. Ferrous metals mining and preparation
10. Food manufacturing industry
11. Furniture manufacturing industry
12. Instruments, metres and other measuring equipment manufacturing industry
13. Leather, furs and manufactured goods
14. Logging and transport of timber and bamboo
15. Universal machine manufacturing industry
16. Medical and pharmaceutical products
17. Metal products
18. Non-metal mineral products
19. Papermaking and manufactured goods
20. Petroleum and natural gas extraction
21. Plastic manufactured goods
22. Power generation, steam and hot water production and supply
23. Printing and record medium manufacturing industry
24. Rubber manufactured goods
25. Running water production and supply
26. Smelting and pressing of ferrous metals
27. Textile manufacturing industry
28. Timber processing, bamboo, cane, palm fibre and straw products
29. Tobacco manufacturing industry
30. Transportation equipment manufacturing industry

APPENDIX 4.2 ISARD INDICATOR OF REGIONAL SPECIALIZATION

Regions	Beijing	Tianjin	Hebei	Shanxi	Neimeng	Liaoning	Jilin	Heilon-gjiang
1988	25.52	18.39	16.38	34.23	27.57	20.42	24.58	43.89
1989	24.90	20.43	16.67	34.51	24.06	19.68	25.00	42.98
1990	28.70	18.39	15.16	36.16	28.47	20.68	26.60	47.71
1991	24.98	21.77	15.01	37.82	29.85	20.67	25.64	47.65
1992	26.70	24.14	15.06	38.75	30.87	18.45	31.50	47.75
1993	25.46	20.14	17.57	36.80	35.21	21.37	30.71	48.98
1994	25.63	20.96	18.55	39.37	32.15	20.82	33.54	52.13

	Shanghai	Jiangsu	Zejiang	Anhui	Fujian	Jiangxi	Shandong
1988	22.17	20.60	20.93	18.71	24.70	16.12	15.95
1989	21.56	20.79	20.66	15.72	24.92	13.72	15.75
1990	22.38	22.93	22.26	17.36	22.87	16.23	15.56
1991	23.24	22.84	22.25	16.93	24.30	16.35	16.19
1992	21.49	22.53	23.00	17.05	23.74	15.91	16.09
1993	24.88	24.16	26.81	20.59	27.80	19.52	17.72
1994	25.84	24.83	26.48	18.25	28.39	17.51	16.66

	Henan	Hubei	Hunan	Guang-dong	Guangxi	Hainan	Sichuan	Guizhou
1988	16.94	20.01	15.64	23.74	20.09	45.99	10.44	30.84
1989	16.53	18.69	15.65	22.90	19.71	47.18	10.92	31.51
1990	15.93	17.94	17.61	24.17	21.83	50.21	9.64	32.46
1991	15.84	17.58	18.92	25.21	22.74	47.79	12.62	33.26
1992	16.48	18.72	18.74	25.98	21.42	42.23	12.92	34.93
1993	15.81	15.97	18.22	27.25	25.61	42.70	14.59	28.32
1994	15.16	18.09	19.15	28.49	26.17	47.20	16.92	30.45

	Yunnan	Tibet	Shaanxi	Gansu	Qianghai	Ningxia	Xinjiang
1988	41.25	73.70	20.59	16.10	29.35	28.65	37.21
1989	45.51	63.21	21.06	14.96	28.02	27.66	33.90
1990	47.17	61.17	20.14	18.96	28.77	30.58	31.66
1991	47.89	60.34	20.67	22.82	25.07	30.18	35.38
1992	48.01	60.35	19.92	18.50	23.38	33.07	36.46
1993	47.43	57.81	22.21	22.49	31.19	35.27	38.50
1994	56.41	63.69	21.12	22.95	33.70	35.62	45.20

5. Productivity growth, catch-up and convergence in China's reforming economy

Yanrui Wu

The role of productivity in economic growth has recently attracted a lot of attention among both researchers and policy makers. In particular, several empirical studies presented some highly provocative finding that East Asian growth is largely driven by factor inputs rather than technological progress and therefore growth in this region is unlikely to be sustainable in the long run (Young, 1995; Kim and Lau, 1994). Those studies have led to a flourishing literature on this topic. Among them, few studies focused on China. The purpose of this chapter is to examine productivity growth in China's reforming economy and hence to contribute to the ongoing debate on East Asian economic growth.

China's economic reform was initiated in the late 1970s. Since then, the Chinese economy has achieved an average annual growth rate of about 10%. This growth is unprecedented in world history, with the exception of small, diamond-rich Botswana (World Bank, 1996). Economic reform was the key to the Chinese success. The reforms can boost productivity growth in two conceptually different ways. One way is by increasing the efficiency with which the existing resources are utilized in production. Due to well-known systemic reasons, centrally-planned economies like the Chinese economy produce well below their best practice outputs. Economic reform aims to raise production close to the frontier (that is, improvement in technical efficiency). Another way to boost productivity growth is by stimulating innovation, that is, technological progress. Centrally-planned economies have recorded low levels of technological progress according to international standards (Lau and Brada, 1990). Nishimizu and Page (1982) define productivity growth as the sum of technical efficiency change and technological progress. This definition allows the identification of productivity growth due to either improvement in efficiency (that is, catch-up) or technological progress (that is, innovation). An investigation of China's productivity performance, in particular the two components of productivity growth, can provide valuable insights into the understanding of that country's spectacular growth in the 1980s and 1990s. The next section briefly reviews the literature. This is followed by discussion of the modelling issues. Explanations of the data and estimation results are then presented. The last section summarises the main findings in this study.

1 PREVIOUS STUDIES

Empirical studies of East Asian economies have focused on examining the contribution of total factor productivity (TFP) to economic growth. On the one hand, it is argued that the rate of productivity growth in the East Asian NICs is not high even though the growth of output and manufacturing exports in these countries is unprecedented (Young, 1992). This line of thinking is supported by Kim and Lau (1994) whose findings have shown that technical progress was virtually zero in the NICs during the post-war growth period. On the other hand, the World Bank (1993) and other authors have shown empirical evidence of rapid productivity growth in the high performing Asian economies (HPAEs).[1] The existing literature covers both cross-country and industry studies. Several authors also presented empirical analyses of regional economies within countries.[2]

Studies of productivity performance in the Chinese economy are more sector-oriented. In particular, there is an abundant literature on China's agricultural and industrial productivity.[3] It is now widely accepted that agricultural productivity increased considerably after the initiative of economic reform in 1979, in particular in the first half of the 1980s (McMillan et al., 1989; Lin, 1992; Wu, 1995). However, researchers are still uncertain about whether industrial productivity has increased since the reform. Early studies such as the World Bank (1985), Tidrick (1986), and Chow (1985) argued that industrial TFP declined in the initial years of the reform. However, more recent studies, including Chen et al. (1988), Jefferson et al. (1992, 1996) presented evidence of significant TFP growth during the reform period.

There are several economy-wide studies on growth in China. Wei (1995) and Fleisher and Chen (1997) applied city-level and regional panel data, respectively, to examine the impact of economic openness and productivity on growth. Borensztein and Ostry (1996) and Maddison (1998) employed a simple growth-accounting method by assuming ad hoc factor shares for labour and capital.[4] The existing literature has some common features such as (i) productivity growth and technological progress are used interchangeably, (ii) in some cases, the value of capital stock is substituted by the value of gross investment, (iii) no regional price deflators are used. This chapter attempts to extend previous studies and shed some light on the issues associated with productivity convergence, catch-up and growth using China's regional economies as the setting. Specifically, this study differs from the existing literature in the following ways:

- The approach employed in this chapter distinguishes technological progress from productivity growth. Thus, this study can investigate the impacts of catch-up and innovation on economic growth separately.
- Regional price deflators are used to deflate the value-based variables.
- A unique technique is applied to estimate capital stock series for the Chinese regions.
- This study links productivity growth with regional convergence or divergence.

2 MODELLING PRODUCTIVITY GROWTH

The Theoretical Models

The econometric model used in this study, hereafter called the frontier model, is related to the concept of output-oriented technical efficiency first proposed by Farrell (1957) and popularized by Aigner et al. (1977), and Meeusen and van den Broeck (1977).[5] The important difference between the traditional growth accounting method and the production frontier technique is that the latter allows for production below the best practice output. The panel data version of this model can be presented as follows:

$$y_{it} = y_{it}^F TE_{it} = f(x_{it}, t) TE_{it} \; y_{it} \quad t = 1,..., \quad \text{and } i = 1,..., N \qquad (5.1)$$

where, given technology $f(\bullet)$ and input x_{it}, y_{it}^F represents the frontier production level or the so-called 'best practice' output for the *i*th country or region at time *t*, y_{it} the observed output, and TE_{it} technical efficiency, defined as the ratio of the observed output over the best practice output. Equation (5.1) can be transformed into

$$\dot{y}_{it} = f_x \dot{x}_{it} + f_t + \dot{TE}_{it} \qquad (5.2)$$

where dotted variables denote time derivatives, and f_X and f_t represent, respectively, output elasticities with respect to x and t.

Solow (1957) attributed output growth to input growth and technical change. The decomposition in equation (5.2) enriches Solow's dichotomy by attributing growth in observed output to movement along a path on or beneath the production frontier (input growth), movement toward or away from the production frontier (technical efficiency change), and shifts in the production frontier (technological progress). According to this decomposition, total factor productivity growth ($\dot{TFP}$), defined as the growth in output not explained by input growth, is the sum of technological progress and changes in technical efficiency, that is

$$\dot{TFP}_{it} = \dot{TP}_{it} + \dot{TE}_{it}, \qquad t = 1,\ldots, T, \qquad i = 1,\ldots, N. \tag{5.3}$$

The conventional growth-accounting method cannot distinguish between technological progress and changes in technical efficiency, yet the former can be assumed to be the consequence of innovation or adoption of new technology by best practice countries or economies, and the latter due mainly to the effect of catching up. These two are analytically distinct and may have quite different policy implications, as argued by Nishimizu and Page (1982). Qualitatively, this decomposition emphasises a distinction between 'level' and 'growth' effects of economic reform on the long-run growth (Huang, 1995; Lucas, 1988). On the one hand, the level effect of economic reform causes upward shifts in actual production (that is, movement towards the frontier). On the other hand, the growth effect implies that economic reform not only raises the level of production in the short run but also stimulates technological progress and hence leads to sustained growth in the economy. The fundamental difference between these two effects is that level effects can be drawn out over time but not growth effects which can be large and sustainable.

Isolation of changes in efficiency and technological progress is also embodied in the increasingly popular Malmquist productivity approach which is, however, nonparametric.[6] This approach has recently attracted a lot of interest and has been widely used in empirical analyses partly due to the fact that it typically employs linear programming models. Though this approach has a number of virtues, its main drawback is that it is deterministic (Lovell, 1996). In contrast, the econometric approach employed in this chapter is stochastic, and it is capable of distinguishing the effects of statistical noise from those of inefficiency.

The Empirical Model

To estimate equation (5.3), consider the following specification of a frontier production function:[7]

$$\ln Q_{it} = \alpha_0 + \alpha_1 t + \frac{1}{2}\alpha_2 t^2 + (\beta_0 + \beta_1 t)\ln L_{it} + (\gamma_0 + \gamma_1 t)\ln K_{it}$$

$$+\frac{1}{2}(\eta_1 \ln L_{it} \ln L_{it} + 2\eta_2 \ln L_{it} \ln K_{it} + \eta_3 \ln K_{it} \ln K_{it}) + \varepsilon_{it} \qquad (5.4)$$

where

$\varepsilon_{it} = v_{it} - u_{it}$,

$u_{it} = \varsigma_0 + \varsigma_1 t + \omega_{it} \geq 0$,

$$\beta_0 + \gamma_0 = 1,\ \beta_1 + \gamma_1 = 0,\ \eta_1 + \eta_2 = \eta_2 + \eta_3 = 0,$$

Q, L and K represent GDP, labour and capital stock, respectively; α_i's, β_j's, γ_k's, η_l's and ς_m's are parameters to be estimated; ε_{it} is the error term combining the white noise, v_{it}, and the term associated with technical inefficiency, u_{it}; v_{it} and u_{it} are assumed to be independently distributed, and have normal distributions with zero means and variances σ_v^2 and σ_u^2, respectively; ω_{it} is defined by the truncation of the normal distribution with zero mean and variance σ_u^2 such that the point of truncation is $(-\varsigma_0 - \varsigma_1 t)$, that is, $\omega_{it} \geq -\varsigma_0 - \varsigma_1 t$; thus, u_{it}'s are non-negative and obtained by truncation at zero of the normal distribution with mean $(\varsigma_0 + \varsigma_1 t)$ and variances, σ_u^2; and the restrictions ensure constant returns to scale.[8]

The above specification allows the estimation of both technological progress in the stochastic frontier and time-varying technical efficiency. The distributional assumptions on the inefficiency effects, the u_{it}'s, permit the coefficients of the two t-terms to be identified in addition to the coefficients of other terms (Battese and Coelli, 1995). The above model can be estimated by the maximum likelihood method using the computer program, FRONTIER 4.1.[9] Finally, given the estimates of the parameters in equation (5.4), the rates of technical efficiency change and technological progress for the ith region at the tth period can be computed. Both rates vary over time and across the regions.

3 DATA AND RESULTS

Data Issues

China is divided into 30 provinces. Data for Tibet are incomplete in the original source. Hainan Island became a province in 1988 and has been listed independently only since 1989. An initial plot of all variables against time indicates that there are serious problems with statistics from Qinghai province. As a result, all three regions are dropped from the final estimation. Thus, the empirical model specified in the preceding section is applied to the panel data of 27 Chinese provinces during the period 1981–95. GDP data are from the statistical yearbooks of each province. Labour statistics are from the statistical yearbooks of China for the period 1985–95 and are estimated for the period 1981–84 by extrapolation. The total numbers of people employed are used instead of man hours, due to the lack of data on the latter. The data of net capital stock are estimated from gross investment in each year. For this purpose, the capital stock in the first period is assumed to be the sum of all past investments and a rate of 5% is allowed for capital depreciation.[10] Symbolically,

$$K(1) = \int_{-\infty}^{1} I(t)dt = \frac{I(0)e^{\theta}}{\theta} \tag{5.5}$$

where $I(t) = I(0)e^{\theta t}$, and θ and $I(0)$ are estimated by linear regressions using the investment series (1981–95). Therefore, given a depreciation rate, δ

$$K(t)=(1-d)K(t-1)\delta+I(t) \qquad t = 2, ..., 15 \tag{5.6}$$

GDP and capital stock data are measured in 1980 constant prices. The price deflator is estimated from GDP data which are available in both current and constant prices. The final sample has 405 observations. On the average, during the period 1981–97, the regions together recorded an annual growth of 10% in GDP, 21.5% in capital stock and 2.4% in employment. Among the regions, Guangdong, the province adjacent to Hong Kong, had the fastest growing economy (14% per annum) followed by other coastal regions such as Jiangsu (13%), Zhejiang (13%), Fujiang (13%) and Shandong (12%). At the same time, these regions also showed relatively high growth in capital stock.

Estimation Results

The initial estimates of the parameters in equation (5.4) are presented in Table 5.1. All coefficients are statistically significant. The negative sign of α_1 indicates the deterioration of technological progress in the initial years. This is typical of all reforming economies. At the beginning of the reform, economic restructuring can actually retard technological progress. This probably happens due to the large changes in relative prices which may adversely affect the choice of factor inputs (Färe et al., 1995). In other words, economic reform may have to undertake an initial cost as argued by some observers (Portes, 1992; Reynolds, 1987). The positive sign of α_2, however, implies the acceleration in the change of technological progress. This will be discussed further in the following section.

Table 5.1 Estimation results of frontier production functions

Parameters	Estimates	Standard errors
α_0 (intercept)	1.3224	0.0898
$\alpha_1(t)$	-0.2381	0.0189
$\alpha_2\left(\frac{1}{2}t^2\right)$	0.0229	0.0021
$\beta_0(\ln L)$	0.3160	0.0354
$\beta_1(t \ln L)$	0.0238	0.0061
$\gamma_0(\ln K)$	0.6839*	n.a.
$\gamma_1(t \ln K)$	-0.0238*	n.a.
$\eta_1\left(\frac{1}{2}\ln L \ \ln L\right)$	0.2364	0.0252
$\eta_2(\ln L \ \ln K)$	-0.2364*	n.a.
$\eta_3\left(\frac{1}{2}\ln K \ \ln K\right)$	0.2364*	n.a.
σ^2	0.0554	0.0038
λ	0.6159	0.0504
ς_0 (intercept)	0.7032	0.0882
$\varsigma_1(t)$	-0.1475	0.0256

Note: * These figures are derived from the restrictions on the coefficients.

Next the estimates of technical efficiency, technological progress and total factor productivity are derived by applying the above-described techniques. Technical efficiency estimates show that the Shanghai economy was the most efficient (closest to the frontier). The scatter plot of technical efficiency rates is presented in Figure 5.1. As shown in this chart, there has been significant catching up among the regional economies. Thus, China's economic reform has brought about significant improvement in efficiency, that is, a level effect as also concluded by Borensztein and Ostry (1996). The regions did not hesitate to exploit the opportunity brought about by the reforms to catch up to each other rapidly. However, the potential in efficiency improvement was almost exhausted in the 1990s, and hence economic growth in the future will mainly rely on innovation, that is, technological progress which, in contrast, may continue indefinitely.

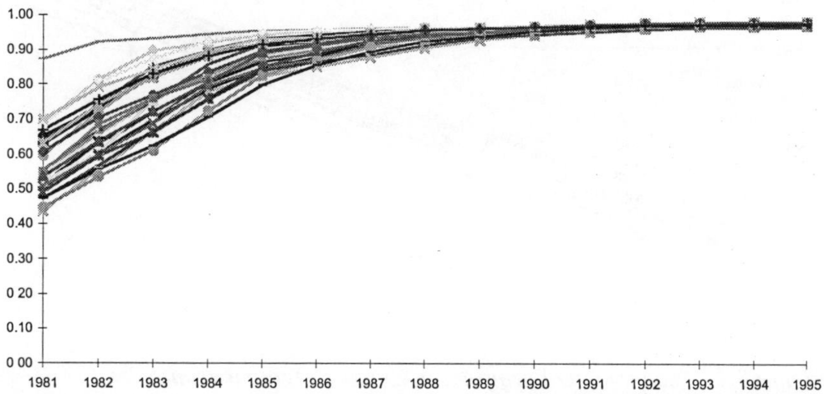

Figure 5.1 Technical efficiency in China's regional economies, 1981–1995

As for technological progress, the (estimated) record for the Chinese regions is a poor one (Figure 5.2). As discussed early, the results show that economic reform has overshadowed technological progress in exchange for efficiency improvements. In the decade of the 1980s, all regional economies registered poor technological progress according to the estimates in this study. Significant technological progress was not recorded until the early 1990s in all regions. This process coincided with the take-off of the Chinese economy which recorded an average annual growth rate of 12% during 1991–1995. In particular, the three largest cities (Beijing, Shanghai and Tianjin) have the worst record of technological progress. There are three possible explanations for this. First, these cities all have a dominant state sector which has undergone painful changes during the reform. Second, it is commonly accepted that China's rural reform in the late 1970s was successful in raising agricultural income and productivity (McMillan et al., 1989; Lin, 1992). The three largest cities might have gained less from the rural success due to their relatively small agricultural sectors. Third, other regions have performed better in terms of technological progress perhaps because they have exploited the so-called 'advantages of backwardness'. As Abramovitz (1986) argued, backwardness may carry an opportunity for modernization in disembodied, as well as embodied, technology. Regions who are behind may have the potential to leap forward and thus to catch up with the leaders.

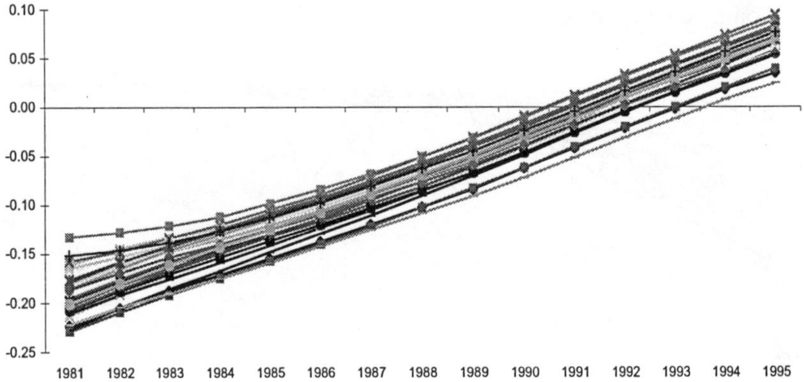

Figure 5.2 Technological progress in China's regional economies, 1981–1995

Due to the dominance of technological progress, TFP growth has also shown a poor record among the Chinese regions (Figure 5.3). Positive rates of TFP growth were recorded only in the 1990s. However, the pattern of productivity change among the regions does show the learning process during the period of economic reform: as shown in Figure 5.3, the pattern of TFP growth among the regions forms a J-curve during 1982–95. Immediately after the implementation of the reform procedures in the early 1980s, productivity performance deteriorated continuously and bottomed out in 1986 in most regions. This finding supports the view on the effects of the reform, as argued by some observers such as Lau and Brada (1990), Reynolds (1987b) and Woo et al. (1994). In addition, Figure 5.3 shows that the three largest cities which embody the relatively advanced economies have recorded the lowest rates of TFP growth among the regions. This again supports the argument of the so-called 'advantages of backwardness' observed in the rest of the world.

Figures 5.1, 5.2 and 5.3 can also be used to examine whether TFP growth, technical efficiency and technological progress among the regions have converged or not. Visual examination of the three charts clearly indicates the tendency of convergence in these performance indexes over time. To gain more insight into this issue, the coefficients of variation, an indicator of convergence, defined as the ratio of the standard deviation to the mean are computed (Table 5.2). All coefficients have declined over time, and therefore indicate substantial convergence among the regions. In particular, the Chinese regions have converged rapidly in terms of technical efficiency performance and the process of convergence was almost completed in the early 1990s.

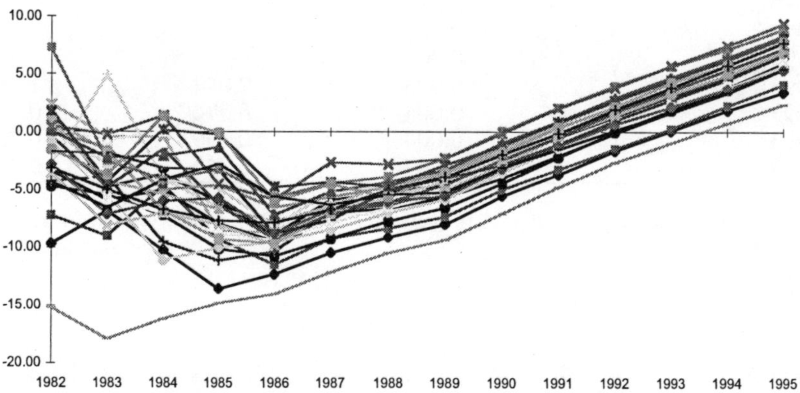

Figure 5.3 Total factor productivity growth in China's regional economies, 1982–1995

In order to shed more light on the dynamics of productivity, the scatter plot of the rates of TFP, TP and TE changes are presented in Figures 5.4, 5.5 and 5.6. According to these charts, TFP growth, TP and TE changes have all shown the tendency of acceleration over time (that is, positive rates). Figure 5.4 shows the trend of rapid convergence of the rate of technical efficiency changes during 1982–1995. It also shows that the catching-up process was almost completed by 1994. TP performance across the regions shows a mixed trend according to Figure 5.5. It tended to converge in the 1980s but has become slightly divergent in the first half of the 1990s. Finally, the phenomenon of convergence in TFP growth performance is evident in

Figure 5.6. It is shown that TFP growth has accelerated in all regions since the late 1980s, and the acceleration is mainly due to the improvements in the performance of technological progress.

Table 5.2 Coefficients of variation

Year	TE	TP	TFP
1981	0.169		
1982	0.138		
1983	0.111		
1984	0.074		
1985	0.046		
1986	0.034		
1987	0.024		
1988	0.017		
1989	0.011		
1990	0.008		
1991	0.007		
1992	0.005	2.044	1.182
1993	0.004	0.576	0.524
1994	0.004	0.339	0.331
1995	0.004	0.245	0.247

Note: The coefficients of variation are negative for TP and TFP before 1991 and hence not reported.

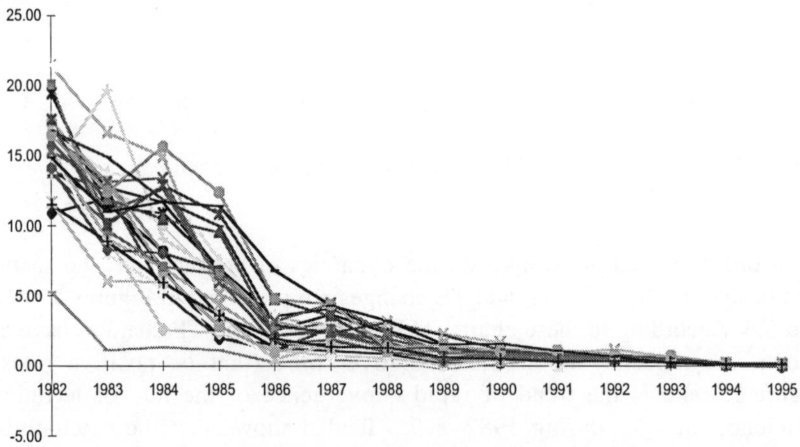

Figure 5.4 Rate of TE changes in China's regional economies, 1982–1995

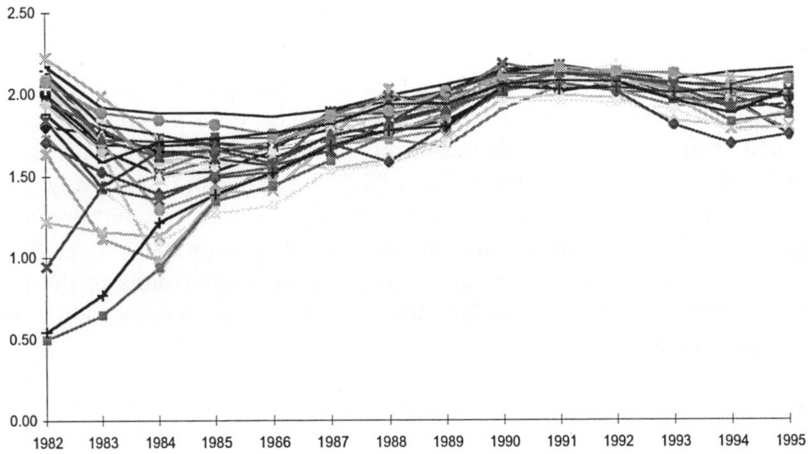

Figure 5.5 Rate of TP changes in China's regional economies, 1982–1995

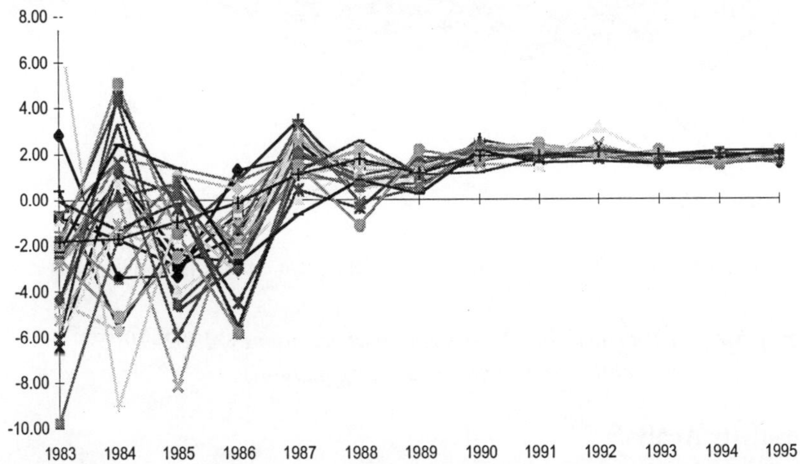

Figure 5.6 Rate of TFP changes in China's regional economies, 1982–1995

A Comparison

As a comparison, the estimates of TFP growth applying the conventional growth accounting method are computed as follows:

$$T\dot{F}P = \dot{Q} - (a\dot{L} + b\dot{K}) \quad (5.7)$$

where dots indicate percentage changes, and the parameters a and b are the factor shares to be estimated from a Cobb-Douglas production function with constant returns to scale. In this case, the estimated a and b are statistically significant, and have estimated values of 0.527 and 0.473, respectively. The calculated TFP growth rates are shown in Figure 5.7. It is apparent that both Figures 5.3 and 5.7 show the similar trend of TFP performance over time. However, the magnitude of changes varies between the results of the two methods. Färe et al. (1994) attribute these variations to the difference in the techniques applied.

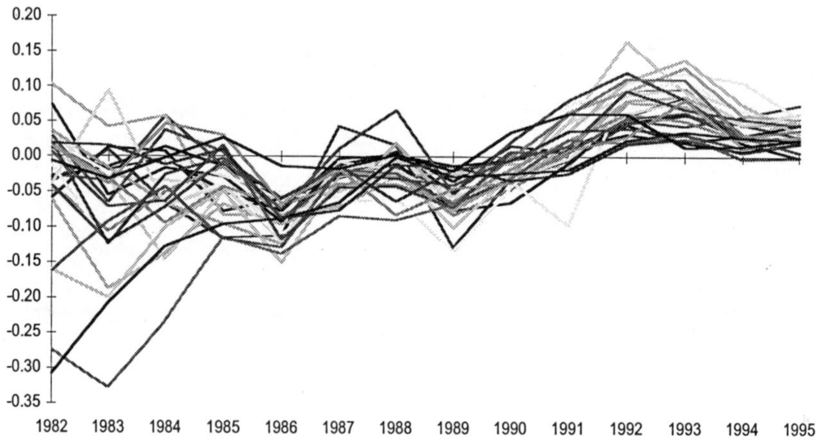

Figure 5.7 TFP growth in China's regional economies, 1982–1995 (conventional growth-accounting method)

Sensitivity Analysis

Finally, a sensitivity analysis is applied to shed some light on the possible impact of effective depreciation rates. The estimation process of capital stock has become an important issue in the growth literature partly because time series data on capital stock are not available in many countries. This problem is particularly acute in the developing Asian countries, and makes it difficult to carry out quantitative studies. The above analysis is based upon the assumption of a depreciation rate of 5%. To make a comparison, the preceding exercise is repeated using data generated from high depreciation rates, that is, 10, 15 and 30%, respectively. Apart from this purpose, a sensitivity analysis can also shed light on the impact of possible embodied technological progress. As Young (1992) argued, capital could become scrapped not because of wear-out but due to the introduction of new technology such as joint ventures. In this case, the depreciation rate should be endogenous. For a comparison with Figure 5.3, the estimates of productivity growth under the assumption of a depreciation rate of 30% are shown in Figure 5.8. The results under the assumption of a depreciation rate of 5 and 30% can be treated as the lower and upper bounds of productivity growth, respectively. Obviously, TFP changes in Figures 5.2 and 5.7 show a similar J-curve trend. The only difference is that, under the assumption of a higher rate of depreciation, productivity growth bottoms out about two years earlier in most regions. The findings on technical efficiency change, convergence and catch-up remain more or less the same as in the previous case.

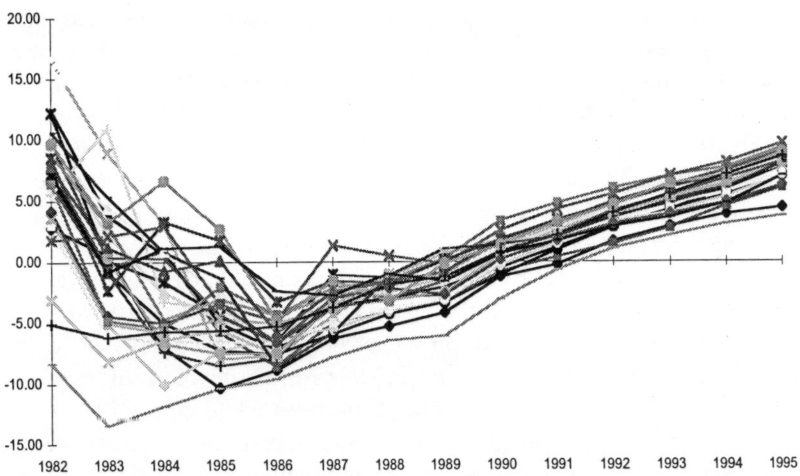

Figure 5.8 TFP growth in China's regional economies, 1982–1995

4 SUMMARY AND CONCLUSIONS

Applying a stochastic frontier technique to regional statistics, this chapter examines productivity growth in China's reforming economy during the period 1981–1995. In particular, the analysis focuses on the trend of technological progress and technical efficiency change among the regions. The principal findings are that, since the initiative of economic reform, the pattern of TFP growth resembles a J-shaped curve: productivity growth declined sharply in the initial years of the reform and recovered gradually over time. This finding holds even when variations in the rate of capital depreciation are allowed. In addition, it is found that China's economic growth in the 1980s was mainly due to efficiency improvement and growth in inputs. This however, changed in the 1990s. Technological progress has become an important factor propelling China's economic growth. This change is very favourable for sustained growth.

Specifically, this study shows that technical efficiency performance in China's regional economies has converged rapidly since the early 1980s. This indicates the success of economic reform which helped stimulate the Chinese regional economies to catch up with the best practice producers. However, the growth potential in efficiency was almost exhausted by the middle of the 1990s. Further growth in the regions will rely largely on improvement in innovation, that is, technological progress, as has been argued by the World Bank and other China watchers. The record of technological progress among the regions is poor, especially in the 1980s. However, the rate of change of technological progress has been positive for all regions. Due to this upward trend, most regions have shown a positive rate of technological progress in the early 1990s. As a result, the rate of TFP changes across the region has become positive and shown the tendency of convergence in the 1990s.

Finally, although the findings in this study provide important insight into productivity performance in Chinese regional economies, further research is called for. Relative price changes may be an important factor influencing technological progress. Other factors may also be attributed to the rapid decline in technological progress in the early 1980s. The quality of regional statistics can be improved in the future when more detailed information is available. For example, various depreciation rates could be used to estimate capital stock in different categories, and labour statistics could be based upon the employed man hours instead of the number of employees, as is used widely in the literature at present. In terms of methodology, though the applied model has its advantages, there is still room for technical improvement. Furthermore, no matter how refined and how elaborate the analysis, 15 years of high growth in China is not sufficient to indicate high and sustained growth in the long run. Thus, further theoretical and empirical work is required to obtain a better understanding of economic growth in China.

NOTES

1. Other authors include Kawai (1994), Oshima (1995) and Sarel (1995).
2. Such as Holtz-Eakin (1993) and Evans and Karras (1994).
3. See Wu (1993), Putterman and Chiacu (1994) and Jefferson and Singh (1999) for surveys of the literature.
4. Other recent studies include Hu and Khan (1997), World Bank (1997) and Woo (1998).
5. Comprehensive surveys of efficiency measurement techniques are documented in Fried et al. (1993) and Lovell (1996), for instance.
6. The name of Malmquist (1953) productivity index was introduced by Caves et al. (1982). This approach has become popular largely due to Färe et al. (1992).
7. This function form was proposed by Christensen et al. (1971), and Griliches and Ringstad (1971), and applied to productivity studies by, for instance, Nishimizu and Page (1982), Lau and Brada (1990), and Young (1995).
8. The original model was proposed by Battese and Coelli (1995). Other similar models include, for example, Reifschneider and Stevenson (1991), and Huang and Liu (1994).
9. Readers may refer to Coelli (1992) for further details about the FRONTIER program.
10. The same technique was also used in Chou (1995).

REFERENCES

Abramovitz, M. (1986), 'Catching up, forging ahead, and falling behind', *Journal of Economic History*, 46(2), pp. 385–406.

Aigner, D.J., C.A.K. Lovell and P.J. Schmidt (1977), 'Formulation and estimation of stochastic frontier models', *Journal of Econometrics*, 6(1), pp. 21–37.

Battese, G. and T. Coelli (1995), 'A model for technical inefficiency effects in a stochastic frontier production function', *Empirical Economics*, 20, pp. 325–32.

Borensztein, E. and J.D. Ostry (1996), 'Accounting for China's growth performance', *American Economic Review (Papers and Proceedings)*, 86, pp. 225–8.

Caves, D.W., L.R. Christensen and W.E. Diewert (1982), 'Multilateral comparisons of output, input and productivity using superlative index numbers', *Economic Journal*, 92, pp. 73–86.

Chen, K., H.C. Wang, Y.X. Zheng, G.H. Jefferson and T.G. Rawski (1988), 'Productivity change in Chinese industry, 1953–85', *Journal of Comparative Economics*, 12, pp. 570–91.

Chou, J. (1995), 'Old and new development models: the Taiwan experience', in *Growth Theories in Light of the East Asian Experience*, edited by Takatoshi Ito and Anne O. Krueger, University of Chicago Press, Chicago and London.

Chow, G. (1985), *The Chinese Economy*, Harper and Row, New York.

Christensen, L.R., D.W. Jorgensen and L.J. Lau (1971), 'Conjugate duality and the transcendental logarithmic production function', *Econometrica*, 39, pp. 255–6.

Coelli, T.J. (1992), 'A computer program for frontier production function estimation: FRONTIER, version 2.0', *Economics Letters*, 39, pp. 29–32.

Evans, P. and G. Karras (1994), 'Are government activities productive: evidence from a panel of US states', *Review of Economics and Statistics*, 76, pp. 1–11.

Färe, R., S. Grosskopf and W.F Lee (1995), 'Productivity in Taiwanese manufacturing industries', *Applied Economics*, 27, pp. 259–65.

Färe, R., S. Grosskopf, B. Lindgren and P. Roos (1992), 'Productivity changes in Swedish pharmacies 1980–1989: a nonparametric Malmquist approach', *Journal of Productivity Analysis*, 3, pp. 85–101.

Färe, R., S. Grosskopf, M. Norris and Z. Zhang (1994), 'Productivity growth, technical progress and efficiency change in industrialised countries', *American Economic Review*, 84(1), pp. 66–83.

Farrell, M.J. (1957), 'The measurement of productive efficiency', *Journal of the Royal Statistical Society, Series A, General*, 120, pp. 253–82.

Fecher, F. and P. Pestieau, 1993, 'Efficiency and competition in OECD financial services', in *The Measurement of Productive Efficiency*, edited by H. Fried, C.A. K. Lovell and S. Schmidt, Oxford University Press, New York.

Fleisher, B.M. and J. Chen (1997), 'The coastal-noncoastal income gap, productivity and regional economic policy in China', *Journal of Comparative Economics*, 25(2), pp. 220–36.

Fried, H., C.A.K. Lovell and S. Schmidt (eds) (1993), *The Measurement of Productive Efficiency*, Oxford University Press, New York.

Griliches, Z. and V. Ringstad (1971), *Economies of Scale and the Form of the Production Function*, North-Holland Publishing Company, Amsterdam.

Holtz-Eakin, D. (1993), 'Solow and the states: capital accumulation, productivity and economic growth', *National Tax Journal*, 46, pp. 425–39.

Hu, Z.F. and M.S. Khan (1997), 'Why is China growing so fast?', *IMF Staff Papers*, 44, pp. 103–31.

Huang, C.J. and J.T. Liu (1994), 'Estimation of a non-neutral stochastic frontier production function', *Journal of Productivity Analysis*, 5, pp. 171–80.

Huang, Y. (1995), 'Can institutional transition stimulate long-run growth?', Economics Division Working Papers 95/8, Australian National University.

Jefferson, G.H. and I. Singh (eds) (1999), *Enterprise Reform in China: Ownership, Transition, and Performance*, Oxford: Oxford University Press.

Jefferson, G.H., T.G. Rawski and Y. Zheng (1992), 'Growth, efficiency and convergence in China's state and collective industry', *Economic Development and Cultural Change*, 40(1), pp. 239–66.

Jefferson, G.H., T.G. Rawski and Y. Zheng (1996), 'Chinese industrial productivity: trends, measurement issues and recent developments', *Journal of Comparative Economics*, 23, pp. 146–80.

Kawai, H. (1994), 'International comparative analysis of economic growth: trade liberalisation and productivity', *Developing Economies*, 17(4), pp. 373–97.

Kim, J-I and L. Lau (1994), 'The sources of economic growth in the East Asian newly industrialised countries', *Journal of the Japanese and International Economies*, 8, pp. 235–71.

Lau, K.T. and J.C. Brada (1990), 'Technological progress and technical efficiency in Chinese industrial growth: a frontier production function approach', *China Economic Review*, 1, pp. 113–24.

Lin, J.Y. (1992), 'Rural reforms and agricultural growth in China', *American Economic Review*, 82, pp. 34–51.

Lovell, C.A.K. (1996), 'Applying efficiency measurement techniques to the measurement of productivity change', *Journal of Productivity Analysis*, 7, pp. 329–40.

Lucas, R.E. (1988), 'On the mechanics of economic development', *Journal of Monetary Economics*, 22, pp. 3–42.

Maddison, A. (1998), *Chinese Economic Performance in the Long Run*, OECD Development Centre, Paris.

Malmquist, S. (1953), 'Index numbers and indifference curves', *Trabajos de Estatistica*, 4, pp. 209–42.

McMillan, J., J. Whalley and L. Zhu (1989), 'The impact of China's economic reforms on agricultural productivity growth', *Journal of Political Economy*, 97(4), pp. 781–807.

Meeusen, W. and J. van den Broeck (1977), 'Efficiency estimation from Cobb-Douglas production functions with composed error', *International Economic Review*, 18(2), pp. 435–44.

Nishimizu, M. and J.M. Page (1982), 'Total factor productivity growth, technological progress and technical efficiency change: dimensions of productivity change in Yugoslavia, 1965–78', *Economic Journal*, 92, pp. 920–36.

Oshima, M. (1995), 'Trends in productivity growth in the economic transition of Asia and long-term prospects for the 1990s', *Asian Economic Journal*, 9(21), pp. 89–111.

Portes, R. (1992), 'Structural reform in Central and Eastern Europe', *European Economic Review*, 36, pp. 661–69.

Putterman, L. and A.F. Chiacu (1994), 'Elasticities and factor weights for agricultural growth accounting: a look at the data for China', *China Economic Review*, 5(2), pp. 191–204.

Reifschneider, D. and R. Stevenson (1991), 'Systematic departures from the frontier: a framework for analysis of farm inefficiency', *International Economic Review*, 32, pp. 715–23.

Reynolds, B.L. (ed.) (1987), *Reform in China: Challenges and Choices*, M.E. Sharpe, New York.

Sarel, M. (1995), 'Growth in East Asia: what we can and what we cannot infer from it', in *Productivity and Growth*, proceedings of a conference, edited by Palle Andersen, Jacqueline Dwyer and David Gruen, Reserve Bank of Australia.

Solow, R.M. (1957), 'Technical change and the aggregate production function', *Review of Economics and Statistics*, 39(3), pp. 312–20.

Statistical Yearbook of China, various issues, State Statistical Bureau, Statistical Publishing House of China, Beijing.

Tidrick, G. (1986), 'Productivity growth and technological change in Chinese industry', World Bank Working Papers No. 761, World Bank, Washington, DC.

Wei, S-J. (1995), 'The open door policy and China's rapid growth: evidence from city-level data', in *Growth Theories in Light of the East Asian Experience*, edited by Takatoshi Ito and Anne O. Krueger, University of Chicago Press, Chicago and London.

Woo, W.T. (1998), 'Chinese economic growth: sources and prospects', in *The Chinese Economy* edited by M. Fouquin and F. Lemoine, Economica Ltd, Paris.

Woo, W.T., W. Hai, Y. Jin and G. Fan (1994), 'How successful has Chinese enterprise reform been? Pitfalls in opposite biases and focus', *Journal of Comparative Economics*, 18, pp. 410–37.

World Bank (1985), *China: Long-Term Development Issues and Options*, Johns Hopkins University Press, Baltimore.

World Bank (1993), *The East Asian Miracle, a World Bank Policy Research Report*, Oxford University Press, New York.

World Bank (1996), *From Plan to Market, World Development Report*, Oxford University Press, New York.

World Bank (1997), *China 2020: Development Challenges in the New Century*, Washington, DC.

Wu, Y. (1993), 'Productive efficiency in Chinese industry: a review', *Asia-Pacific Economic Literature*, 7(2), pp. 58–66.

Wu, Y. (1995), 'Productivity growth, technological progress and technical efficiency change in China: a three-sector analysis', *Journal of Comparative Economics*, 21, pp. 207–29.

Young, A. (1992), 'A tale of two cities: factor accumulation and technical change in Hong Kong and Singapore', *NBER Macroeconomic Annual*, MIT Press, Cambridge, Mass.

Young, A. (1995), 'The tyranny of numbers: confronting the statistical realities of the East Asian growth experience', *Quarterly Journal of Economics*, 110, pp. 641–80.

6. The impact of WTO accession on income disparity in China*

Fan Zhai and Shantong Li[a]

1 INTRODUCTION

Since the beginning of economic reform and its opening to the outside world, China's economy has been growing at a rate of nearly 10% annually and its external trade has expanded by more than 15% a year. In 1997 China's trade volume reached US$325.0 billion, ranking 10th in the world, with export volume reaching US$182.7 billion. China has emerged as an important player in the world trading system. A World Trade Organization (WTO) without China as a member will have difficulty in claiming to represent the global economy. Integration of China into WTO's global trading system would significantly expand world trade, and strength the multilateral trade system's integrity and credibility. The negotiations over China's membership in the WTO are still ongoing. Substantial trade liberalization is expected in China to further reform its foreign trade regime and bid for WTO accession.

Accompanying rapid economic growth, the household income gap has widened sharply. In China, the income disparity between rural and urban households dominates overall income inequality. Between the late 1970s and the mid-1980s, when reform was largely confined to agriculture, rural household income was growing more rapidly than urban income and hence urban–rural income distribution improved. But after 1984, income growth in rural areas slowed and urban income accelerated. As a result, the rural–urban income gap began to enlarge. At the same time, income disparities among regions were also on the rise, as economic growth in coastal areas grew more

* Funding for this research was supported by a grant from the Washington Center for China Studies and Ford Foundation. We thank Wang Huijiong, David Roland-Holst, Dominique van der Mensbrugghe and Wang Zhi for their help in development of the Chinese CGE model. The views expressed in the chapter are those of the authors and should not be attributed to their affiliated institution.

a Development Research Center, The State Council, P.R. China - 225 Chaoyangmen Nei Street, Beijing 100010, CHINA - Fax: (86 10) 65236060 - Email: fzhai@drc.gov.cn.

rapidly than inland areas. In addition, income distribution within both rural and urban areas has also become less equitable.

Statistics indicates that about five million households, approximately 2% of all households in China, have annual incomes of more than 50 000 yuan (about US$6 000) in 1995. One million of these households have personal assets of more than one million yuan (about US$120 000). However, most Chinese working families still have very low incomes and 12.5 million urban residents, about 5% of the urban population, fall beneath the poverty line, having less than 1200 yuan (about US$150) income per capita a year. Moreover, 60 million people in rural areas still live in poverty. The incomes of the top 20% urban households are 13 times the incomes of the lowest 20% of the rural households, which is very high even by international standards (Huang, 1996).

These widening gaps are the result of profound structural changes in the Chinese economy. Some empirical literature has addressed the issue of the development of income disparity and its determining factors in China (Khan et al., 1993; Zhao and Li, 1998). However, existing literature has not clearly revealed how trade expansion has affected income disparity since economic reform and opening up. But undoubtedly, it will have important implications for income disparity in China if China becomes a member of WTO. In fact, the effect on income distribution has significance for the political feasibility of any trade policy reform. While overall welfare gains may arise from the WTO accession, the uneven distribution of the gain may result in strong opposition to trade liberalization. Therefore, evaluation of the distributional effects of trade policy reform is important for the successful implementation of this reform.

This chapter investigates the impact of China's WTO accession on income disparity in China. This analysis uses a 41 sector, 10 representative households recursive dynamic computable general equilibrium (CGE) model of China. We provide some empirical evidence for policy makers to evaluate the effects of China's WTO accession from the perspectives of efficiency and equality.

The conflict between economic efficiency and income equality has long been recognized in economics. CGE models provide a unified quantitative framework to analyse the various trade-offs. Dervis et al. (1982) have argued that analysis of income distribution requires a general equilibrium rather than a partial equilibrium framework. In the CGE framework, the income flows between factors and agents are completely and explicitly specified. The linkage between returns from various production factors and income flows to major groups of households permits the analysis of both functional and size distribution among economic agents (Adelman and Robinson, 1988). This capability provides a valuable means for economists and policy makers to capture the efficiency–equality trade-offs induced by different policy scenarios and thus obtain a better understanding of the possible social consequences of the proposed policy changes. (Wang and Zhai, 1998).

Section 2 of this chapter outlines the basic structure of the CGE model for China and presents major assumptions. Section 3 describes the basic characteristics of the base year data, and highlights the structure, sources and distribution of household income in China. Section 4 describes the simulation scenarios and Section 5 uses simulation results to assess the efficiency and equality consequences of China's WTO accession. Section 6 concludes by drawing policy implications.

2 THE MODEL

The starting point for the model used in this study is the prototype CGE model developed for the Trade and Environment Programme of the OECD Development Centre (Beghin et al., 1994). Some significant modifications were made to this model to capture the major features of the trade and tax system in the current Chinese economy. First, a value-added tax and export rebate mechanism is incorporated into the model to capture the major changes in China's taxation reform in 1994 (Wang and Zhai, 1998). Second, two separate trade regimes – an ordinary trade regime and a processing trade regime – are introduced into the model. As pointed out correctly by Naughton (1996), China had established two separate trading regimes by 1986–87. One is the export processing or export promotion regime, which is extremely open and in which most foreign-invested firms and parts of domestic firms participate. The other is the traditional, but increasingly reformed, ordinary trade regime. Since the 1990s export processing has grown rapidly to the point where it accounts for more than half of all exports. Obviously, to analyse external trade behaviour and the impact of alternative changes of trade policy in such an economy, it is very important to have an explicit treatment of its dualistic foreign trading regimes in the model. Finally, labour is classified by agricultural labour, production workers and professionals. We added migration behaviour between agricultural labour and production workers in this model to specify the partial mobility of the labour force.

Forty-one production sectors and ten representative households (low, middle–low, middle, middle–high and high income households in both urban and rural areas) are specified in this model. There are five primary factors of production in the model, namely, agricultural land, capital, agricultural labourers, production workers, and professionals. Production and professional workers have basic education in common, but professionals usually have more advanced training. Agricultural labourers are those who have little or no education and work only in farm sectors.

This section provides a brief description of the structure of this model and the data issue.

2.1 Production and Factor Markets

Suppose there are two types of competitive firm – *ordinary firms* and *export processing firms* – that produce the same product in the same industry. The products of ordinary firms are assumed to be sold on the domestic market or to be exported to the rest of the world by a constant elasticity of transformation (CET) function, while for the latter –export processing firm– their products are exported only.

The production technology is represented by a set of nested constant elasticity of substitution (CES) and Leontief functions. Technology in all sectors is assumed to exhibit constant returns to scale. At the first level, firms are assumed to use a composite of primary factors plus energy inputs, that is, value added plus the energy bundle, and aggregate non-energy intermediate input according to a CES cost function. At the second level, the division of intermediate non-energy demand is assumed to follow a Leontief specification, therefore, there is no substitution among other intermediate inputs. At the same level, the value-added plus energy bundle is divided between aggregate labour and energy–capital bundles, that are further split into energy and capital–land bundles. Finally, the energy bundle is decomposed into different base fuel components. All composite bundles in each nest are assumed to substitute smoothly in a CES cost function. The degree of substitutability among them depends on their base year share in production and on the elasticity of substitution, which is assumed to be constant.

The model distinguishes between *old* and *new* capital goods. This assumption of vintage capital allows the substitute elasticity in production function to differ according to the vintage of capital. The model also includes adjustment rigidities in a capital market. It is assumed that new capital goods are homogeneous and old capital good supply second-hand markets. The installed old capital in a sector can disinvest when this sector is in decline. The supply curve of old capital is a simple constant elasticity function of the relative rental rates. The higher the rental rate on old capital, the higher the supply of old capital. But the rental rate on old capital is not allowed to exceed the rental rate on new capital. Within each sector, the capital is fully mobile among ordinary firms and export processing firms.

Each type of labour force is assumed to be fully mobile across sectors and across the two types of firms. The agricultural labourers work only in farm sectors and production workers work only in non-farm sectors. There is no substitute between agricultural labourer and production worker in production functions. In China, despite reforms, there are still large barriers to the migration of rural labourers to urban areas. These barriers include the household registration regime, discrimination in employment, education and social security and so on. This segmented labour market is modelled by incorporating partial mobility between agricultural labourer and production worker. We assumed agricultural labourer and production worker could be converted from one to another. A CET function is used here to capture this specification, that is, this transfer is determined by the relative wages of agricultural labourer and production worker, as well as the constant elasticity of transformation.

2.2 Trade

The rest of the world supplies imports and demands exports. Given China's small trade share in the world, import prices are exogenous in foreign currency (an infinite price-elasticity), that is, the local consumption of imports does not affect the border price of imports. Exports are demanded according to constant-elasticity demand curves, the price-elasticities of which are high but less than infinite (Pomfret, 1997).

The ordinary firms allocate their output between export and domestic sales to maximize profits, subject to imperfect transformation between the two alternatives. All the output of export processing firms is sold to overseas markets. We assume that exports by ordinary firms and export processing firms are heterogeneous, a CES aggregation function with relative high substitute elasticities is employed to form the composite export. In other words, we assume the buyers of the rest of the world choose a mix between the two types of export to minimize their cost.

Three types of import are differentiated in the model. The first one is the ordinary trade import, which is operated under the ordinary trade regime, subjected to import tariff and non-tariff barriers (NTB). The second one is the duty-free import of raw materials and components into processing trade export. Most of these imports are used as intermediate input of export processing firms, but part of them is transferred to the domestic market. The third one is duty-free import of investment goods for foreign invested enterprises and export processing enterprises.

Agents are assumed to consider products from domestic supply and imports as imperfect substitutes, that is, the Armington assumption. A two-level nesting CES aggregation function is specified for each Armington composite commodity. At the top level, agents choose an optimal combination of the domestic good and an import aggregate, which is determined by a set of relative prices and the degree of substitutability. At the second level of the nest, the import aggregate is further split into ordinary import, duty-free import of investment and the import of processing trade which is transferred into the domestic market, again as a function of relative import prices and the degree of substitution across different import types. Note that the import prices are specific by import type because of the duty-free element of the last two types of import.

We establish the difference between domestic price and world price in two parts, that is, the tariff rate and non-tariff barriers. NTB is modelled as the tariff equivalent, which creates a pure rent to households. The quantitative restriction on agricultural products is modelled explicitly through a Leontief specification, where imports cannot exceed the quota allocation. The rates of agricultural quota rent are solved endogenously.

In the textile and apparel sectors, China faces the multi-fibre agreement (MFA) quota in the markets of the USA, Canada, EU and other countries. In our model, we treat this voluntary export restrictions (VER) quota as an export tax equivalent that is added to the domestic export price. The quota premium is assumed to be obtained by households. In the simulations, the MFA quotas are exogenous, with export tax rates adjusted endogenously.

2.3 Demands

The representative households are assumed to maximize a Stone-Geary utility function over the 46 composite (Armington) goods subject to their budget constraints, which leads to an extended linear expenditure system (ELES) of household demand functions. Household savings are treated as a demand for future consumption goods with zero subsistence quantity (Howe, 1975). An economy-wide consumer price index is specified as the price of savings. It represents the opportunity cost of giving up current consumption in exchange for future consumption. Other final demands, including social consumption and investment demand, are based on constant expenditure share functions for each composite commodity.

Stock change is assumed as a demand for domestic products. The intermediate inputs for ordinary firms are provided by the Armington composite goods, while the intermediate inputs for export processing firms are composed of composite goods and duty-free import of raw materials and components into processing trade export through a CES function. The intermediate inputs for ordinary firms, the domestic part of intermediate input for export processing firms, household consumption, and other final demands constitute the total demand for the same Armington composite of domestic products and imported goods from the rest of the world.

2.4 Income Distribution

Production generates income, which is distributed to four major institutions, namely, enterprises, households, the government and extra-budget public sectors. Enterprise earnings equal a share of gross operating surplus, that is, the sum of capital remuneration across all sectors, minus government corporate income taxes. The tax rate is taken as a parameter in the model. However, it can be endogenized to meet government fiscal targets, in which case an adjustment parameter becomes endogenous. A part of net company income is allocated to households as distributed profits based on fixed shares, which are the assumed shares of capital ownership by households. Another part of net company income is allocated to extra-budget public sectors as fee. Retained earnings, that is, corporate savings for new investment and capital depreciation replacement, equals a residual of after-tax company income minus the distributed profits and fee.

Household incomes consist of labour earnings and the returns from land and capital that households own. Additionally, households receive distributed corporate profits, transfers and subsidies from the government and remittances from the rest of the world. Households also receive all kinds of import and export quota rent. Assume the rural households earn all the land returns. Rural households earn their labour income from both agricultural labourers and production workers, while urban households obtain their wages from both production and professional workers. But this can change when agricultural labourers and production workers change roles. If some agricultural labourers transfer to the non-agricultural sector and become production workers, their labour income would be allocated to rural households, on the other hand, if production workers transfer to the agricultural sector and become agricultural labour, their wages are still distributed to urban and rural households according to the distribution share of production worker's wages. The household income tax rate is set as a parameter, but an associated adjustment factor can be endogenous if government budgets are exogenous. In this case, household tax schedules shift in or out to achieve government budget balance. Household disposable income equals total household income less taxes.

2.5 Government and Extra-budget Public Sector

The government collects taxes from producers, households and the foreign sector, transfers money to the household sector, and purchases public goods. It derives revenues from direct corporate and household income taxes, import tariffs, and various types of indirect taxes. Subsidies and export tax rebates enter as negative receipts. There are two types of indirect taxes in the model. The value-added tax, which is the most important part of indirect tax in China after 1994 tax reform, is treated as a tax levied on production factors. Its revenues equal total sector value-added multiplied by a tax rate. The value-added tax is also levied on imports while firms obtain rebates when they export. The other indirect tax, including various agricultural taxes, and business taxes on construction and services, is treated as a production tax levied on sectoral outputs.

Extra-budget public sectors collect fees from enterprise and households. Their income is allocated to consumption and saving. The consumption of extra-budget public sectors and government spending compose a type of final demand, that is, the social consumption.

2.6 Equilibrium and Macro Closure

Equilibrium is defined as a set of prices and quantities for goods and factors such that (i) demand equals supply for all goods and factors; (ii) each industry earns zero profit; and (iii) gross investment equals aggregate savings, which is the sum of domestic savings plus foreign capital inflows.

Macro closure in a CGE model involves both macroeconomic accounting balances and assumptions about adjustment behaviour. It determines the manner in which the following three accounts are brought into balance: (i) the government budget; (ii) aggregate savings and investment; and (iii) the balance of payments.

Real government spending is exogenous in the model. All tax rates and transfers are fixed, while real government savings are endogenous. This government closure rule has significant consequences on the level of investment since investment is driven by savings in the model.

The total value of investment expenditure equals total resources allocated to the investment sector; it includes retained corporate earnings, total household savings, government savings, extra-budget saving and foreign capital flows. In this model, the aggregate investment is the endogenous sum of the separate saving components. This specification corresponds to the 'neoclassical' macroeconomic closure in CGE literature.

The last macroeconomic identity is the balance of payments. The value of imports, at world prices, must equal the value of exports at border prices, that is, inclusive of export taxes and subsidies, plus the sum of net transfers and factor payments and net capital inflows. An exchange rate is specified to convert world prices, for example, in dollars, into domestic prices. Either this exchange rate or total foreign capital inflow can be fixed while the other is allowed to adjust providing alternative closure rules. With foreign saving set exogenously, equilibrium would be achieved through changing the relative price of tradables to nontradables, or the real exchange rate.

Since the purpose of this chapter is to estimate the efficiency and equality trade-off induced by trade liberalization, we keep the domestic savings and investment gap constant across all the simulations conducted. This is achieved by keeping balance of trade fixed at foreign currency. Thus, any changes in real absorption do not result from changes from lending to, or borrowing from, overseas. This makes it easy to compare the efficiency impacts of different simulations.

2.7 Recursive Dynamics

The current version of China's CGE model has a simple recursive dynamic structure as agents are assumed to be myopic and to base their decision on static expectations about prices and quantities. Dynamics in the model originate from accumulation of productive factor and productivity changes

The within-period, static model is solved for several single-period equilibria from 1995–2010. Between the static model solutions, selected parameters are updated in the dynamic (between-period) module, either using lagged endogenous variables (from solution in previous periods) or exogenously (on the basis of trend).

The growth rate of population, labour forces, labour productivity and an autonomous energy efficiency improvement in energy use (known as the AEEI factor) are exogenous. The growth of capital is endogenously determined by the saving/investment relation. In the aggregate, the basic capital accumulation function equates the current capital stock to the depreciated stock inherited from the previous period plus gross investment. At the sectoral level, the specific accumulation functions may differ because the demand for (old and new) capital can be less than the depreciated stock of old capital. We assume the producer decides the optimal way to divide production of total output across vintages. If sectoral demand exceeds what can be produced with the sectoral installed old capital, the producer will demand new capital. Otherwise, the producer will disinvest some of the installed capital.

In defining the reference simulation, a single economy-wide Hicks neutral efficiency factor (TFP) and sector specific agricultural productivity are determined endogenously to get a pre-specified growth path of real GDP and agricultural output. When alternative scenarios are simulated, the TFP growth rate is exogenous, and the growth rate of real GDP is endogenous.

2.8 Data

The model is calibrated to the 1995 Chinese Social Accounting Matrix (SAM) developed from the most recent 1995 input-output table (Zhai, 1998). The SAM provides a consistent framework to organize the relevant flow of value statistics for China's economy to satisfy the requirements of a benchmark data set for CGE modelling. Some key parameters of the model – essentially substitution and income elasticities – were derived from a literature search. All other parameters – mainly shift and share parameters – are calibrated in the base year using the key parameters and the base data.

3 CHINA'S ECONOMIC STRUCTURE, MARKET OPENNESS AND INCOME DISTRIBUTION

Our CGE model for China is constructed according to a SAM for 1995. This section outlines the basic features of industrial structure, market openness and income distribution of the Chinese economy in 1995 based upon the SAM.

Table 6.1 summarizes the sectoral structure of China's economy in the base year. For each of the 41 sectors, the base year data for shares of output, employment, imports, exports, and trade dependence are reported. Column 7 gives data on net exports. Columns 8 to 11 give information about the degree of import protection. As may be seen in columns 1 to 4, the data are notably asymmetric among the shares of output, employment, and trade. For example, the crop sectors (sector 1-5) accounts for more than 45% of China's labour employment but only produces 7% of its output and constitutes about 2% of China's total trade. While textile, apparel and leather industries employ less than 3% of China's labour force, they produce 8.7% of its total output and account for more than 27% of the country's total exports. The sectors with the largest shares in imports are machinery and chemicals as they account for 19 and 13% of China's total imports, respectively.

Export dependency is high for the apparel, leather and electronic sectors as more than 30% of their products depend on foreign markets. Textile and other light consumption goods (sawmills and furniture, paper and social articles) are the other export-oriented sectors in which almost 20% of output is sold on international markets. The wool, instruments, electronics and machinery and two raw materials sectors (crude oils and metal mining) have higher market penetration ratio. The electronics sector has both high export and import dependency, reflecting the fact that a large percentage of production in this sector represents processing and assembling products from abroad, that is, processing trade.

The trade balances by industry in column 7 reflect China's comparative advantage. China is a net exporter of labour-intensive manufactures and a net importer of capital-intensive manufactures. The largest share of the trade surplus in China comes from the apparel and textile sectors. In the agricultural sector, China is a net importer of grain, but has a trade surplus in other agricultural products.

Another notable feature of the base year data is the significant difference between China's nominal tariff rate and the actual collected rate. It is well known that China's tariff collection is significantly below its nominal tariff level because of a large volume of processed trade, extensive import duty exemptions and widespread smuggling activities (World Bank, 1994). The final three columns of Table 6.1 provide the nominal tariff rate, actual collected rate for total import and collected rate for *ordinary trade* import. This indicates the dramatic variation of the nominal/actual tariff rate ratio among sectors as this statistic ranges from 92 in apparel industries to around 3.1 in transportation equipment industries. It also indicates that in some sectors, such as textile and apparel, the share of *ordinary trade* import is very small, less than 10%. In general, the more export-oriented sectors have the higher nominal/actual rate gaps because of the tariff exemptions applied to their imports of intermediate inputs and processed trade.

The sectoral actual tariff rates for *ordinary trade* indicates that China's tariff structure is typical that of developing countries, that is, providing high protection for the manufacturing sector, especially the capital-intensive manufacturing sector and final consumption goods sector. But in the aggregated level, China's actual tariff rate is moderate. Automobiles are subject to the highest tariff rate of 28%. The tariff rates in other manufacturing, sugar, textile and apparel sectors are also relatively high, but their effects are limited because the share of duty import (*ordinary trade* import) is very small in these sectors.

Table 6.2 presents the sources and structures of household income with its distribution in China captured by the base year SAM. It provides a snapshot of the growing income inequality in China today. Urban households are less than 30% of China's total population but they account for more than half of total household income. Per-capita annual income of a middle-income family in a rural area is still well below a low-income family living in urban areas.

Table 6.1 Economic structure and market openness in China, 1995 (%)

	Output	Employment	Imports	Exports	Import/ Domestic Use	Export/ Output	Net Export (bn. Yuan)	Nominal Tariff Rate	Collect Tariff Rate for Total Imports	Collect Tariff Rate for Ordinary Imports	Tariff Equiv. of NTBs
Rices	1.82	11.79	0.12	0.01	0.6	0.0	-1.4	0.3	0.1	0.3	
Wheat	0.94	6.09	0.85	0.00	7.2	0.0	-10.3	0.3	0.1	0.2	
Other grain	1.39	9.03	0.30	0.26	2.0	1.6	-0.1	0.3	0.1	0.4	
Cotton	0.43	2.79	0.69	0.03	11.8	0.6	-7.9	6.8	1.4	3.1	
Other non-grain crops	2.47	16.05	0.18	1.46	0.6	5.1	17.7	6.8	1.4	2.2	
Forestry	0.45	0.72	0.34	0.06	5.8	1.1	-3.4	29.3	2.0	7.7	
Wool	0.02	0.02	0.39	0.01	56.9	2.9	-4.6	15.8	0.7	3.7	
Other livestock	3.84	3.42	0.07	0.64	0.2	1.5	7.9	15.8	0.7	3.0	
Other agriculture	0.53	2.09	0.01	0.01	0.2	0.2	0.0	25.1	6.5	9.4	
Fishing	1.09	0.92	0.07	0.62	0.5	4.9	7.7	11.9	1.7	4.2	
Coal mining	0.85	0.78	0.05	0.62	0.7	6.7	7.8	12.0	3.0	3.7	45.7
Crude oil	0.96	0.16	1.63	1.37	17.9	13.9	-1.1	1.5	0.4	0.5	45.7
Metal mining	0.47	0.16	1.36	0.25	19.9	5.6	-13.1	0.1	0.0	0.0	3.3
Other mining	1.20	0.45	0.48	0.60	3.3	4.1	2.3	6.0	0.6	1.8	5.7
Grain mill and vegetable oil	1.56	0.35	1.16	0.31	6.2	1.6	-9.8	18.3	3.3	9.1	2.7

Sugar	0.32	0.18	0.30	0.12	8.1	3.0	-1.9	30.5	4.4	24.0	2.7
Processed food	4.96	0.81	1.61	5.07	2.9	9.0	49.6	58.3	4.0	7.3	2.7
Textiles	5.12	1.68	7.90	12.87	13.5	21.0	80.0	58.7	1.1	16.7	24.3
Apparel	2.20	0.59	0.22	9.18	1.18	33.76	122.65	64.5	0.7	20.9	18.4
Leather	1.39	0.39	1.51	5.23	11.39	33.33	53.09	30.8	0.5	10.4	18.4
Sawmills and furniture	1.03	0.43	0.89	2.35	9.1	16.9	21.3	23.0	3.4	6.8	32.5
Paper and social articles	2.78	0.87	3.12	6.34	10.4	21.8	48.7	24.6	1.9	6.7	0.0
Electricity	1.87	0.33	0.02	0.24	0.1	1.0	3.0	3.0	0.7	0.9	
Petroleum refineries	1.44	0.16	1.60	0.63	9.7	3.4	-10.7	9.5	2.3	2.9	15.0
Coking and coal	0.28	0.03	0.00	0.44	0.2	14.6	5.9	6.1	1.5	1.9	
Chemicals	7.72	1.89	14.47	9.48	14.7	10.6	-45.9	16.1	2.0	4.7	3.3
Building materials	3.97	2.30	1.21	2.83	2.6	5.6	24.0	32.3	3.8	10.4	0.0
Basic metals	5.12	0.97	7.27	4.21	11.5	7.0	-30.6	12.0	1.3	3.5	15.9
Metal products	2.23	0.72	1.41	3.25	5.7	11.8	27.3	29.7	4.5	10.8	
Machinery	4.90	1.70	20.50	7.35	29.3	15.3	-148.0	21.0	2.9	7.7	5.1
Road vehicles	1.54	0.43	1.56	0.38	11.1	2.4	-13.7	78.1	24.1	27.9	26.3
Transport equip.	1.05	0.37	1.91	1.45	15.2	13.2	-3.3	8.8	2.8	3.2	0.0
Electrical mach.	2.55	0.65	3.76	4.06	12.8	14.6	9.9	26.9	3.5	9.8	7.8

Table 6.1 (continued)

	Output	Employment	Imports	Exports	Import/ Domestic Use	Export/ Output	Net Export (bn. Yuan)	Nominal Tariff Rate	Collect Tariff Rate for Total Imports	Collect Tariff Rate for Ordinary Imports	Tariff Equiv. of NTBs
Electronics	2.40	0.38	9.82	8.54	33.2	30.8	-2.5	25.1	3.3	9.2	5.6
Instruments	0.23	0.19	1.38	0.41	37.9	15.8	-11.2	12.7	2.3	4.7	5.6
Machinery repairing	0.32	0.18	0.00	0.00	0.0	0.0	0.0				
Other industries	0.26	0.57	0.32	0.27	9.7	8.0	-0.2	68.9	1.6	26.5	
Construction	8.56	5.32	0.55	0.47	0.5	0.5	-0.3				
Infrastructure	3.37	4.26	2.61	3.96	6.3	10.3	22.4				
Commerce	7.03	9.46	3.27	1.24	3.5	1.5	-22.7				
Service	9.35	10.23	5.07	3.38	4.2	3.2	-15.3				
Total/Average	100.00	100.00	100.00	100.00	8.4	8.7	153.2	20.2	2.6	6.5	

Notes: (1) Imports/Domestic Use and Exports/Output are at domestic price. The sectoral share of imports and exports are at world price. (2) The imports of rice, wheat, other grain, cotton, wool, grain mill and vegetable oil, and sugar are averages of 1993–97.

The urban to rural income gap reached 3.1:1 in 1995.

The data in Table 6.2 show that earnings from agricultural labour and wages of production workers are both the major source of income for China's rural households. It reflects the importance of the village and township enterprises in a rural household's earnings. A large part of urban households' income comes from enterprise transfer, that is, the distributed corporate profits. Return from capital is an important portion of urban households' income, indicating the growing role of profits from property in urban household's income. Rural households earn income from the return of land. The government price subsidies favour urban residents, but its influence is already very little. On the expenditure side, high-income households have higher propensities to save, while low-income households are at a subsistence level with no savings. The household's burden from income tax was very low in 1995 at less than 1% of income. But the burden of fees is heavier than income tax.

The Lorenz Curve in Figure 6.1 summarizes the information regarding income inequality reflected by the data in the first block of Table 6.2. It is interesting to compare our data with data used previously in other studies. Despite differences in the definition of household income, data sources, and the derivation method, the resulting pattern of income inequality in China from our data is quite similar to that of other recent studies, for example

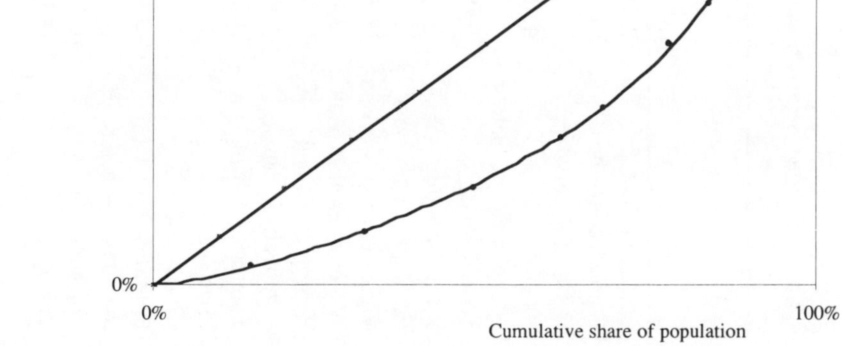

Figure 6.1 Lorenz curve for China, 1995

Table 6.2 Sources, structure and distribution of household income in China, 1995 [a]

	Urban						*Rural*					
	Total	Low	Medium –low	Medium	Medium –high	High	**Total**	Low	Medium – low	Medium	Medium –high	High
Population (%)	29.0	6.4	6.0	5.8	5.6	5.2	71.0	14.6	17.2	16.3	13.2	9.6
Disposable income (%)	56.1	6.3	8.5	10.4	12.7	18.2	43.9	4.3	7.1	9.2	10.4	13.0
Per capita disposable income	6,428	3,249	4,754	5,959	7,531	11,647	2,048	950	1,343	1,854	2,620	4,521
Per capita income before tax (yuan/year)	6,582	3,322	4,809	6,072	7,717	12,028	2,105	990	1,395	1,917	2,687	4,589
Income Structure[b] (%)												
Earnings of ag. labour	-	-	-	-	-	-	33.6	39.7	41.5	37.8	32.7	25.1
Wages of prod. workers	37.5	58.0	50.1	43.7	35.6	22.3	34.5	27.9	33.1	33.9	35.1	37.6
Wages of professionals	22.1	8.9	14.7	19.2	23.5	30.7	4.7	1.8	3.0	3.2	4.9	7.6
Returns from land	-	-	-	-	-	-	5.1	5.0	4.5	4.4	4.7	6.1
Returns from capital	7.7	4.7	4.8	5.3	6.8	12.1	3.3	3.2	2.9	2.9	3.1	4.0
Enterprise transfer	31.8	27.2	29.4	31.0	33.3	33.9	16.7	7.1	14.3	17.0	19.0	19.0
Price subsidy	0.1	0.2	0.1	0.1	0.1	0.1	-	-	-	-	-	-
Gov. transfer	0.6	0.8	0.6	0.5	0.5	0.6	1.7	15.0	0.5	0.4	0.3	0.2
Remittent from ROW	0.3	0.3	0.2	0.2	0.2	0.3	0.3	0.3	0.3	0.3	0.3	0.3
Expenditure structure (%)												
Consumption	63.0	80.6	71.5	66.5	61.5	51.9	76.1	96.0	84.8	76.7	72.2	67.4
Saving	34.7	17.2	27.3	31.6	36.1	44.9	21.2	0.0	11.5	20.0	25.3	31.1

Income tax	0.4	0.1	0.1	0.2	0.3	0.9	0.2	0.3	0.3	0.2	0.2	0.1
Fee[c]	1.9	2.1	1.1	1.7	2.2	2.3	2.5	3.6	3.5	3.0	2.3	1.3

Notes:
a. The grouping of urban and rural households is based on the urban household survey and the rural household survey in 1995 from State Statistical Bureau (SSB). The urban households were grouped by the income available for living per capita, while the rural households were grouped by net income of rural households.
b. To derive this income distribution matrix, we constructed an initial matrix based on the household survey data. The RAS method (Stone, 1962) is used to generate a balanced income distribution matrix from the initial matrix using macroeconomic data as control totals (the 'RAS' method takes its name from the notation used in Stone's original equations). The resulting matrix is presented here in percentage form. We derived all the distribution coefficients of factor incomes in our model from this matrix.
c. Fee is the extra-budget income of government such as various administration fees paid to local governments and other public sectors by households and enterprises.

Source: 1995 Social Accounting Matrix for China.

Zhao and Li (1998). Both data sets show that income inequality between rural and urban households dominates inequality within each area, as reflected by substantially higher overall Gini coefficients. Based on the data of Zhao and Li, the Gini coefficients for rural, urban, and overall were 0.429, 0.286, and 0.445 respectively in 1995, while based on data from our SAM, they were 0.285, 0.247, and 0.406 respectively.[1] Moreover, both data show that the Gini coefficient in rural China is larger than the one in urban China.

This SAM-based data analysis provides an overview of the characteristics of economy structure and market openness in China. It has important implications for the impact of trade liberalization and facilitates the understanding of simulation results reported later in this chapter.

4 BASE CASE PROJECTIONS AND SIMULATIONS DESIGN

China's WTO accession includes a complex package of reform of trade and investment liberalization. This chapter quantifies the impact of the following four major aspects: (1) tariff reduction in industrial products; (2) elimination of non-tariff barriers in industrial sectors; (3) agricultural trade liberalization, that is, the accelerated growth of import quotas of agricultural products and foods, and elimination of import quotas in 2005; and (4) the phasing out of the MFA quota on textile and clothing, which was included in the Uruguay Round agreement. Once China becomes a member of the WTO, China's exports in textile and apparel to North American and EU markets will be subjected to accelerating MFA quota growth from 1996–2004 in line with other developing countries, and the remaining export quota restrictions will be terminated in the year 2005.

Since China's WTO accession schedule will be phased in over a transition period of 8–10 years, we utilized the recursive dynamic model to assess the impact of China's WTO membership. The dynamic model captures the changes of industrial structure, factor composition and comparative advantage of China in the next 15 years.

The base case projection for the next 15 years is established first, which determines a reference growth trajectory, in the absence of trade or other reforms. Then we consider five scenarios in reference to the baseline scenario. The first scenario looks at the impact of the Uruguay Round trade liberalization excluding China. The world price shocks due to the Uruguay Round, which were generated from a multi-region world CGE model, is imposed on this scenario. The change in trade environment due to the Uruguay Round will also be imposed on all the following WTO accession scenarios. Second, we consider the tariff reduction and NTB elimination that China offered for the WTO accession. The average nominal tariff for industrial products will be lowered to 10% in the year 2005, and those industrial sector NTBs subject to elimination will be phased out over eight years (1997–2005). A linear formula was used to calculate the cut in each simulation period. The third scenario focuses on agricultural trade liberalization. The growth rate of import quota of agricultural products and foods will be increased to 5% from the growth rate of 3% in the base case, and the import quota will be eliminated in 2005, in place of a 10% tariff. The fourth scenario looks at the impact of MFA elimination. In this case, China faces accelerated quota growth rate for its textile and clothing export, and the quantitative restriction will be terminated in 2005. The last scenario combines all the four aspects of China's WTO accession. We want to see the whole effects of China's WTO accession. All the assumptions for baseline scenario and five policy scenarios are summarized in Table 6.3.

Table 6.3 Summary of simulations design

Experiment	Description
E1	Base case - Real GDP and agricultural output exogenous - TFP growth rate endogenous - 3% growth rate of import quota of foods and agricultural products subjected to quantitative restriction (Rice, wheat, other grain, cotton, wool, grain mill and vegetable oil, sugar) - exogenous export quota growth for textile and apparel textile: 5.0% apparel: 6.2% - In 1997, tariff rate reduced to the level of its recently applied new tariff schedules. NTBs in industrial sectors are cut 10% - All other tax rates are fixed at its base year level - Balance of payment gradually declines to 30% of its base year level in 2010
E2	Uruguay Round trade liberalization excluding China - TFP growth exogenous at base case rates - World import prices and export prices shock due to Uruguay Round
E3	Tariff reduction and NTBs elimination and E2 combined

	- A gradual 40% cut of 1997 tariff level across all sectors from 1998–2005 - Phased elimination of NTBs in the following nine sectors from 1998–2005 food, textile, refined petroleum, chemical, machinery, automobiles, electrical machinery, electronics, instruments
E4	Agricultural trade liberalization and E2 combined - 5% growth rate of import quota of foods and agricultural products from 1998–2004 - Elimination of import quota in 2005, in place of a uniform 10% tariff for these agricultural and food sectors
E5	Phase out of MFA and E2 combined - Acceleration of MFA quota growth rate from 1998–2004 - Zero export tax of textile and apparel in 2005
E6	The whole WTO accession package - E3, E4 and E5 combined

5 MAJOR SIMULATION RESULTS

Table 6.4 reports the main efficiency, inequality, and other macroeconomic indicators under the four scenarios of China's WTO accession. They are deviations from E2 (the case of Uruguay Round without China) in the year of 2005. The results show that China will benefit from its WTO accession in terms of real GDP and social welfare. In 2005, China's real GDP will increase 1.53% compared with E2. The welfare gains represented by Hicksian equivalent variations (EV), are smaller compared to GDP (1.24% of 2005 GDP), because of a 1.57% deterioration in terms of trade. Private consumption would increase 0.58%, indicating the benefits to consumers from trade liberalization. Investment increases by 1.75%. China's trade expansion is significant when it becomes a member of WTO. Exports and imports would increase 26.9% and 25.8% respectively.

The interaction of many factors determines these general equilibrium results. Generally, the large gains in GDP result from the enhanced efficiency of resource allocation through increased specialization according to comparative advantage. But two other reasons also contribute to GDP growth: (1) Removal of high protection rates induces real depreciation, enhancing the international competitiveness of China's industries; (2) Elimination of the MFA further increases the competitiveness of China's textile and apparel sectors, leading to export expansion of these sectors, while these sectors have comparative advantage in China.

Table 6.4 Major macroeconomic results under China's WTO accession scenarios, 2005 (percentage change relative to E2, except Gini coefficient)

	Whole WTO accession package (E6)	Tariff and NTBs reduction (E3)	Agricultural trade liberalization (E4)	MFA elimination (E5)
EV (% of GDP)	1.24	0.02	1.14	0.02
GDP	1.53	0.15	1.02	0.20
Absorption	0.95	0.04	0.80	0.02
Consumption	0.58	0.05	0.42	0.01
Investment	1.75	0.02	1.60	0.04
Exports	26.93	3.53	5.13	8.74
Imports	25.79	3.14	4.49	8.38
Government revenue	3.51	-0.72	4.46	-0.01
Urban households income	4.56	-0.15	5.08	-0.06
Rural households income	-2.05	0.18	-2.67	0.05
Terms of trade	-1.57	-0.47	-0.76	-0.58
Real exchange rate	1.85	2.39	3.39	-1.10
Change of Gini coefficient	0.00531	-0.00036	0.00730	-0.00016
In urban area	-0.00105	0.00001	-0.00030	-0.00006
In rural area	-0.00445	0.00004	-0.00430	-0.00004

Note: The results of E6 do not equal the sum of E3, E4 and E5 due to the interactive effects.

The result of significant expansion of trade is a little surprising at first. However, even in the WTO accession scenario, the average annual growth rate of export is 9.1%, which is not high compared to the average growth rate of 15.8% in the period of 1980–1998. As we stressed in previous sections, processing trade accounts for more than half of China's total trade. There are high import contents in its exports. A growth of exports will result in corresponding growth of imports, thus formulating the pressure of real depreciation, and contributing to further growth of exports. This characteristic partly contributes to the rapid increase of China's trade dependence, and explains the significant trade expansion effect of China's WTO accession.

The decomposition of the overall WTO accession package helps further understanding of the impact of various components of trade reform. Given the scarcity of agricultural land and predictions of population growth in the next ten years, and the import restriction policy for agricultural products, it is not surprising that agricultural trade liberalization is a crucial aspect of China's WTO accession. The elimination of import quotas of food and agricultural products will raise China's real GDP by 130.6 billion yuan in 2005, which accounts for almost two-thirds of the overall gains of China's WTO accession. Agricultural trade liberalization results in an adverse terms of trade effect, but the welfare gains are similar to GDP, indicating the significant price distortion in agricultural products in the pre-reform case.

Due to the low actual rate of tariff collection and the relatively open policy adopted towards processing trade, the gains from MFA elimination and reduction of tariff and non-tariff barriers are relatively small. Real GDP will increase by 25.0 billion yuan and 19.6 billion yuan under the MFA elimination scenario and tariff reduction scenario, respectively. The welfare gains are smaller compared to real GDP due to adverse terms of trade effects.

While the aggregate results of the WTO accession scenarios show the overall welfare gains resulting from lower price distortions and expanded trade, they reveal only part of the story. In fact, the welfare gains are rarely distributed evenly. Overall Gini coefficient would increase by 0.00531 in the experiment for the whole WTO accession package, illustrating the deterioration in income equality and conflict between efficiency and equality. But in the meantime the Gini coefficients for urban and rural areas both decline, indicating that the enlarged rural–urban income disparity is the major contributory factor in increasing income inequality resulting from China's WTO accession.

The patterns of changes of Gini coefficient are different across components of China's WTO accession package. Under the scenario for agricultural trade liberalization, the changes of Gini coefficients are quite similar to the scenario of whole accession package, indicating the dominant role of agricultural trade liberalization. But under the scenario for reduction of tariff and non-tariff barriers, overall income equality improves while income distribution in both rural and urban areas becomes less equitable. Under the scenario for MFA elimination, all the Gini coefficients for overall, rural and urban decline slightly.

Table 6.5 presents the equivalent variation (EV) of different types of households affected by China's WTO accession. Estimation of the distribution of welfare gains among the different types of households is helpful in obtaining a better understanding of the distributional effect of trade liberalization. The results reported in Table 6.5 show that the distribution of welfare gains among households at different income levels is quite different under all the experiments. Under the experiment for the whole WTO accession package, the welfare of urban households increases by 4.86% of disposable income in base case, while rural households decline by 1.5% of their disposable income. In rural areas, only the poorest households gain from China's WTO accession. The richest rural households lose the most at around 2.6% of their disposal income in base case. All urban households gain, and poorer urban households benefit more than richer urban households.

Table 6.5 Households, welfare changes under China's WTO accession scenarios, 2005 (percentage change from disposable income in E2)

	Whole WTO accession package (E6)	Tariffand NTBs reduction (E3)	Agricultural trade liberalization (E4)	MFA elimination (E5)
Rural	**-1.53**	**0.16**	**-2.09**	**0.04**
Low	0.63	0.08	0.24	0.02
Medium-low	-1.17	0.19	-1.89	0.06
Medium	-1.13	0.16	-1.76	0.05
Medium-high	-1.47	0.14	-2.00	0.04
High	-2.63	0.16	-3.13	0.02
Urban	**4.86**	**-0.16**	**5.43**	**-0.06**
Low	5.37	-0.16	5.69	-0.05
Medium-low	5.13	-0.16	5.54	-0.05
Medium	4.96	-0.16	5.45	-0.05
Medium-high	4.76	-0.18	5.38	-0.06
High	4.60	-0.15	5.31	-0.08

The reason for increasing inequality from China's WTO accession is the import restriction of agricultural products and food in the base case. High import protection results in high domestic costs of agricultural production. Elimination of the quantitative restriction of import in agriculture in 2005 would sharply decrease the domestic price of agricultural products, resulting in a contracting effect, decreasing the return of agricultural production factors and pushing labour and capital away from it. The change in functional income distribution reported in Table 6.6 indicates that the wages of skilled labour and the rental price of capital increase much more than the wages of agricultural labour and production workers, while the rent of agricultural land decreases sharply. Obviously, rural households are the main losers during this process. An increase in rural–urban disparity would accompany China's WTO accession.

Table 6.6 Changes of factor prices under China's WTO accession scenarios, 2005 (percentage change relative to E2)

	Whole WTO accession package (E6)	Tariff and NTBs reduction (E3)	Agricultural trade liberalization (E4)	MFA elimination (E5)
Agricultural labour	2.19	0.51	0.10	0.45
Production worker	2.19	0.51	0.11	0.45
Professionals	6.05	0.52	5.52	0.11
Agricultural land	-18.38	0.58	-19.95	0.21
Capital	6.60	0.47	5.59	0.38

As the income of richer rural households relies on agricultural land to a greater extent than that of poorer rural households, the changes of factor return tend to improve rural income distribution. But the changes of functional distribution tend to make urban income distribution less equitable. The poorer urban households rely on income from production workers more than richer households. Because of the competition coming from the migration of the rural agricultural labour force, the wages of production workers increase much less than the wages of skilled labour and the rental price of capital.

But the net effect of China's WTO accession on income distribution within both rural and urban areas tends to reduce inequality. Two reasons account for it: (1) poorer households in both rural and urban areas consume more agricultural commodities, whose prices decline much more than the prices of industrial goods because of the heavy protection in agricultural sectors in the pre-reform case, therefore they benefit more than richer households. (2) Given our assumption that quota premiums are distributed to households, and that usually households at higher income levels can obtain quota premiums much more than lower income households, the replacement of import quantitative restrictions with tariff favours income equality.

The distributional effects of agricultural trade liberalization are quite similar to that of the whole WTO accession package. But things are very different under the scenarios for MFA elimination and reduction of tariff and non-tariff barriers. Urban households are losers in these two cases, while rural households' welfare would increase. It is easy to understand when we note that the manufacturing sectors are highly protected by tariff and NTBs, and that most textile and apparel exports are produced by village and town enterprises.

6 CONCLUSION

This chapter analyses the distributional effects of China's WTO accession. The simulation results show that China would gain significantly in economic efficiency when the country becomes a member of the WTO. But the gains are not evenly distributed among either sectors or households groups. Due to the shortage of arable land per capita in China, the comparative advantage of the agricultural sector will be weakened. The protection of agricultural imports will imply a high social cost in a long-term perspective. Therefore trade liberalization in agriculture may reduce rural household's income. Because of the dominant role played by agricultural trade liberalization, rural households will be the main losers during China's entry to the WTO, although a part of the agricultural labour force can be shifted to other sectors. The rural–urban disparity will enlarge, but income distribution within rural and urban areas will improve.

These results have important implications for China's WTO accession. First, overall income distribution would deteriorate after China enters the WTO. But the rise of income disparity is due largely to the food self-sufficiency policy that would continue in the future, rather than to trade liberalization. Protection in agriculture can improve the farmer's income temporarily, but not sustainably. The later the reform, the larger the distortion and the more serious the problem of income distribution. The appropriate strategy for China's WTO accession is for the nation to open its agricultural and food market in exchange for the developed countries lifting their limits on labour-intensive products from China, to phase in cutting the protection of manufacturing sectors over a period of time, and to create the necessary economic and social conditions for the shift of the agricultural labour force. This will benefit both efficiency and equality in China.

Second, the domestic taxation policy should target redistribution of income in order to reduce the impact of income inequality resulting from the accession to the WTO. One of our previous studies has investigated the welfare and distributional effects of tariff reduction under alternative tax replacement assumptions (Wang and Zhai, 1998). This study suggested that imposing a progressive household income tax seems to be an appropriate policy choice to replace the lost tariff revenue, it reduces the Gini coefficient and retains most of the efficiency gains.

These results do depend on a number of assumptions about the model and the base year data. The assets market is important for household incomes and wealth, especially from the long-term perspective, but it is not taken into account in the model. A lot of work on data collection and model updating are necessary for policy analysis in the future.

NOTE

1. Our figure on overall Gini coefficient is quite similar to the estimation by the World Bank. It is reported in *World Development Report 1997* that the overall Gini coefficient of China is 0.415 in 1995.

REFERENCES

Adelman, I. and S. Robinson (1988), 'Income Distribution and Development: A Survey', in Chenery, H.B. and T.N. Srinivasan (eds), *Handbook of Development Economics*, 2, pp. 950–1003, Amsterdam: North-Holland.

Beghin, J., S. Dessus, D. Roland-Holst and D. van der Mensbrugghe (1994), 'Prototype CGE Model for the Trade and the Environment Programme – Technical Specification', OECD Development Centre, Paris.

Dervis, K., J. de Melo and S. Robinson (1982), *General Equilibrium Models for Development Policy*, Cambridge: Cambridge University Press.

Howe, H. (1975), 'Development of the Extended Linear Expenditure System from Simple Savings Assumptions', *European Economic Review*, 6, pp. 305–10.

Huang, Y. (1996), 'How Should the Personal Income Pie Be Cut', *China Reform (Zhong Gou Gai Ge)*, 4, April, pp. 32–4. (in Chinese.)

Khan, A.R., K. Griffin, C. Riskin and R. Zhao (1993), 'Sources of Income Inequality in Post-reform China', *China Economic Review*, 4(1), pp. 19–35.

Naughton, B. (1996), 'China's Emergence and Prospects as a Trading Nation', *Brookings Paper on Economic Activity*, 2.

Pomfret, R. (1997), *Is China a 'Large Country'?* – China's Influence on World Markets, OECD Development Centre, Paris.

Stone, R. (1962), *A Computable Model of Economic Growth. A Programme for Growth*, Cambridge, U.K.: Chapman and Hall.

Wang, Z. and F. Zhai (1998), 'Tariff Reduction, Tax Replacement and Implication for Income Distribution in China', *Journal of Comparative Economics*, 26, June.

World Bank (1994), 'China Foreign Trade Reform', A World Bank Country Study, The World Bank, Washington, DC.

World Bank (1997), *The State in a Changing World*, World Development Report 1997, Oxford: Oxford University Press.

Zhai, F. (1998), 'A Social Accounting Matrix of China, 1995', mimeo, Development Research Center of the State Council, PRC.

Zhao, R. and S. Li (1998), 'Increasing Income Inequality and its Causes in China', *Economic Research Journal (Jing Ji Yan Jiu)*, 9, September, pp. 19–28. (in Chinese.)

7. Changes in income inequality in China's transition*

Shi Li

1 INTRODUCTION

Since the end of the 1970s, China has experienced a transition towards a market economy. From the point of view of economic growth, China has achieved an impressive record. The average annual growth rate of GDP per capita was as high as 8.36% during the period 1978–1997. All indicators of economic performance show that the 'pie' baked by the Chinese economy has become larger and larger. Important socio-demographic indicators also point towards better living conditions on average for the Chinese population. At the same time, China has been deeply involved in the integration of the world economy. Chinese exports grew annually on average by 16.7% in the last two decades. China has absorbed US$205 billion of as foreign direct investment during the period 1990–1997.

Transition towards an economy with market allocation and openness to the world economy, however, is not without problems. One cannot be sure that rapid economic growth implies that the 'tide lifts up all boats'. In other words, fast average income growth does not automatically lead to the improvement of the well-being of all individuals in a society (Tam and Zhang, 1996). Looking at how the 'pie' is distributed in a country like China with rapid economic growth would provide us with an alternative criterion to evaluate its performance. This is the primary topic of the present chapter.

In this chapter we attempt to evaluate changes in the distribution of income in China. The strategy is to make comparisons based on two household income surveys made in very similar ways for 1988 and 1995. Both surveys are large in size and cover large parts of rural as well as urban China.

* This chapter has been published in a special issue of Revue d'Economie du Développement, no. 1-2, 1999.

The chapter is laid out in the following way. In the next section we discuss the main changes in the Chinese economy and trends of income inequality. In Section 3 we briefly describe the data, how the target variable is constructed and describe some key variables in the samples. In Section 4 we present results from decomposition analysis for income types for both urban and rural China. In Section 5 we investigate the changed relations between location variables and personal and household characteristics on the one hand and personal income on the other. Meanwhile we decompose total inequality by population subgroups. Finally we sum up the results in Section 6.

2 ECONOMIC TRANSITION AND THE TREND OF INCOME INEQUALITY IN CHINA

Economic transition in China has gone hand in hand with industrialization. Since the end of the 1980s there have been large changes in the composition of the industrial sector. According to the national accounts, gross product value in agriculture grew by 57.6% between 1988 and 1995 while for the service sector the increases were 73.3% and the manufacturing sector grew by an astonishing 138.5%. Rural industry in China has also grown remarkably, with an annual average growth rate of 24.1% during the period 1985–1995. Rural industry absorbed 28.6% of the total labour force in rural China in 1995. Results from earlier studies point out that shifts away from the traditional agricultural economy would lead to increased inequality in rural China.[1] The impact of the rapid growth of rural industry and the correspondingly larger share of non-farm income of rural households on increased inequality will be examined in this chapter.

It is not surprising that the economic reforms led to a significant change in structure of ownership in Chinese industries. Table 7.1 presents the changes in gross output value of industry and the shares contributed by enterprises with different ownership since 1988. The general picture shows that the share of gross output value of industry by state-owned enterprises has been declining, from 57% in 1988 to 27% in 1997, while that of non-publicly owned enterprises has increased considerably, from 7% in 1988 to 33% in 1997. Workers in joint-venture and foreign-capital enterprises are, on average, paid substantially higher wages than their counterparts in public enterprises. It would be interesting to know if the changes in structure of ownership have an impact on changes in total inequality in China, by investigating the income differences between workers among different ownership sectors.

Table 7.1 Gross output value of industry by ownership in China (billion)

	1988	1991	1993	1995	1997
Gross value	1822.5	2662.5	4840.2	9189.4	11212.8
%	(100)	(100)	(100)	(100)	(100)
State-owned enterprises	1035.1	1495.5	2272.5	3122.0	2976.0
	(56.8)	(56.2)	(47.0)	(34.0)	(26.5)
Collectively-owned enterprises	658.8	878.3	1646.4	3362.3	4543.0
in which:	(36.2)	(33.0)	(34.0)	(36.6)	(40.5)
Township enterprises	184.7	240.1	537.4	1193.2	
	(10.1)	(9.0)	(11.1)	(13.0)	
Village enterprises	170.4	234.7	516.3	1184.7	
	(9.4)	(8.8)	(10.7)	(12.9)	
Joint enterprises	43.9	56.9	132.2	213.4	
	(2.4)	(2.1)	(2.7)	(2.3)	
Individual and privately-owned	79.1	128.7	386.1	1182.1	1785.2
enterprises	(4.3)	(4.8)	(8.0)	(12.9)	(15.9)
Other ownership	49.5	163.1	517.4	1523.1	1908.6
in which:	(2.7)	(6.1)	(10.7)	(16.6)	(17.0)
Shareholding			146.1	318.3	
			(3.0)	(3.5)	
Foreign-owned			185.3	540.8	
			(3.8)	(5.9)	
Overseas Chinese from HK,			176.1	556.4	
Macao, Taiwan			(3.6)	(6.1)	

Notes: Gross output values are in current prices. In parentheses are shares of components, which are calculated by the author.

Sources: State Statistical Bureau, (SSB) (1996a): 401, 406–7; (SSB) (1994); (SSB) (1998).

In urban China, employment in the publicly-owned sector increased modestly by only 3.1% from 1988 to 1997, while employment in the non-public sector, such as private, self-employed, and joint-venture and foreign-capital enterprises, increased enormously, by 730.7%. Moreover in 1997 the latter accounts for nearly 31.1% of total employment in urban China according to official statistics. As the non-public sector has grown fast, the public sector has suffered financial difficulty. During the last decade in particular more and more state-owned enterprises (SOE) became financial loss-makers. As a result, the loss-making enterprises were unable to pay high wages. This led to an increasing differential between the wages of workers in enterprises making profits and those in loss-making enterprises in the state-owned sector.

Additional reasons for expecting that income inequality has increased are institutional changes in wage determination within the state-owned sector. State-owned enterprises have been allowed to take more decisions regarding distribution of wages, bonuses and various subsidies. Wages thus can be set with emphasis on productivity improvement, education and skill can be more rewarded than before and consequently wage differences between workers of different skill-levels have increased. It is also possible that managerial staff have acted to increase their own wages. To find some relevant evidence for this supposition, we will investigate changes in income inequality between occupation sub-groups,

There are several reasons why we expect the income gap between well-educated workers and less well-educated workers to have increased during the transition period. First, more emphasis placed on productivity in the state-owned sector would result in increasing returns to skill associated with education level. Second, the rapid growth of the non-public sector, especially joint-venture and foreign-capital enterprises, implies rising demand for skilled workers, technicians and professional staff, which would inevitably give rise to demand-pulled increase in wages for skilled and well-educated workers. Third, there are an estimated 50–70 million rural migrants, most of them among the less well-educated, employed as unskilled workers in urban China. A large number of rural migrants entering the labour market in urban areas would have an impact on depressing the wage levels of unskilled workers there.

Economic transition in China has a very clear regional dimension as reforms were first institutionalized in the coastal provinces. The coastal provinces have attracted a disproportionately large share of foreign investments, and economic growth has been most rapid there. The other extreme is the less populated western part. In Table 7.2 we report how between-province inequality in term of provincial per capita income has developed. The table shows a narrowing of between-province income inequality during the 1980s but increases thereafter.[2] Our micro-data analysis will provide some evidence of how large growth in regional inequality occurred during the period 1988–1995.

The economic reforms and corresponding changes in all aspects of economic life have had significant impacts on changes in inequality of income distribution in China. As a result, income inequality has been increasing within rural China and urban China as well as between rural and urban areas. Table 7.3 presents the results estimated by SSB, which show the changes in income growth and income inequality in terms of the Gini coefficient in rural and urban China from 1978 to 1997.

Table 7.2 Spatial inequality in China: by provincial GNP per capita

Inequality index		1980	1984	1988	1993
Coefficient of variation		0.951	0.753	0.675	0.685
Gini coefficient		0.350	0.304	0.298	0.321
Quintile	1	0.10236	0.10967	0.10606	0.09123
	2	0.22254	0.23710	0.23407	0.21521
	3	0.36083	0.38511	0.38770	0.36680
	4	0.52284	0.57373	0.58887	0.58229
	5	1.00000	1.00000	1.00000	1.00000
Number of provinces		30	30	30	30

Source: State Statistical Bureau (1996b).

Table 7.3 Changes in income inequality in China, 1978–1997

Year	Gini-coefficient in rural China	Gini-coefficient in rural China	Ratio of urban income to rural income
1978	0.21	0.16	2.36
1984	0.26	0.16	2.13
1988	0.30	0.23	2.40
1992	0.31	0.25	2.71
1995	0.34	0.28	2.79
1997	0.33	0.29	2.45

Sources. Appendix 7A.1 and Appendix 7A.2.

Then Gini coefficient increased by 57% in rural areas during this period, from 0.21 in 1978 to 0.33 in 1997. At the same time, the Gini coefficient increased by 88% in urban areas, from 0.16 in 1978 to 0.30 in 1997.

Meanwhile, the income gap between urban and rural parts of China was decreasing at the beginning of economic reform owing to the substantial growth of rural household income. However since the mid-1980s, the rural–urban income gap has been increasing. As shown in Table 7.3, the real ratio of urban income over rural income rose from 2.13 in 1984 to 2.79 in 1995.

Due to the increasing inequality of income distribution within rural and urban China and the income gap between rural China and urban China, it is not surprising that the inequality in China as a whole has been rising since the end of the 1970s. The results from our two surveys indicate that the Gini coefficient for the whole country increased from 0.382 in 1988 to 0.452 in 1995 (Khan and Riskin, 1998).

3 DESCRIPTION OF DATA

The data used in this chapter for the detailed analysis are from two surveys, conducted by the Institute of Economics, Chinese Academy of Social Sciences, with assistance from the State Statistical Bureau in Beijing. The first survey of household income in 1988 was implemented in the spring of 1989 and has been intensively analysed by the project team led by Keith Griffin and Zhao Renwei (1993) and in some extended studies (Gustafsson and Li, 1997 and 1998). More details of the survey can be found in Eichen and Zhang (1993) and Khan et al. (1992).

The second survey of household income refers to 1995 and was conducted during January to March 1996. Similar to the first survey in some ways, the second survey had different sample procedures and different instruments for households in rural and urban areas. Both samples were derived from large samples of the State Statistic Bureau. Subject to budget constraints the sample size for the second survey was reduced from about 20 000 households (10 515 in the rural sample and 9001 in the urban sample) in the first survey to 15 000 households (with 8000 in rural areas and 7000 in the urban sample). The rural sample covered 109 countries in 19 provinces and the urban sample 11 provinces.[3] The provinces were chosen by a consideration of geographic differences in China as a whole.[4]

The questionnaires were designed by members of the research team. Most questions in the questionnaires in the first survey reappeared in the second. In addition some new questions were added. In the urban questionnaires, income questions were posed with the objective of deriving household disposable income, so households were required to answer questions regarding income in kind and the market value of housing subsidies as well as imputed rent of privately-owned houses. In the rural questionnaires, the present values of private houses were asked in order to derive their imputed values by adopting a discount rate. Both the rural and the urban questionnaires have fairly comprehensive questions about household consumption and its components as well as on household assets, both financial and physical.

Household disposable income consists of individual income and household income which cannot be attributed to individuals. The former includes earnings, pensions, monetary and in-kind subsidies. The latter include household income from farming, family enterprise and property. As over 70% of the urban households were still living in public apartments in 1995, paying rents much lower than market rates, housing subsidies for those households were a crucial part of their income. This was calculated as a differential between the respondents' estimate of the market rent and the rents actually paid.[5] It was also considered important to include imputed rent of privately-owned houses and apartments. For rural China this was done by applying the discount rate of 8% to the present value of the house (as estimated by the respondent).

In all tables here, reported disposable income for 1995 has been expressed in the 1988 prices. This has been done using price indexes specific for rural and urban parts of each province as published by the State Statistical Bureau (1996).

4 DECOMPOSITION ANALYSIS OF INCOME COMPONENTS

Changes in inequality as measured by the Gini coefficient can be traced to changes in size and share of the different income types. Following the methodology initiated by Rao (1969) and Pyatt et al. (1980), the Gini coefficient of disposable income can be decomposed into:

$$G = \sum \mu_i C_i \tag{7.1}$$

where μ_i is the mean value of an income type Y_i is a proportion of disposable income, and C_i is the concentration ratio of income type Y_i. The concentration ratio is based on the concentration curve which shows cumulated proportions of income type ranked according to disposable income. It is defined as the area between the concentration curve and the diagonal. Unlike the Gini coefficient which is bounded by 0 and 1 it can take values ranging from -1 to +1.

Assume first an income type taking positive values. In this case a positive value of the concentration coefficient means that the income type contributes positively to total inequality. For taxes, taking negative values, the reverse holds. It should be noted that the Gini coefficient is one of many possible ways to summarize inequality into one index. Each type of income contributes to the Gini coefficient of disposable income by the product of its concentration coefficient and its average share in disposable income.

Many studies argue that the non-farm incomes of rural households have played an important role in increasing inequality of income distribution in rural China (Khan et al., 1993; Khan and Riskin, 1998; Zhu Ling, 1994; S. Li et al., 1998). To provide further evidence for the contribution of non-farm incomes of rural households to the increase of inequality in rural China, we have conducted decomposition analysis of income components by using the approach above. The disposable income is decomposed into three components, that is, household production income, individual wage income and other income, which includes household property income, imputed rental value of privately-owned housing, transfer income and so on. The results of this decomposition analysis are presented in Table 7.4.

Table 7.4 Decomposition analysis of income inequality in rural China, 1988 and 1995

Income and its components	1988			1995		
	U_i (x 100)	C_i or G	e_i (x 100)	U_i (x 100)	C_i or G	e_i (x 100)
1. Household production income	74.21	0.282	61.8	59.56	0.286	39.7
2. Individual wage income	8.73	0.710	18.3	23.62	0.745	41.0
3. Other income	17.06	0.394	19.9	16.82	0.492	19.3
Total income	**100**	**0.338**	**100**	**100**	**0.429**	**100**

Notes:
U_i is share of income component Y_i in total income; C_i is concentration ratio of income component Y_i; e_i is contribution of income component Y_i to total inequality, which is expressed as U_iC_i/G, G being the Gini coefficient of total income.
The other income includes household property income, imputed rental value of private owned housing, transfer income and so on.
Concentration ratio of other income is calculated by the author.

Sources: S. Li, et al. (1998); Khan, et al. (1993).

As we can see in Table 7.4, the rural inequality in terms of the Gini coefficient increased by nearly 27% between 1988 and 1995, from 0.338 to 0.429. Meanwhile, the concentration ratios of the three income components increased by 1.4%, 4.9% and 24.9% respectively. It is obvious that the increase of inequalities of the three income components can only explain a small part of the overall increasing inequality. The greater part of it can be explained by the changes in share of three income components. To illustrate this point, we do two exercises.[6] In one exercise, assuming the disposable income to have the same pattern of share of income components in 1995 as in 1988, we could calculate a simulated Gini coefficient as 0.360, which is 6.8% higher than the actual Gini in 1988. The difference between the simulated Gini and the actual Gini is due merely to the changes in distribution of income components.

In another exercise, assuming each income component in 1995 to have the same distribution as that in 1988, we could compute a different simulated Gini for rural China of 0.402. This simulated Gini is 18.9% higher than the actual one in 1988. The increase is interpreted as due to the changes in the share of income components alone. Therefore, we conclude that increased inequality in rural China has mainly been caused by the changes in share of income components of household income, which reflect rapid but unbalanced growth of non-farm income associated with the development of rural industry.

Turning to urban China, the results from decomposition analysis indicate a different pattern for the changes in the inequality of income distribution. Household disposable income per capita is decomposed into five components, workers' wage income, workers' non-wage income, income of retirees, income in kind, and other income. It can be seen that distribution of all income components except for the income of retirees, was more unequal in 1995 than in 1988. The concentration ratio of workers' wage income increased by 30%, non-wage income by 33%, and income in kind by 24%. Our simulation analysis using the same approach as in the rural analysis, shows that over 95% of the increased inequality in urban China is due to the changes in distribution of income components, while only a very small part is due to the changes in share of income components, as shown in Table 7.5.

5 INEQUALITY AND PERSONAL CHARACTERISTICS

In this section we decompose the population into mutually exclusive subgroups according to alternative breakdowns of the sample. Using an additively decomposable inequality index, that is, the Theil index and mean logarithmic deviation (MLD), we investigate inequality in various subgroups at the two time points and analyse changes in total inequality.

Table 7.5 Decomposition analysis of income inequality in urban China, 1988 and 1995

Income and its components	1988 U_i (x 100)	1988 C_i or G	1988 e_i (x 100)	1995 U_i (x 100)	1995 C_i or G	1995 e_i (x 100)
1. Worker wage income	32.57	0.130	18.2	32.83	0.169	19.4
2. Worker non-wage income	25.33	0.253	27.5	24.58	0.336	28.9
3. Income of retirees	6.83	0.335	9.8	10.96	0.324	12.4
4. Income in kind	29.51	0.276	9.5	25.20	0.341	30.0
5. Other income	5.76	0.384	35.0	6.43	0.451	9.3
Total income	**100**	**0. 233**	**100**	**100**	**0. 289**	**100**

Notes:
U_i is share of income component Y_i in total income; C_i is concentration ratio of income component Y_i; e_i is contribution of income component Y_i to total inequality, which is expressed as U_iC_i/G , G being the Gini coefficient of total income.
Income in kind includes subsidies in kind for public housing, in-kind income from work units, imputed rental value of private owned housing and so on.
Other income covers property income, earnings of private owners and the self-employed and private transfer income.

Sources : Khan, et al. (1993); S. Li, et al. (1998).

The Theil index is defined as:

$$T\left(y;N\right)=\frac{\sum_i\left(\frac{y_i}{\mu}\right)\log\left(\frac{y_i}{\mu}\right)}{N}$$

and the MLD is defined as:

$$\text{MLD}\left(y;N\right)=\frac{\sum_i\log\left(\frac{\mu}{y_i}\right)}{N}$$

Where y_i is income of ith individual, μ the mean income and N the total number of individuals.

It should be noted that while the Theil index uses income as weights for the various groups when obtaining the between-group component this role is taken by the number of units for MLD. Both the Theil and MLD can be employed for decomposition of total inequality into between-group and within-group inequalities (Shorrocks, 1983). It turns out that the overwhelming part of the results are similar for the two indices and therefore we concentrate the comments on those obtained by the Theil index, as it is more commonly used.

Table 7.6 shows the size of the within-subgroup inequality and between-subgroup inequality and their relative contribution to total inequality for both years under observation when decomposition is made according to the characteristics of individuals and household heads. The results come mainly from the more detailed analysis of Gustafsson and Li (2001). The individuals are divided into sub-groups using their location variables and the personal characteristics of their household heads. As for the location, we have three dimensions: rural–urban divide, east-central-west subgroups and rural–urban and east-central-west combined. Regarding the household heads, we focus on characteristics of particular interest to us, such as education, occupation and ownership. In the following we comment on the results of each location dimension in turn.

Starting with the *rural–urban* divide, we find that more than two-fifths of total inequality in China as a whole in 1988 could be attributed to differences in mean income between urban and rural China, as shown by Theil index. Inequality between urban and rural areas measured by the Theil index in absolute terms has increased by 22% during the period 1988–1995. However, as discussed above the inequality within each part, especially in rural China, increased even more strikingly over the same period, the within-group inequality having risen by 66% in absolute terms. This means that although the rural–urban income gap has widened, the proportion of total inequality which can be attributed to this dimension in 1995 was down to 35% from 43% in 1988. An analysis conducted by Gustafsson and Li (1998) also illustrates that one-sixth of the increase in inequality in China as a whole is due to the increased income gap between rural and urban China.

As for the dimension of *east-central-west* (three 'belts'), we can see that between-group inequality contributed nearly 8% of the total inequality in the entire country in 1988 and that its contribution had increased to almost 10% in 1995. Moreover, the between-group inequality increased by 84% in absolute terms, as shown by the Theil index during this period. As Gustafsson and Li (1998) show, 13% of the increase in inequality in China as

Table 7.6 Decomposition of within-group and between-group inequality in 1988 and 1995

Sample partition	Year	1000 $\mathbf{I}_o$ Average inequality	1000 $\mathbf{I}_o$ Within-group inequality	1000 $\mathbf{I}_o$ Between-group inequality	1000 $\mathbf{I}_1$ Average inequality	1000 $\mathbf{I}_1$ Within-group inequality	1000 $\mathbf{I}_1$ Between-group inequality
Rural-Urban	1988	258.31	159.6	98.7	253.3	145.6	107.7
	(%)	(100)	(61.8)	(38.2)	(100)	(57.5)	(42.5)
	1995	378.41	255.9	122.5	373.14	242.3	130.9
	(%)	(100)	(67.6)	(32.36)	(100)	(64.9)	(35.1)
Three 'Belts'	1988	258.31	238.8	19.5	253.3	233.6	19.7
	(%)	(100)	(92.5)	(7.5)	(100)	(92.2)	(7.8)
	1995	378.41	343.1	35.4	373.14	336.9	36.2
	(%)	(100)	(90.7)	(9.3)	(100)	(90.3)	(9.7)
Six regions	1988	258.31	138.4	119.9	253.3	125.8	127.5
	(%)	(100)	(53.6)	(46.4)	(100)	(49.7)	(50.3)
	1995	378.41	206.6	171.8	373.14	202.7	170.4
	(%)	(100)	(54.6)	(45.4)	(100)	(54.3)	(45.7)
Education of head	1988	258.31	226.0	32.3	253.3	218.3	35.0
	(%)	(100)	(87.5)	(12.5)	(100)	(86.2)	(13.8)
	1995	378.41	322.6	55.8	373.14	311.3	61.8
	(%)	(100)	(85.3)	(14.7)	(100)	(83.4)	(16.6)

Employment status of head	1988	258.31	256.7	1.6	253.3	251.6	1.7
	(%)	(100)	(99.4)	(0.6)	(100)	(99.3)	(0.7)
	1995	378.41	361.7	16.7	373.14	353.4	19.7
	(%)	(100)	(95.6)	(4.4)	(100)	(94.7)	(5.3)
Work unit's ownership of head	1988	258.31	159.2	99.4	253.3	149.5	103.8
	(%)	(100)	(61.6)	(38.4)	(100)	(59.0)	(41.0)
	1995	378.41	241.2	137.2	373.14	233.2	139.9
	(%)	(100)	(63.7)	(36.3)	(100)	(62.5)	(37.5)
Occupation of head	1988	258.31	160.4	97.9	253.3	150.8	102.4
	(%)	(100)	(62.1)	(37.9)	(100)	(59.6)	(40.6)
	1995	378.41	237.5	140.9	373.14	229.3	143.8
	(%)	(100)	(62.8)	(37.2)	(100)	(61.5)	(38.5)

Notes:
Unit of analysis is individual.
Subgroups are defined as follows: rural-urban: Rural, Urban; three-belts: East, Middle, West; six regions: Rural-East, Rural-Middle, Rural-West, Urban-East, Urban-Middle, Urban-West.
Education of head: 4-year college or above, 2-3-year college, technical or professional school, upper-middle school, lower-middle school, primary school, less primary school.
Employment status of head: worker, pensioner, unemployed, housewife, disabled person, other.
Work unit's ownership: state-owned public, other public, urban collective, private and self-employed, foreign and joint venture, family farming, other (such as TVEs).
Occupation of head: owner of private enterprises, professional, manager or director of enterprise, branch manager or director of enterprise, office worker, skilled worker, unskilled worker, rural cadre, farmer.
1000 I_o is index I_o multiplied by 1000; 1000 I_1 is index I_1 multiplied by 1000.

Sources: Gustafsson and Li (2001).

a whole can be attributed to increased differences in means between the three parts, and an increasing part of Chinese inequality is due to differences in means between the parts. Compared to the rural–urban dimension, the importance of the dimension of *east-central-west* is less notable, but it is growing.

When integrating the *rural–urban* and *west-central-east* dimensions, we come up with six subgroups (regions). The contribution of the between-group inequality to total inequality in China as a whole was as large as 50.3% in 1988, and fell to 45.7% in 1995, but was still very large by international standards. Nevertheless, the between-group inequality still grew by 34% in absolute terms, as shown by the Theil index, during this period. The decline of the relative contribution of the between-group inequality implies the increasing importance of the within-group inequality. It has increased by 61% in absolute terms and by almost 5% in its relative contribution.

As we discussed in Section 2, education and skill have become important determinants for individual and household income. The education levels of individuals cannot be applied to our classification of subgroups, as educational variables are not appropriate for all individuals, such as very young children and retired people. The same applies to variables of occupation and ownership of work units. Thus, we have to link the income of individuals with the relevant variables of their household heads. Here we concentrate on the impact of education, occupation and work-unit ownership of household heads on income inequality between groups and within groups of individuals.

When all individuals are broken down into seven subgroups by the educational level of their household heads, the within-group inequality has increased by 42.6% and the between-group inequality by 76.6% in the period 1988–1995. Consequently, the relative contribution of between-group inequality to total inequality in China as a whole went up from 13.8% in 1988 to 16.6% in 1995, as shown in Table 7.6. Moreover, one-fifth of the increase in inequality in China as a whole from 1988 to 1995 can be attributed to increased differences in means between different educational categories (Gustafsson and Li, 2001). The results indicate that returns to education are increasing and education is playing a more important role in the determination of income than before.[7]

We have six subgroups for the employment status of household head – workers, pensioners, unemployed, housewife, disabled persons and others. The between-group inequality was too small to be relevant, with its contribution less than 1% in 1988. However, it became of more importance in 1995. As reported in Table 7.6, over 5% of total inequality in China as a whole can be attributed to the between-group inequality related to the employment status of household head. One reason for this could be the rise in unemployment in urban areas.[8]

In both cases, the breakdown after *occupation of household head* and *work unit's ownership* overlap with the rural–urban breakdown and gives a similar pattern. It can be seen that over two-fifths of total inequality is attributable to between-group inequality in 1988. While the relative contribution of between-group inequality decreased slightly in 1995, the between-group inequality itself continued to rise in absolute terms (Theil index) for the two dimensions. For the dimension of work-unit's ownership of household head, the between-group inequality increased by 35%, largely due to a notable widening of the income gap between public sector and private sector and urban workers as a whole and rural farmers. For the dimension of occupation of household head, the between-group inequality increased by 40%, mainly due to a rising income gap between skilled workers and unskilled workers in urban areas.

6 CONCLUSIONS

A first, uncontroversial result is that income inequality has increased, which is indicated by the official data and the data from the two surveys. In moving to a market economy, China is becoming a society with a more unequal distribution of income. Indeed the increase in total inequality in China as a whole is astonishingly large even by international standards. Moreover, the growth of Chinese income inequality is general, and has taken place along a number of different dimensions.

Our analysis of decomposition by income components indicates that a large part of the increased inequality in rural China can be explained by the changes in share of income components, resulting from a rapid but unbalanced growth of rural industry. In contrast, the increased inequality in urban China can nearly be completely explained by the changes in distribution of income components.

Unlike in other countries, a large part of income inequality in China is due to location. The urban–rural income gap was large, and has widened during the period studied. However, inequality within urban China and particularly within rural China has widened more remarkably and therefore in the mid-1990s a somewhat smaller proportion of Chinese inequality can actually be attributed to the rural–urban gap. The increasing gap would become a stronger incentive for rural people to move to urban areas. This process has been occurring and will endure for a long period.

The better-off households in the eastern part of China have, on average, experienced a much faster income growth than their counterparts living in central and western parts. As slow-down in income growth, we can not rule out possibility that some poor households were facing unfortunate decline of their income in the western part. Although the proportion of total inequality attributed to differences in mean income between eastern, central and western China was not very large in 1988, it has increased by a considerable percentage since then.

Regarding some characteristics of household heads, we have found that the relation between education of household heads and income of individuals in China was stronger in 1995 than in 1988. Along with education, occupation and work unit's ownership of household heads have also played an increasing role in the growth in total inequality in China as a whole.

NOTES

1. See Khan et al. (1992), and Zhu Ling (1994), who studied non-agriculture income and Gustafsson and Li (1997) who studied money income.
2. The figures might overestimate the real development due to migration. In the Chinese statistics, migrants are usually included in the population of the provinces of origin, not in the province of destination. Moreover migrants' remittances are included in total GDP for the province of destination, not in the province of origin. However, it is difficult to have a well-based view on the size of the bias.
3. The provinces in the rural sample are Beijing, Hebei, Shanxi, Liaoning, Jilin, Jiangsu, Zhejiang, Anhui, Jiangxi, Shandong, Henan, Hubei, Hunan, Guangdong, Sichuan, Guizhou, Yunnan, Shaanxi and Gansu. The provinces in the urban sample are Beijing, Shanzi, Liaoning, Jiangsu, Anhui, Henan, Hubei, Guangdong, Sichuan, Yunnan and Gansu.
4. A striking difference in household income can be found between eastern coastal areas and western areas. Liaoning, Jiangsu, Zhejiang, Shandong and Guangdong represent the eastern coastal area; Hebei, Shanxi, Jilin, Anhui, Jiangxi, Henan, Hubei and Hunan the interior areas; and Sichuan, Guizhou, Yunnan, Shaanxi and Gansu the western areas. Beijing is a representative of the three large province-level municipalities.
5. The question in the urban questionnaire was phrased: 'If you could rent out your house or apartment estimate the per month rent'.
6. The corresponding formula is derived in this way. The growth of inequality of total income can be expressed as $\Delta G = G95 - G88 = \Sigma\mu95C95 - \Sigma\mu88C88 = \Sigma\mu95C95 - \Sigma\mu88C95 + \Sigma\mu88C95 - \Sigma\mu88C88 = \Sigma\mu88\,(C95 - C88) + \Sigma C95\,(\mu95 - \mu88)$. The first term in the formula is change in inequality of total income merely due to change in concentration ratio of income components, holding share of income components in 1988 as constant. The second term is change in inequality of total income merely due to change in share of income components, holding concentration ratio of income components in 1995 as constant.
7. Using Mincerian formula, the rate of private returns to education is estimated as 3.8% in urban China in 1988 and the corresponding figure is 5.3% in 1995. Knight and Song (2001) also found increasing rewards to well-educated workers.
8. In 1995, the official statistics showed an unemployment rate of 2.9% in urban China, while the actual unemployment rate from a population survey is 5.4%, if Xiagang workers (redundant workers) are included.

REFERENCES

Eichen, M. and M. Zhang (1993), 'The 1988 Household Sample Survey – Data Description and Availability' in Griffin, K. and Zhao, R. (1993), *The Distribution of Income in China*, Basingstoke: Macmillan.

Griffin, K. and R. Zhao (1993), *The Distribution of Income in China,* Basingstoke: Macmillan.

Gustafsson, B. and S. Li (2001) 'A More Unequal China? Industrialisation, Economic Transformation and Changes in the Distribution of Equivalent Income', to be published in Riskin, Zhao and Li (eds), *China's Retreat from Equality: Income Distribution and Economic Transition,* New York: M.E. Sharpe.

Gustafsson, B. and S. Li (1998), 'Inequality in China at the End of the 80s – Location Aspects and Household Characteristics', *Asian Economic Journal*, 12(1), March, pp. 35–63.

Gustafsson, B. and S. Li (1997), 'Types of Income and Inequality in China at the End of the 1980s', *Review of Income and Wealth,* 43(2), June, pp. 211–26.

Khan, A. and C. Riskin (1998), 'Income and Inequality in China: Composition, Distribution and Growth of Household Income. 1988 to 1995', *China Quarterly,* 154, pp. 221–53.

Khan, A., K. Griffin, C. Riskin and R. Zhao (1992), 'Household Income and its Distribution in China, *China Quarterly*, 132, pp. 1029–61.

Khan, A., K. Griffin, C. Riskin, and R. Zhao (1993), 'Sources of Income Inequality in Post-Reform China', *China Economic Review*, 4, pp. 19–35.

Knight, J. and L. Song (1993), 'The Spatial Contribution to Income Inequality in Rural China', *Cambridge Journal of Economics*, 17, pp. 195–213.

Knight, J. and L. Song (2001), 'Increasing Wage Inequality in China: Efficiency versus Equity?', to be published in Riskin, Zhao and Li (eds), *China's Retreat from Equality: Income Distribution and Economic Transition,* New York: M.E. Sharpe.

Li S., R. Zhao and P. Zhang (1998), 'Economic Transition and Income Distribution in China', *Economic Research*, April (in Chinese).

Pyatt, G., C.N. Chen and J. Fei (1980), 'The Distribution of Income by Factor Components', *Quarterly Journal of Economics*, 95, pp. 451–73.

Rao, V.M. (1969), 'Two Decompositions of the Concentration Ratio', *Journal of the Royal Statistical Society*, 132, pp. 418–25.

Ren, F. and X. Cheng (1996), 'To Investigate Income Differential from Income Urban Households', *Reference of Economic Research.* No. 157 (in Chinese).

Rozelle, S. (1994), 'Rural Industrialisation and Increasing Inequality: Emerging Patterns in China's Reform Economy', *Journal of Comparative Economics*, 19, pp. 362–91.

Shorrocks, A.F. (1983), 'Ranking Income Distributions', *Economica*, 50, pp. 3–17.

State Statistical Bureau (1994), *China Statistical Yearbook 1994*, Beijing: China Statistical Publishing House.

State Statistical Bureau (1996a), *China Statistical Yearbook 1996*, Beijing: China Statistical Publishing House.

State Statistical Bureau (1996b), *China Regional Economy. A Profile of 17 Years of Reform and Open-up*, Beijing: China Statistical Publishing House.

State Statistical Bureau (1998), *A Statistical Survey of China 1998*, Beijing: China Statistical Publishing House.

Tam, M.-Y. and R. Zhang (1996), 'Ranking Income Distributions: The Trade-off between Efficiency and Equality', *Economica*, 63, pp. 239–52.
Tang Ping (1995), 'Analysis on Income Level and Inequality in Rural Households in China', *Management World*, No 2 (in Chinese).
World Bank (1997), *Sharing Rising Incomes: Disparities in China*, Washington, DC: The World Bank.
Zhu L. (1994), 'Inequality and Non-farming Income in Rural China', in Zhao Renwei et al. (eds), *Distribution of Household Income in China*, Beijing: Chinese Social Science Press (in Chinese).

APPENDIX

Table 7A.1 The trend of income growth and income inequality in rural China, 1978–1997

	Gini Coefficient		*Real income per capita*	
Year	Level	Change (%)	Level (yuan)	Change (%)
1978	0.212	-	134	-
1979	0.237	11.8	140*	4.5
1980	0.238*	0.4	146	4.3
1981	0.239	0.4	161	10.3
1982	0.232	-2.9	191	18.6
1983	0.246	6.0	210	10.0
1984	0.258	4.9	231	10.0
Annual growth rate, 1978–84 (%)	**3.33**		**9.50**	
1985	0.264	2.3	238	3.0
1986	0.288	9.1	240	0.8
1987	0.292	1.4	246	2.5
1988	0.301	3.1	247	0.4
1989	0.300	0.3	228	-7.7
1990	0.310	3.3	249	9.2
Annual growth rate, 1985–90 (%)	**3.11**		**1.26**	
1991	0.307	1.0	252	1.2
1992	0.314	2.2	266	5.6
1993	0.320	1.9	275	3.4
Annual growth rate, 1991–93 (%)	**1.06**		**3.37**	
1994	0.321	0.3	295	7.3

1995	0.341	6.3	325	10.2
1996	0.323	-5.3	368	13.1
1997	0.329	1.9	397	7.9
Annual growth rate, 1994–97 (%)	**0.7**		**9.61**	

Notes: * are estimated as mean of figures of the previous year and the next year due to omitted value of this year.

Sources: Tang Ping (1995); SSB, *China Statistical Yearbook* (various years). Gini coefficients for 1994–97 are provided by General Team of Rural Household Survey, SSB.

Table 7A.2 The trend of income growth and income inequality in urban China, 1978–1997

	Gini Coefficient		*Real income per capita*	
Year	Level	Change (%)	Level (yuan)	Change (%)
1978	0.16	-	316	-
1979	0.16*	0.0	359*	13.6
1980	0.16	0.0	401	11.7
1981	0.15	-6.3	408	1.8
1982	0.15	0.0	433	6.1
1983	0.15	0.0	451	4.2
Annual growth rate, 1978–83 (%)	**-1.3**		**7.4**	
1984	0.16	6.7	507	12.4
1985	0.19	18.8	510	0.6
1986	0.19	0.0	577	13.1
1987	0.20	5.3	586	1.6
1988	0.23	15.0	594	1.4
1989	0.23	0.0	575	-3.2
Annual growth rate, 1984–89 (%)	**7.4**		**2.1**	
1990	0.23	0.0	625	8.7
1991	0.24	4.4	662	5.9
1992	0.25	4.2	721	8.9
1993	0.27	8.0	794	10.1
1994	0.30	11.1	864	8.8
Annual growth rate, 1990–94 (%)	**5.5**		**10.9**	
1995	0.282	-6.0	906	4.9

1996	0.284	0.7	940	3.8
1997	0.292	2.8	972	3.4
Annual growth rate, 1995–97 (%)	**-0.9**		**4.0**	

Sources: Ren Fangcai and Cheng Xuebin (1996); SSB, *China Statistical Yearbook* various years. Gini coefficients for 1994–97 are provided by General Team of Urban Household Survey, SSB.

8. Infant mortality and external openness in Chinese provinces

Martine Audibert, Jacky Mathonnat and Ningshan Chen*

1 INTRODUCTION

Since 1949, China has achieved some remarkable results in improving the health status of its population. Taken as a whole, the situation is better than might be expected when looking at per capita income. This can be illustrated by the fact that in 1995, the life expectancy at birth in developing countries which had a standard of living comparable to that of China was 63 years, whilst in China itself, it was 69 years (World Bank, 1997a). Over a period of around 35 years there was a spectacular decline in the mortality rate for children under five which fell from 173 per 1000 live births in 1960 to 43 in 1997, for the infant mortality rate as we will see below, and for the maternal mortality rate[1]. As a whole, these indicators compare with the level reached by the middle income countries.

In 1978, China undertook an ambitious programme of economic reforms aimed at what has been called 'socialist market economy'. One of the elements of these reforms was the gradual opening up of the economy. Amongst other things, this entailed from the very beginning giving a progressive freedom to enterprises to engage in international trade. The

* Martine Audibert and Jacky Mathonnat, Centre d'Etudes et de Recherches sur le Développement International/Centre National de la Recherche Scientifique CERDI/CNRS, UMR 6537, Clermont-Ferrand, Auvergne University (France); Ningshan Chen, Department of Health Economics, Weifang Medical College, Shandong, and National Health Economics Institute (NHEI), Beijing Medical University. The authors thank Professor Wei Ying, Director of NHEI and his colleagues for their invaluable discussions about the functioning and the challenges of the Chinese health system, and are indebted to J.-L. Arcand and S. Guillaumont Jeanneney, Professors at CERDI, for their suggestions. They also thank G. Boyreau-Debray for providing a number of the macroeconomic variables used in this study. However the analyses contained within this chapter are the responsibility of the authors alone.

openness of China has subsequently expanded and accelerated, particularly since the second half of the 1980s, both in the fields of international trade and of foreign investment, both having contributed to its impressive growth (Jian et al., 1996; Démurger, 1997; Sachs and Woo, 1997; Jammes, 1998).

It is proposed here to analyse the effects of external openness on infant mortality rates (IMR) in Chinese provinces between 1983 and 1994. The first part of this study contains a brief look at the main features of the evolution of IMR. There follows the theoretical framework for analysis and the modelling of the relationship between external openness and the other determinants of IMR. The results of the econometric analysis are discussed in the final section.

2 THE EVOLUTION OF INFANT MORTALITY RATES

There exists a vast amount of literature given over to the measurement of health. We limit here the present analysis to that of infant mortality rates. Before a brief comment on the evolution of the IMR, two points have to be mentioned.

Firstly, the official data regarding mortality statistics indicate a higher death rate in China as a whole and in rural China for the mid-1980s than had been achieved by the country in 1979. Independent estimations lead to the same conclusion, mainly because female infant mortality apparently had an upward jump, while male IMR has continued to decrease (Drèze and Sen, 1989; Sen, 1992). But, for several reasons pointed out by Sen, the interpretation of these figures is not obvious and 'it is not unreasonable to hope that ... the picture is considerably more satisfactory than it looks from the official death rates' (Sen, 1992, p. 1308). Thus comparing the data of the first years of the reform period with the last one of the pre-reform period is misleading.

Secondly, there has been for a long time a phenomenon of under-reporting of infant deaths and associated births, which lowers the IMR. Some authors have argued that the failure to record infant deaths is especially likely in the event of suspicious deaths or when the death concerns an infant born outside the family planning plan (Merli, 1998).[2] This under-reporting does not relate only to population policies, although enforced limitation of population size may have well-known negative effects on female children. It also reflects 'the complex relationship between Chinese peasant society and the bureaucratic structure' (Merli, 1998), and a tendency in traditional Chinese peasant culture to ignore the births of infants who die in the early stages of infancy.

Bearing this in mind, the national average for China's IMR declined from 1990 per live births in 1965 to 33 in 1997; looking at provinces and since the beginning of the 1980s, the declining trend in infant mortality rates has been appreciable, with the median falling from 35 deaths per 1000 live births to 29 in 1992–94, accompanied by a lowering of the maximum (Table 8.1). It can be seen that the situation in coastal provinces is better than that in the country as a whole.

Table 8.1 Changes in infant mortality rates in Chinese provinces (per 1000 live births)

	1979–81	1990	1992–94	Coastal provinces 1992–94
Minimum	14	10	10	10
Maximum	100	74	71	46
Median	35	28	29	18
Coef. variation	0.55	0.56	0.63	0.50

Data sources: See appendix.

However, since the beginning of the decade, a period of overall stagnation that could be called – at least – a 'plateauing phase' can be observed because the IMR have increased in several provinces. This is a phenomenon which has also been recorded since the middle of the 1980s for child mortality rates (under five; World Bank, 1997a). Moreover, a study of 30 poverty counties found that the average IMR in China's poorest region deteriorated from a level of 50 in the late 1970s to more than 70 in the late 1980s (Liu et al., 1996). There appears also to be an increase in overall disparity levels between provinces, as measured by standard deviation from the mean. One finds a confirmation of this trend when provinces are classified by quintile of per capita income: over the period 1983–93, the percentage of change is of around -4% for the poorest quintile and of -33% for the richest one (Hossain, 1997). The gap has also widened between rural and urban area. In 1981, the ratio rural to urban IMR was around 1.7. The change was moderate in 1990, but the ratio jumped up close to three in 1995 (from studies quoted in Liu et al., 1999).

In short, the best situation is found in the coastal provinces, than in central ones, the less favourable being in the western region with levels which compare with those of the low income countries group.

3 THEORETICAL FRAMEWORK OF THE DETERMINANTS OF INFANT MORTALITY RATES IN CHINESE PROVINCES

Endogenous and Exogenous Risk Factors of IMR

Infant mortality rate is determined by two broad types of causes or risk factors; those that are endogenous and those that are exogenous. The first type, linked to biogenetic factors (malformation, incidence of twin births etc.), depends largely on the degree of development of medical science (Stoddart, 1997; Kodio and Etard, 1997) and are difficult to measure. Those of the second type are made up of factors which fall into four major categories in the literature: the socio-health environment, the supply of care characteristics (quality, accessibility…), the family characteristics and behaviour (household income, parental education, migrant or non-migrant status…) and the characteristics of the child (position in family hierarchy, amount of time between births, breast-feeding…).[3] The IMR may thus be expressed as:

$$IMR = s\,(HE, HCS, F, Z) + \mu \tag{8.1}$$

where HE, HCS, F and Z are the vectors of the determinants of IMR and represent respectively the health environment, the health care supply, the family characteristics and the characteristics specific to the individual (child, mother); μ incorporates the non-measurable endogenous risk factors, as well as exogenous risk factors for which no data is available. These different elements have both a direct and an indirect influence on infant mortality rates and may also affect each other.

The Effects of the Level of External Openness on IMR

External openness may have effects on IMR by 'directly' or 'indirectly' influencing the main types of factors mentioned above, which have been demonstrated to differing degrees by both theoretical analysis and empirical studies to be important determinants in the incidence of infant mortality.

'Direct' effects

These derive largely from certain characteristic traits in the development of the Chinese economy. It is hypothesized that a comparatively high level of openness in the provinces gives rise to more dynamic progress, particularly industrial progress (World Bank, 1997b). This is then reflected in more prosperous firms, with comparatively positive effects on employment, as there is evidence that the output elasticity of employment in industries under private and other new forms of ownership is high (Khan et al., 1999). There is also evidence that benefit coverage for employees is influenced by the wealth of the enterprise (Hu et al., 1999). As a result, and in contrast to the situation which has been observed in the case of other firms, more prosperous enterprises with relatively high profit margins are less likely to be obliged to reduce the medical cover they offer to their employees. They also have more capacity to offer comprehensive benefits to their workers. In addition, the more widespread presence of foreign businesses in the comparatively more open provinces, particularly those on the coast, taken together with the previous point, suggests that the population in these areas is generally better covered by health care mechanisms, in a context where the decline in the population covered by the different health insurance schemes (state, 'public' sector industries,[4] and rural health co-operatives) is one of the key health problems facing China today. But the above effects may be more or less mitigated or disappear altogether in some cases (areas), where state and collective enterprises responded to increased competition by reducing the disguised unemployment arising from the previous policy of 'employment for all'.

'Indirect' effects

Different hypotheses suggest that the external openness of China has had an indirect positive effect on the determinants of the IMR through three principal channels: (i) on the demand for health care; (ii) on the education and behaviour of the individual; (iii) on the characteristics of the health care supply. These channels may be approached through the five following points:

1. The per capita GDP is on average higher in provinces that are comparatively open which, as well as encouraging better nutrition,[5] promotes the use of health care services, as those are in the main not free even (and increasingly so) for preventive care such as vaccinations.
2. External openness has helped in the development of the education and training of men and women in provinces that are relatively more open, because of a comparatively greater need for qualified labour in these areas (as has been suggested for a number of developing countries in Coe et al., 1994). This has also induced spillover effects (Chen, 1983; Jammes, 1998).
3. Since income is generally higher in the more open provinces, private health expenditures per capita are normally also higher, which

encourages the existence and maintenance of a more 'functional' and effective[6] health care supply.

4. In addition, the higher per capita GDP leads to the raising of more public resources,[7] not only because the theoretical average fiscal basis per capita is greater, but also because it is easier to tax it. The so-called 'extra-budgetary' funds, which are based upon production taxes and which are not subject to the system of resources sharing between central government and decentralized units are therefore all the greater (Wong et al., 1995; Raiser, 1998). It can therefore be assumed, all other things being equal, that public health spending per capita in comparatively open provinces is greater than in those that are less open, and that this applies not only to curative care but also to preventive care (mainly prenatal and immunisation), the financing of which rests largely with local administrative levels and structures. These programmes receive provincial and county government budgets and collect fees for service. These sources of funding depend on economic conditions which are directly influenced by external openness.[8] In the poor provinces of China, the financing of vertical health programmes[9] is an acute problem. The lack of resources is worrying as it has been observed in China as well as in many countries that preventive care (most notably vaccinations) and primary curative health care play an important role in bringing down the infant mortality rate (Beenstock and Sturdy, 1990; Hojman, 1996; Filmer and Pritchett, 1997).
5. It is reasonable to assume that households in more open provinces live in a better health environment mainly through having more developed sanitation services and wider access to safe water, although it must be noted that the relationship between access to safe water and infant mortality is somewhat controversial (Galavardin, 1998).

Figure 8.1 shows the theoretical relationship between openness and level of IMR.

The direct and indirect effects of openness on the IMR can therefore be expressed as:

$$IMR = s\,(EO, HE(EO), HCS(EO), F(EO), Z) + \mu \qquad (8.2)$$

EO being external openness, the other vectors as previously mentioned in equation (8.1).

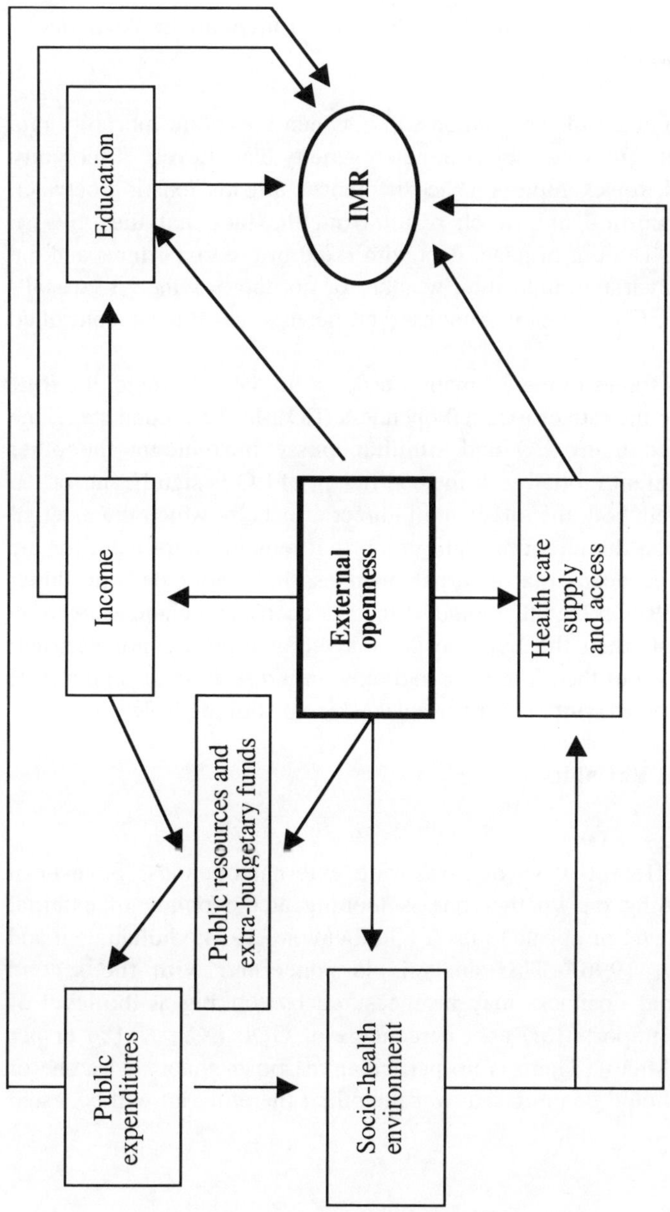

Figure 8.1 Effects of external openness on the IMR

4 DETERMINANTS SPECIFICATION AND DATA

Unobserved Heterogeneity, Correlation between Independent Variables and the Estimation Process

The estimation process of the relationship between the infant mortality rate and its determinants may be subject to heterogeneity bias. Levels of mortality may also depend, for example, on the differences already existing between individuals or families and which result from the fact that they live in different regions. The use of panel data with fixed or random effects and the introduction of a variable indicating whether or not the province is coastal[10] (dummy variable, Coast) enables unobserved heterogeneity to be controlled for.

There are two stages to the estimation process. In the first stage, the IMR is estimated using the rate of external openness (EO). In the second stage, the IMR is estimated using EO and simultaneously introducing the other determinants of infant mortality. If the coefficient of EO is significant for the first stage, it covers both the direct and indirect effects by which the external openness acts upon the infant mortality rate. If it remains significant for the second stage, this means that external openness has had a definite direct impact on the IMR. On the other hand, if the EO coefficient changes to be no longer significant, then the hypothesis of a direct effect is not verified: external openness will therefore have had only an indirect effect on the IMR via the influence it has on the other variables which determine IMR.

The Independent Variables

External openness (EO)

A number of different ways of measuring external openness have been proposed depending on whether one is looking at the policy of external openness or the level of openness itself (Guillaumont, 1994; Guillaumont and Boyreau-Debray, 1996). This analysis is concerned with the second approach. External openness may be measured by looking at the level of exports (X) and imports (M) as a percentage of GDP (XY; XMY) or per capita (Xhab; XMhab). There is no particular reason in theory why one of these measures should be preferred over the other; therefore all will be tested here.

The socio-health environment and initial situation in the province (HE)
The environmental situation is traditionally measured by looking at the percentage of the population having access to safe water (Water). The initial situation in each province at the beginning of the period of research may be assessed using life expectancy (Life), which we know depends largely on the behaviour of the mother, illiteracy, access to potable water and income (Barlow and Vissandjée, 1998). The relationship between initial life expectancy and mortality rate is a priori difficult to determine: (i) the better the environment and personal circumstances at the start, the harder it is comparatively to improve level of health; inversely, (ii) a healthy environment to start with promotes the dissemination of skills and knowledge which help to reduce mortality rates.

Healthcare supply (HCS)
It is generally accepted that basic health care and preventive health care, particularly vaccination programmes against target diseases (tetanus, rubella, diphtheria, tuberculosis, whooping cough and polio) are most effective in bringing down the mortality rate. In Chinese provinces for the period 1982–1992, Hammer (1996a) found a negative correlation between vaccinations and IMR, as did Hossain (1997) with DPT3.

In the absence of data on the number and characteristics of health facilities per province and on the main vertical health programmes, it has been necessary to fall back on somewhat approximate indicators, specifically, the number of doctors (Docth) and the number of beds (Bedh) per thousand inhabitants. The traditional limitations of these indicators are well known. In China, they are all the more acute given that, in general, the country does not suffer severe problems of geographical accessibility to healthcare and that excess staffing levels and excess structural capacity can frequently be found across all levels of the health pyramid above that of the village (Wilkes et al., 1997). This excess of capacity has several causes, coming mainly from duplication and overlapping between the three-tier and the vertical services, along with other overlapping between the county, the township and the state-owned enterprise facilities. Therefore in this field the main issue is the degree of functioning of the health structures. But although in the urban areas of coastal provinces the level of availability of health structures compares with that of developing countries, at the village level in poor areas, the situation might be very different. A survey in 320 poor districts in six provinces (Gansu, Qinghai, Sichuan, Yunnan, Guizhou, Guangxi) shows there is no medical staff in 15 407 villages (quoted by Caillez, 1998). Another study on 30 poor counties found that only 55% of the villages had a functioning health post in 1993 (Liu et al., 1996). So, in poor and mountainous areas where most of the poor live, there might be acute physical barriers to accessing basic health care.

Nevertheless it appears globally reasonable to assume that a relatively larger pool of doctors indicates that there is comparatively less of a shortage of operational resources per inhabitant, which translates, all other things being equal, into comparatively more efficient health care supply. On average, there was an increase in the general availability of health provision per head measured by the two indicators mentioned above. But it is relevant to make a distinction between 'availability' and 'entitlement' as Sen and Drèze have shown in another context. Here the core of the issue is certainly financial accessibility to the given health care supply. We return to this question later.

Hammer (1996a) has shown for 1992 a positive correlation between per capita GDP in the provinces and vaccination levels. If this relationship remains stable over time, it may be supposed that the variable income, when introduced into the model (see below) also reflects this aspect of health care supply, which cannot be measured in any other way because of a lack of data.

A number of studies across several different sample countries have questioned the role that public health expenditure plays in influencing level of health, including IMR (Anand and Ravallion, 1993; Calipel and Guillaumont, 1994; Hammer, 1996b; Jamison et al., 1996; Bidani and Ravallion, 1997; Brun and Mathonnat, 1997; Filmer and Pritchett, 1997; Hojman, 1996). The results are contrasting. All but three of these studies[11] conclude that there are no statistically significant discernible effects. It is still necessary however to look at their impact on IMR in the provinces of China, although here too statistical limitations prevent us from directly analysing their effects. But two studies provide useful information and indicate that public health expenditures are regressive since the early 1990s. First, Hammer (1996b) has shown that in Chinese provinces, public health care expenditures are a function of the level of per capita GDP per province. These observations tend to agree with those of Luo (1995) for a sample of 20 counties. Second, Hossain (op cit.) points out that poor provinces in which IMR are higher than the national average have low health budgetary expenditures. That is the case among others for Henan, Guizhou, Yunnan, Sichuan, Guangxi, contrasting with the opposite situation prevailing in Beijing, Shandong, Shanghai, and Tianjin for example. It may therefore be assumed that per capita GDP is an indicator that also partly reflects public expenditures on health care.

Family and province characteristics (F)

Income and openness

Per capita GDP has been retained as an income measure (Yhab) with an expected negative relation with IMR. Numerous studies of China have shown that the increase in per capita income in the more open provinces, particularly those on the coast, has been more rapid than in other provinces, and that it has been more pronounced in rural areas than in urban ones. This means, all other things being equal, and particularly if these differences in revenue growth are not counteracted in those provinces experiencing more 'rapid' growth than others by higher increased costs in access to health care, that the growth dynamic linked to external openness leads to provincial divergence on two counts: first, to a widening of the differences in IMR between open/coastal provinces and others, and second, to greater IMR disparities between urban and rural areas in provinces which are less open than others. The interactive variable Cotinc (Yhab x Coast) enables this hypothesis to be partly tested. It is also advisable to retain a multiplicative variable in order to identify any possible additional effect, which may result from the combination of income and degree of openness (Multi).

However, in any given province, the effects of an average level of per capita income on IMR will vary from the point of view of nutrition and access to health care, according to whether the income is more or less equally distributed. Within a household, the income effects on IMR will be influenced by the existing or not of an insurance scheme and by the constraints arising from the composition of that household.

Income distribution

The literature shows that, all other things being equal, income distribution is a matter of importance for health status. Greater concentration of income tends to be associated with a higher IMR (Bidani and Ravallion, 1997; Filmer and Pritchett, 1997). The indicators used here for hypothesis testing purposes are the Gini coefficient,[12] the incidence of poverty (Pover)[13] and, as an additional proxy, the percentage of the population employed in agriculture (Agr), most of the poor being in rural areas although urban poverty is increasing. The introduction of variables to capture the effects of poverty is theoretically justified for three reasons. First, because the poor are more likely than others to be faced with the risk of illness. Second, because the way in which they go about seeking health care is different from the non-poor. These issues have been empirically confirmed by studies, which looked simultaneously at the effects of income and the incidence of poverty

(Behrman, 1990; Carrin and Politi, 1996). In China, Wilkes et al. (1997) have shown that the poor spend less than others in total on health care, but proportionately more as a percentage of their income (Carrin et al., 1996). Hao et al. (1997) found that within a sample of counties more than half those individuals with low income and claiming to be ill had not sought health care for financial reasons, compared with less than a quarter of those who enjoyed a relatively high income. Third, the poor are more exposed than others to sizeable income risk. In a study on southern China, Jalan and Ravallion (1999) calculated that the poorest of their sample passed on 40% of an exogenous income shock to consumption, contrasting with the behaviour of richer[14] individuals who passed on only 10% to consumption. The authors also find in another study (1998; quoted in Jalan and Ravallion, 1999) that higher income risks at the origin limit out-migration of labour, which obviously reduces additional revenue from internal remittances. So, one might expect these elements to have important negative effects on IMR, through the channel of their influence on nutrition and health care demand.

Income and insurance

Any system of health insurance help to soften the link between income and health care demand. In China, the percentage of the total population which is not insured has gone from 30% in 1981 to 80% in 1993 (Wei, 1996). In rural areas, the percentage of the population covered by the system of rural medical co-operatives has fallen from 48% to 7% (Carrin et al., 1996; World Bank, 1997b). The advantage of co-operative medical schemes and of other pre-reform mechanisms of insurance was that they covered most of the poor and vulnerable people, providing an entitlement to basic health care and guaranteeing financial accessibility to health care. A number of empirical studies have shown that income and the price paid (out-of-pocket) by those seeking treatment has an effect on access to care. Evidence for rural areas is reported in the studies edited by Bloom and Wilkes (1997). Especially, Hao et al. (1997) found that the main factor influencing the non-use of services was not the unavailability of medical services at the local level, but the inability of villagers to pay for care. Henderson et al. (1992) reached the same conclusion and quoted additional figures from a Ministry of Health survey in 1988 showing than 16% of households in the survey had ill members who failed to get needed in-patient care because they could not bear the cost. An other more recent survey (National Health Services Survey; Liu et al., 1999) gives further evidence for 1993: almost 60% of the rural patients who had refused to be hospitalised reported inability to pay as the major reason for disregarding the medical staff advice; for urban areas, the figure is

40%.[15] Although one can't strictly compare all these results, they are going along the same lines. Let's add that a new survey conducted by MoH and Unicef at the village level in 40 counties found that 70% of women could not afford prenatal exams (MoH and Unicef, 1999).

Lu (1997) found that outpatient health care demand amongst those who were insured in the town of Hang Zhou was more price sensitive (in terms of elasticity) where the poor were involved, serving to underline the importance of income. It has also been shown that employees under labour health insurance plans have, on average, higher utilization rates and level of health expenditures than those with partial or no coverage. In a study covering 400 urban enterprises and 6000 workers, Hu et al. (1999) found that workers with no insurance coverage have to bear an expected average amount of out-of-pocket expenditure which is roughly twice the amount borne by a worker with partial assurance coverage. Knight and Song (1993) considered two samples each of 52 villages, one with rural co-operative medical schemes and the other with private payment schemes. They estimate that 'health insurance reduces crude death rate by 14 per cent' (p. 83).

So they are numerous direct or indirect evidence regarding the importance of insurance on the access to healthcare. But one has to quote here the puzzling results of a recent study by Henderson et al. (1998). Using data from the China Health and Nutrition Survey in 1989, 1991 and 1993 for height provinces (urban and rural areas)[16] they found that 'people with medical insurance seem to be no more likely to seek care when ill than those with no insurance coverage' (p. 1967). They add that similar relationships were drawn out from calculations based on the data from the Nation Health Services Survey of 1993 (p. 1967). One notices that these results seem to contradict the intuitive interpretation of the above figures. One can suggest it might be because the level of reimbursement appears to be often low as a recent study by Carrin et al. (1999) has documented it for 14 counties in 11 provinces.

However, waiting for more research on this issue, one can assume that the most probable current picture may be summarised as one of a dual process: on the one hand, growing economic prosperity is leading to more health care demand from those who can afford to pay for growing health care prices (and move often to the growing private providers in urban areas). On the other hand, the average income level of most of the uninsured (and of the 'poorly' insured) has increased, but for most of them certainly not enough to make up for the negative effect of the wreck of the health insurance schemes, especially in rural areas.

The share of the population opting for the system of agricultural household contracted responsibility (Respon) and the percentage of the population living in rural areas (Poprur) are variables which help to account for the breakdown of the system of health insurance in rural areas where it is of most importance. Since the vast majority of health care is monetary cost, this change strengthens still further the potential impact of income on health care demand, and no doubt most especially on the demand for preventive, compared with curative care.

Income and family composition

The composition of the family changes the impact of income on IMR for two reasons: (i) demand for health care increases with level of dependence and (ii) in a situation of equal income, the likelihood of not being able financially to deal with illness is less in the case of a household made up of relatively young adults than it is in one of the same size, but which contains old people and children. This effect is tested by introducing the dependence rate resulting from the presence of old people (over 65, Aged), children under 15 (Child) and a combination of the two (Depen). It is worth explaining why the level of dependence of children has been taken into account. In the first place, it is justified by the great differences in child dependency which exist between provinces. In effect, each province issued its own rules concerning the number of births allowed, and as Attané (1998) has shown, the degree of adherence to these directives varies in rural areas according to province.[17] For example, in provinces with a high proportion of ethnic minorities, 70% of women have the right to bear two children; in Xianjing, 40% are allowed to have three (Attané, 1998). However, these provinces are comparatively poor, which further accentuates the income constraints resulting from child dependency. In addition, it is possible that the children of individuals insured through the three main insurance schemes[18] are not covered or covered only to a limited degree.

Education

The role of education in the reduction of infant mortality has been dealt with in a number of previous studies (Schultz, 1993; Murray and Chen, 1993; Filmer and Pritchett, 1997). Whilst older empirical studies showed that the mother's education had a greater influence on IMR than that of the father (Barrera, 1991),[19] more recent studies have tended to demonstrate that the influence of the father is by no means negligible (Baya, 1998). We have retained a variable of 'stock' of knowledge, the adult illiteracy rate (Illite), in order to avoid the difficulties posed by the issue of time lag when 'flow' variables such as the number of years of schooling are introduced in a model.

The other characteristics of both individuals and families (Z), such as position of the child within the family hierarchy and time between births are difficult to monitor and consolidate at province level. They are covered by μ. On the whole, the analysis of the effects of these factors on IMR has led to some very controversial results (Guilkey and Riphahn, 1998).

5 THE DETERMINANTS OF THE INFANT MORTALITY RATE IN CHINESE PROVINCES

The relationship between the infant mortality rate and the degree of openness at the first stage is expressed by:

$$\log(IMR_{it}) = \alpha + \beta_1 \log(XY_{it}) + u_{it} \tag{8.3}$$

The relationship between the infant mortality rate and its determinants at the second stage is expressed by equation (8.4) as follows:

$$\begin{aligned}\log(IMR_{it}) &= \alpha + \beta_1 Coast_{it} + \beta_2 \log(XY_{it}) + \beta_3 \log(Water_{it}) + \beta_4 \log(Life_{it}) + \beta_5 \log(Docth_{it}) \\ &+ \beta_6 \log(Bedh_{it}) + \beta_7 \log(Yhab_{it}) + \beta_8 Gini_{it} + \beta_9 \log(Pover_{it}) + \beta_{10} \log(Poprur_{it}) \\ &+ \beta_{11} \log(\mathrm{Re}\,spon_{it}) + \beta_{12} \log(Agr_{it}) + \beta_{13} \log(Cotinc) + \beta_{14} \log(Multi_{it}) + \beta_{15} \log(Depen_{it}) \\ &+ \beta_{16} \log(Illite_{it}) + \mu_{it}\end{aligned} \tag{8.4}$$

where $i = 1$, n provinces; $t = 1$ to T years, the other variables having been defined above. We used the software Limdep.

Direct and Indirect Effects of External Openness on Infant Mortality

As hypothesized, (stage 1) external openness, as measured by the level of exports (*XY*, exports as a percentage of GDP),[20] positively influences the reduction of the IMR (Table 8.2, equation 8.1). However, as we have seen, this effect may be direct or may work indirectly if the degree of openness also affects the other determinants of IMR. Either way, its impact is confirmed (appendix Table 8A.1) since relationships which are both significant and with the sign anticipated, have been observed between the level of exports and the per capita GDP (positive relationship), the illiteracy level (negative relationship) and the density of medical practitioners (positive relationship).

It is then appropriate to introduce into the second stage all of the potential determinants of IMR alongside that of degree of openness. The final results can be seen in Table 8.2 (equation 8.2). It should be noted that the presence of random effects attests to an unobserved heterogeneity between provinces.

Table 8.2 Estimate of the parameters of infant mortality

	Model 1		Model 2		Model 3	
Variables	coefficient	*t*	coefficient	*t*	coefficient	*t*
XY	- 0.276	- 3.475**	0.181	1.011ns	0.201	0.821ns
Life			-7.479	-6.177*		
ResYhab			-0.380	-1.879**	-0.687	-2.232*
Poprur			0.104	-1.825**	0.202	2.222*
Depen			0.545	2.539*	0.922	4.149*
Constant	2.714	12.847*	36.084	6.806*	5.527	1.746***
R^2 ddl	0.748		0.783		0.882	
F	15.31		17.29		18.37	
N	73		73		73	
Effects$^{\mu}$	R		R		R	

Notes:
*Significant at 1%; **significant at 5%; **significant at 10%.
µ The value of the LM test leads to the rejection of the OLS, and the Hausman test (null hypothesis – fixed effects, versus alternative hypothesis – random effects) leads to the rejection of the fixed effect model in favour of the random effect model at normal confidence levels.
R = random effects

The export ratio coefficient is no longer significant. That means that the effect of external openness on IMR is only indirect: its influence is felt through the other variables, principally that of income, as medical coverage (*Docth* and *Bedh*) and education (*Illite*) – variables with which the degree of openness was correlated – are not significant. Knight and Song had already highlighted in the 1970s that level of literacy had no effect on the IMR (1993, p. 68). It may be assumed that since overall literacy rates are only fair,[21] the differences between provinces are too small for this factor to stand out as a determinant of infant mortality. A certain number of other variables have also no effect on IMR. These are the interactive variables, level of export with income (*Multi*) and coastal province with income (*Cotinc*), as well as the variables, access to safe water (*Water*), two indicators of income distribution (*Gini* and *Pover*)[22] and the dummy variable, coastal province (*Coast*).

Income and Infant Mortality

As the per capita GDP was correlated with the level of exports, a regression analysis was carried out on it against export level, and the residual (*ResYhab* in Table 8.2) was introduced into the model in place of the observed values. The coefficient is both significant and negative as per the proposed hypothesis.[23] Thus it confirms in the case of Chinese provinces one of the conclusions most clearly seen in the existing literature as to the determinants of infant mortality. This first value of elasticity – another is obtained from equation 8.3 (see comments below) – is equal to 0.38, which is around the lower end of the bracket generally found in studies for developing countries.

The indirect impact of the degree of openness on the IMR raises the question of the impact of export levels on the differences in mortality rates between provinces because external openness widens the income gap between more open provinces and the others.[24] As we have seen, the variables *Cotinc* and *Multi* used to try to capture these effects are not significant.

In addition, the question was also posed as to whether the effect of income on the IMR might not increase over time, for four main reasons:

1. The increase in the cost of access to care has in general been more rapid than the increase in income. Outpatient and inpatient costs went up by 400–500% from 1990 to 1997, mainly because of the boosting of drugs prices. The annual average growth rate of GDP has been around 8%. This means that a higher share of income is necessary in order to be able to purchase the same amount of health care.
2. The proportion of the population benefiting from social insurance has declined strongly since the beginning of the 1980s (compare above).
3. The mother and children health facilities at county level, as all health care facilities, tends to lack funds to pay for staff and operating expenditures. For several years, they had to raise a large part of their resources from user fees. This has encouraged them to cut down on services which do not produce income and to give priority to treatment rather than to preventive activities (such as vaccinations) which are in themselves less financially rewarding,[25] but more efficient in fighting infant mortality. An additional aspect of this issue being that treatment practices are often modified in a more costly (and if not in a less

efficient) way. One example of this is the treatment of diarrhoea, an important contributor to infant mortality. For some years it has been quite frequently treated at hospital level, which is expensive, but more financially rewarding for the health care provider. It may even involve hospitalisation of the infant, instead of the use of traditional treatments such as dehydration salts and intestinal antiseptics administered at out-patient level (World Bank, 1997b). An other example comes from the MoH-Unicef survey in 40 counties (1999, op cit.): 47–65% of the mothers reported that their children received intramuscular injections during their latest visit to health facilities for a common cold. Generally speaking, as selling drugs is the main source of revenue by the health structures and agents, there is a general trend in overprescribing and in favouring prescriptions of costly products, with the consequence of pushing out of the system those who cannot pay for. It is not uncommon for families to become heavily indebted to access to health care, and consequently have to face with poverty. The corollary of this are negative effects on nutrition, morbidity and infant mortality.

4. Economic growth in the last 20 years has brought progressively specific factors of contamination which lead to new reasons to seek infant health care: development of unchecked pollution, risks introduced by the itinerant population. But one can argue that this does not offset the decreasing incidence of infectious diseases since the beginning of the nineteenth century.[26] However this two opposite arguments don't tell us very much about the associated infant mortality.

The hypothesis that the influence of income on IMR increased with time was tested in two ways. The first involved dividing the sample into two periods (1978–89 and 1990–94) and comparing the elasticities of each of them. No significant differences were found between the two periods (Chow test).

The second way consisted of introducing, as follows, the multiplicative variables which had been set up: a dummy variable was created which successively took the value one for the years 1994–89, 1994–90, 1994–91 and zero for the other years. Each variable was then multiplied by the per capita GDP and introduced one by one into the model. The coefficients were not significant. Thus there is no evidence from the results obtained here that the IMR becomes increasingly sensitive to income. Leaving aside issues of methodology, one of the reasons for this may be that the decline in medical insurance and the increase in the relative price of health care are uneven between provinces and counties, making an increasing effect of income very difficult to capture. For example, a study[27] in the relatively poor province of Shanxi, has shown that around one-third of the villages had continued to maintain some form of community financing of health care, whilst in the much poorer province of Guizhou any such form of financing had practically disappeared. Conversely, in the district of Taichang, the scheme of medical co-operatives is still very dynamic and is expanding (Khan et al., 1996). Carrin et al. (1999) provide additional evidences of the uneven situation in the field of rural insurance.

Initial Situation, Family Characteristics and infant mortality

Three other variables offer a significant explanation for the differences in the IMR between provinces: life expectancy at the beginning of the period, the degree of dependence and the percentage of the population living in rural areas. Life expectancy at the start of the period (*Life*) comes up with a negative value, which is a reflection of the length of time the effects of acquired learning – including individual behaviour, which has a positive effect on the IMR – last for. The global level of dependence (*Depen*) appears to be of more significance than the level of dependence of children and old people taken separately, which is not really surprising. The coefficient has the expected positive sign which suggests, as hypothesized, that a comparatively high level of dependence slows down the reduction of the IMR: on the one hand, it imposes more constraints on income, and on the other it may be translated into the mother having less time to devote to younger children. Finally, the results show that the greater the proportion of the population in rural areas (*Poprur*), the higher the IMR, which confirms the initial hypothesis.[28]

A study of the correlation matrix shows that life expectancy at the start of the period (*Life*, equation 8.2), is correlated with the other independent variables. The model was therefore recalculated leaving out this variable (equation 8.3), which resulted in higher coefficients and higher significance levels for the other variables. Thus, for example, income elasticity increases from 0.38 (equation 8.2) to 0.68, which corresponds approximately with the upper bracket of estimates found in existing literature concerning the effect of income on infant mortality in developing countries.

6 CONCLUSION

External openness does not appear to have a direct effect on the infant mortality rate in Chinese provinces after controlling for other factors. The results of this study show that its influence is indirect, mainly through the positive effects of openness on per capita income. This relationship between external openness, income and infant mortality rate suggests, bearing in mind the conclusions concerning external openness and the growth of Chinese provinces in existing literature, that external openness will spur on thc differences in the rates of infant mortality between the more open provinces, particularly those on the coast, and the others. Consequently it suggests it might be advisable to adopt measures in order to correct the health effects of the widening of income disparities among provinces.[29] Conversely, within the relatively more open provinces, external openness will tend to narrow the IMR gap between rural and urban areas because it tends to reduce the income gap between both, as shown by the literature on growth in China.

Amongst the variables which have emerged as being significant determinants of the infant mortality rate, three – per capita income, level of dependence and percentage of the population living in rural areas – underline strongly the need to rebuild medical insurance schemes in China, which is one of the objectives of the government. In March 1996, the National Peoples' Congress approved the *Outline of the Ninth Five-Year Plan (1996–2000) for National Economic and Social Development and the Long Term Targets for the Year 2010*. It is stated that in rural areas regions will develop and improve rural co-operative health care delivery according to local conditions, and in urban areas, a medical insurance system will be implemented combining municipality-wide centralized funds and individual accounts (*Peoples' Daily*, 20 March 1996). Several 'pilot' schemes or experiments have been already set up in various places giving results which seem promising.[30] It also appears advisable to strengthen public health programs and to shift the actual pattern of public health expenditure on a pro poor province fashion. The case is supported by the present situation (regressive public expenditure and breakdown of basic health services due to a lack of resources) and by the results of Hossain (1997) who found the reduction of the IMR to be more positively influenced by public health expenditures in poorer provinces than in high income provinces. Taking into consideration that health funding is mainly decentralised and that the transition call for new social responsibilities for the State – some of them being formerly financed by the state-owned enterprises – these objectives require central regulation and fiscal transfers to assure that the local funding reaches some threshold set up as a 'minimum level', at least for basic health care.

Broadly speaking, the picture portrayed in this chapter regarding the influence of external openness on IMR within the current context calls for wide-ranging and more efficient public action to support health promotion and remove destitution, without waiting for health improvement mainly coming from individual behaviour and collective transformations induced by growth.[31] As a consequence, one part of the task ahead will be to make new improvements in IMR a national issue and not one which has to be tackled mainly by the MoH alone.

Finally, the presence of random effects in the econometric results demonstrates the (expected) existence of non-observed heterogeneity. Outside of a lack of homogeneity in the data, which cannot be ruled out, these random effects confirm how great are the disparities existing between provinces and within these, between counties, the subject of which invites further investigation. Several case studies have already revealed that the reality of the health situation in Chinese provinces is extremely complex. These call for further microeconomic analyses to be undertaken to complement the more global approaches, such as the study carried out here.

NOTES

1. Ninety-five per 1000 live births in 1990, 64 in 1997.
2. Early births, resulting from early marriages (*zaohun zaohy*), out-of-wedlock births (*feihun zaoyu*) and above quota births (*chaosheng*) (Merli, 1998, p. 641).
3. Mostley and Chen, 1984; Murray and Chen, 1993; Schultz, 1993; World Bank, 1993; Kodio and Etard, 1997; Baya, 1998; Akin et al., 1998; Guilkey and Riphan, 1998.
4. Whatever their status.
5. In the western region and in poor counties in others provinces, childhood malnutrition is still a cause of infant mortality although it has drastically declined over decades.
6. Nevertheless it is clear that the inefficiency of health care facilities is one of the main challenges that China needs to address in the area of health care. However this question raises issues that are outside the scope of this chapter.
7. Revenues mobilisation is largely decentralized and the transfers from central government to decentralized units do not (and cannot) compensate for the inequalities in fiscal potential between provinces.
8. They are also and obviously influenced by the political willingness to support or not a 'pro-health' structure of public expenditure.
9. Especially in the case of the Epidemics Prevention Service, the Extended Programme of Immunisation (under the Ministry of Health authority) and the Mother and Infant Health Programme (depending on the Family Planning Commission). As example of lack of funding, in Shaanxi and Guizhou provinces, measles coverage is as low as in many sub-Saharan African countries.
10. Regions along the coast benefited earlier than others from external openness measures and their coastal characteristics significantly contribute to the 'explanation' as to why they had more rapid growth between 1978 and 1993 (Jian et al., 1996). These regions are: Tianjin,

Hebei, Liaoning, Shanghai, Jiangsu, Zhejiang, Fujian, Shangdong, Guangdong and Guangxi. Heilongjang, situated in the north west on the border with Russia, with whom it has strong trade links, has also been included here as 'coastal', as it enjoys a comparable status to coastal provinces since much of its agricultural production is exported (Guillaumont Jeanneney and Hua, 1998).

11. Jamison et al. (1996), Anand and Ravallion (1993), Bidani and Ravallion (1997).
12. For 1992, in the absence of other available years.
13. The incidence of poverty relates to the years 1992–93 (using a threshold of 500 yuan per month), which is clearly a statistical constraint.
14. Respectively the poorest decile and the richest third.
15. The average cost of inpatient care at the county hospital level was around 20–25% of GDP per capita in 1995.
16. Conducted by the Chinese Academy of Preventive Medicine with the University of North Carolina in Liaoning, regarding Shangdong, Jiangsu, Henan, Hubei, Hunan, Guangxi and Guizhou.
17. The one-child rule is enforced in urban areas.
18. Public employee's health scheme, workplace health insurance, rural medical co-operative system.
19. Good education enables mothers to take better care of their offspring and encourages a lower birth rate; this last element applies in rural area mostly in provinces with a high proportion of ethnic minorities.
20. This indicator appears to be more significant than the alternative measures of openness (higher t-Student).
21. Around an average of 16%, with 14% for eastern and 22% for western provinces.
22. The fact that the variables *Gini* and *Pover* are not significant might be due to the way in which they were measured (one year available).
23. The same approach has also been used for *Docth* and *Bedh*, but these variables remain insignificant.
24. Compare above paragraph 'Income and openness'.
25. For example, it as been argued that no one wants to do poorly-paid immunization work (*China News Analysis*, no. 1562, 15 June 1996).
26. But the incidence of tuberculosis and hepatitis is increasing as a direct consequence of a lack of funding.
27. 'The Five Provinces Survey', cited in World Bank (1997b).
28. The share of the population opting for the agricultural household contracted responsibility system (*Respon*) is not significant.
29. Generally speaking, the central government intends to put a break on the growing disparities among regions (Fifth Plenary Meeting of the Fourteenth Central Committee, 1995). Among recent measures adopted, a proactive fiscal policy is being implemented to favour investment in werstern provinces and the building of a new railways between Beijing and Ningxia has been announced in November 1999.
30. Some examples: Sichuan Health Insurance Experiment, Taichang (near Shanghai) reform of the medical scheme of medical co-operative; in urban areas, the three tiers of financing for health services in cities of Juijang (Jiangxi province) and Zhenjiang (Jiangsu province).
31. Focused on the field of health, this is closely akin to what A. Sen calls in the broader conext of growth 'the strategy of support-led-security' (1989, p. 183 and sq).

REFERENCES

Akin, J., D. Guilkey, P. Hutchinson and M. McIntosh (1998), 'Price elasticities of demand for curative health care with control for sample selectivity on endogenous illness: an analysis for Sri-Lanka', *Health Economics*, 7, pp. 509–31.

Anand, S. and M. Ravallion (1993), 'Human development in poor countries: on the role of private incomes and public services', *Journal of Economic Perspectives*, 7(1), pp. 133–50.

Attané, I. (1998), *La politique de contrôle des naissances en Chine*, Institut National d'Etudes Démographiques, Paris, 28 pp.

Barlow, R. and B. Vissandjée (1998), 'Determinants of national life expectancy', School of Public Health, Michigan State University, mimeo, 22 pp.

Barrera, A. (1991), 'The interactive effects of mother's schooling and unsupplemented breastfeeding on child health', *Journal of Development Economics*, 34, pp. 81–98.

Baya, A. (1998), 'Instruction des parents et survie de l'enfant au Burkina-Faso, cas de Bobo-Dioulasso', *Dossiers du CEPED*, 48, pp. 6–27.

Beenstock, M. and P. Sturdy (1990), 'The determinants of infant mortality in regional India', *World Development*, 18(3), pp. 443–53.

Behrman, J. (1990), 'The action of human resources and poverty on one another', LSMS Working Paper no. 74, World Bank, Washington, DC.

Bidani, B. and M. Ravallion (1997), 'Decomposing social indicators using distributional data', *Journal of Econometrics*, 77, pp. 125–39.

Bloom, G. and A. Wilkes (eds) (1997), 'Health in transition: reforming China's rural health services', *IDS Bulletin*, 28, Institute of Development Studies, University of Sussex, England.

Brun, J.F. and J. Mathonnat (1997), 'Les effets du financement extérieur sur le niveau des dépenses publiques d'éducation et de santé dans les pays en développement – une analyse économétrique sur données de panel', *Etudes et Documents*, CERDI., Université d'Auvergne, 35 pp.

Caillez, C. (1998), 'L'effondrement du système de santé rurale', *Perspectives Chinoises*, no. 47, May–June.

Calipel, S. and P. Guillaumont (1994), 'L'évolution des dépenses publiques d'éducation et de santé: déterminants et conséquences', in Guillaumont P. and Guillaumont S. (eds), *Ajustement et Développement – L'expérience des pays ACP*, Paris: Economica.

Carrin, G., A. Ron, Y. Hui, W. Hong, Z. Tuhohong, Z. Licheng, Z. Shuo, Y. Yide, C. Jiyaying, J. Qicheng, Z. Zhaoyang, Y. Jun and L. Xuescheng (1999), 'The reform of the rural cooperative medical system in the PR of China: interim experience in 14 pilot counties', *Social Science and Medicine*, 48, pp. 961–72.

Carrin, G., and C. Politi (1996), *Exploring the Health Impact of Economic Growth, Poverty Reduction and Public Health Expenditure*, Division of Intensified Cooperation with Countries, Geneva: World Health Organization.

Carrin, G., S. Wang, Y. Hui (1996), *The Reform of the Rural Cooperative Medical System in the People's Republic of China*, Division of Intensified Cooperation with Countries, Geneva: World Health Organization.

Chen, J. (1983), *Multinational Corporations, Technology and Employment*, Macmillan, London.

Coe, D., E. Helpman, and A. Hoffmaister (1994), 'North south R&D spillovers', IMF Working Paper WP/94/144, Washington, DC.

Démurger, S. (1997), 'Ouverture et croissance: le cas de la République Populaire en Chine', PhD Thesis, Université de Panthéon-Sorbonne, Paris, 248 pp.

Drèze, J. and A. Sen (1989), *Hunger and Public Action*, Oxford University Press, New York.

Filmer D. and Pritchett L. (1997), 'Child mortality and public spending on health', Policy Research Working Paper no. 1864, World Bank, Washington, DC, 41 pp.

Galavardin, S. (1998), 'Les déterminants de la mortalité infantile et l'ajustement structurel - Une étude empirique sur le continent Africain', Mémoire de DEA, Cerdi, Université d'Auvergne, Clermont-Fd, France.

Gu, X. and T. Shenglan (1995), 'Reform of the Chinese health care financing', *Health Policy*, 32, pp 181–91.

Gu, X-Y., G. Bloom, S-L. Tang and H. Lucas (1995), 'Health Expenditures and Finance in Three Poor Counties of China', *IDS Working Paper* no. 21, Institute of Development Studies, University of Sussex, England.

Guilkey, D. and R. Riphahn (1998), 'The determinants of child mortality in the Philippines: estimation of a structural model', *Journal of Development Economics*, 56, pp. 281–305.

Guillaumont, P. (1994), 'Politique d'ouverture et croissance économique: les effets de la croissance et de l'instabilité des recettes d'exportation', *Revue d'Economie du Développement*, (1), pp. 92–114.

Guillaumont, P. and G. Boyreau-Debray (1996), 'La Chine et la convergence', *Revue d'Economie du Développement*, (1), pp. 33–67.

Guillaumont, S. and P. Hua (1998), 'Taux de change réel et inégalité entre les revenus ruraux et les revenus urbains en Chine', Communication au Colloque International sur l'Economie Chinoise 'Ouverture et disparités en Chine', CERDI - IDREC, Université d'Auvergne, 22–23 Octobre, 23 pp.

Hammer, J. (1996a), 'Health and Poverty in China', The World Bank, Policy Research Department, mimeo, Washington, DC, 19 pp.

Hammer, J. (1996b), 'Setting the context of health care finance in China', The World Bank, Policy Research Department, mimeo, Washington, DC, 19 pp.

Hao, Y., C. Suhua and H. Lucas (1997), 'Equality in the utilisation of medical services: a survey in poor rural China', *IDS Bulletin*, 28(1), Bloom and Wilkes (op cit.), eds.

Henderson, G et al. (1992), 'Equity and the utilisation of health services: report of an eight provinces survey in China', Paper presented at the Annual Meeting of the Association for Asian Studies, Washington.

Henderson, G., J. Akin, P. Hutchinson, S. Jin, J. Wang, J. Dietricht and L. Mao (1998), 'Trends in health services utilisation in eight provinces in China', *Social Science and Medicine*, 47(12), pp. 1967–71.

Hojman, D. (1996), 'Economic and other determinants of infant and child mortality in small developing countries: the case of Central America and the Caribbean', *Applied Economics*, 28, pp. 281–90.

Hossain, S. (1997), 'Tackling health transition in China', Working Papers, *Transitional Economies*, 18 13, 35 pp.

Hu, T.-W., M. Ong, Z.-H. Lin. and E. Li (1999), 'The effects of economic reform on health insurance and the financial burden for urban workers in China', *Health Economics*, 8, pp. 309–22.

Jalan, J. and M. Ravallion (1999), 'Are the poor less well insured? Vulnerability to income risk in rural China', *Journal of Development Economics*, February, pp. 61–82.

Jamison, D., W. Jia, K. Hill and J.-L. Londono (1996), 'Income, mortality and fertility control in Latin America: Country Level Performance 1960–90', mimeo, LAC Technical Department, The World Bank, Washington, DC.

Jammes, O. (1998), 'Investissements étrangers directs, capital humain et rattrapage en Chine', Communication au Colloque International sur l'Economie Chinoise, 'Ouverture et disparités en Chine', CERDI - IDREC, Université d'Auvergne, 22–23 Octobre, 23 pp.

Jian, T., J. Sachs and Warner A. (1996), 'Trends in regional inequality in China', NBER Working Paper 5412, Cambridge

Khan, A.R., K. Griffin and C. Riskin (1999), 'Income distribution in urban China during the period of economic reform and globalization', *American Economic Review, Papers and Proceedings*, May, pp. 296–300.

Khan, M., N. Zhu and J. Ling (1996), 'En Chine, l'assurance-maladie à base communautaire s'adapte à l'évolution de la situation', *Forum Mondial de la Santé*, 17, pp. 139–43.

Knight, J. and L. Song (1993), 'The length of life and the standard of living: economic influence on premature death in China', *Journal of Development Studies*, 30(1), pp. 58–91.

Kodio, B. and J.F. Etard (1997), 'Evolution récente de la mortalité infantile à Bamako, Mali', *Population*, 2, pp. 381–98.

Lu, Y. (1997), 'An analysis of the demand for outpatients services in Hang Zhou City', Department of Health Economics, Shangai Medical University, mimeo, 28 pp.

Luo, W.J. (1995), 'Study of health financing and organisation in poor rural areas of China'; Paper presented at the IHPP Research Workshop, Washington, 1–9 March, mimeo.

Ma, Y. (1994), 'Macro-economic management and intergovernmental relations in China', Policy Research Working Paper, World Bank, Washington, DC.

Merli, G. (1998), 'Underreporting of births and infant deaths in rural China: evidence from field research in one county of northern China', *The China Quarterly*, no. 155, pp. 637–55.

MoH (Ministry of Health) and UNICEF (1999), '40-Counties Survey', Beijing, mimeo.

Mosley, W. and L. Chen (1993), 'An analytical framework for the study of child survival in developing countries', *Population and Development Review*, 36, pp. 143–55.

Murray, C. and L. Chen (1993), 'In search of contemporary theory for understanding mortality change', *Social Science and Medicine*, 36, 143–55.

Raiser, M. (1998), 'Subsidising inequality: economic reforms, fiscal transfers and convergence across Chinese provinces', *Journal of Development Studies*, 34(3), pp. 1–26.

Sachs, J. and W. Woo (1997), 'Understanding China's Economic Performance', NBER Working Paper, 5935, Cambridge, 54 pp.

Schultz, T. (1993), 'Mortality decline in the low-income world: causes and consequences', *American Economic Review, Papers and Proceedings*, 83(2), pp. 337–41.

Sen, A. (1992), 'Life and death in China: a Reply', *World Development*, 20(9). pp. 1305–12.
Stoddart, G. (1997), 'Les défis de la santé dans les économies modernes', in Jacobzone (ed.), Economie de la santé - Trajectoires du futur, *Economica*, Paris, 69 pp.
Wei, Y. (1996), *An Introduction to Health Financing Patterns in China*, National Health Economic Institute, Peking.
Weigel, J.Y. (1997), 'The quest for the "socialist-market economy" in China and Vietnam', *Mondes en Développement*, 99, pp. 19–25.
Wilkes, A., Y. Hao, G. Bloom and X. Gu (1997), 'Coping with the costs of severe illness in rural China', IDS Working Paper, no. 58, Institute of Development Studies, University of Sussex, England.
Wong, C., C. Heady and W. Woo (1995), *Financing Local Government in the People's Republic of China*, Hong-Kong: Oxford University Press.
World Bank (1992), China, long-term issues and options in the health transition, *A World Bank Country Study*, Washington DC.
World Bank (1993), *Rapport sur le Développement dans le Monde – Investir dans la Santé*, Oxford University Press for the World Bank.
World Bank (1995), China, macroeconomic stability in a decentralized economy, *A World Bank Country Study*, Washington DC.
World Bank (1997a), *World Development Report*, Oxford University Press for the World Bank.
World Bank (1997b), *China 2020–Financing Health Care*, Washington DC.
World Bank (1997c), *China Engaged*, Washington DC
World Bank (1997d), *Sharing Rising Income: Disparities in China*, Washington DC.
UNICEF (1995), *Mother and Children in China*, Beijing Office, Beijing, PR of China.

APPENDIX

Table 8A.1 Relations between external openness and other determinants of IMR

	Yhab		*Illite*		*Docth*	
Variables	coefficient	*t*	coefficient	*t*	coefficient	*t*
XY	0.708	9.411*	-0.345	-8.938*	0.060	9.41*
R^2 ddl	0.461		0.851		0.702	
F	62.3		51.03		18.4	
N	73		73		73	
Effects α	R		F		R	

Notes:
α Fixed effects (F), random effects (R).
*Significant at 1%.

Data Sources Used

Health indicators: National Health Economic Institute and data from the Chinese government; incidence of poverty and Gini coefficient, World Bank, (1997b). All other data has been taken or calculated from the *China Statistical Yearbook* for different years. Where possible, missing data for certain years were estimated using growth rates.

9. The regional distribution of foreign direct investment in China: the impact of human capital*

Qiumei Yang[a]

1 INTRODUCTION

In the standard neoclassical model (Cass, 1965; Koopmans, 1965; and Solow, 1956), the level of physical capital per worker is the only determinant of the rate of return to physical capital. The marginal product of capital is higher in the less productive (that is, in the poorer) economy where the ratio of capital to labour used in the production process is relatively low.[1] Without barriers to international factor movements, capital will tend to flow from developed to developing countries until capital–labour ratios, and hence wages and capital returns are equalized. Why have these capital flows not occurred in practice?

Traditionally, economists emphasized risk and uncertainty regarding capital returns, the high costs associated with production, the level of taxation, and the overall availability of economic and social infrastructure in developing regions or countries. They argued that improvements in any of these determining factors could relocate international production, as capital is redistributed to the country offering the highest real return on its investment.

In the new endogenous growth models by Romer (1986, 1990), Lucas (1988)[2] and others, however, human resources become central to the growth process. Human resource investment can yield positive externalities and increasing returns, knowledge and per capita output thus do not necessarily have to slow down and eventually converge to the familiar steady state,

* This chapter has been published in Revue d'Economie du Développement, no. 3, 1999.

[a] An earlier version of this chapter was presented at the Sixth Convention of the East Asian Economic Association in Kitakyushu, Japan (4–6 September 1998). The author is grateful to participants, especially Robert McCleery, for valuable comments. The author would also like to thank Sylvie Démurger, William Maloney, David O'Connor, Helmut Reisen, Peter Schran, Akiko Suwa-eisenmann, Julia Von Maltzan, and an anonymous referee for helpful comments and suggestions. All views expressed in this chapter are the author's own and not necessarily those of OECD Development Centre.

instead, they can grow without bounds. Therefore, countries with a skilled labour force, supporting services and infrastructure are becoming more attractive to foreign investors from technologically advanced industries. Previous research incorporating human capital and R&D externality effects in production functions include Romer (1994), Barro (1992) and Mankiw, Romer and Weil (1992).

Lucas (1990) adjusted for differences in human capital, that is, the skill level of workers, in the standard neoclassical model. He found that the skill level of workers is so low in India that the marginal product of capital is no greater than in the United States. He then concluded that correcting for human capital differentials reduces the predicted return ratios between very rich and very poor countries, if knowledge spillover is local enough to unity. Ratcliffe (1994) applied Lucas's methodology to 105 countries and found that the predicted differences in marginal products of capital are smaller after adjusting for human capital, but the differences are still too large to be consistent with the small capital flows observed. Adjusting for financial development, however, yields lower rates in poor countries than in the US.

Large amounts of foreign investment have been flowing into China since the beginning of the 1980s. China now is a major host country for foreign investment, second only to the United States. However, the regional distribution of these inflows is heavily tilted to coastal areas. As shown in Table 9.1, from 1987 to 1997, nine coastal provinces attracted 71% of the (actually utilized) national total foreign direct investment (FDI), among which Guangdong province alone accounted for 30%. In terms of per capita FDI, Shanghai topped all the other regions. What are the factors that have shaped such an uneven regional allocation of foreign investment in China? How important is the level of human resources in each region to foreign investment?

Motivated by these questions, this chapter will, for the first time, use China's provinces as a controlled environment to examine how Lucas's evidence fits in the case of China and what determines the regional distribution of FDI. We first review, respectively, the theoretical arguments and empirical evidence on the determinants of foreign direct investment and the developments of FDI in China in Sections 2 and 3. Then we compute the rates of return to capital for regions of China[3] in Section 4. Comparing the neoclassical and the human capital-adjusted return rates allows us to predict the regions to which foreign investment should flow in search of the highest real returns. In Section 5 we conduct an empirical test to examine the impact of human capital, among other factors, on the actual regional inflows of foreign direct investment within China. Concluding remarks offer a view on how to improve the investment environment and how to achieve a more balanced distribution of foreign investment in China.

Table 9.1 The regional distribution of foreign direct investment in China[a]: 1987–1997

	Total Foreign Direct Investment (millions of US$)	Percent	Per Capita Foreign Direct Investment (US$)
Regional Total[b]	**229 441**	**100.0**	**18.03**
Major Cities	**37 630**	**16.4**	**101.63**
Beijing	8 698	3.8	70.84
Tianjin	9 080	4.0	91.32
Shanghai	19 852	8.7	134.08
Coastal Provinces	**163 381**	**71.2**	**33.47**
Hebei	3 838	1.7	5.63
Liaoning	11 187	4.9	25.48
Jiangsu	24 952	10.9	33.20
Zhejiang	7 381	3.2	15.78
Fujian	22 242	9.7	65.46
Shangdong	14 301	6.2	15.33
Guangdong	69 682	30.4	97.57
Guangxi	4 499	2.0	9.39
Hainan	5 298	2.3	70.48
Inland Provinces	**28 430**	**12.4**	**3.8**

Notes:

a. Actually used through contracts or agreement.

b. Regional total is not equal to national total due to the discrepancy of foreign direct investment attracted by ministries and departments.

Source: *China Statistical Yearbook*, various years.

2 THE DETERMINANTS OF FOREIGN DIRECT INVESTMENT INFLOWS: A LITERATURE REVIEW

The determinants of foreign direct investment inflows into a region can be grouped by microeconomic and macroeconomic determinants.

The theories of return rates, portfolio diversification, international organization, internalization, product cycle, and industry structure are the main arguments for the microeconomic determinants of FDI inflows into a country. Specifically, the *differential rates of return* (Agarwal, 1980) theory argues that foreign direct investments flow from countries with low rates of return to countries with high rates of return. Assuming that the marginal cost of capital is the same in both home and foreign countries, if expected marginal returns are higher abroad than at home, there is an incentive to invest abroad rather than at home.

The *portfolio diversification* theory claims that when a firm has to choose among different projects, it is guided not only by their expected returns but also by their expected risks. Because the returns on activities in different countries are likely to have a less than perfect correlation, a firm could reduce its overall risk by undertaking projects in more than one country. Foreign direct investment can therefore be viewed as international portfolio diversification at the corporate level (Hufbauer, 1975; Agarwal, 1980).

Macroeconomic indicators that are important to foreign investors include the rate of economic growth, the size of the economy in terms of per capita GDP, industrial capability, infrastructure condition, educational facility, research and development capacity, and investment environment (regulatory framework or foreign investment regime and fiscal incentives). Pfefferman and Madarassy (1994) argued that market size is one of the most important considerations when investors make investment location decisions, along with high literacy rates and skill levels in the workforce.

Host country FDI policies can provide important incentives to prospective investors, for example, monetary and fiscal policies, capital controls, transfer pricing regulations, competition policy, labour relations policies, and intellectual property rights enforcement (UNCTC, 1992; Becky et al., 1991; Brewer, 1991). In developing countries a positive attitude toward FDI and efforts to improve the investment environment and to strengthen industrial capabilities all render crucial to promotion of foreign capital inflows.

A phenomenon of the 1980s was that FDI was unevenly distributed among developing countries. Regarding the underlying causes, the literature mainly emphasizes the demand-side aspects. The changing nature of FDI supply, however, has been ignored. Technical innovations (such as robotics and artificial intelligence) have led to reductions in production costs, particularly those of the labour component. The implications of these technological innovations are several. First, they reduce the attractiveness of low labour cost countries as investment locations. Second, countries with a skilled labour force, supporting services and infrastructure are becoming more attractive to foreign investors from technologically advanced industries.

Grub et al. (1990) conducted a study of the factors influencing the attitude and motivations of American investors in China and found out that market size is the most important determinant of their investment, followed by low labour cost. But, to what extent and at what level is human capital an important variable for foreign investors to decide whether to invest in China or not? The answer to this question will be analysed empirically in Section 4 after the development of FDI in China is reviewed in Section 3.

3 FOREIGN DIRECT INVESTMENT IN CHINA

China's Foreign Joint Venture Law, promulgated in July 1979, effectively ended the country's 30-year period of isolation from the outside world by permitting foreign investment. By the end of 1997 China had approved a total of 304 821 foreign invested projects and actually used an accumulated fund of US$221.9 billion. The foreign funded enterprises (FFEs) employed 17.5 million workers, which was about 12% of China's non-agricultural labour force, and contributed to 47% of the national total foreign trade.

Factors behind FDI Growth

Several factors have contributed to encouraging inflows of FDI into China. First, the country's continuous efforts on economic reforms have brought a sustained rapid growth of the national economy. Between 1979 and 1995 the Chinese economy grew at one of the highest rates in the world – an annual rate of 9% on average. The high-speed economic growth has raised the income level of the Chinese and generated a growing demand for products produced by the FFEs.

Second, the low cost of the labour force and the complete range of industrial sectors bestow on China a comparative advantage in attracting foreign investment.

Third, the regional opening initiative and the preferential policies (such as import and export duty exemption, income tax exemption or reduction, and value-added tax exemption) available to foreign investors within the open regions have significantly boosted FDI inflows to China. Since the establishment of four special economic zones[4] (SEZs) along the southeast coast in 1980, the country has open regions[5] of numerous categories such as SEZs, border areas, technological development zones, open cities, and so on.

Last, China has improved its legal structure and infrastructures steadily. The government has promulgated laws[6] that are imperative to the operation of FFEs and directed financial resources into the construction of infrastructures such as power supply, telecommunication, highways, railroads, airports, and wharfs. These efforts have positively influenced FDI inflows into the country.

The Regional Distribution of Foreign Direct Investment

As shown in Table 9.1 Guangdong, Jiangsu, Fujian and other coastal provinces have attracted the majority of FDI inflows into China. Eighteen inland provinces attracted only 12.4% of the national total FDI between 1987 and 1997. In terms of per capita FDI inland areas achieved only a modest \$3.8, lower than the national average of \$18.04, and far behind the average level of coastal provinces at \$33.47.

Natural resource-oriented FDI has gone where the resources are (such as in the coal mine in Shanxi province and the oil-related FDI along the south China coast), while joint ventures and hotels are mostly built in the major cities and tourist destinations. Foreign investors seeking Chinese partners in large enterprises generally flock to the industrial centres of Shanghai, Beijing, Tianjin, Wuhan and the cities of the north east and of southern Jiangsu. By the late 1980s, export-oriented FDI in labour-intensive manufacturing activities had moved up the coast and was spreading quickly (Pomfert, 1993).

In conclusion, over the past 20 years, China's open economy reforms have attracted a tangible amount of FDI. The majority of FDI, however, has flowed to the coastal provinces or relatively developed areas. Sections 4 and 5 will attempt to shed light on the explanations about this phenomenon.

4 THE RATES OF RETURN TO CAPITAL: REGIONS OF CHINA

In this section we apply Lucas's methodology (1990) to compute the rates of return to capital in the regions of China.

The Model

Suppose that production in the regions of China follows a Cobb-Douglas type constant returns technology with a common intercept, homogeneous capital and labour inputs

$$y = Ax^{\beta},$$

where y is income per worker and x is capital per worker. Then the marginal product of capital is

$$r = A\beta\, x^{\beta-1}$$

in terms of capital per worker, and

$$r = \beta A^{1/\beta} y^{(\beta-1)/\beta}$$

in terms of production per worker.

Now we include h, human capital per worker, in the production function,

$$y = Ax^{\beta}h^{\gamma}$$

where h^{γ} can be considered as an external effect. It multiplies the productivity of a worker at any skill level h', exactly as does the intercept A. Then the marginal productivity of capital is

$$r = \beta A^{1/\beta} y^{(\beta-1)/\beta} h^{\gamma/\beta}.$$

We use SH to denote Shanghai municipality and i to denote one of the Regions.[7] The ratio of return rates to physical capital in Region i over Shanghai, $r_{k,i}/r_{k,SH}$, can be expressed by

$$\left(\frac{y_i}{y_{SH}}\right)^{\frac{\beta-1}{\beta}}$$

in the neoclassical production function, and by

$$\left(\frac{y_{h,i}}{y_{h,SH}}\right)^{\frac{\beta-1}{\beta}} \left(\frac{h_i}{h_{SH}}\right)^{\frac{\gamma}{\beta}}$$

in the human capital-adjusted neoclassical model.

If $r_{k,i}/r_{k,SH}$ exceeds 1, foreign investment should flow to Region i rather than to Shanghai.[8] We select Shanghai as the representative *rich* region because its level of economic development, human capital endowment, and attracted per capita FDI are among the highest of all the regions in China.

The Data

For y, income per worker, we use the ratio of regional GDP over its total employed social labour force. Due to the lack of data availability on the skill level of the labour force, the human capital variable is approximated by h_p, h_s, and h_u, where h_p is the ratio of the total number of graduates from primary schools, secondary schools, and universities over a region's total population, h_s is the ratio of the total number of graduates from secondary schools and universities over a region's total population, and h_u is the ratio of the total number of graduates from universities over a region's total population. We do, however, acknowledge that the selection of h_p, h_s, and h_u is a second-best solution because the brain drain of relatively well-educated workers to urban areas means that the ratio of graduates to the population is an overestimate of the ratios of graduates in the labour force. Table 9.2 lists h_p, h_s, and h_u for 1994.

The external benefit of human capital is difficult to measure. Estimates for γ range from 0.15 in Bartlesman et al. (1991) to 0.36 in Lucas (1988, 1990). Mankiw et al. (1992) estimate that both β and γ equal roughly 0.33. Barro, et al. (1992) take β and γ as 0.5 and 0.3 respectively. We first take the values of $\beta = 0.36$ and $\gamma = 0.40$, as Lucas did,[9] in the computation and then apply a range of values of $\beta = 0.3, 0.4, 0.5$ and $\gamma = 0.15, 0.2, 0.3$ to show the sensitivity of capital return rates to the changes in β and γ.

The data covers the period of 1985–94 for 27 regions in China. Hainan, Gansu, and Tibet are not included for lack of data. Chongqing was separated from Sichuan province as the fourth central government administrated city in China in 1997. This chapter does not reflect such a change, that is, all the data referring to Sichuan province include Chongqing.

The Results

The sensitivity tests reveal that as β, the share of capital used in production, goes up, the return rates in Shanghai increase faster than those in Regions[10] (that is, the ratios of return rates in regions over in Shanghai become smaller). The computed return rates to capital when $\beta = 0.36$ and $\gamma = 0.40$ are presented in Tables 9.3 to 9.5.

In the neoclassical model the rates of return to physical capital in Regions are higher than in Shanghai with $r_{k,i}/r_{k,SH}$ ranging from 1.36 to 45.53 (Table 9.3). Foreign investment thus should flow to Regions rather than to Shanghai. But why has Shanghai received an amount of per capita FDI higher than all Regions? Is human capital an important explanatory variable?

To answer the question, we adjust the neoclassical return rates by incorporating the impact of primary, secondary, and university education, which are represented by h_p, h_s, and h_u respectively, on the production function. The results are displayed in Tables 9.4a–c.

Table 9.2 Human capital variables, 1994 (%)

Rank	Region	Ratios of Total Number of Graduates from Primary Schools, Secondary Schools and Universities over a Region's Total Population $h_p=(Hp+Hs+Hu)/popu$	Rank	Region	Ratios of Total Number of Graduates from Secondary Schools and Universities over a Region's Total Population $h_s=(Hs+Hu)/popu$	Rank	Region	Ratios of Total Number of Graduates from over a Region's Total Population $h_u=Hu/popu$
1	Liaoning	96.26	1	Beijing	60.58	1	Beijing	7.23
2	Beijing	94.84	2	Shanghai	60.15	2	Shanghai	5.45
3	Heilongjiang	93.90	3	Tianjin	50.29	3	Tianjin	3.48
4	Shanghai	93.24	4	Liaoning	48.71	4	Liaoning	1.72
5	Jilin	93.08	5	Jilin	44.83	5	Jilin	1.52
6	Shanxi	92.60	6	Heilongjiang	44.32	6	Shaanxi	1.42
7	Tianjin	88.58	7	Shanxi	41.22	7	Heilongjiang	1.25
8	Hunan	86.89	8	Inner Mongolia	38.86	8	Jiangsu	1.22
9	Inner Mongolia	85.73	9	Xinjiang	38.20	9	Hubei	1.18
10	Zhejiang	85.63	10	Shaanxi	37.49	10	Qinghai	1.10
11	Xinjiang	82.81	11	Jiangsu	36.95	11	Xinjiang	1.10
12	Shangdong	82.05	12	Hubei	35.12	12	Shanxi	1.06

13	Hubei	81.99	13	Shangdong	34.93	13	Fujian	1.03
14	Jianxi	81.64	14	Ningxia	34.50	14	Ningxia	0.97
15	Guangdong	81.54	15	Zhejiang	34.17	15	Inner Mongolia	0.91
16	Sichuan	81.49	16	Hebei	34.07	16	Guangdong	0.85
17	Jiangsu	80.02	17	Henan	33.44	17	Zhejiang	0.80
18	Hebei	79.99	18	Hunan	32.59	18	Shangdong	0.77
19	Shaanxi	79.43	19	Guangdong	32.29	19	Hunan	0.77
20	Henan	78.18	20	Qinghai	31.62	20	Jianxi	0.76
21	Guangxi	76.99	21	Jianxi	29.15	21	Sichuan	0.73
22	Fujian	73.17	22	Sichuan	28.08	22	Hebei	0.72
23	Ningxia	71.54	23	Guangxi	27.68	23	Anhui	0.69
24	Anhui	69.62	24	Anhui	26.98	24	Guangxi	0.60
25	Qinghai	66.40	25	Fujian	25.78	25	Yunnan	0.60
26	Yunnan	60.70	26	Guizhou	21.14	26	Guizhou	0.59
27	Guizhou	60.48	27	Yunnan	20.23	27	Henan	0.57

Notes:
H_p is the total number of graduates from primary schools. H_s is the total number of graduates from secondary schools. H_u is the total number of graduates from universities. *Popu* is the total population in a region.

Table 9.3 The ratios of neoclassical return rates: regions over Shanghai

$$\left(\frac{y_i}{y_{SH}}\right)^{\frac{\beta-1}{\beta}}, \text{ where } \beta = 0.36$$

Region	1985	1986	1987	1988	1989	1990	1991	1992	1993	1994	1995
Beijing	1.66	1.54	1.47	1.36	1.41	1.47	1.41	1.72	2.13	2.28	2.08
Tianjin	2.19	2.08	2.02	2.00	1.96	1.87	2.05	2.40	2.76	2.58	2.48
Hebei	10.27	9.90	9.22	8.72	8.37	8.53	8.81	10.62	10.17	10.12	9.63
Shanxi	7.76	7.97	8.60	8.63	7.99	7.47	8.54	10.27	10.99	12.35	11.87
Inner Mongolia	8.68	8.54	8.37	7.18	7.37	7.01	7.73	9.56	9.79	9.83	10.31
Liaoning	3.85	3.42	3.13	3.03	2.86	3.00	3.24	3.81	3.20	3.56	4.23
Jilin	6.09	6.03	4.93	5.25	6.00	6.02	6.86	8.29	8.41	8.20	8.67
Heilongjiang	4.28	4.06	3.73	3.80	3.73	3.58	3.91	4.80	4.85	4.53	4.65
Jiangsu	6.70	5.94	5.47	5.07	5.47	5.53	5.78	5.61	4.91	4.40	4.25
Zhejiang	8.17	7.22	6.53	6.25	6.19	6.33	6.21	6.98	5.91	5.11	4.61
Anhui	13.94	12.49	12.27	12.27	12.34	13.11	17.28	20.78	19.96	17.66	16.12
Fujian	9.19	8.88	7.94	6.70	6.04	5.97	6.15	6.95	5.55	4.36	4.20
Jiangxi	13.79	13.26	7.46	12.92	12.36	11.45	12.42	14.77	17.28	17.99	18.02
Shandong	8.18	7.97	7.38	7.05	6.47	6.59	6.45	7.38	7.56	6.60	6.34
Henan	14.21	13.30	12.36	12.71	12.56	12.98	14.27	16.88	18.16	17.32	15.51
Hubei	8.24	7.73	7.26	7.39	7.19	6.87	7.65	9.41	9.40	9.14	8.95
Hunan	14.22	13.01	12.30	12.00	12.47	12.48	13.34	16.73	17.41	16.74	16.06

Guangdong	6.54	5.84	4.91	4.09	3.75	3.62	3.45	3.70	3.83	3.75	3.76
Guangxi	20.52	20.42	19.20	18.87	17.34	16.67	17.12	18.99	16.51	14.70	14.17
Sichuan	17.30	17.70	16.54	15.89	17.01	15.43	16.83	21.67	21.38	19.97	19.55
Guizhou	24.64	23.14	21.86	21.32	21.59	22.96	24.19	31.85	39.44	42.30	45.53
Yunnan	22.22	22.32	20.61	19.39	17.88	14.43	16.39	20.47	18.24	19.26	19.91
Shaanxi	13.56	12.86	12.39	11.27	11.08	11.32	12.07	15.59	16.62	18.29	19.21
Qinghai	7.94	7.05	7.07	6.56	6.63	6.59	7.36	9.40	10.77	11.32	12.33
Ningxia	9.46	8.36	8.64	8.18	7.79	7.87	8.59	11.30	13.00	13.10	13.39
Xinjiang	6.94	6.34	5.83	5.22	4.68	4.26	4.10	4.51	5.11	4.72	4.89

Table 9.4a The ratios of neoclassical return rates to capital adjusted by primary education: regions over Shanghai [a]

$$\left(\frac{y_{h,i}}{y_{h,SH}}\right)^{\frac{\beta-1}{\beta}}\left(\frac{h_i}{h_{SH}}\right)^{\frac{y}{\beta}}, \text{ where } \beta = 0.36 \text{ and } y = 0.4$$

Region	1985	1986	1987	1988	1989	1990	1991	1992	1993	1994	1995
Beijing	1.86	1.75	1.71	1.58	1.62	1.64	1.55	1.90	2.34	2.48	1.89
Tianjin	2.08	2.00	1.95	1.94	1.85	1.84	1.91	2.20	2.51	2.32	2.44
Hebei	6.63	6.61	6.36	6.04	5.82	6.04	6.19	7.61	7.24	7.16	7.54
Shanxi	6.44	7.14	8.32	8.72	8.31	8.13	9.31	11.26	12.04	13.43	14.14
Inner Mongolia	4.92	5.07	5.38	4.84	4.76	5.83	6.56	8.30	8.54	8.48	9.81
Liaoning	3.71	3.42	3.22	3.18	3.04	3.48	3.81	4.45	3.71	4.11	5.42
Jilin	4.98	5.23	4.57	5.14	5.99	6.44	7.41	9.01	9.17	8.90	10.42
Heilongjiang	3.40	3.48	3.43	3.68	3.75	3.91	4.31	5.31	5.35	4.92	5.55
Jiangsu	3.80	3.55	3.41	3.23	3.58	3.85	4.03	3.88	3.39	3.01	3.22
Zhejiang	5.15	4.76	4.46	4.34	4.42	5.44	5.34	5.94	4.99	4.28	4.26
Anhui	4.38	4.27	4.56	4.82	5.09	5.92	8.03	9.85	9.64	8.57	8.72
Fujian	3.98	4.12	3.88	3.35	2.81	3.15	3.23	3.71	2.95	2.31	2.42
Jiangxi	7.08	7.27	4.33	8.05	8.11	8.35	9.31	11.28	13.34	13.82	15.22
Shandong	4.18	4.40	4.36	4.36	4.12	4.47	4.46	5.29	5.57	4.93	5.34
Henan	7.16	7.18	7.10	7.63	7.81	8.40	9.35	11.23	12.25	11.73	11.67
Hubei	5.18	5.17	5.15	5.34	5.19	5.31	5.90	7.31	7.24	6.92	7.43
Hunan	11.07	10.54	10.35	10.00	10.58	11.77	12.40	15.63	16.19	15.34	16.16

Guangdong	4.40	4.07	3.45	3.09	2.82	2.72	2.53	2.73	2.79	2.69	2.84
Guangxi	11.74	11.89	11.46	11.33	10.44	10.88	11.06	12.58	10.81	9.46	10.02
Sichuan	10.75	11.51	11.29	11.20	12.47	12.84	13.92	17.80	17.07	15.32	16.03
Guizhou	5.73	5.78	5.92	5.75	5.99	7.12	7.61	10.69	13.36	14.18	16.72
Yunnan	4.74	5.03	4.97	4.91	4.79	4.39	5.12	6.75	6.02	6.32	7.19
Shaanxi	7.73	7.79	7.94	7.32	7.23	8.21	8.68	11.41	12.03	12.99	14.88
Qinghai	2.00	1.84	2.02	2.02	2.19	2.54	2.93	3.86	4.52	4.70	5.62
Ningxia	2.63	2.52	2.82	2.87	2.96	3.44	3.92	5.53	6.68	6.79	7.73
Xinjiang	3.73	3.73	3.78	3.64	3.41	3.26	3.11	3.51	4.00	3.58	4.00

Note:

a. Human capital variable $h_p = (Hp + Hs + Hu)/popu$.

Table 9.4b The ratios of neoclassical return rates to capital adjusted by secondary education: regions over Shanghai [a]

$$\left(\frac{y_{h,i}}{y_{h,SH}}\right)^{\frac{\beta-1}{\beta}}\left(\frac{h_i}{h_{SH}}\right)^{\frac{y}{\beta}}, \text{ where } \beta = 0.36 \text{ and } y = 0.4$$

Region	1985	1986	1987	1988	1989	1990	1991	1992	1993	1994	1995
Beijing	1.72	1.60	1.59	1.48	1.53	1.57	1.49	1.81	2.20	2.33	1.79
Tianjin	1.38	1.32	1.29	1.28	1.23	1.23	1.28	1.47	1.67	1.56	1.66
Hebei	1.71	1.72	1.68	1.64	1.62	1.71	1.77	2.13	2.05	2.06	2.21
Shanxi	1.74	1.94	2.28	2.43	2.39	2.41	2.82	3.46	3.76	4.28	4.61
Inner Mongolia	1.52	1.58	1.69	1.54	1.54	1.91	2.17	2.76	2.87	2.89	3.37
Liaoning	1.65	1.52	1.43	1.42	1.38	1.59	1.74	2.07	1.75	1.97	2.62
Jilin	1.79	1.93	1.72	1.95	2.27	2.46	2.84	3.49	3.60	3.60	4.31
Heilongjiang	1.24	1.27	1.25	1.34	1.37	1.44	1.61	2.00	2.05	1.93	2.21
Jiangsu	1.24	1.17	1.14	1.09	1.21	1.31	1.39	1.37	1.22	1.13	1.23
Zhejiang	0.93	0.88	0.85	0.86	0.91	1.15	1.15	1.33	1.17	1.05	1.09
Anhui	0.85	0.83	0.90	0.96	1.02	1.20	1.64	2.04	2.03	1.87	1.96
Fujian	0.56	0.59	0.56	0.50	0.44	0.49	0.52	0.60	0.50	0.41	0.45
Jiangxi	0.91	0.96	0.60	1.11	1.15	1.21	1.39	1.75	2.16	2.37	2.72
Shandong	1.02	1.08	1.09	1.11	1.07	1.19	1.22	1.46	1.57	1.44	1.60
Henan	2.12	2.09	2.04	2.16	2.20	2.36	2.62	3.15	3.44	3.35	3.38
Hubei	1.35	1.36	1.36	1.44	1.43	1.49	1.66	2.06	2.07	2.03	2.23

Hunan	1.77	1.71	1.72	1.72	1.85	2.10	2.26	2.89	3.07	3.01	3.27
Guangdong	0.85	0.80	0.70	0.65	0.61	0.61	0.59	0.64	0.66	0.66	0.71
Guangxi	1.94	1.95	1.87	1.85	1.74	1.84	1.89	2.11	1.85	1.67	1.82
Sichuan	1.29	1.42	1.42	1.43	1.60	1.69	1.90	2.52	2.52	2.36	2.56
Guizhou	0.79	0.81	0.84	0.84	0.92	1.11	1.21	1.63	2.07	2.26	2.73
Yunnan	0.52	0.56	0.57	0.58	0.59	0.56	0.67	0.88	0.83	0.91	1.08
Shaanxi	2.46	2.51	2.60	2.48	2.57	2.99	3.21	4.13	4.42	4.87	5.66
Qinghai	0.59	0.57	0.66	0.69	0.79	0.94	1.10	1.46	1.74	1.87	2.27
Ningxia	0.86	0.86	1.00	1.05	1.11	1.31	1.52	2.17	2.65	2.76	3.19
Xinjiang	0.99	1.02	1.08	1.09	1.07	1.08	1.09	1.24	1.44	1.32	1.51

Note:

a. Human capital variable $h_s = (Hs + Hu)/popu$.

Table 9.4c The ratios of neoclassical return rates adjusted by higher education: regions over Shanghai [a]

$$\left(\frac{y_{h,i}}{h_{h,SH}}\right)^{\frac{\beta-1}{\beta}}\left(\frac{h_i}{h_{SH}}\right)^{\frac{y}{\beta}}, \text{ where } \beta = 0.36 \text{ and } y = 0.4$$

Region	1985	1986	1987	1988	1989	1990	1991	1992	1993	1994	1995
Beijing	4.44	4.10	3.89	3.52	3.56	3.53	3.32	3.96	4.78	5.04	3.86
Tianjin	0.67	0.64	0.61	0.60	0.58	0.57	0.59	0.70	0.79	0.74	0.80
Hebei	0.02	0.02	0.02	0.02	0.02	0.02	0.02	0.03	0.03	0.03	0.04
Shanxi	0.06	0.06	0.07	0.07	0.06	0.06	0.07	0.10	0.11	0.12	0.13
Inner Mongolia	0.04	0.04	0.04	0.04	0.03	0.04	0.04	0.07	0.07	0.06	0.08
Liaoning	0.12	0.10	0.10	0.10	0.09	0.10	0.11	0.15	0.12	0.14	0.19
Jilin	0.11	0.11	0.10	0.11	0.13	0.14	0.16	0.22	0.23	0.23	0.28
Heilongjiang	0.05	0.05	0.05	0.05	0.05	0.05	0.06	0.08	0.08	0.07	0.09
Jiangsu	0.08	0.07	0.07	0.06	0.07	0.07	0.08	0.08	0.07	0.07	0.07
Zhejiang	0.02	0.02	0.02	0.02	0.02	0.02	0.02	0.03	0.03	0.02	0.02
Anhui	0.03	0.03	0.03	0.03	0.03	0.04	0.05	0.06	0.06	0.05	0.06
Fujian	0.06	0.06	0.06	0.05	0.04	0.05	0.05	0.07	0.05	0.04	0.04
Jiangxi	0.03	0.03	0.02	0.04	0.04	0.04	0.04	0.06	0.07	0.07	0.08
Shandong	0.02	0.02	0.02	0.02	0.02	0.02	0.02	0.03	0.03	0.03	0.03
Henan	0.01	0.01	0.01	0.02	0.02	0.02	0.02	0.03	0.03	0.03	0.03
Hubei	0.06	0.06	0.07	0.07	0.07	0.08	0.09	0.13	0.13	0.13	0.14
Hunan	0.03	0.03	0.03	0.03	0.04	0.04	0.04	0.07	0.07	0.07	0.08

Guangdong	0.03	0.02	0.02	0.02	0.02	0.02	0.02	0.02	0.02	0.02	0.02
Guangxi	0.04	0.04	0.04	0.04	0.03	0.03	0.03	0.04	0.03	0.03	0.03
Sichuan	0.04	0.04	0.04	0.04	0.04	0.05	0.05	0.08	0.08	0.07	0.08
Guizhou	0.06	0.05	0.05	0.04	0.04	0.05	0.04	0.07	0.08	0.08	0.10
Yunnan	0.02	0.02	0.02	0.02	0.02	0.02	0.02	0.04	0.04	0.04	0.05
Shaanxi	0.22	0.21	0.22	0.21	0.21	0.24	0.26	0.35	0.38	0.43	0.52
Qinghai	0.12	0.10	0.09	0.08	0.08	0.08	0.09	0.12	0.13	0.13	0.15
Ningxia	0.07	0.06	0.06	0.06	0.05	0.06	0.06	0.09	0.10	0.10	0.11
Xinjiang	0.07	0.07	0.06	0.06	0.05	0.04	0.04	0.05	0.06	0.05	0.06

Note:

a. Human capital variable $h_u = Hu/popu$

Table 9.5 The ratios of human capital adjusted over neoclassical return rates: regions over Shanghai [a]

$$\frac{\left(\frac{y_{h,i}}{y_{h,SH}}\right)^{\frac{\beta-1}{\beta}}\left(\frac{h_i}{h_{SH}}\right)^{\frac{y}{\beta}}}{\left(\frac{y_i}{y_{SH}}\right)^{\frac{\beta-1}{\beta}}}, \text{ where } \beta = 0.36 \text{ and } y = 0.4$$

Region	1985	1986	1987	1988	1989	1990	1991	1992	1993	1994	1995
Beijing	1.12	1.13	1.16	1.17	1.15	1.11	1.10	1.10	1.10	1.09	0.91
Shanxi	0.83	0.90	0.97	1.01	1.04	1.09	1.09	1.10	1.09	1.09	1.19
Liaoning	0.96	1.00	1.03	1.05	1.06	1.16	1.17	1.17	1.16	1.16	1.28
Jilin	0.82	0.87	0.93	0.98	1.00	1.07	1.08	1.09	1.09	1.09	1.20
Heilongjiang	0.79	0.86	0.92	0.97	1.01	1.09	1.10	1.11	1.10	1.09	1.19

Note:

a. Human capital variable $h_p = (Hp + Hs + Hu)/popu$.

First, we examine the effect of primary education on production by inserting h_p into the neoclassical production function. The difference in the return rates to capital between Shanghai and Regions has reduced. The adjusted $r_{k,i}/r_{k,SH}$ ranges from 1.55 to 17.8 (Table 9.4a). Next, when secondary education effect h_s is modelled into the neoclassical production function, the gap between $r_{k,i}$ and $r_{k,SH}$ and is further abridged and the adjusted $r_{k,i}/r_{k,SH}$ falls between 0.41 and 5.66 (Table 9.4b). Finally, we test the impact of higher education by employing h_u as the human capital variable in the neoclassical model, except Beijing, the adjusted return rates in all the other Regions have become smaller than those in Shanghai (Table 9.4c).

Last, the ratios of the h_p-adjusted $r_{k,i}/r_{k,SH}$ and neoclassical $r_{k,i}/r_{k,SH}$ are computed. Table 9.5 reports the results for Beijing, Liaoning, Jilin, Heilongjiang, and Shanxi. For these regions, the ratios of the adjusted $r_{k,i}/r_{k,SH}$ over the neoclassical $r_{k,i}/r_{k,SH}$ are bigger than 1 for certain years. They also have a level of h_p higher than or comparable to that of Shanghai.

In conclusion, the neoclassical return rates to capital in Regions ($r_{k,i}$) are higher than those in Shanghai ($r_{k,SH}$), the *rich* region, in China. However, when we adjust for human capital, the differences between $r_{k,i}$ and $r_{k,SH}$ have become smaller. These results confirm Lucas's result in his paper (1990) – human capital equalizes the return rates to capital between a *poor* region and a *rich* region. They also corroborate that like physical capital, human capital contributes positively to production and raises the return rates to capital in regions of China. The higher the education level in a region, the higher its return rates to capital. For example, the level of higher education in Beijing, measured by h_u, is the highest among all regions of China. Its return rates to capital adjusted by h_u are also ranked as the number one in the country. The relatively high level of education in Shanghai, compared with other regions, has contributed, among other factors, to its high return rates to capital.

Nevertheless, does FDI in China actually flow to regions that offer the highest human capital-adjusted return rates to capital? Or, in general, is the level of human resources in a region an important factor in foreign investment? The next section will elaborate on answers to these questions.

5 THE DETERMINANTS OF FDI REGIONAL DISTRIBUTION IN CHINA: AN EMPIRICAL TEST

Many factors might affect foreign capital flows into a country. However, the factors that determine the regional distribution of foreign capital within a country are associated solely with region-specific factors such as variations in product, education, labour cost, location, infrastructure, financial development, natural resources, urbanization, marketization, and industrialization.

Lu (1994, 1997), Wei (1995), Chen (1996), and Démurger (1998) have contributed empirical analyses about the regional distribution of foreign direct investment in China. They have found out that market size, infrastructure, and government policies are important factors for foreign investors to decide which regions to invest in China. Démurger (1998) employed a model of simultaneous equations and confirmed the fundamental role played by foreign investment in provincial economic growth in China and the importance of the potential for future growth to foreign investors. However, none of them have studied the impact of human capital.

In this section, we test empirically the role of human capital in attracting FDI to the regions of China. We include h_p and the h_p-adjusted return rates to capital ($\beta = 0.36$ and $\gamma = 0.40$) in the test, along with the following region-specific variables based on the availability of data: regional share of national total FDI, GDP, industrial output value, fixed investment, freight traffic volume (railway and highway), trade volume, the share of private ownership (other than state and collective) in a region's industrial output value, and the ratio of urban population over total population within a region. The definitions of these variables are described in Table 9.6. The test covers the period 1985–94 for 26 regions of China. Gansu, Hainan, Qinghai, and Tibet are not included due to lack of data. The data are denoted in Chinese currency RMB and deflated by the provincial general retail price index (1990 = 100) wherever applicable.

The expected impact of these explanatory variables on the amount of FDI inflows into a region is analysed as follows. First, gdp_{ns} measures the scale of a regional economy and its size of market relative to the country as a whole. FDI tends to flow to regions with a large scale of economy and a big size of domestic market. $indus_{ns}$ and fix_{n} indicate a region's relative level of industrialization and fixed investment. Higher $indus_{ns}$ and fix_{ns} imply better investment environment. $freight_{ns}$ indicates a region's transportation capacity. Infrastructure facilities such as power supply, telecommunications, highways, railroads, airports, and wharfs are crucial factors for foreign investment. Foreign investors are naturally drawn to regions with better infrastructure conditions. $trade_{ns}$ reflects the degree of trade opening-up. Regions with an open trade policy attract more foreign investment. In sum, the better the conditions defined by gdp_{ns}, $indus_{ns}$, fix_{ns}, $freight_{ns}$, and $trade_{ns}$, the more attractive a regional economy is to foreign investment. Therefore, we expect that gdp_{ns}, $indus_{ns}$, fix_{ns}, $freight_{ns}$, and $trade_{ns}$ are all positively related to fdi_{ns}.

Table 9.6 Description of variables

Dependent Variable	**Definition**	
fdi_{ns}	Regional share in national total FDI	
Independent Variable	**Definition**	**Expected Sign on**
		fdi_{ns}
h_p	The ratio of the total number of graduates from primary schools, secondary schools, and universities over a region's total population	+
$rate_p$	A region's neoclassical return rates to capital adjusted by h_p	+
gdp_{ns}	Regional share in national total GDP	+
$indus_{ns}$	Regional share in national total industrial output value	+
fix_{ns}	Regional share in national total fixed investment	+
$priv_{rs}$	The share of private ownership (other than state and collective) in a region's industrial output value	+
$trade_{ns}$	Regional share of national total trade volume	+
$urban_{rs}$	Ratio of a region's urban population out of its total population	+
$freight_{ns}$	Regional share of national total freight traffic volume (railway and highway)	+

Moreover, $priv_{rs}$ measures the strength of the private economy and indicates the speed of market reforms. Regions with a relatively higher share of industrial output contributed by the private sector have often reformed their economies more extensively and economic transactions are more often market and rule based, and thus more attractive to foreign investors. In a conventional market economy, the scale of urbanization, defined by $urban_{rs}$, is often positively related to foreign investment. Last, foreign investments are expected to flow to regions offering the highest real return rates and highest endowment of human capital, that is, fdi_{ns} should be positively related to h_p and $rate_p$.

Since we need to analyse data over multiple time periods and multiple regions and to capture the variations both within groups and across time, a two-factor time series cross-sectional (TSCS) model is chosen for the empirical test. According to the Hausman test (Hausman, 1978), the fixed effect is selected for our regression results (Table 9.7).

Table 9.7 Regression result

Dependent variable:	fdi_{ns}					
Independent variables:						
h_p	$rate_p$	gdp_{ns}	$indus_{ns}$	fix_{ns}	$priv_{rs}$	$trade_{ns}$
0.05	2.84	0.87	0.25	0.28	0.06	0.03
(3.27)	(3.21)	(4.01)	(1.30)	(2.52)	(4.49)	(3.32)
Number of obs.	260					
R-square	0.94					
Adjusted R-square	0.93					
Hausman test	80.37					

Note: The numbers in parentheses are t-statistics.

First, human capital (h_p) and the adjusted return rates to capital ($rate_p$) have a positive impact on foreign direct investment inflows as expected. 1% of increase in a region's h_p and $rate_p$ induces a 0.05 and 2.84% of increase in its share of national total FDI (fdi_{ns}). This result attests the positive and notable role of human capital in attracting foreign direct investment into a region.

Next, the size of a regional economy and its level of industrialization are determining factors for foreign investment inflows. If gdp_{ns} grows by 1%, fdi_{ns} will go up by 0.87%. When $indus_{ns}$ and fix_{ns} expand by 1%, fdi_{ns} will rise by 0.25 and 0.25% respectively.

The share of the private sector in a region's industrial output value ($priv_{rs}$) also influences fdi_{ns} positively. 1% of increase in $priv_{rs}$ causes fdi_{ns} to increase by 0.06%. Démurger (1998) tested the impact of a region's state share of industrial output value on its FDI inflows and found out they were negatively correlated.

Furthermore, 1% change in $trade_{ns}$ will see a 0.03% of change in fdi_{ns}. Two main effects might serve as an explanation. First, the dynamic effect, that is, the more foreign investment a region attracts, the more foreign trade it conducts, and the more often foreign investment flows back; moreover, the higher the degree of trade openness, the faster the growth of trade, and so the growth of foreign direct investment. Second, the agglomeration effect, that is, people go where others are. The fact that one person is investing in a host region might create an image of a positive future investment environment for the host region, which will attract more investors.

$urban_{rs}$ and $freight_{ns}$ are not identified as influential factors for the regional allocation of foreign investment in China between 1985 and 1994 and thus are not reported in Table 9.7.[11] Such a result seems to be puzzling because in a conventional market economy foreign investment inflows tend to be positively related to its degree of urbanization and transportation capacity. However, an analysis about the special situation in China might render us a conventional explanation. For example, in 1994 the level of urbanization in Jilin province (measured by $urban_{rs}$) was ranked as the second in the nation, advanced only by Guangdong. Yet, Jilin received only 0.9% of national total FDI in the last ten years. In Hubei, Heilongjiang, Guizhou, Anhui, and Shaanxi, $urban_{rs}$ was higher than in Tianjin and Liaoning, yet these five regions received a smaller amount of FDI than most other regions. An explanation for this non-positive correlation between $urban_{rs}$ and fdi_{ns} could be traced to the fact that the high level of $urban_{rs}$ in most of China's regions was achieved during the pre-reform period (before 1979), which might be associated with a strong state sector and tight government control.

In terms of $freight_{ns}$ Sichuan province was ranked second only to Guangdong province in 1994, while Shaanxi province was above Zhejiang, and Henan, Hunan, Anhui, Yunnan, Hubei, Heilongjiang, and Inner Mongolia were ahead of Fujian. However, as in the case of ranking by urbanization, the provinces with a higher $freight_{ns}$ have attracted much less FDI than those with a lower capacity of transportation such as Zhejiang and Fujian. To further capture the freight effect, we conduct two more tests. First, we construct the ratio of a region's freight traffic over its gross domestic product and compare it with the attracted foreign direct investment (to eliminate the bias caused by the size of a region). Shaanxi's freight capacity becomes the highest, followed by Inner Mongolia, Yunnan, Ningxia, and Hubei. However, none of these regions have attracted a large amount of FDI. Furthermore, considering that a high $freight_{ns}$ is often associated with an industrial structure tilted to heavy industries, we insert the ratio of heavy industry output value over total industry output value (production structure variable) in the regression, along with the residuals from a regression of the freight variable on the production structure variable, in order to catch the pure effect of freight. These changes did not significantly alter our regression results. Nevertheless, the condition of infrastructures is an important factor when foreign investors decide whether to invest or not in a region. In this respect, better proxies for infrastructure variables are needed to improve the efficacy of the model.

Overall, human capital has a positive effect on FDI, so do gdp_{ns}, $indus_{ns}$, fix_{ns}, $priv_{rs}$, and $trade_{ns}$.

6 CONCLUSION

Endogenous growth models have built human capital as an endogenous variable into the neoclassical production function. In the case of China, when education level is incorporated into the neoclassical model, the difference in the return rates to capital between Shanghai and *poor* regions has reduced. This result conforms to Lucas's argument (1990) – the important role of human capital in equalizing rates of return to capital between a rich region and a poor region. Moreover, the empirical results prove that foreign direct investment inflows to a region of China are positively related to its level of human capital development, size of market, and growth of private sector.

Human capital accumulation drives economic growth. Low levels of human capital in poor regions affect production internally by reducing the productivity of individual workers and affect production externally by reducing the productivity of other factors. Thus the difference in human capital among regions helps to explain the unbalanced regional pattern of FDI in China.

These findings imply that in order for the middle and western regions to attract foreign investment and for China to achieve a balanced FDI regional distribution, local governments should implement policies focused on affecting the accumulation of human capital and reform their economies to attract foreign investment on competitive terms. However, since poorer regions are poorer, and thus likely to suffer a brain drain to coastal regions and Beijing, funds for a human resource development push should come at least initially from the central government. Moreover, domestic investment will respond favourably to these initiatives as well. In the short run, workers in poor regions may continue to migrate to existing jobs that offer a higher pay, however, in the long run increased FDI should bring jobs to better qualified workers.

NOTES

1. King and Rebelo (1993) have shown that the standard neoclassical growth model predicts post-war return rate differentials of 799% between the US and a sample of poor countries along the transition to a steady state.
2. Romer (1986) expanded the Solow neoclassical growth model by incorporating externalities related to the accumulation of knowledge driven by endogenous policies. Lucas (1988) explicitly identified this as human capital raising productivity within firms, together with externalities raising productivity elsewhere.
3. They are provinces, autonomous regions, and municipalities directly under the administration of the central government.
4. Shenzhen, Zhuhai, Xiamen, and Shantou.
5. China now has five Special Economic Zones (SEZs), 32 Economic and Technological Development Zones, 52 New and High Technology and Industry Development Zones, 13 Border Areas, 14 Border Economic Co-operation Zones, 11 Tourist Resort Areas, and designated Open Coastal Cities, Open Cities along the Yangtze River, Open Border Cities and Open Provincial Capitals.
6. The Chinese-Foreign Equity Joint Ventures, the Law on Chinese-Foreign Co-operative Joint Venture, the Law on Wholly Foreign-Owned Enterprises, and the Income Tax Law Concerning Foreign Invested Enterprises.
7. For ease of use, in the following text we use Regions denoting all the regions in China except Shanghai.
8. As in Lucas (1990) the cross-region comparison is based on the assumption that the external benefits of a region's stock of human capital accrue entirely to producers within that region.
9. Note that Lucas (1990) states $\gamma = 0.36$ but uses $\gamma = 0.40$ in his calculation.
10. For reason of space, these sensitivity results are not listed here.
11. When these two variables are included in the regression, the results remain similar as reported in Table 9.7.

REFERENCES

Agarwal, J.P. (1980), 'Determinants of Foreign Direct Investment: A Survey', *Weltwirtschaftliches Archiv*, 116(4).

Barro, R.J. (1992), 'Human Capital and Economic Growth', Policies for long-run economic growth: A symposium sponsored by the Federal Reserve Bank of Kansas City, *Symposium Series*, pp. 199–216.

Barro, R.J., N.G. Mankiw and X. Salai-Martin (1992), 'Capital Mobility in Neoclassical Models of Growth', *NBER Working Paper*, No. 4206.

Bartelsman, E.J., R.J. Caballero and R.K. Lyons (1991), 'Short and Long Run Externalities', *NBER Working Paper*, No. 3810.

Becky, G., H.L. Young and A. Ordu (1991), 'Foreign Direct Investment in Selected Developing Counties in the Last Two Decades', Washington, DC, The World Bank.

Brewer, T.L. (1991), 'Foreign Direct Investment in Developing Countries: Patterns Polices and Prospects', Washington, DC, The World Bank.

Cass, D. (1965), 'Optimum Growth in an Aggregative Model of Capital Accumulation', *Review of Economic Studies*, 32, pp. 233–40.

Chen, C.H. (1996), 'Regional Determinants of Foreign Direct Investment in Mainland China', *Journal of Economic Studies*, 23(2), pp. 18–30.

Démurger, S. (1998), 'Determinants and Role of Foreign Investment in China: Evidence from Provincial Data', forthcoming in W. Andreff and X. Richet (eds), *Foreign Direct Investment in Transforming Economies*, Edward Edgar, Cheltenham, UK.
Grub, Lin, and Xia (1990), in P. Schran and A.R. Negandhi (eds), 'Research in International Business and International Relations', *China and India: Foreign Investment and Economic Development*, JAI Press Inc., London, pp. 96–97.
Hausman, J. (1978), 'Specification Tests in Econometrics', *Econometrica*, 46, pp. 1251–71.
Hufbauer, G.C. (1975), 'The Multinational Corporation and Direct Investment', in Peter B. Kenen (ed.), *International Trade and Finance: Frontiers for Research*, Cambridge, Cambridge University Press.
King, R.G. and S.T. Rebelo (1993), 'Transitional Dynamics and Economic Growth in the Neoclassical Model', *American Economic Review*, 83, pp. 908–31.
Koopmans, T. (1965), 'On the Concept of Optimal Economic Growth'. The Econometric Approach to Development Planning, North-Holland, Amsterdam, pp. 225–87.
Lu, M.H. (1994), 'Evaluation and Comparison of Investment Environment in Regions of China' (in Chinese), *Economic Studies* (Beijing), 2.
Lu, M.H. (1997), 'Foreign Direct Investment Regional Distribution and China's Investment Environment' (in Chinese), *Economic Studies* (Beijing), 12.
Lucas, R.E. (1988), 'On the Mechanics of Economics Development', *Journal of Monetary Economics*, 22, pp. 3–42.
Lucas, R.E. (1990), 'Why Doesn't Capital Flow from Rich to Poor Countries?', *American Economic Review Papers and Proceedings*, 80, pp. 92–6.
Mankiw N.G., D. Romer and D.N. Weil (1992), 'A Contribution to the Empirics of Economic Growth', *Quarterly Journal of Economics*, 107(2), pp. 407–37.
Pfefferman, G.P. and A. Madarassy (1994), 'Trends in Private Investment in Developing Countries', International Finance Corporation, Discussion Paper, No. 14, Washington, DC, The World Bank/International Finance Company.
Ratcliffe, R.C. (1994), '*Why Doesn't Capital Flow From Rich to Poor Countries? An Evaluation of Lucas' Evidence*', Global Economic Research, Bankers Trust Company, New York.
Romer, P. (1986), 'Increasing Returns and Long-Run Growth', *Journal of Political Economy*, October, pp. 1002–37.
Romer, P. (1990), 'Endogenous Technological Change', *Journal of Political Economy*, 98(5), October, pp. S71–S102.
Romer, P. (1994), 'The Origins of Endogenous Growth', *Journal of Economic Perspectives*, 8(1), pp. 1–23.
Solow, R. (1956), 'A Contribution to the Theory of Economic Growth', *Quarterly Journal of Economics*, 70, pp. 65–94.
UNCTC (United Nations Centre on Transitional Corporations) (1972), 'Government Policies and Foreign Direct Investment', UNCTC Current Studies, Series A, No. 17, New York: United Nations.
Wei, S.J. (1995), 'Attracting Foreign Direct Investment: Has China Reached Its Potential?', *China Economic Review*, 6(2), pp. 187–99.

10. Foreign direct investment, human capital and catching up: the Chinese case

Olivier Jammes

1 INTRODUCTION

Many studies have already focused on the outstanding results of China regarding economic growth, most of them being empirical. Many research streams have been explored in order to explain how the most populated country in the world, running under a planned economy and initially closed, or almost, has been benefiting from such a success in terms of economic growth for the last 20 years.

This chapter focuses on the mechanisms through which foreign direct investment (FDI) may promote economic growth in the Chinese provinces. Our approach deviates somehow from the literature regarding this issue. Indeed, FDI is generally considered either as local investments, or as imports of technologically more advanced goods within the framework of international trade theory. While the estimated growth functions may differ, all these works treat FDI, empirically, as annual flows. This approach can been seen as being incomplete since one essential and specific aspect of FDI is left out: the embodied or joined knowledge which can lead to a diffusion process within the beneficiary economy, a process whose achievement is both cumulative and time consuming. This acknowledgement prompted us to introduce FDI not only as annual flows, so as to take in account their short-term impact on growth (just like local investment), but also as a cumulated form (through a specific indicator especially developed for this chapter) so as to take into account the new incorporated knowledge which can diffuse according to a long-term process.

Moreover, we consider, just as the catching up theory does, that FDI impact on growth may vary depending on the technological level already attained by the beneficiary economy. Considering the difficulties in measuring this technological level, especially for a developing country, as well as the available variables at the provincial level in the case of China, we use an indicator of the available human capital level as a proxy for this technological level. Therefore, we introduce multiplicative variables in order to estimate the joint effect of FDI and human capital on economic growth. Final results, even if one can consider them as counter-intuitive, are consistent with the catching up theory.

Finally, we share the idea that underdevelopment is defined by a knowledge deficit which reduction can allow for rapid growth gains (P. Romer, 1993).

Results may confirm that FDI has played a crucial role on the growth of Chinese provinces through two distinct channels:

- On one side, a direct short-term effect, widely studied in the literature, which can be considered as a Keynesian effect (increase of the available investment for the economy);
- On the other side, an indirect, cumulative and longer-term effect of FDI on growth, linked to positive externalities.

Moreover, results seem to indicate quite a complex relation between FDI, human capital and growth. Indeed, if these two variables have, each being taken separately, a positive impact on the growth of the Chinese provinces, human capital can, indirectly, play negatively by diminishing the positive impact of FDI through the reduction of the technological gap. In other words, the lower the available human capital level, the more benefits in terms of growth can be provided by FDI, if the minimal absorption capability level is reached. These results may legitimate, under certain conditions, the use of FDI as a mean of rapid development.

The first section gathers some stylized facts regarding growth, FDI inflows and human capital in China. In the second section, a brief statement of the theory is set out as well as our theoretical assumptions. Finally, the third section presents our empirical methodology and the econometric results.

2 FOREIGN DIRECT INVESTMENT, HUMAN CAPITAL AND GROWTH IN THE CHINESE PROVINCES: SOME STYLIZED FACTS

The main characteristic of the general trend regarding inflows of FDI to China between 1979 and 1995 is its tremendous rate of growth. This phenomenon is one of the more impressive consequences of the course change decided by the Chinese authorities, from a planned and introverted policy to a market economy open to the rest of the world. The annual total amount of FDI inflows has been rising without a break from US$109 million in 1979 to US$37 521 billion in 1995, which represents an annual average growth rate of 44%. Thus, in less than 20 years, China has become the first destination for FDI among developing countries, and the second largest recipient in the world after the USA. Together with high economic growth and booming external trade, FDI has exposed and integrated the Chinese economy to the rest of the world. This opening process has been done through a step by step process, because of both the concern of the local authorities to experiment with the market economy on a small scale, and because of the initial fears of foreign investors regarding this new open market, fears that have softened over time thanks to the positive evolution of reforms towards them.

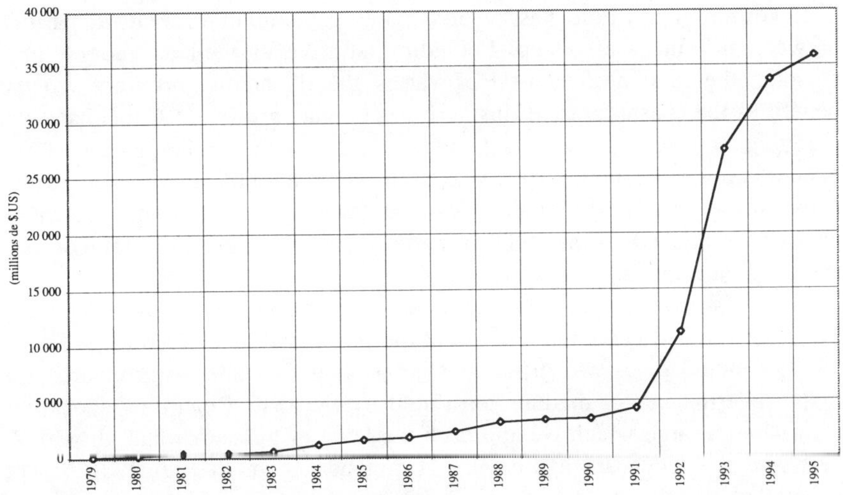

Source: The World Bank, World Tables, 1998.

Figure 10.1 *Annual inflows of foreign direct investment to China*

One may also notice a change in the shares of FDI inflows according to their geographical origin, as shown by Figure 10.2. During the first years of openess, industrial countries (USA, Europe and Japan) on the one hand, and the new industrialized Asian countries (NIAC) as well as the ASEAN countries on the other hand, shared investment to China about equally (respectively 42 and 52%), the rest of the world representing a very small share of the total flows (less than 10%). From this moment, the share of the former has been continually decreasing to the benefit of the latter group of countries, with the rest of thc world maintaining about the same share. This evolution has been taking place in two steps: during the 1986–91 period, the share of industrialized countries fell to under 30%, and at the end of the 1991–95 period, they represented only 20% of the total flows, while Asian countries counted for 75%. However, this distribution, which is calculated from Chinese official statistics, may not reveal the reality of FDI inflows accurately. Indeed, a fair amount of FDI originating from industrialized countries transits through Asia (Hong Kong in particular) before being effectively invested in China. Their real origin is therefore not taken into account. Moreover, part of recorded FDI is in fact Chinese investments which are subject to a round-tripping operation, in order to enjoy the special benefits granted by local authorities to FDI (this phenomenon represented 25% of total FDI in 1992, according to a World Bank non-published study).

If China as a whole has received a huge amount of FDI, disparities between provinces are deep. For administrative as well as geographical reasons, the total amount of FDI varies greatly among provinces to the benefit of the coastal areas. Considering economic growth, if China has been enjoying an impressive annual average rate since the beginning of the openness reforms (about 10% a year), one can again notice strong disparities between the provinces. Figure 10.3 shows for 27 provinces (those for which data are available over the 1982–96 period) the total amount of FDI received, and the annual average growth rate.

Point distribution may allow consideration of a positive relation between FDI received and economic growth at the provincial level. Démurger (1996, 1997) concluded, in two different studies, that FDI are, with exports, the major determinants of medium-term industrial growth. Regarding education, a variable through which we approach the level of human capital, disparities between provinces are again very strong as shown in Figure 10.4. The calculated variable is the number of people who attended secondary and higher education, for 1000 people. This ratio is for example three times higher for Beijing than for the Yunnan province. It is worth noticing that Beijing, Shanghai, Liaoning and Tianjin, which have been facing poor performances in terms of economic growth relative to other provinces, are also those which enjoy the highest ratios of highly educated persons. This remark, which could be interpreted as paradoxical, is at the heart of the set of problems developed in this chapter.

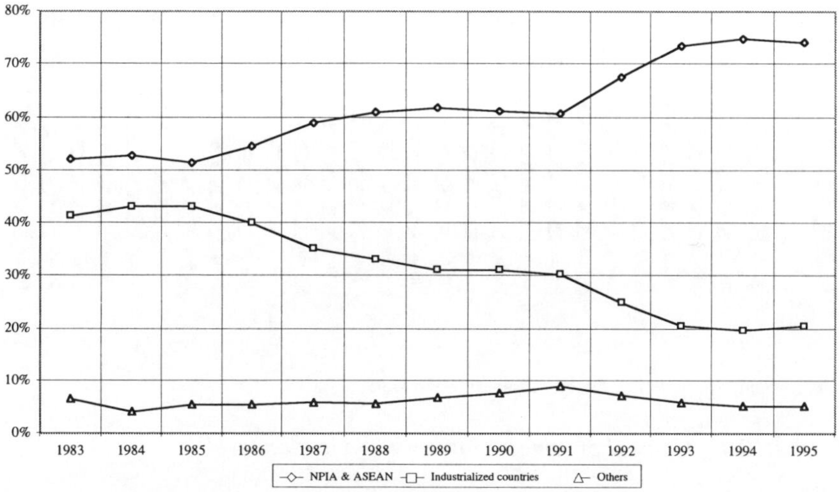

Source: Chinese statistical directory, several years.

Figure 10.2 China: Evolution of FDI inflows by origin

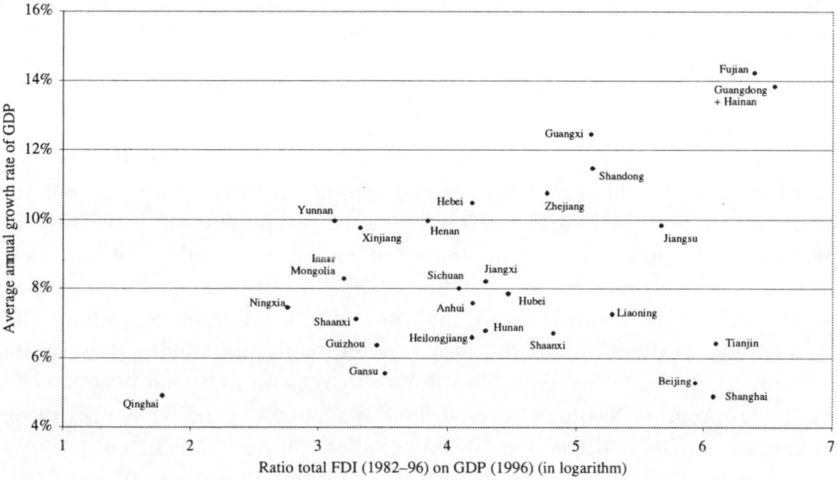

Source: Chinese statistical directory, several years.

Figure 10.3 Chinese provinces: Average annual growth rates and total FDI received

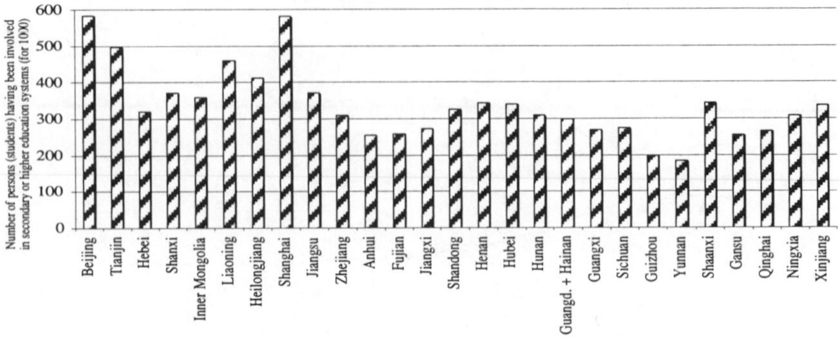

Source: Chinese statistical directory, several years.

Figure 10.4 Chinese provinces: Advanced education level

3 THEORETICAL ASPECTS

If technical progress was already involved in the neoclassical model (Solow, 1956), it suffered from two assumptions, theoretically questioned and refuted by number of empirical studies: the exogenous nature of technical progress and its steadiness around the world.

The new theories of endogenous growth (from the seminal works of Romer, 1986 and Lucas, 1988) have put these two assumptions into question. If Solow remains sceptical regarding several points of this theoretical stream, he admits that '... the real value of endogenous growth theory will emerge from its attempt to model the endogenous component of technological progress as an integral part of the theory of economic growth' (Solow, 1994). Among others, Romer emphasizes that technical progress has a dual impact on growth: it acts directly on the production function by raising the productivity of other inputs, but also acts indirectly, by making new capital investment opportunities possible through increasing marginal productivity. Technical progress has thus become the key element of the debate regarding economic growth, and has been widely studied. However, technical progress or the technological level (its equivalent in terms of stock) are subject to various definitions, more or less restrictive. We embrace here the widest definition: technical progress is made of all the elements that allow for an increase of production for an unchanged quantity of inputs (capital and labour).

Although many local factors have been identified which affect the technological level attained by an economy, external factors induced by international relations have also been taken into account. Thus, many works have focused on the diffusion of technical progress, most of them within the framework of international trade, namely through the imports of more advanced goods. Over the last years, growing interest has been devoted to the role of FDI as a source of financing, due to the slowdown of international aid flows. These theoretical studies can be divided into three major groups:

- One group focuses more on the determinants of FDI than on their consequences on growth. It uses the industrial organization theory (Hymer, 1960) or the eclectic theory (OLI) (Dunning, 1981) and tries to explain why firms do invest overseas to produce the same goods that are already produced locally. They answer that FDI takes place when goods or input markets are imperfect or when multinational companies (MNCs) enjoy specific benefits: they finally tell us more about the behaviour of MNCs than about the consequences for the beneficiary economy.
- The issue of the role of FDI is also often treated as the issue of trade openness. Indeed, authors use, in this case, the standard theory of international trade (MacDougall, 1960; Kemp, 1966). However, it appears to us that there are fundamental differences between the consequences of a bare openness to international trade and openness to FDI, among other reasons because international trade theories deal with the physical capital deficit issue (the well-known 'object gap' of Romer, 1993) rather than with knowledge deficit (the 'idea gap').
- Endogenous growth models like the one developed by Borensztein and De Gregorio (1994) give more emphasis to openness to international trade than they really give to the specific characteristics of FDI. Moreover, their results are more or less identical to those of Romer's initial model, regarding the equilibrium growth rate.

Nevertheless, one can find in an older literature some attempts at formalization focusing directly on the role of FDI on technological transfers and economic growth. Indeed, Gomulka (1971, 1990), Koizumi and Kopecky (1977), Findlay (1978), and Rodriguez (1981) among others have considered FDI as an essential vector and developed a brand of original models regarding this issue. They make use of the catching up assumption regarding the international diffusion of technical progress generally attributed to Veblen (1915) and Gershenkron (1962). According to this assumption, the wider the technological gap between source and beneficiary countries, the easier productivity gains are to be realized. As noted by Findlay, the disparity must not be too wide in order not to fall in a 'cargo cult' situation in which there cannot be any technology transfer, because of the lack of absorption capability. The rate of technical progress of the FDI host country depends, in these models, on the technological gap with the financing source country and on the penetration rate of the latter in the local economy. This assumption has recently been introduced in some more sophisticated models with intermediary goods, on the basis of the works of Grossman and Helpman (1991) (Barro and Sala-i-Martin, 1997, for example). Yet, the core idea remains the same: the catching up rate slows down as the gap is filled because of the increase of imitation costs. These models are thus more closely attuned to the issue of knowledge deficit as defined by Romer (1993).

This chapter, first and foremost empirical, stands within the catching up theory. A simple neoclassical production function with technical progress is used:

$$Y = AF(K,L) \tag{10.1}$$

were Y is production, K the physical capital, L is labour, and A is technical progress. F() is a Cobb–Douglas function endowed with all the classical properties.

Within the neoclassical framework, technical progress has the following form:

$$A_t = A_0 e^{at} \tag{10.2}$$

where:

A_t: the technological level attained at date t;

A_0: the initial technological level (supposed equal to 1 for simplification)

a: the technical progress rate that is assumed to be exogenous.

This leads us to the well-known result in terms of product growth rate:

$$GY = \frac{dY}{dt.Y} = a + \alpha.GK + (1-\alpha).GL$$

We focus now on the role played by FDI on the value of the a coefficient. Let us assume that for the rest of the world (or at least for FDI source countries of the host country considered) the technological level function can be written:

$$H_t = H_0 e^{ht} \tag{10.3}$$

with the same characteristics as previously.

For a closed economy, the *a* coefficient is given constant, such as $a < h$. Indeed, we consider the case of a developing country which does not have enough means to compete with the rest of the world, and more particularly industrialized countries, regarding research and development activities. We can even assume that $A_t < H_t$, for each $t > 0$. Thus, the technological gap between the closed economy and the rest of the world increases with time.

$$\frac{H_{t+1}}{A_{t+1}} > \frac{H_t}{A_t}; \forall t \tag{10.4}$$

Equation (10.4) can show how, *ceteris paribus*, differences in technical progress alone may explain the growth rate gap between a closed developing country and the rest of the world. Moreover, considering that technical progress has a multiplicative effect on the accumulation of physical capital, this growth rate difference would be more than proportional. Thus, this result may simply explain the lack of convergence between economies if the required conditions for technical progress in developing countries are not present (weakness in research and development activities, shortfall in human capital investment and/or in international economic relations).

Let us consider now the case where the economy will open and benefit from FDI inflows, as has been the case for China since 1979. We shall use the catching up assumption we have seen before. We thus consider that a stock of new knowledge is associated with an inflow of FDI, knowledge that will spread in the host economy. This diffusion requires time while stock of new knowledge lasts, or in other words until knowledge has been diffused throughout the whole economy.

FDI operations are likely to imply technology transfers (embodied in the equipment provided by the foreign investor) and easier access to new markets (thanks to international contacts provided by the foreign partner), but they also obviously lead to an improvement in capabilities in many fields within the firm. Indeed, not only must the technical staff be trained to use new equipment, the workers in charge of production must also take into account new constraints for production in order to improve productivity and final product quality, managerial staff have to learn new management and marketing standards, and so on. Types of training range from learning by doing, through seminars, to formal overseas training sessions with the parent company according to the capabilities required. Gerschenberg (1978) studies enterprises with foreign capital settled in Kenya and concludes that they offer more training to their staff than local private firms. Chen (1983) indicates, in a study regarding technology transfer in Hong Kong, that the major contribution of enterprises running with foreign investment in the industrial sector is staff training rather than production of new techniques and products. These new capabilities can then diffuse in the rest of the local economy when the workers move to new firms or set up their own businesses. Katz (1987) notes in the case of Latin America that local firm managers often started their careers in firms with foreign capital where they were trained.

Moreover, foreign investor entrance leads to some indirect effects for the rest of the economy. Enterprises financed by FDI may contribute to increasing efficiency in other firms:

- local enterprises competing with the new foreign capital firm have to adapt themselves to remain competitive (Caves, 1971; Jenkins, 1990);
- local enterprises competing directly with the new foreign capital firm, and probably, although to a lesser extent, those working in other fields of activity, benefit from a demonstration effect. This is what King and Robson (1992) call 'learning by watching';
- Lall (1980) identifies upstream externalities to the benefit of suppliers (assistance for the setting up of production infrastructure, technical support and information in order to improve product quality, management training and assistance, support for diversification outlets and so on);
- Blomström (1991) finds downstream externalities to the benefit of customers, thanks to the price fall of intermediate goods and/or their higher quality or technological content.

Thus, FDI implies positive externalities through both learning by doing (Arrow, 1962) and learning by watching (King and Robson, 1992). The first situation is to the benefit of local firms which are in contact with foreign capital firms (suppliers, customers) and to the benefit of their staff while the second situation benefits firms in competition or any enterprise which has the opportunity to observe the way in which FDI-financed firms function.

Therefore, if the introduction of FDI annual inflows in a growth function, as generally treated in the literature, is necessary to take into account the direct impact of FDI, in terms of additional investment capability, this methodology may appear inadequate to measure all the benefits attributable to FDI that we have just reviewed. This explains why it has been decided to introduce in the following econometric study not only FDI annual inflows but also an additional indicator in order to take in account the longer term and indirect effect of FDI on economic growth. These two different aspects of the role of FDI legitimate the use of two different variables.

In order to take into account the FDI effect on the increase of the technological level and the fact that diffusion takes time, we have produced an original indicator of FDI efficiency in terms of spillovers. It is a dispersion indicator which penalizes more recent investments. Indeed, the more recent FDI is, the less time there is for embodied knowledge to be diffused. This indicator can be interpreted, conceptually, as the inverse of a capital depreciation indicator. The general formulation is:

$$\Phi_t = \sum_{i=t-x}^{t} \left(IED_i - \sum_{j=i}^{t} IED_j \right)^2$$

For a given year *t*, the Φ_t coefficient will be the weaker, the more recently FDI has occurred during the *t-x* to *t* considered period, in comparison with the total amount of FDI received during the same period (and vice versa). In order to make this indicator more easily interpretable, it is normalized thanks to the following transformation:

$$SO = \frac{(x+1).IT^2 - \Phi}{(x+1).IT^2}$$

with

$$IT = \sum_{i=t-x}^{t} IE_i$$

Thus, 0 and 1 always bound the *SO* coefficient. According to this formulation:

- The best allocation is: $IED_{t-x} = IT\ (IED_i = 0; \forall i \neq t-x)$, all FDI occur during the first year of the period for which $\Phi = 0$, and which implies $SO = 1$.
- The worst allocation is: $IED_t = IT\ (IED_i = 0; \forall i \neq t)$, all FDI occur during the last year of the period for which $\Phi = x.IT^2$, which implies $SO = 0$.

Finally, to take into account the fact that the more the host economy is linked to the rest of the world, the more important spillover opportunities are, the efficiency indicator is multiplied by the ratio sum of FDI inflows for the *t-x* to *t* period on production in *t*. This ratio is therefore an indicator of openness to FDI by analogy with indicators of trade openness.

$$SOINDEX_t = \frac{\sum_{i=t-x}^{t} IE_i}{Y_t} \times \frac{\left((x+1) \times \sum_{i=t-x}^{t} IE_i\right)^2 - \Phi}{\left((x+1) \times \sum_{i=t-x}^{t} IE_i\right)^2}$$

One may notice that if FDI of the current year *t* are included in the calculation, these are weighted by a zero coefficient in terms of diffusion.

According to our assumptions, the rate of technical progress *a* in equation (10.2) is an increasing function of *SOINDEX* and a decreasing function of the technological gap.

It is impracticable to measure precisely the technological level attained by an economy. We have here considered, as is often done, that the level of human capital should be a good proxy of the technological level. Considering the available variables for the Chinese provinces, we use an education variable including higher and secondary education levels, which are supposed to be representative of the technological capability. Indeed, the level of primary education cannot be considered as a good indicator of the technological level considering that it is a minimum knowledge level (which is thus irrelevant to the technological level reached by the economy). Moreover, the value of this variable is quite homogeneous whatever the level of development of the economy is. In the case of China, primary education is compulsory for all. However, the proportion of persons having received at least a secondary education in the total population seems to be a good proxy for the technological level.

It is even more difficult to measure the average technological level of FDI source countries to China. It has been assumed that during the considered period this level was constant. This simplification should not be of consequence for the results since this average foreign technological level (which is the numerator of the ratio H_t/A_t) is the same for all provinces. Therefore, the technological gap is measured by the level of higher education of each province, which can be considered to give a good idea of the level of knowledge in each province.

4 MODEL AND ECONOMETRIC RESULTS

Chinese data, at least at the provincial level, require quite deep reprocessing since series are either interrupted or have their definition changed over time. Moreover, the small number of series actually available has led us to restrain the study within the 1986–96 period and to put aside some variables which could have completed or sharpened the analysis.

Our cross-section sample has been split into two sub-periods, 1986–91 and 1991–96, initially for statistical reasons, since the number of provinces for which all data were available for the 1986–96 period was too small. But this division is also justified by the evolution of the economic environment. First, FDI profiles have been modified from 1991 if one considers their distribution by origin (compare Figure 10.2) since the share of the new industrial Asian countries has been rising during the second sub-period. Since this noticeable modification in the origin of FDI implies a difference in the average associated technological level, it can be relevant to take this phenomenon into account by splitting the sample and using a dummy variable (0 for 1986–91, 1 for 1991–96). On the other side, the Chinese economy has been facing structural changes between the two periods, such as a sharp fall of its nominal effective exchange rate from 1991 and the restructuring of public enterprise.

The following equation will be tested:

$$GYREG = c + \alpha.GLF + \beta.LI + \chi.RTFDI + \delta.SOINDEX + \varphi.SHK + \gamma.GHK \\ + \lambda.RTFDI \times SKH + \mu.SOINDEX \times GHK + \nu.Y_0 + \sigma.DUM + \varepsilon$$

The regression has been estimated with the ordinary least squares method with White correction. Variables are the following:

GYREG: the annual average growth rate for each province and under each sub-period, using the World Bank method (estimation by fitting a least squares linear regression trend line to the logarithmic annual values of the variable in the relevant period). A six-year average is used in order to stand within the long-term neoclassical framework, and to limit the impact of short-term economic fluctuations;

GLF: the annual average rate of growth of the labour force (total number of employees), for each province and under each sub-period;

LI: the annual average of the ratio of local investments to GDP for each province and under each sub-period;

TFDI: the annual average ratio of FDI to GDP for each province and under each sub-period; this will allow us to compare this variable with *GLF* in order to see if FDI has a direct effect on growth significantly different from local investments;

RTFDI: the same variable as *TFDI* but controlled for the effect of *SOINDEX* (the two variables being closely connected); this variable is used in regressions where *SOINDEX* is also introduced;

SOINDEX: the spillover indicator defined above; according to our assumptions, this variable should allow us to detect potential indirect and longer-term effects on economic growth;

SHK: the stock of human capital at the beginning of the period, calculated as the number of persons having received secondary or higher education for one thousand persons; this variable is used as a proxy for the technological level of each province;

GHK: the growth rate of human capital calculated as the annual average growth rate of *SHK*;

Y_0: the initial per capita GDP in order to take in account a potential convergence phenomenon;

DUM1: a dummy variable which takes the value 0 for the first sub period (1986–91) and 1 for the second (1991–96);

Finally, two multiplicative variables have been introduced in order to take in account joint effects of FDI inflows and technological level (approached through the education level). These two variables are supposed to allow for testing the catching up assumption through two different approaches:

TFDI_SHK: should allow for measuring FDI annual inflow productivity according to the human capital stock of each province: *TFDI_SHK* = *RTFDI* × *SHK*. The issue raised here is whether a difference in the stock of human capital may imply difference in the impact of FDI on economic growth;

SO_GHK: is used to measure indirect effects of FDI according to the development of the level of human capital: *SO_VHK* = *SOINDEX* × *GHK;* this variable should allow us to estimate how externalities generated by cumulated FDI are diffusing according to the development of the level of local human capital.

These variables should allow us to confront on the one hand the catching up theory, which supposes that FDI is the more productive the lower the human capital level, and on the other hand the capability absorption assumption, which implies that FDI is the more efficient the higher the human capital level. The multiplicative variable should allow a more direct test on the issue of catching up, while the second is much more oriented towards the issue of substitutability between knowledge coming from FDI and knowledge generated by the local education system.

Thus, this equation uses a number of variables usually employed within the framework of the empirical study of growth. Its originality comes from the joint analysis of the impact of FDI and human capital on growth. Unlike a good number of studies, FDI is not only introduced through annual flows with a one year lag (*t*-1), but also as a sum of the period inflows and weighted by an efficiency coefficient in terms of diffusion. Chung et al. (1995), considering the role of FDI on China's economic development have used, as is often the case, FDI with a one year lag, but they admit that this choice is highly subjective and that rigorously speaking, determination of the necessary lag for FDI to have an impact on GDP remains an unsolved empirical issue. Therefore, a different approach has been adopted in this chapter.

Results appear rather strong. Indeed, adjusted R^2 of the different regressions are reasonably high which indicates that our model offers a good explanation level. Moreover, we have used several White correction formulas proposed by Davidson and MacKinnon (1993) and none of them has put the stability of our results into question. Finally, all the tests carried out (variable omission, Chow test, Ramsey-Reset test) have confirmed that the formulation used is both justified and robust. Results are summarized in Table 10.1.

Regression 1

This first regression comprises only additive explanatory variables. Variables traditionally used in growth models are not significant (labour force, local investment, initial per capita revenue, human capital stock) or even not of the expected sign (local investment and human capital stock are negative). Regarding local investment, this issue has been underlined in several studies focusing on China, and is generally explained by the low actual efficiency of local investment in China. The fact that the labour force variable is not significant has been highlighted by several authors (Guillaumont and Boyreau Debray, 1996, for example) and can be explained by problems in measuring the labour force in China, particularly at the province level. Indeed, *floating workers* are not taken into account by official statistics. For the initial per capital revenue, the last studies which have taken into account the new GDP deflator (just as we have done) have led to the same result.

Table 10.1 Econometric results

Dependant Variable: GYREG – 56 Observations – OLS with White correction				
Variable	Reg. 1	Reg. 2	Reg. 3	Reg. 4
C	-0.016	0.097	-0.078	-0.079
	(74%)	(0%)	(14%)	(14%)
GLF	0.287	0.304	0.283	0.345
	(58%)	(59%)	(55%)	(42%)
LI	-0.015	-0.081	-0.028	0.033
	(81%)	(18%)	(66%)	(58%)
TFDI		0.942		
		(0%)		
RTFDI	0.846			2.154
	(9%)			(0%)
SOINDEX	0.192		1.828	3.756
	(2%)		(2%)	(0%)
Y_0	1.3^E-06	1.2^E-05	-3.5^E-06	1.1^E-05
	(75%)	(13%)	(46%)	(1%)
GHK	0.636		0.999	0.954
	(2%)		(0%)	(0%)
SHK	-3.5^E-0.5	-7.2^E-05		-9.4^E-05
	(57%)	(25%)		(14%)
SO_GHK			-8.618	-15.713
			(3%)	(0%)
TIED_SHK		-0.002		-0.003
		(15%)		(2%)
DUM	0.017	0.028	0.018	0.014
	(3%)	(0%)	(3%)	(11%)
Adjusted R^2	0.538	0.515	0.543	0.628
Stat. Proba.	0%	0%	0%	0%

Note: Percentages between brackets under each coefficient are statistical probabilities for each variable.

However, the human capital growth variable (*VHK*) is positive and highly significant; this result confirms the major role played by human capital in economic growth. Nevertheless, the human capital stock variable is not significant (as in the following regressions). This can be explained by the way this variable has been constructed. Indeed, it has been produced according to the permanent inventory method but with no data prior to 1985 which is a rather short period. Finally, the two variables related to FDI are significant and have the expected sign (positive). Thus, it appears that FDI has positive and significant effects on the growth of Chinese provinces: a direct and short-term effect through the *RTFDI* variable (Keynesian effect) and an indirect and longer-term effect through the *SOINDEX* variable (knowledge diffusion).

Regression 2

In this second regression, we focus on the impact of annual FDI inflows on economic growth and on their interactivity with the stock of human capital. With this aim in view, we introduce not only the annual FDI inflows and human capital stock variables through an additive way in the regression, but also a multiplicative variable of these two indicators. The latter should allow us to measure the effect of the joint impact, in other words the impact of FDI annual inflows on the growth of the Chinese provinces depending on the stock of human capital.

As expected, the model loses slightly in terms of overall significance (the adjusted R^2 falls) with the removal of *SOINDEX* and *GHK,* but this intermediary stage has been presented in order to clarify the different effects (short and long-term) of FDI on growth. One should notice that *RTFDI* has been replaced by *TFDI,* which is the same indicator but not controlled for the effect of *SOINDEX* since the latter does not appear in this regression. Variables that were not significant in the first regression remain non-significant (even if some of them benefit from an increase of their statistical probability). The inflow variable (*TFDI*) greatly improves its significance (probability of 0%), so does the dummy variable (*DUM*). Moreover, the multiplicative variable *TFDI_SHK* (equals to *TFDI* × *SHK*) should allow us to assess the impact of annual FDI inflows on the growth of the Chinese provinces, according to level of human capital, that is, the direct short-term impact of FDI on growth depending on the level of human capital. Thus, depending on the sign obtained, we will be able to assess if, for an equivalent amount of FDI, a more or less high level of human capital allows for a more or less substantial gain in terms of economic growth. This variable is not significant at the moment (15% probability), but one can notice that the sign is negative, which is consistent with the catching up theory.

Regression 3

The idea here is the same as in the previous regression: to focus on a particular aspect of the impact of FDI on growth, on long-term effects this time. Compared with regression 2, we have reintroduced *SOINDEX* and removed all variables regarding FDI annual inflows and human capital stock (*TFDI*, *SHK*, *TFDI_SHK*). As in regression 2, non-significant variables of regression 1 are still non-significant. Results allow us not to reject the assumption according to which FDI has a positive longer-term effect on growth, since the variable *SOINDEX* is both positive and strongly significant. Moreover, they corroborate the major role played by the growth of human capital (here estimated by *GHK*) since this variable is both positive and very significant.

The multiplicative variable *SO_GHK* (equal to *SOINDEX* × *GHK*) should allow us to assess for longer-term externalities, following from the use of FDI jointly with the evolution of human capital. This particular formulation has been chosen in order to assess if an increase over time of the level of human capital leads to an improvement or a deterioration of externality diffusion following from FDI inflows. This boils down to a kind of substitutability test. This variable is negative and strongly significant. This can be interpreted as follows: the less human capital has increased, the higher are the gains from long-term FDI generated externalities, in other words the substitutability assumption cannot be rejected. One could say that in the case of Chinese provinces, high knowledge progress can be achieved through two separate and alternative channels: either through a traditional way via the local education system (*GHK* is a measure of the evolution of the population share having received higher education), or thanks to knowledge embodied in or coming with FDI through a learning by doing process.

Regression 4

In this final regression, all effects are combined: short and long-term effects of FDI, human capital stock and variation effects, FDI–human capital joint effects.

The simultaneous introduction of all variables improves the significance of our model (adjusted R^2 grows to 0.628) and none of the tests implemented (variable oversight, Chow test and Ramsey-Reset test) reveal any problem.

Even if variables traditionally used in growth functions remain non-significant (*LF*, *LI*, *SHK*) or of non-expected signs (Y_0 positive but close to zero, *SHK* negative but statistically not-different from zero), it has already been indicated that these results were common in the case of studies regarding China, or justified by some construction issues.

However, all results related to variables on FDI (*RTFDI* and *SOINDEX*), human capital stock growth (*GHK*), and FDI-human capital joint effect (*SO_GHK* and *TFDI_SHK*) are significant and consistent with our predictions.

To summarize, one may observe:

- Annual FDI inflows (*RIED*) have direct and short-term positive impacts on economic growth. This result stands apart from a number of studies which find marginal or even no effect of FDI on growth (Sigh, 1988, for example on a sample of 73 developing countries, or Hein, 1992, on a sample of 41 developing countries).
- Our indicator *SOINDEX* (cumulated and weighted FDI) is also very significant and positive. This allows us not to reject the assumption that FDI has indirect and longer-term effects on growth, apart from the short-term effects of increasing production capacity, related to the externality diffusion phenomenon. We have tried to introduce the total sum of inflows (always for a 6-year period) without any weighting within intermediary regressions. This variable was highly significant and positive also, but less than our *SOINDEX* variable. We have also made the attempt to introduce all past FDI inflows (not only for the last 6 years) but this variable did not return significance which lets us assume that there is actually a phenomenon of 'drying up' of externalities generated by FDI inflows and that it is not the investment stock which is relevant.
- Human capital improvement (measured by *GHK*) has a positive effect on economic growth. This usual result implies no particular comment.
- The use of the multiplicative variable *FDI_SHK* allows us to conclude that FDI is more effective in the short term where the knowledge gap is wider, in accordance with the catching up theory. But this result should have just reflected the fact that FDI in China is oriented to labour-intensive activity with low human capital endowment. From this assessment, we have tested the role of the human capital level on FDI inflows but no correlation has been statistically detected between these two variables. Thus, from a statistical point of view, FDI does not seem to be particularly attracted by provinces with lower endowment of human capital.
- Finally, the negative sign of the multiplicative variable *SO_GHK* leads us to conclude that the weaker the human capital generated by the local education system, the greater the long-term gains (knowledge diffusion) coming from cumulated FDI will be. We consider this result as a form of substitutability between diffusion of knowledge generated by the Chinese education system on the one hand, and learning by doing within activities financed by FDI on the other hand.

5 CONCLUSION

China has been enjoying, since the beginning of its economic policy reforms and notably openness reform, an impressive annual average growth rate and this chapter was an attempt to show the crucial role played both by FDI inflows and the level of human capital in this process.

However, this average rate for China as a whole hides deep disparities between provinces, not only concerning economic growth, but also in terms of FDI inflows and human capital level. The econometric study has shed light on the crucial role of FDI in growth, either directly or indirectly, through generated externalities. We have made an attempt to assess two distinct effects (short and long term) of FDI on economic growth. Moreover, results suggest, thanks to multiplicative variables that have been introduced, that the lower the human capital level is, the more efficient FDI is (assuming the existence of absorption capability). This should encourage this kind of investment in developing countries with low human capital endowment, even bearing in mind that China is a special case. Indeed, this country benefit from the required absorption capability in order for knowledge transfer to take place.

But results also let us foresee a natural slowdown of Chinese growth as the economy moves closer to the technological frontier. Thus, it seems important that the Chinese authorities stimulate local research and development to make China achieve innovator status. However, even once China has reached this new position, foreign economic relations in general and FDI inflows in particular will still matter in order that China continues to benefit from externalities and to maintain absorption of the knowledge gap.

Finally, one may consider, even if the tested growth equation is not expressed in per capita values, that these results may explain the convergence process. Indeed, it appears that economies converge insofar as they reach a common technological frontier. This conclusion accords with Guillaumont and Boyreau Debray (1996) who considered this possibility in a study regarding convergence of Chinese provinces.

Even if this study has helped us to better understand the complex relations between FDI, human capital and growth in the case of the Chinese provinces, many points still have to be clarified. Future work should focus, among other issues, on the functional formulation of the spillover indicator in order to specify its dynamics. Moreover, it will be useful to analyse the differentiated impact of FDI according to its origin in order better to understand what stands behind the dummy variable we have used. Finally, we will have to go deeper into the relationship between FDI and human capital.

REFERENCES

Aitken, B. and A. Harrison (1994), 'Do Domestic Firms Benefit from Foreign Direct Investment? Evidence from Panel Data', Policy Research Working Paper No. 1248, The World Bank.

Arrow, K. (1962), 'The Economic Implications of Learning by Doing', *Review of Economic Studies*, 29, pp. 155–73.

Barro, R. Jr. and X. Sala-i-Martin (1995), *Economic Growth*, New York: McGraw-Hill.

Barro, R. Jr. and X. Sala-i-Martin (1997), 'Technological Diffusion, Convergence, and Growth', *Journal of Economic Growth*, 2, pp. 1–26.

Blomström, M. (1991), 'Host Country Benefits of Foreign Investment', in D.G. McFetridge, ed., *Foreign Investment, Technology and Economic Growth*, Toronto and London: Toronto University Press.

Blomström, M. and A. Kokko (1997), 'How Foreign Investment Affects Host Countries', Policy Research Working Paper No. 1745, The World Bank.

Borensztein, E. and J. De Gregorio (1994), 'How Does Foreign Investment Affect Economic Growth?', Working Paper No. 94/110, International Monetary Fund.

Caves, R. (1971), 'International Corporations: The Industrial Economics of Foreign Investment', *Economica*, 38, pp. 1–27.

Chen, J. (1983), *Multinational Corporations, Technology and Employment*, London: Macmillan.

Chung, C., L. Chang and Y. Zhang (1995), 'The Role of Foreign Direct Investment in China's Post-1978 Economic Development', *World Development*, 23, pp. 691–703.

Davidson, R. and J.G. Mackinnon (1993), *Estimation and Inference in Econometrics*, Oxford University Press.

De Melo, J. and J.M. Grether (1997), *Commerce International, Théories et Applications*, Balises, De Boeck Université, Paris.

Démurger, S. (1996), 'Ouverture et Croissance Industrielle des Villes Chinoises', *Revue Economique*, 3, pp. 841–50.

Démurger, S. (1997), 'Différences Régionales de la Croissance Industrielle en Chine', *Revue d'Economie du Développement*, 1996, 1–2, pp. 145–68.

Dunning, John, 1981, 'International Production and the Multinational Enterprise', London: George Allen and Unwin.

Findlay, R. (1978), 'Relative Backwardness, Direct Foreign Investment, and the Transfer of Technology: A Simple Dynamic Model', *Quarterly Journal of Economics*, 92, pp. 1–16.

Gerschenberg, I. and T. Ryan (1978), 'Does Parentage Matter? An Analysis of Transnational and Other Firms: An East African Case', *Journal of Developing Areas*, 13, pp. 3–10.

Gershenkron, A. (1962), *Economic Backwardness in a Historical Perspective, a Book of Essays*, Harvard/Belknap, Cambridge, Massachusetts

Gomulka, S. (1971), *Inventive Activity, Diffusion and the Stages of Economic Growth*, Aarhus.

Gomulka, S. (1990), *The Theory of Technological Change and Economic Growth*, London: Routledge.

Grossman, G.M. and E. Helpman (1991), *Innovation and Growth in the Global Economy*, Cambridge, MA: MIT Press.

Guillaumont, P. and G. Boyreau Debray (1996), 'La Chine et la Convergence', *Revue d'Economie du Développement*, 1, pp. 33–67.

Hsueh, T.T., Q. Li and S. Liu (1993), *China's Provincial Statistics, 1949–1989*, Boulder, Co: Westview Press.

Hymer, S. (1960). *The International Operations of National Firms: a Study of Foreign Direct Investment*. Cambridge, MA: MIT Press.

Jenkins, R. (1990) 'Comparing Foreign Subsidiaries and Local Firms in LDCs: Theoretical Issues and Empirical Evidence', *Journal of Development Studies*, 26, pp. 205–28

Jorgenson, D. and Z. Griliches (1967), 'The Explanation of Productivity Change', *Review of Economic Studies*, 34, pp. 349–83.

Katz, J. (1987), *Technology Creation in Latin American Manufacturing Industries*, New York: St Martin's Press.

Kemp, M.C. (1966), 'The Gain from International Trade and Investment: A Neo-Heckscher Ohlin Approach,' *American Economic Review*.

King, M. and M. Robson (1992), 'Investment and Technical Progress', *Oxford Review of Economic Policy*, 8–4, pp. 43–56.

Koizumi, T. and K. Kopecky (1977), 'Economic Growth, Capital Movements and the International Transfer of Technological Knowledge', *Journal of International Economics*, 7, 45–66.

Kumar, N. (1996), 'Foreign Direct Investments and Technology Transfers in Development: A Perspective on Recent Literature', Discussion Paper No. 9606, INTECH, Maastricht.

Lall, S. (1980), 'Vertical Interfirm Linkages in LDCs: An Empirical Study', Oxford Bulletin of Economics and Statistics, Vol. 42, pp. 203–26.

Lucas, R. Jr. (1988), 'On the Mechanics of Economic Development', *Journal of Monetary Economics*, 22, pp. 3–42.

MacDougall, G.D.A. (1960), 'The Benefits and Costs of Private Investment from Abroad: A Theoretical Approach', *Economic Record*, Vol. 36, pp. 13–35.

Mody, A., J. Sanders, R. Suri, C. Rao and F. Contreras (1991), *International Competition in the Bicycle Industry: Keeping Pace with Technological Change*, The World Bank.

Rodriguez, C. (1981), 'The Technology Transfer Issue', in S. Grassman and E. Lundberg (eds), *The World Economic Order: Past and Prospect*, London: Macmillan.

Romer, P. (1986), 'Increasing Returns and Long-run Growth', *Journal of Political Economy*, 94, pp. 1002–37.

Romer, P. (1989), 'What Determines the Rate of Growth and Technological Change?', Policy, Planning, and Research Working Paper No. 279, The World Bank.

Romer, P. (1993), 'Idea Gaps and Object Gaps in Economic Development', *Journal of Monetary Economics*, 32, pp. 543–73.

Solow, R. (1956), 'A Contribution to the Theory of Economic Growth', *Quarterly Journal of Economics*, 70, pp. 65–94.

Solow, R. (1994), 'Perspectives on Growth Theory', *Journal of Economic Perspectives*, 8, pp. 45–54.

Veblen, T. (1915), *Imperial Germany and the Industrial Revolution*, New York: Macmillan.

Wang, Y. and M. Blomström (1992), 'Foreign Investment and Technology Transfer: A Simple Model', *European Economic Review*, 36, pp. 137–55.

11. Some observations on the ownership and regional aspects in financing the growth of China's rural enterprises*

Wing Thye Woo[a]

1 INTRODUCTION

The hallmark of Chinese economic growth since 1984 is that rural enterprises (popularly known as township and village enterprises, TVEs) have constituted the main engine of economic growth.[1] The industrial output alone from rural enterprises accounted for about 31% of the increase in GDP between 1984 and 1993.[2] It has been clear since the fifteenth Party Congress in September 1997 that China has decided to sharply reduce the importance of state-owned enterprises (SOEs) by accelerating the diversity of ownership forms. The amendment of the constitution in March 1999 to accord private ownership the same legal status as state ownership is a logical development from the 1997 policy decision. Implicitly, TVEs are expected to become an even more important engine of growth in the future.

This expectation of continued high TVE growth may be unrealistic however, given recent investment trends. TVE investment in the 1990s has declined relative to both GDP and total fixed investment, in a period in which total investment went from 30% of GDP in 1987 to 33% in 1997.[3]

So far, the TVEs have increased their output share[4] not only without getting any of the investment share released by the shrinking SOE sector but doing so with a decreased investment share, from 29% in 1987 to 23%

* This chapter has been published in a special issue of Revue d'Economie du Développement, no. 1-2, 1999.

a An earlier draft of this chapter was presented at the International Conference on Chinese Economy: Openness and Disparities in China, Centre d'Etudes et de Recherches sur le Développement International (CERDI), Université D'Auvergne, Clermont-Ferrand, France, 22-23 October 1998. I am grateful to Sylvie Démurger, Fan Gang, Patrick Guillaumont, Aart Kraay, Chingboon Lee, Françoise Lemoine, Li Shantong, Pascal Mazodier, Mary-Francoise Renard, Wu Yanrui, Zhai Fan, and an anonymous referee for insightful and helpful comments. The results reported here are from the Economic Geography Project being undertaken at the Center for International Development, Harvard University.

in 1997. This is unlikely to be a sustainable situation. It is hard to see how the TVEs could move up the value added chain in production without significant capital investments in the near future. So, if China's market capitals continue not to allocate sufficient investment funds to the most dynamic sector of the economy, China's high growth rate is probably not going to continue in the medium run unless there are drastic reductions in the restrictions on non-state enterprises in the urban areas, and on the movement of rural labour into urban centres.

Table 11.1 Investment in different forms of ownership

	Fixed investment as % of GDP		Share of fixed investment, %		Share of industrial output, %	
	1987	1997	1987	1997	1987	1997
All ownership forms	30.4	33.4	100.0	100.0	100.0	100.0
SOEs	19.2	17.5	63.1	52.5	59.7	25.5
TVEs	8.9	7.7	29.1	23.0	32.5	47.6

According to the standard core-periphery spatial model of economic development, an emerging core would grow by attracting resource inflows from the periphery (the backwash effects). Over time, as production costs, like congestion, land prices and wages, rise, capital and skilled manpower would move from the core to the neighbouring provinces (the spread effects). Applying this model to China, the prediction would be that TVEs would first blossom in the coastal provinces because of easier integration into the international division of labour, and then later in the neighbouring inland provinces. This implies that when TVE growth in the coastal provinces slows down, it is not necessarily a cause for national concern. The problem in China after 20 years of rural deregulation is that the investment slowdown by the TVEs in the five coastal provinces does not seem to have been accompanied by an increase in investment by TVEs in their neighbouring provinces (the eight central provinces).[5] Investment by both coastal TVEs and central TVEs have fallen as a share of GDP, as well as a share of total national investment! (See Table 11.2.)

The three indicators in Table 11.2 do not show any signs of a positive spread effect on the TVEs in the central provinces. The central TVEs' share of total TVE investment has in fact dropped from 29.8% in 1987 to 26.0% in 1997. However, as we shall show later in the chapter, that data from another source appear to suggest the existence of spread effects on collectively-owned TVEs (rural collectives).

Table 11.2 Investment in coastal and central provinces

	Investment as % of GDP		Share of national investment, %		Share of investments by all TVEs, %	
	1987	1997	1987	1997	1987	1997
TVEs in coastal provinces	4.0	3.5	13.0	10.3	44.5	44.9
TVEs in central provinces	2.6	2.0	8.7	6.0	29.8	26.0

The level of TVE investment and the existence of spread effects are important not only for economic reasons but also for political reasons. If the economic forces unleashed by the post-1978 reforms do not naturally generate sustained economic growth, and 'trickling-down' to the rural areas and to the non-coastal provinces, then political forces could rise to push for the amelioration of rural–urban inequality and regional inequality. And there is no reason to believe that these political forces, without an understanding of the causes of the barriers to financing TVE investment, would not choose direct administration to address these problems (which would worsen long-run economic performance, and create social instability at the same time).

The aims of this chapter are to study the financing of investments by rural enterprises, and to recommend the institution of appropriate investment-financing mechanisms to accelerate the growth of rural enterprises, especially in the non-coastal provinces.

2 THE PROFILE OF TVEs ACROSS GEOGRAPHICAL GROUPINGS

Nineteen of China's 30 provinces[6] can be quite naturally classified under four geographical groupings that are analytically distinct in economic terms:

- the five fast-growing coastal provinces of Fujian, Guangdong, Jiangsu, Shandong, and Zhejiang;
- the eight agricultural central provinces of Anhui, Henan, Hubei, Hunan, Jiangxi, Shaanxi, Shanxi, and Sichuan;
- the three industrial northeastern provinces of Heilongjiang, Jilin and Liaoning, and;
- the three prosperous cities with province-level status, Beijing, Shanghai, and Tianjin.

The remaining 11 provinces – Gansu, Guangxi, Guizhou, Hainan, Hebei, Inner Mongolia, Ningxia, Qinghai, Tibet, Xinjiang, and Yunnan – do not fit the criteria, in the broad sense, of being geographically similar or contiguous, having similar economic structure, and being at similar development level. We lump them under a fifth (residual) grouping called 'other mainly non-coastal' because eight of them (that is excluding Guangxi, Hainan and Hebei) are inland provinces. These provinces vary widely in economic characteristics, for example, landlocked Xinjiang has a per capita income higher than the national average, while landlocked Gansu and Guizhou are the two poorest provinces in China.

The key economic indicators of these five provincial groupings are shown in Appendix Table 11A.1. The city-provinces are major industrial, trade and administrative centres, with over 87% of their labour-force employed in secondary and tertiary industries. The average city-province has a per capita income that is 78% above the average province in the second richest provincial grouping – the coastal provinces. The location of the biggest and most prosperous SOEs in these city-provinces provides linkages (supplier opportunities) for TVEs to develop around these cities. This linkage effect may be an important reason why the TVEs in city-provinces are significantly larger than in the other provincial groupings, 22 workers in an average city-province TVE versus eight in an average coastal province TVE. The proportion of workforce employed by TVEs is naturally lower than the national average of 21%.

Under the pre-1984 central planning regime, the three northeastern provinces became the industrial heartland of China, and the core of the state enterprise sector. This is the part of China that bears the closest resemblance to the heavy industry bias of the classic Soviet economic structure. The strong legacy of traditional socialism has resulted in active legal discrimination against the establishment of non-state enterprises, and this has helped to render TVEs in the northeastern provinces the smallest in scale in China – four workers in a typical northeastern province TVE, despite the existence of linkage opportunities.

All the five coastal provinces have per capita income levels that are significantly above the national average. It is important to note that the above-average income of the coastal provinces is recent when compared with the city-provinces and the northeastern provinces.[7] Prosperity came to the coastal provinces only after 1978 when the policies of economic reform and opening were implemented. A large part of the big income increases in the coastal provinces in the 1978–84 period was due to the agricultural boom. The post-1984 (even bigger) income increases were primarily the result of the industrialization of the coastal provinces led by their dynamic TVEs. Almost 30% of their workforce are employed by TVEs.

All the eight central provinces have per capita incomes that are below the national average. Less than 20% of their labour force are employed in secondary industry compared to 47% for the city-provinces, 33% for the northeastern provinces, and 29% for the coastal provinces. While the average number of TVEs in a central province is higher than in a coastal province, the average size of a central province TVE is smaller than that of a coastal province TVE – five persons and eight persons respectively. Both the average size of TVEs and the proportion of labour force working in TVEs are at the national average.

It is clear that the experience of the coastal provinces is more relevant for the economic development of the central provinces than the experiences of the city-provinces and the northeastern provinces. The unusually high incomes of the city-provinces come from being industrial enclaves with no rural hinterlands, and the above-average incomes of the northeastern provinces were artificially created by the industrialization dictated by the central plan. The northeastern provinces are now in fact in the throes of restructuring their Soviet-type economies to be compatible with the working of a market economy. The coastal provinces, in contrast, owe their above-average incomes to the fast development of the TVEs after 1984. So for the purpose of this chapter, we will use the coastal provinces as the comparator when we analyse the reasons for the relative backwardness of the TVEs in the other provinces.

3 THE FINANCIAL SYSTEM IN RURAL CHINA[8]

The Agricultural Bank of China (ABC) was established in 1955 to provide financial services to the rural sector, and channel funds for grain procurement purchases. Small-scale collectively-owned rural credit cooperatives (RCCs, *Nongcun Xindai Hezuoshe*) were started in the early 1950s, under the supervision of ABC, to be the primary financial institutions serving the rural areas. Although RCCs are independent accounting units owned by townships, or towns, or villages, or several villages jointly, they are, in practice, grassroot units of the ABC. RCCs operate an extensive network of branches, savings deposit offices, and credit stations in market towns and remote areas. The number of RCC units rose from 389 726 in 1981 to 421 582 in 1984, and then fell steadily to 365 492 in 1995.[9] We want to highlight this decline in the number of RCC units after 1984 because this decline means a decrease in the effort to mobilize rural saving, and a decrease in the access of the rural community to investment financing.

Appendix Table 11A.2 outlines the changes in the operations of RCCs in the reform era. It shows three turning points that coincide with other changes in China's economy. In 1978, RCCs lent only 27% of the deposits they collected in rural areas to finance rural economic activities. The first turning point was 1984 when the legal barriers against non-agricultural economic activities undertaken by farm households, and the establishment of rural enterprises were lowered, and the RCCs were allowed to make more loans in rural areas. RCCs' loans to rural areas jumped from 34% of RCC deposits in 1983 to 57% in 1984. The proportion of RCC deposits going to rural loans increased every year in the 1984–1988 period, reaching 65% in 1988. 1984 was also a turning point for the SOE sector, which received its first significant dose of operational autonomy.

The second turning point was 1989 when the incremental dismantling of discrimination against rural lending was suspended. It marked the beginning of a period of tight credit, reintroduction of some administrative curbs on investment spending, and uncertainty as to future state policies on economic reform and trade opening. The loan–deposit ratio of RCCs stayed at about 66% in the 1989–1991 period. The third turning point was 1992 when economic deregulation accelerated after Deng Xiaoping's inspection tour of southern China (*nanxun*) in early 1992.

These three turning points produced distinctive economic responses. The suspension of reform saw average annual investment (fixed capital formation) decline from 30% of GDP in 1984–88 to 25% in 1989–91, and the re-starting of economic deregulation saw the RCCs' loan–deposit ratio jump to 71% in 1992 and investment to rise to 34% of GDP in 1992–97. We will use the three distinct policy regime periods identified here in analysing the discussion in the subsequent sections.

It would be right to say that until the mid-1980s, the RCCs, by relending the bulk of their deposits to ABC, served primarily as tributaries by which rural savings were channelled to finance economic activities in the urban areas. RCCs still divert a significant proportion of their deposits to finance activities outside of the rural area, 27% of their deposits in 1995. The fact is that non-SOEs face great difficulties in raising funds. The financial system is dominated by the state banks, and the state banks lend primarily to the SOEs. The access to bank loans by non-SOEs is particularly bad during periods of tight credit. In 1989, ceilings were imposed on loans to rural collectives (township, village and production team enterprises, TVEs); and working capital credit from banks to private enterprises was severely curtailed. (Banks gave virtually no fixed capital credit to private enterprises before then.) The result was that the number of private enterprises dropped from 225 000 in mid-1988 to 98 000 in early 1991.

Private and small collective enterprises have always paid higher interest rates in informal credit markets. A 1992 field investigation reported that a fast-growing private electronics company[10] paid an interest rate of 2.5% each month on its working capital; and its original start-up capital came from the savings of the partners and informal loans from friends. These informal credit markets, popularly referred to as 'folk finance' (*minjian rongzhi*), appear to have increased greatly in scope in recent years.

Given the heavy reliance by rural collectives and individual enterprises on informal investment financing, a new informal financial instrument called employee bond (*jizi*) has emerged as a significant source of funds. An employee bond is purchased by the new employee when he joins the enterprise, and it carries an interest rate at least equal to that of a time deposit with the same maturity. Many non-SOEs also issue a hybrid equity-bond instrument which, in addition to paying a fixed base rate, also pays a bonus rate – the size of which is contingent on the profitability of the enterprise. In many cases, especially with collectives, tax exemption turned out to be an important source of investment financing. Since many counties, towns and villages are on tax contracts with upper levels that specify a fixed amount, they typically start exempting taxes once their tax quotas are reached provided that the extra retained funds are invested.[11]

4 INVESTMENT PERFORMANCE OF RURAL ENTERPRISES

Appendix Table 11A.3 summarizes the financing of investment by enterprises of different ownership forms.[12] Part A compares the absolute size of investment from each ownership type by expressing investment spending as a percentage of GDP for each of the three analytical periods identified previously. Part B shows the relative size of investment by expressing investment spending of each ownership type as a percentage of total investment.

While it is desirable that total investment has risen from 30% in 1985–88 to 34% in 1992–96 – a confirmation of the well-known international experience that economic deregulation increases economic efficiency and capital accumulation – it is extremely troubling that investment by rural enterprises (rural collectives and rural individuals) has actually shrunk over time, from 8.5% of GDP in 1985–88 to 7.7% in 1992–96. SOE investment, on the other hand, rose slightly from 19% of GDP in 1985–88 to 20% of

GDP in 1992–96. This anomalous situation is a bad sign for future economic growth, and for the reduction of rural poverty.

The biggest absolute increase in investment was from foreign-owned firms (including those owned by overseas Chinese). Their investment rose from negligible levels in 1985–92 to 4.1% of GDP in 1995. This big increase in investment in such a short time indicates the tremendous investment potential of foreign firms because of their access to international capital markets. Naturally, the obvious question is how to increase the access of TVEs in the central provinces to foreign capital.

Parts C and D track the financing of investments undertaken by enterprises of different ownership type. Part C focuses on where enterprises of each type of ownership get their investment funds by calculating the percentage of investment that is funded by each financing source. Part D emphasizes the destination of the funds from each financing source by calculating the share of funds from each source received by enterprises of each ownership type. The definitions of the funding sources are as follows:

(a) *State Budget*: This source primarily finances projects specified in the state investment plan. The funds come from (1) direct budget appropriations, and (2) policy loans from state banks (that are often backed by government deposits). The Chinese economic reforms have drastically reduced the scope of the state investment plan, and hence reduced 'state budget' as a source of investment funding.

(b) *Domestic Loans*: Until the early 1990s, domestic loans were largely loans from the state banks that were backed by the banks' own funds and non-government deposits. Domestic loans also include investment loans from local governments, and from finance companies.

(c) *Foreign Investment*: Funds from (1) bonds and shares sold to foreigners (including Chinese from Taiwan, Hong Kong, and Macao) – who may hold the controlling shares – and (2) loans from international organizations that are managed or guaranteed by the government.

(d) *Self-Raised Funds*: These funds come mostly from (1) retained earnings, (2) bonds/shares sold to workers within the enterprises, and (3) the supervising agencies of the SOEs.

(e) *Other Funds*: This is more than a residual category. It also encompasses funds that are raised in the formal and informal bond and stock markets. In our usage, there are only two formal bond and equity markets in China because only those in Shenzhen and Shanghai have legal recognition. So we call all the other bond and equity markets

(quite numerous but less developed in the poorer regions) 'informal financial markets'.

Parts C and D suggest five immediate policy issues for promoting the growth of the more dynamic TVE sector. The first policy issue is that even though the SOE share of domestic loans has declined, SOEs continue to have disproportionate access to domestic loans and hence are retarding the growth of TVEs. The reasoning follows from that:

(loans to SOEs/output of SOEs) = (loans to SOEs/GDP)/(output of SOEs/GDP)

The (loans to SOEs/output of SOEs) ratio has increased very significantly in the 1985–96 period because (a) the annual average (loans to SOEs/GDP) ratio has gone up from 4.1% in the 1985–91 period to 5.1% in the 1992–96 period, and (b) the (output of SOEs/GDP) ratio has gone down greatly as evidenced by the drop in the SOE share of total industrial output from 65% in 1985 to 28% in 1996.

The second policy issue is that despite the drop in SOE share of total domestic loans, the rural sector's share did not go up. The rural sector's share averaged 18% in both the 1985–88 and 1992–95 periods. The loan share 'released' by the SOEs went entirely to help finance the investments of foreign-owned firms. The absolute amount of resources transferred by domestic loans to rural enterprises showed little change over time, 1.1% of GDP in 1985–88 and 1.3% in 1992–95, a paltry increase of 0.2%.

The third policy issue is that while rural enterprises have recently gained access to 'foreign investment', their share of this fund is disproportionately small. TVEs received only 8.2% of the total foreign capital inflow into China in the 1992–96 period; and foreign funds financed only 3.4% of TVE investment in this period. In the same period, the SOEs absorbed 49.6% of the foreign investment.

The fourth policy issue is that access of the rural enterprises to funds from the fast growing 'other funds' has recently declined precipitously. 'Other funds', which we take to be a proxy for informal credit, has grown from 2.9% of GDP in 1985–88 to 4.7% in 1992–96, but the TVEs' share of it has fallen from 31% in 1985–88 to 27% in 1992–96, with the share being 6.1% in 1995 and 11.4% in 1996.

The fifth policy issue from Parts C and D is that in light of the limited access that TVEs have to foreign funds and domestic loans, it is troublesome that the chief source for financing TVE investments – self-raised funds – has declined in size over time, from 6.4% of GDP in 1985–88 to 4.8% of GDP in

1992–96. The drop in self-raised funds deserves serious study to determine whether it is the result of increased competition from the entry of new TVEs or the result of increased compensation to managers and workers. If the drop in retained earning is due to over-compensation of personnel in rural collectives, then the *corporate governance structure* and *ownership form* of rural collectives has become a barrier to the dynamic growth of the TVE sector.

5 REGIONAL CONTRAST IN THE FINANCING OF INVESTMENTS BY RURAL COLLECTIVES

The only data set that is consistent over time on the sources of investment financing for rural enterprises in different provinces is from the *Township-Village Enterprises Yearbook* (TVEY) published by the Ministry of Agriculture, and we face several difficulties in using it.[13] The first difficulty is that the TVEY data set covers only the component of the TVE sector that is registered as collectively-owned, that is, only rural COEs.

The second difficulty is that the classification scheme for the sources of funds in TVEY is also different from the classification scheme in the *China Statistical Yearbook* (CSY), displayed in Table 11A.3, with the former being more detailed. From our analysis of the data and from our conversations with the statistical authorities, it appears that the approximate correspondence between the two classification schemes is as follows:

China Statistical Yearbook		*Township-Village Enterprise Yearbook*
State Budget	=	State Budget
Domestic Loans	=	Bank and Credit Union Loans
Foreign Investment	=	Foreign Funds
Self-Raised Funds	=	Funds from Supervising Agency + Bonds Sold to Employees + Other Internal Funds
Other Funds	=	Other Sources + Other Funds Raised Outside of the Firm

The third difficulty we face in using the investment data in TVEY is that, in some years, their values differ significantly with those in the investment data from the CSY. The CSY, as noted earlier, does not separate provincial COEs into rural and urban categories until 1993 onwards. If the data in both sources are correct, then the data on investments by rural COEs in TVEY should always be smaller than the data investment by all (rural and urban) COEs in CSY. Such is not the case however. The TVEY data on investment by rural COEs data is smaller than the CSY data on investment by all COEs in the 1987–91 period, but larger in the 1992–96 period. The former is 66% of the latter in 1987, and 112% in 1996.

The larger investment figures in TVEY in the first half of the 1990s could be due to exaggeration by local officials to make themselves look good. The exaggeration of TVE output is a well-documented phenomenon. For example, the 1996 CSY revised significantly downward the 1991–1994 gross industrial output from COEs and IOEs reported in the 1995 CSY, which were compatible with figures in TVEY. After the data revision, CSY reported 1993–95 gross industrial output from COEs and IOEs that were smaller than in TVEY. So it is likely that the TVEY investment data are also exaggerated. The implication is that we should not draw any conclusions based on the levels of investment reported in TVEY (for example, investment as percentage of GDP). To the extent that the degree of exaggeration in values are roughly uniform across provinces, and across funding sources, then some ratios of these numbers could provide some useful information.[14]

With this point in mind, Appendix Table 11.4 is constructed to contrast the financing of investments by rural collectives in the coastal provinces and in the central provinces in the 1987–95 period in two ways: (a) the group's share of funds from each source, that is, the group's share of the national total of each type of fund, and (b) the proportion of each group's total investment that is funded by each of the funding sources. Since the use of the group average can mis-state the situation of a particular member of the group, we have also included the data for Shandong and Sichuan. Shandong is the most populated coastal province, and Sichuan is the most populated central province.[15] Since Shandong is the poorest of the coastal provinces, and Sichuan has a per capita income that is lower than the average per capita income of the central provinces, our discussion will be more sensitive to the financing situation in the poorer provinces within each provincial grouping.

The detailed data show a highly unequal distribution of investment funds. Up to 1994, rural collectives in the *five* coastal provinces raised more funds from each financing source than rural enterprises in the *eight* central provinces. During the 1987–96 period, the coastal provinces attracted 47 to 60% of the national total of investment funds going to rural collectives while the central rural collectives attracted 16 to 28%. The disparity is even greater when we compare the poorer provinces within each provincial grouping. In 1996, rural collectives in Shandong accounted for 17% of the investment by all rural collectives, while rural collectives in Sichuan accounted for just 4%.

The data also show that state-directed investment funds did not seek to ameliorate this disproportional flow of funds to the coastal rural collectives. Until 1995, the state budget had always invested much more in the coastal rural collectives (over 40%) than in the central rural collectives (under 30%). The disbursement of investment funds by the supervising agencies is even more skewed than the state budget allocations, and the volume of funds from the supervising agencies is two to three-and-a-half times higher than that from the state budget.

In our judgement, the unequal outcome is largely due to incomplete economic reforms, unequal regional policies, and natural geography, which together rendered the rate of return to capital higher in the coastal provinces than in the central provinces. The gradual dismantling of the central credit allocation plan started in the second half of the 1980s, and the permitted degree of financial market liberalization differed across provinces. The official toleration of informal financial markets occurred earliest, and is greatest, in the coastal provinces, and hence the informal financial markets in the coastal provinces have become the most developed in China. Because the interest rate in the liberalized financial markets are higher than the regulated interest rates of the state banking system, funds have flowed to the coastal provinces from the provinces which lag in financial deregulation and financial development.

The central government has extended special development incentives to many regions in the coastal provinces. These coastal regions are exempted from many economic regulations (for example, those governing foreign investments), and from several type of taxes (for example, import duties). The central government also allocates more funds (via the budget and state banks) for infrastructure investment in the coastal provinces. In short, throughout the 1980s and the beginning of the 1990s, central government actions raised the rate of return on capital in the coastal provinces relative to the rate of return on capital in the central provinces by deregulating and favouring the coastal provinces above the central provinces.

Finally, natural geography has also contributed to the higher rate of return to capital in the coastal provinces. The inadequate transportation network in China meant that the economic opening of China inevitably allowed the coastal provinces not only to be the first to be integrated into the international division of labour, but also to be the only provinces (for a considerable period of time) to be integrated into the international economy.

6 A SPREAD EFFECT IN THE MAKING?

The comparison at the beginning of this chapter of 1987 and 1997 data from CSY on the regional investment pattern of TVEs suggested that the coastal provinces were not yet generating a spread effect to benefit the central provinces. This suggestion was based on two observations. First, the coastal provinces' share of investment by all TVEs was 36% in both 1987 and 1997, while the central provinces' share had dropped from 24% to 21%. Second, the decline in the investment of coastal TVEs from 4.0% of GDP in 1987 to 3.5% in 1997 was mirrored in the investment of central TVEs which went from 2.6% to 2.0%. These two observations still held when we restricted the sample to rural collectives.

We must emphasize that the TVEY data do not contradict the above two observations even though:

- Part A of Table 11A.4 shows that the central rural collectives' share of investment by all of China's rural collectives rose from 18% in 1989–91 to 23% in 1992–96 (the coastal rural collectives' share was about 53% throughout 1989–96); and
- the investment of rural collectives in the central provinces (in calculations not shown here) rose from 0.6% of GDP in 1987 to 1.3% in 1996.[16]

There is no contradiction because, first, the periods of comparison do not correspond due to data limitations. The CSY data allow us to compare investment between two periods with roughly the same policy regime (1985–88 and 1992–96), while the TVEY data require us to compare investment across two different policy regimes (the dirigiste period 1989–91 versus the more liberal period of 1992–96). Second, we know that investment values in TVEY (even when transformed to be a proportion of GDP) are exaggerated.

We think that while it is likely that there has not been a spread effect from the coastal TVEs, Table 11A.4 appears to show that one may be in the making. Table 11A.4 indicates that proportionally more investment funds are following to the rural collectives in the central provinces. Compared to the austerity period of 1989–91, the TVEs in the central provinces have increased their shares of funds from all eight financing sources in the post-*nanxun* period of 1992–96. Coastal rural collectives generally received smaller shares of funds from domestic funding sources in the post-*nanxun* period. If not for the large increase in the volume of foreign capital inflow in the 1992–96 period, of which the coastal provinces absorb a disproportionate amount, their share of total investment by rural collectives would not have been maintained.

The most dramatic increases in shares of funds received by central rural collectives occurred where the financing sources are most market-oriented: 'foreign funds' and 'other funds raised outside of the firms'.[17] A significant part of the increased foreign capital inflow since 1992 has gone to the central rural collectives, lifting their share of foreign funds from 4% in 1989–91 to 11% in 1992–96. For 'other funds raised outside of the firm', the central rural collectives have increased their share of this category of funds from 21% to 32% over these periods. In fact, by the end of 1996, the central rural collectives' share of 'other funds raised outside of the firm' was twice the share of the coastal rural collectives, 45% and 22% respectively.

There are many reasons why domestic funds that are market-driven have flowed in greater proportions to the central provinces in the post-*nanxun* period. The three important reasons in our opinion are (a) significant economic deregulation, (b) de facto clarification of the property rights of the rural collectives, and (c) the decrease in underemployment of the labour force of the coastal provinces.

The first important reason is that in the post-*nanxun* period, there has been more economic deregulation in the central provinces than in the coastal provinces. This is because the coastal provinces had already undertaken the same deregulation steps in the 1980s – and so the additional deregulation steps implemented in the coastal provinces after 1992 were not equivalent in scope to those implemented earlier in the coastal provinces, and to those implemented in the central provinces after 1992. In brief, there has been a diminution of the central–coastal gap in economic regulation.[18]

Economic deregulation in the central provinces mainly meant the creation of a more business-friendly economic environment. The most basic of such deregulation involved the reduction of legal barriers to the formation of new businesses; the reduction of the supervisory role of local officials in production, investment, and hiring/firing decisions of firms; and the reduction of taxes and levies (formal and informal). The point here is that economic deregulation in the central provinces has raised the productivity of capital, and this has attracted more capital flows from abroad and elsewhere in China.[19]

The second important reason for the reallocation of domestic funds is that many central provinces have followed the lead of the coastal provinces in allowing their rural collectives to change to ownership forms that have clearly defined and legally protected property rights that are (potentially, if not already) freely tradable. The most common practice is to transform rural collectives into shareholding cooperatives.[20] With the movement towards clear, legal, and tradable property rights for rural collectives in the central provinces, outside investors have become more confident that their investments are now better secured against embezzlement. Outside investors have hence sent a larger share of their funds to invest in the now more deregulated (that is, more profitable) economies of the central provinces.

The third important reason for the new tendency of market-driven funds to flow to the central provinces is that labour costs in the coastal provinces have risen significantly. The fast growth of rural enterprises in the coastal provinces in the 1980s have now largely eliminated underemployment in the rural labour force, and this caused rural wages to rise. The result is two opposite flows between the coastal provinces and the central provinces. Labour has been flowing from the central provinces to the coastal provinces in response to the higher wages in the coastal provinces, and capital is now beginning to flow from the coastal provinces to the central provinces in response to lower wages in the central provinces. It must be emphasized however that until China's transportation system is significantly improved to give the central provinces much easier access to the ports, this type of capital inflow into the central provinces will be temporary.

7 IMPROVING THE FINANCING OF RURAL ENTERPRISES

As pointed out earlier, the general prospects for future TVE growth is actually not very promising. TVE investment dropped by 1.8% of GDP during the 1985–96 period, even though total domestic investment increased by over 4% of GDP; and the TVE share of total domestic investment has dropped from 28% in 1985–88 to 22% in 1992–96. In our opinion, the primary reason for this drop in TVE investment (as a share of GDP and as a share of total domestic investments) is that TVEs suffer from two big disadvantages in investment financing.

The first disadvantage suffered by TVEs is that the still heavily-regulated financial system is directing too much of the investment funds to the SOE sector, thus starving the TVE sector of investment funds. SOE investment has actually risen as a share of GDP despite the facts that the share of SOE output in GDP has fallen, and that the SOE sector is less profitable and less efficient than the TVE sector.

The second major disadvantage of the TVEs in raising capital is that TVEs generally still do not have forms of property rights that attract market-driven investment funds. We see this clearly in the failure of the TVE sector to significantly increase their shares of funds from the banking sector, foreign capital flows, and funds raised in the formal and informal financial markets. As the banking sector began to commercialize its lending activities in the 1990s, a smaller proportion of bank loans flowed to the SOE sector, but the 'released share' went entirely to firms of other ownership structure, for example, shareholding companies and foreign-owned companies.

The three most important issues that must be addressed in order to overcome the above two crippling disadvantages faced by TVEs in getting investment financing are: the financial system is over-regulated, the RCC-ABC system lacks the organizational flexibility and incentive to focus on efficient local financial intermediation, and some ownership forms of TVEs discourage outside investment into TVEs.

8 DEREGULATING THE FINANCIAL SECTOR

This is a much discussed issue in the Chinese press,[21] but unfortunately many of the financial reform proposals are actually proposals for administrative reorganization of the existing financial institutions rather than proposals for using market forces to allocate funds. Marketization of the financial system involves at the minimum: (1) allowing the establishment of privately-owned financial institutions; (2) freeing deposit and loan rates; (3) permitting foreign financial institutions to increase the scale and range of their operations over time; (4) imposing identical supervisory oversight and prudential standards on state-owned, and private-owned banks; and (5) instructing the state banks to stop giving preferential credit to SOEs, and to process loan applications equally without regard to ownership forms of the enterprises.[22]

The above financial reforms will stop the disproportionate flow of credit to the SOE sector,[23] free up funds for more productive projects in the non-state sector; and allow the appearance of new small-scale local financial institutions that will mobilize local savings to finance local TVE investments. Since the adoption of the policies of economic reform and opening in 1978, folk finance (*minjian rongzhi*) has grown impressively despite the absence of legal recognition and legal protection. Folk finance was definitely the source of the development of TVEs in Wenzhou city in Zhejiang province. Liu (1992, pp. 298) reported that:

> Ninety-five per cent of the total capital needed by the local private sector has been supplied by 'underground' private financial organizations, such as money clubs, specialized financial households and money shops.[24]

It is important to keep in mind that financial deregulation has to be accompanied by the introduction of adequate banking supervision and of prudential standards that comply with international norms. The rash of banking crises in Eastern Europe in the early 1990s and in East and Southeast Asia recently should serve as warnings of financial deregulation without adequate improvement in the government's ability to monitor the activities of the financial institutions.

9 REORGANIZING THE RCC–ABC SYSTEM

There is now a wealth of international experience with various schemes in developing countries to direct investment credit to the rural areas where the bulk of the population, as well as where the bulk of the poor, live. In particular, we wish to draw attention to the successful Indonesian experience of establishing a self-sustaining and profitable banking system (the *Unit Desa* system) in the countryside as a starting point for the discussion of the way to accelerate financial development in rural China. Indonesia is very similar to China in key economic and institutional features. Like China, Indonesia is a geographically vast and heavily populated economy, and its rural financial system is dominated by branches of a state bank (Bank Rakyat Indonesia, BRI) which has been designated to serve the rural areas.[25]

The Indonesian experience with the *Unit Desa* system suggests that the reorganization of the RCC–ABC system be guided by five principles. The first key guiding principle is that a large-scale subsidized credit programme for the rural areas cannot be sustained because it is both too expensive and too inefficient. A developing country like China should avoid wasting its scarce capital by using the interest rate mechanism to allocate funds to the projects with the highest rates of return.

The second key principle is that the role of government subsidies is to provide seed money to (1) provide technical training, (2) start the credit unit's lending activities, and (3) cover the losses for the first few years. Over time, the rural credit unit must (1) mobilize local savings to expand its lending activities, (2) improve its loan assessment activities in order to increase profits, and (3) build a reserve fund to cover losses.

The third key principle is that the rural credit unit must be given the incentive to maximize profits in a prudent manner. This third principle necessitates that each credit unit be given a large degree of operational autonomy in return for being financially accountable to the supervising branch of ABC. Bailouts should be used only in exceptional cases where losses are clearly not due to incompetence or recklessness, and bonuses and promotion should be clearly based on contributions to the bank's profitability. Only in an environment with clearly defined individualized rewards and general hard budget constraint, would a credit unit apply itself to mobilize savings diligently, and to assess loan applications carefully.

The fourth key principle is that rural loan rates are generally higher than in the urban areas. This situation does not generally indicate exploitation, it reflects instead the higher costs of making many small loans, and the absence of collateral to cover losses.

The fifth principle is that no rural bank should be given privileges that allow it to monopolize the local market. This is because providing credit to the rural poor is a hard job. The rural poor are often unaware of their eligibility for loans, and can be physically hard to reach. Only a bank that is facing competition will attempt to reach these groups with advertisement campaigns, and with mobile teams. Without competition, a bank may even actually reduce its presence in the rural areas, like the 13% reduction in the number of RCC units in the 1984–95 period – echoing the textbook monopolist who maximizes profit by restricting supply.

The following four steps should be simultaneously implemented in order to strengthen the working of the reorganized RCC-ABC system:

- The existing rural cooperative funds (*nongcun hezuo jijin*), rural credit cooperative (*nongcun xindai hezuoshe*), and other folk finance institutions (*minjian rongzhi*) should be given legal status as independent financial institutions. This will ensure that the RCC–ABC system will no longer enjoy its present near-monopoly status.
- Various departments of rural development within the different ministries may establish and operate rural financial institutions, but none of them should have regulatory power over institutions that they do not own.
- The supervision of these independent rural financial institutions should be the sole responsibility of the People's Bank of China in order to ensure consistent regulation of all financial institutions, and to avoid over-regulation of the rural financial institutions.
- The People's Bank of China should adjust the different mandatory asset–liability ratios to recognize that rural financial institutions face higher transaction costs (due to numerous small loans) and higher risk premia (due to absence of collateral), and that they serve the poorest portion of the population.

It is of fundamental importance to emphasize the point that the proposed ABC credit unit system could work satisfactorily only with competition from other rural financial institutions. Wenzhou's experience with investment financing in the 1980s leaves no doubt about the beneficial effects of vigorous competition from folk finance on state-owned financial institutions:

> In order to compete with [the new folk finance institutions]..., as early as 1980 a local collective credit union, without informing the superior authority, abandoned for the first time the fixed interest rate and adopted a floating interest rate which fluctuated in accordance with market demand but remained within the upper limit set by the state. Despite the dubious legality of the floating interest rate, the local

state bank branches and all the credit unions in Wenzhou had already adopted it before the central state officially ratified it in 1984. Liu (1992, p. 298)

10 ALLOWING RURAL ENTERPRISES TO ASSUME MARKET-DETERMINED OWNERSHIP FORMS

The fact is that profit-maximizing investors do not feel that their interests would be protected in TVEs where their property rights are less clearly defined, less protected legally, and not freely tradable like the property rights of shareholding firms and foreign-owned companies. The present trend of restructuring TVEs into shareholding cooperatives by dividing their assets among the workers (sometimes among the original inhabitants of the community) is hence an important step in addressing the difficulties faced by TVEs in raising investment funds.

The transformation of TVEs into shareholding cooperatives is akin to the present process of transforming most SOEs into shareholding companies. The transformation of TVEs and SOEs into shareholding companies is a natural convergence to an enterprise form which, international experience have shown, assures investors that managers would have the incentives to maximize profits in a prudent manner. If the property rights of TVEs fail to become freely tradable in formal stock markets, their share of total investment funds will be reduced further because the former SOEs (now transformed into normal corporations) will be the more attractive investment vehicle. The failure to turn TVEs into normal corporations will almost certainly mean that foreign institutional investors, who represent the biggest pool of investment fund in the world and who also have less inside information about the operations of TVEs than Chinese investors, will not become significant investors in TVEs.

11 FINAL REMARKS

We attribute the slowdown in TVE investment in the 1990s to continued discrimination against non-state enterprises by the capital markets (which are dominated by state financial institutions), and to ambiguities in the property rights of TVEs. And we think that the best ways to increase the amount of investment in the non-coastal provinces are (1) to implement the proposed economic deregulation in the non-coastal provinces at a pace that should at least equal to that of the coastal provinces; and (2) to improve the transportation links to the coastal provinces to end the tyranny of geography that has prevented the effective integration of the non-coastal provinces into the international economy.

NOTES

1. As in many official Chinese statistical yearbooks, we will use the following terms interchangeably: rural enterprises, TVEs, and collectively-owned enterprises (COEs) and individually-owned enterprises (IOEs) located in the rural areas. TVEs started in the post-1978 era as owned collectively by the local rural communities, but the term now does not connote collective ownership. We will refer to collectively-owned TVEs as rural collectives. For a survey of the different explanations for China's high growth, see Woo (1999) and Woo (2001).
2. Obtained by modifying Woo's (1998a) estimates with the assumption that 85% of the ouput from COEs and IOEs is produced in rural areas. The share of rural enterprises in investment by all COEs and IOEs was 80% in 1987 and 1997.
3. Data are from the 1988 and 1998 issues of the *China Statistical Yearbook*.
4. TVE output is assumed to be 85% of output from COEs and IOEs.
5. The five provinces that constitute our definition of coastal provinces are Fujian, Guangdong, Jiangsu, Shandong, and Zhejiang; and the eight provinces that constitute the central provinces are Anhui, Henan, Hubei, Hunan, Jiangxi, Shaanxi, Shanxi, and Sichuan.
6. In 1996, Chongqing became the fourth city to be given province level status. We have ignored this new province because we do not yet have the information that will allow us to separate the Chongqing data out from the Sichuan data.
7. See Jian et al. (1996), and Démurger et al. (2001).
8. For an overview of China's financial system, see Woo (1998b).
9. The number of RCC units is the number of RCCs plus the number of branches, savings deposit offices and credit stations. The number of RCCs (that is, institutions with independent accounting systems) went up from 55 044 in 1981 to 60 897 in 1988, and then down to 50 219 in 1995. In 1995, RCCs accounted for 13% of deposits in all financial institutions, and 10% of all the loans made.
10. Bao An county factory, 28 September 1992, Case A27 of author's fieldwork.
11. In the author's 1992 fieldtrip, one Chongqing firm raised Y3 million from *jizi* to acquire its Y14 million of fixed assets, while a Chengdu firm raised Y1.5 million from *jizi* for the required fixed asset investment of Y8 million; cases A39 and A34 respectively. One big Chengdu company was given tax concessions worth Y3.5 million a year to allow it to accumulate funds to double its present output; case A35.
12. Data are from various issues of the *China Statistical Yearbook*, and are available only from 1985 onward.
13. The 1989 TVEY does not contain the investment financing information for 1998, so there is a gap in the data set.
14. The difference in magnitude between the TVEY data and the CSY data could also be due to many other reasons, for example, possible differences in definition, changes in definitions over time in one source but not the other. We do know that the two sources generated their estimates from different samples – the TVEY relied on annual reports submitted to the TVE Bureau in the Ministry of Agriculture, and the CSY relied on a survey conducted by the Rural Socio-Economic Survey Organization in the State Statistical Bureau.
15. Sichuan (including Chongqing as is done here) is also the most populated province in China.
16. As is the case in aggregate data, the 1996 investment of the rural and urban COEs in the central provinces in CSY is lower than in TVEY; 0.8% of GDP versus 1.3%.

17. For the central rural collectives, 'other funds raised outside of the firms' mainly refer to revenue obtained by central rural collectives from selling stocks and bonds in informal financial markets.
18. The central provinces have become more deregulated than before, but their level of deregulation is still lower than that of the coastal provinces.
19. In a 1997 fieldtrip, the author found many examples of post-1992 deregulation, for example, a village in Henan which reduced the approval time for new businesses from six months to a month. Furthermore, the Party secretary posted signs on new businesses forbidding local officials who are not members of the village tax bureau from collecting any fines or fees; and a county in Sichuan which established a 'private enterprise development zone' under the direct control of local Party leaders to ensure that the discriminatory regulations against non-state enterprises would no longer be applied.
20. In most cases, the registration status of the enterprise remains as 'collective-owned' despite the transfer of most of the shares of the enterprise to the workers because of the existence of (minority) shares that are designated as collective-owned and are non-tradable.
21. For example, articles in the *China Daily* on 'Financial system to undergo five major changes' (28 February 1998); and 'Reforms to target SOEs and State banks' (17 February 1998).
22. The Export and Import Bank of China has recently decided 'to gradually expand its financial services to collectively-owned firms and joint-stock companies' and to continue making 'the large- and medium-sized State-owned firms ... as its major clients' (*China Daily*, 'Bank loans to non-State enterprise', 22 January 1998). This decision is a step in the right direction, but it is a very inadequate one because of the continued discrimination against private enterprises – which makes a mockery of the heading of the article.
23. The SOE sector has become even more capital-intensive in the post-1978 period of economic deregulation. The subsidized investment funds to the SOE sector are hence offsetting one important thrust of China's economic reforms which is to allow enterprises to choose production techniques that are in line with China's vast endowment of labour.
24. The power of market forces (when tolerated by the local authorities) to induce financial institutional innovations is an old story. Taiwan's small and medium private enterprises exhibited dynamic growth in the 1960–1985 period even though they were heavily discriminated against by the (wholly state-owned) banking system because informal financial markets (curb markets) appeared to cater to their needs, see Shea and Yang (1994).
25. See Patten and Rosengard (1990), Woo (1995), and Yaron et al. (1997) for details of the Indonesian case.

REFERENCES

China Statistical Yearbook (CSY), State Statistical Bureau, Beijing, China, various issues.

Démurger, S., J.D. Sachs, W.T. Woo, S. Bao, G. Hsin Chang and A. Mellinger (2001), 'Geography, Economic Policy and Regional Development in China', *Asian Economic Papers*, 1(1), Fall.

Jian, T., J.D. Sachs and A. Warner (1996), 'Trends in Regional Inequality in China', *China Economic Review*, 7(1), pp. 1–21.

Liu, Y.-L. (1992), 'Reform From Below: The Private Economy and Local Politics in the Rural Industrialization of Wenzhou', *China Quarterly*, 130, June, pp. 293–316.

Patten, R. and J. Rosengard (1990), 'Progress with Profits: The Development of Rural Banking in Indonesia', Harvard Institute for International Development Working Paper.

Shea, J.D. and Y.-H. Yang (1994), 'Taiwan's Financial System and the Allocation of Investment Funds', in Joel Aberbach, David Dollar and Kenneth Sokoloff (eds), *The Role of State in Taiwan's Development*, M.E. Sharpe, Armonk, NY, pp. 193–230.

Township-Village Enterprises Yearbook (TVEY), Ministry of Agriculture, Beijing, China, various issues.

Woo, W.T. (1995), 'Indonesia', in Stephan Haggard and Chung H. Lee (eds), *Financial Systems and Economic Policy in Developing Countries*, Cornell University Press, Ithaca, NY, pp. 76–112.

Woo, W.T. (1998a), 'Zhongguo Quan Yaosu Shengchan Lu: Laizi Nongye Bumen Laodongli Zai Pei Zhi de Shouyao Zuoyong' (Total Factor Productivity Growth in China: The Primacy of Reallocation of Labour from Agriculture), *Jingji Yanjiu*, 3, pp. 31–9.

Woo, W.T. (1998b), 'Financial Intermediation in China', in Olivier Bouin, Fabrizio Coricelli and Francoise Lemoine (eds), *Different Paths to a Market Economy: China and European Economies in Transition*, OECD, Paris, pp. 153–170.

Woo, W.T. (1999), 'The Real Reasons for China's High Economic Growth', *The China Journal*, 41, January, pp. 115–37.

Woo, W.T. (2001), 'Recent Claims of China's Economic Exceptionalism: Reflections Inspired by WTO Accession', *China Economic Review*, 12(2/3), pp. 107–36.

Yaron, J., B. McDonald, and G. Piprek (1997), 'Rural Finance: Issues, Design, and Best Practices', Environmentally and Socially Sustainable Development Studies and Monograph Series 14, World Bank, Washington, DC.

APPENDIX

Table 11A.1 Economic indicators across provinces in 1995

Regions unit	(a) population 10 000	(b) GDP per capita yuan/person	(c) Total number of employees 10 000	(d) Per cent of employees in TVEs	(e) Number of TVEs 10 000	(f) Number of workers per TVE	(g) Distribution of labour force primary industry	secondary industry	tertiary industry
Total	123 669.5	4 631.5	62 388.0	20.6	2 202.7	5.8	52.9	23.0	24.1
Coastal Provinces									
Fujian	3 328.9	6 490.2	1 567.0	30.1	66.7	7.1	50.4	23.7	25.9
Guangdong	7 051.6	7 631.9	3 656.8	29.3	144.7	7.4	37.5	28.6	33.9
Jiangsu	7 273.3	7 087.9	3 765.4	24.6	92.4	10.0	41.7	33.8	24.5
Shandong	8 962.5	5 581.4	4 625.4	31.1	175.2	8.2	54.4	25.1	20.5
Zhejiang	4 446.7	7 926.8	2 700.7	29.5	90.2	8.8	42.7	31.4	25.9
Average	6 212.6	6 832.8	3 263.1	28.9	113.8	8.3	45.3	28.5	26.1
Middle provinces									
Anhui	6 184.4	3 239.7	3 206.8	18.6	60.7	9.8	60.7	17.9	21.4
Henan	9 354.4	3 210.0	4 696.7	15.2	89.5	8.0	60.0	19.8	20.2

Hubei	5 935.8	4 028.8	2 707.0	24.5	146.8	4.5	51.1	22.0	26.9
Hunan	6 586.5	3 333.6	3 506.1	20.6	185.0	3.9	61.4	16.3	22.3
Jiangxi	4 173.4	2 387.6	2 059.2	21.4	106.2	4.1	55.4	18.1	26.5
Shaanxi	3 609.3	2 770.7	1 774.4	18.5	72.2	4.6	59.5	19.2	21.3
Shanxi	3 164.9	3 451.9	1 460.4	27.9	70.9	5.7	43.5	29.8	26.7
Sichuan	11 633.4	3 037.8	6 335.3	18.2	252.4	4.6	63.1	15.9	21.0
Average	6 330.3	3 243.4	3 218.2	20.6	123.0	5.1	56.8	19.9	23.3
Northeast provinces									
Heilongjiang	3 809.4	5 288.3	1 552.4	13.5	62.5	3.4	36.8	34.1	29.1
Jilin	2 668.9	4 231.0	1 254.5	17.0	65.8	3.2	44.8	26.7	28.5
Liaoning	4 213.6	6 629.4	2 034.0	21.3	74.0	5.9	31.1	37.9	31.0
Average	3 564.0	5 552.9	1 613.6	17.3	67.4	4.2	37.6	32.9	29.5
Cities with province status									
Beijing	1 290.1	10 812.3	669.5	14.7	6.3	15.7	10.6	40.1	49.3
Shanghai	1 458.1	16 888.9	768.0	18.2	1.6	87.4	9.2	51.4	39.4
Tianjin	970.4	9 481.8	489.7	21.4	7.6	13.8	16.9	48.4	34.7
Average	1 239.5	12 847.8	642.4	18.1	5.2	22.1	12.2	46.6	41.1
Other mainly non-coastal provinces									
Gansu	2 501.8	2 211.8	1 159.4	17.6	34.0	6.0	58.4	17.5	24.1
Guangxi	4 668.4	3 440.5	2 382.5	7.7	26.5	6.9	66.4	11.8	21.8
Guizhou	3 604.1	1 748.2	1 857.1	4.6	22.2	3.9	73.7	10.0	16.3
Hainan	742.5	4 904.6	335.3	11.3	9.6	3.9	60.7	11.7	27.6

Table 11A.1 (continued)

Regions	(a) population	(b) GDP per capita	(c) Total number of employees	(d) Per cent of employees in TVEs	(e) Number of TVEs	(f) Number of workers per TVE	(g) Distribution of labour force		
							primary industry	secondary industry	tertiary industry
unit	10 000	yuan/person	10 000		10 000				
Hebei	6 621.6	4 303.4	3 367.3	25.3	179.2	4.8	51.4	26.1	22.5
Inner Mongolia	2 349.1	3 545.5	1 024.5	21.9	59.0	3.8	52.4	22.0	25.6
Ningxia	524.9	3 233.9	243.6	5.9	0.6	23.8	58.9	19.1	22.0
Qinghai	494.0	3 346.4	226.0	4.1	1.4	6.6	59.9	18.2	21.9
Tibet	246.5	2 271.0	113.7	0.0	0.0	0.0	77.2	4.6	18.2
Xinjiang	1 705.7	4 892.8	662.2	7.6	14.3	3.5	56.9	18.8	24.3
Yunnan	4 095.0	2 946.7	2 186.3	12.5	85.0	3.2	75.8	9.9	14.3
Average	2 504.9	3 363.8	1 232.5	10.8	39.3	4.5	62.9	15.4	21.7

Sources: Data are from China Statistical Yearbook.

Table 11A.2 Sources and uses of funds in rural credit cooperatives

	Total deposits	Total loans	Loans to agricultural collective units	Loans to township enterprises	Loans to farmer households	**Loans as proportion of deposits, %**	Distribution of loans across borrowers, %		
	(a)	(b)	(c)	(d)	(e)	(b)/(a)	(c)/(b)	(d)/(b)	(e)/(b)
1978	166.0	45.1	21.8	12.1	11.2	27.2	48.3	26.8	24.8
1979	215.9	47.5	22.4	14.2	10.9	22.0	47.2	29.9	22.9
1980	272.3	81.6	34.5	31.1	16.0	30.0	42.3	38.1	19.6
1981	319.6	96.4	35.7	35.5	25.2	30.2	37.0	36.8	26.1
1982	389.9	121.2	34.8	42.3	44.1	31.1	28.7	34.9	36.4
1983	487.4	163.7	28.2	60.1	75.4	33.6	17.2	36.7	46.1
1984	624.9	354.5	38.4	135.0	181.1	56.7	10.8	38.1	51.1
1985	724.9	400.0	41.4	164.4	194.2	55.2	10.4	41.1	48.6
1986	962.3	568.5	44.6	265.9	258.0	59.1	7.8	46.8	45.4
1987	1225.2	771.4	64.5	359.3	347.6	63.0	8.4	46.6	45.1
1988	1399.8	908.6	80.1	456.1	372.4	64.9	8.8	50.2	41.0
1989	1669.5	1094.9	107.3	571.9	415.7	65.6	9.8	52.2	38.0
1990	2144.9	1413.0	134.1	760.7	518.2	65.9	9.5	53.8	36.7
1991	2709.5	1808.6	169.9	1007.3	631.4	66.8	9.4	55.7	34.9
1992	3477.7	2453.9	222.6	1471.8	759.5	70.6	9.1	60.0	31.0
1993	4297.3	3143.9	262.1	2001.2	880.6	73.2	8.3	63.7	28.0
1994	5681.1	4168.6	808.4	2279.4	1080.8	73.4	19.4	54.7	25.9
1995	7172.8	5234.2	1094.9	2779.1	1360.2	73.0	20.9	53.1	26.0

Sources: Constructed from the 1993 and 1995 issues of China Statistical Yearbook.

Table 11A.3 Investment and its financing according to ownership forms

	National total	State-owned enterprises	Rural collectives	Rural individuals	Solely Hong Kong. Taiwan and Macao	Foreign-financed firms	Other forms	*Memo item: Rural sector (collectives & individuals)*
Part A: Fixed asset investment by ownership as percentage of GDP								
1985	28.93	19.11	2.27	5.44	0.00	0.00	2.10	*7.71*
1996	34.19	17.65	4.09	3.71	1.38	2.91	4.44	*7.81*
Average 85–96	30.46	18.64	3.20	4.63	0.31	0.89	2.79	*7.83*
Average 85–88	29.97	19.15	2.72	5.72	0.00	0.00	2.37	*8.45*
Average 89–91	25.10	16.13	2.22	5.03	0.00	0.00	1.72	*7.25*
Average 92–96	34.07	19.74	4.17	3.50	0.75	2.14	3.77	*7.68*
Part B: Share of total investment according to ownership form (%)								
(each row, excluding memo item, sums to 100)								
1985		66.08	7.83	18.81	0.00	0.00	7.28	*26.65*
1996		51.64	11.97	10.86	4.04	8.52	12.97	*22.83*
Average 85–96		61.58	10.34	15.70	0.91	2.55	8.92	*26.03*
Average 85–88		63.93	9.07	19.10	0.00	0.00	7.90	*28.17*
Average 89–91		64.25	8.83	20.06	0.00	0.00	6.87	*28.89*
Average 92–96		58.11	12.26	10.35	2.17	6.12	10.98	*22.61*
Part C: Funding for investment by each type of enterprise according to source (%)								
(for each year, elements within each column sum to 100)								
1985								

a) State budget	17.65	26.42	0.00	0.00			2.59	*0.00*
b) Domestic loans	20.06	23.04	32.12	0.00			31.96	*9.44*
c) Foreign investment	1.98	2.83	0.00	0.00			1.58	*0.00*
d) Self-raised funds	53.62	40.43	51.49	100.00			55.85	*85.74*
e) Others	6.68	7.29	16.39	0.00			8.01	*4.82*
1996								
a) State budget	2.69	4.61	1.77	0.00	0.14	0.30	0.53	*0.93*
b) Domestic loans	19.54	23.58	19.68	4.67	15.21	14.92	20.18	*12.54*
c) Foreign investment	11.73	6.71	9.67	0.00	50.42	53.08	4.25	*5.07*
d) Self-raised funds	53.22	50.79	58.49	93.35	17.33	21.32	56.55	*75.07*
e) Others	12.82	14.32	10.39	1.98	16.90	10.37	18.49	*6.39*
Average 1985–96								
a) State budget	8.00	12.41	0.53	0.00	0.17	0.33	0.90	*0.29*
b) Domestic loans	21.53	24.62	29.22	4.18	14.96	17.30	24.11	*14.30*
c) Foreign investment	6.77	7.28	2.82	0.00	51.69	46.43	3.48	*1.56*
d) Self-raised funds	51.78	44.16	43.75	88.67	18.49	25.09	62.93	*69.85*
e) Others	11.92	11.53	23.69	7.15	14.69	10.85	8.58	*14.01*
Average 1985–88								
a) State budget	13.84	21.33	0.00	0.00			1.48	*0.00*
b) Domestic loans	21.18	23.63	34.06	3.53			29.44	*13.35*
c) Foreign investment	3.98	6.02	0.00	0.00			2.14	*0.00*
d) Self-raised funds	51.30	39.39	44.71	90.24			61.70	*75.52*
e) Others	9.70	9.63	21.22	6.23			5.23	*11.13*
Average 1989–91								
a) State budget	7.91	12.26	0.00	0.00			0.75	*0.00*

Table 11A.3 (continued)

	National total	State-owned enterprises	Rural collectives	Rural individuals	Solely Hong Kong. Taiwan and Macao	Foreign-financed firms	Other forms	*Memo item: Rural sector (collectives & individuals)*
b) Domestic loans	20.11	24.18	25.26	4.39			20.92	*10.78*
c) Foreign investment	6.21	9.20	0.00	0.00			4.45	*0.00*
d) Self-raised funds	53.85	42.69	47.36	86.79			69.26	*74.75*
e) Others	11.92	11.67	27.38	8.82			4.62	*14.47*
Average 1992–96								
a) State budget	3.38	5.35	1.27	0.00	0.17	0.33	0.52	*0.69*
b) Domestic loans	22.65	25.67	27.71	4.58	14.96	17.30	21.77	*17.16*
c) Foreign investment	9.34	7.14	6.76	0.00	51.69	46.43	3.97	*3.74*
d) Self-raised funds	50.92	48.86	40.81	88.54	18.49	25.09	60.11	*62.37*
e) Others	13.71	12.97	23.44	6.89	14.69	10.85	13.63	*16.04*
Part D: Destination of funds from each source, percentage going to each ownership type								
(each row, excluding memo item, sums to 100)								
1985								
a) State budget		98.93	0.00	0.00	0.00	0.00	1.07	*0.00*
b) Domestic loans		75.87	12.54	0.00	0.00	0.00	11.59	*12.54*
c) Foreign investment		94.21	0.00	0.00	0.00	0.00	5.79	*0.00*
d) Self-raised funds		49.82	7.52	35.08	0.00	0.00	7.58	*42.61*
e) Others		72.07	19.21	0.00	0.00	0.00	8.72	*19.21*

1996							
a) State budget	88.44	7.86	0.00	0.21	0.94	2.54	*7.86*
b) Domestic loans	62.30	12.05	2.60	3.15	6.50	13.40	*14.65*
c) Foreign investment	29.52	9.86	0.00	17.38	38.53	4.70	*9.86*
d) Self-raised funds	49.28	13.15	19.05	1.32	3.41	13.78	*32.20*
e) Others	57.68	9.70	1.68	5.33	6.89	18.72	*11.38*
Average 1985–96							
a) State budget	96.35	2.10	0.00	0.03	0.28	1.24	*2.10*
b) Domestic loans	70.57	13.87	2.99	0.67	2.04	9.86	*16.87*
c) Foreign investment	76.28	3.41	0.00	3.99	11.61	4.71	*3.41*
d) Self-raised funds	52.38	8.56	26.72	0.34	1.25	10.75	*35.28*
e) Others	59.86	20.54	9.44	1.13	1.93	7.09	*29.98*
Average 1985–88							
a) State budget	99.14	0.00	0.00	0.00	0.00	0.86	*0.00*
b) Domestic loans	71.41	14.57	3.06	0.00	0.00	10.96	*17.63*
c) Foreign investment	95.49	0.00	0.00	0.00	0.00	4.51	*0.00*
d) Self-raised funds	49.16	7.79	33.50	0.00	0.00	9.54	*41.30*
e) Others	64.22	20.27	10.87	0.00	0.00	4.64	*31.14*
Average 1989–91							
a) State budget	99.35	0.00	0.00	0.00	0.00	0.65	*0.00*
b) Domestic loans	77.25	11.19	4.39	0.00	0.00	7.17	*15.58*
c) Foreign investment	95.06	0.00	0.00	0.00	0.00	4.94	*0.00*
d) Self-raised funds	51.07	7.76	32.35	0.00	0.00	8.81	*40.11*
e) Others	63.10	20.43	13.71	0.00	0.00	2.75	*34.14*

Table 11A.3 (continued)

	National total	State-owned enterprises	Rural collectives	Rural individuals	Solely Hong Kong. Taiwan and Macao	Foreign-financed firms	Other forms	*Memo item: Rural sector (collectives & individuals)*
Average 1992–96								
a) State budget		92.32	5.04	0.00	0.08	0.66	1.90	*5.04*
b) Domestic loans		65.88	14.93	2.11	1.60	4.89	10.59	*17.04*
c) Foreign investment		49.63	8.18	0.00	9.57	27.88	4.74	*8.18*
d) Self-raised funds		55.75	9.66	17.91	0.82	2.99	12.87	*27.57*
e) Others		54.44	20.82	5.74	2.71	4.64	11.65	*26.56*

Note: The national total in Part A is constructed by summing up investment funding data from different funding sources. On the average, the former is smaller by 4%. The national total here is smaller than the fixed asset investment data from the revised national accounts reported in *China Statistical Yearbook* 1996, p. 47.

Table 11A.4 Investment financing of collectively-owned TVEs in the coastal and central provinces

	1. State budget	2. Funds from supervising agency	3. Bank and credit union loans	4. Foreign funds	5. Other funds raised outside of the firm	6. Bonds sold to employees	7. Other internal funds	8. Other sources	Total funds
Part A: TVE Investment Funding: Regional Share of National Total of Funds from Each Source (%)									
(for each year within each column. the sum would be 100 for all 5 geographical groupings. or for all 30 provinces)									
Coastal provinces									
1987	39.0	37.9	50.6	73.9	56.9	55.6	59.3	58.7	52.7
1996	27.4	35.9	46.0	58.7	22.2	40.8	53.6	49.9	47.2
avg 89–91	42.4	43.6	51.3	65.8	44.5	59.3	61.4	63.5	53.8
avg 92–96	36.9	42.3	51.5	68.4	37.5	45.9	57.8	58.5	53.4
Central provinces									
1987	27.2	20.9	24.7	17.5	22.3	30.0	18.8	24.5	23.3
1996	45.5	27.3	28.9	12.6	44.9	34.4	24.4	29.8	27.7
avg 89–91	26.4	19.3	19.4	3.6	20.5	27.3	16.8	15.3	18.0
avg 92–96	32.2	23.8	24.1	10.9	32.4	30.9	20.9	23.5	23.1
Shandong (a coastal province)									
1987	11.5	10.5	12.6	10.0	5.2	14.6	14.7	14.7	12.7
1996	8.9	8.5	17.1	6.6	7.4	11.6	16.1	13.8	13.7
avg 89–91	7.6	11.0	14.1	8.7	4.7	17.8	14.4	18.0	13.0
avg 92–96	7.0	11.9	15.8	9.8	9.7	12.9	17.0	16.5	14.7

Table 11A.4 (continued)

	1. State budget	2. Funds from supervising agency	3. Bank and credit union loans	4. Foreign funds	5. Other funds raised outside of the firm	6. Bonds sold to employees	7. Other internal funds	8. Other sources	Total funds
Sichuan (a central province)									
1987	5.1	3.1	6.3	1.7	5.9	10.5	3.7	11.0	5.9
1996	4.6	1.7	4.1	0.5	4.7	3.0	4.4	5.3	3.9
avg 89–91	4.2	3.3	3.3	0.1	5.4	7.0	3.5	4.6	3.7
avg 92–96	4.4	2.3	4.4	1.2	6.1	4.0	5.1	5.7	4.5
Part B: TVE Investment: Composition of Funding from Each Source (%)									
(each row sums to 100)									
National average									
1987	3.6	7.1	48.4	1.2	5.6	4.7	21.8	7.7	
1996	0.6	1.8	24.6	10.3	10.8	6.6	36.4	8.9	
avg 89–91	3.3	6.7	37.5	5.7	8.5	3.7	25.9	8.8	
avg 92–96	1.0	3.0	29.6	8.8	9.0	7.4	31.9	9.4	
Coastal provinces									
1987	3.5	5.8	46.3	1.7	6.7	5.4	23.1	7.6	
1996	0.3	1.4	23.9	12.8	5.1	5.7	41.4	9.4	
avg 89–91	2.8	5.7	33.5	8.2	6.2	4.4	29.1	9.9	
avg 92–96	0.8	2.4	27.2	13.4	6.2	8.2	32.1	9.6	

Central provinces								
1987	4.9	7.4	51.5	0.9	5.1	5.1	18.8	6.2
1996	0.9	1.8	25.6	4.7	17.4	8.2	32.0	9.6
avg 89–91	5.3	7.7	41.3	0.9	8.3	5.3	23.8	7.4
avg 92–96	1.4	3.2	31.3	4.9	12.2	10.1	27.9	9.2
Shandong (a coastal province)								
1987	3.2	5.9	48.1	1.0	2.3	5.4	25.2	8.9
1996	0.4	1.1	30.7	5.0	5.8	5.6	42.8	9.0
avg 89–91	1.9	5.6	40.7	3.1	3.0	5.1	28.6	12.1
avg 92–95	0.5	2.6	31.6	5.7	5.8	6.5	36.9	10.6
Sichuan (a central province)								
1987	3.1	3.7	51.4	0.3	5.5	8.4	13.4	14.3
1996	0.7	0.8	25.6	1.3	13.0	5.1	41.4	12.1
avg 89–91	3.8	6.2	33.4	0.1	13.0	7.3	25.3	11.0
avg 92–96	1.0	1.5	28.7	2.2	12.1	6.4	36.1	12.0

Sources: Data from various issues of TVE yearbooks. 1988 data are not available.

12. Exports and economic performance: evidence from a panel of Chinese enterprises*

Aart Kraay[a]

1 INTRODUCTION

This chapter investigates whether firms learn from exporting, using a panel data set of 2105 Chinese industrial enterprises between 1988 and 1992. I find that, controlling for past firm performance and unobserved firm characteristics, past exports are a significant predictor of current enterprise performance. These learning effects can be quite large: the estimated coefficients indicate that a 10 percentage point increase in a firm's export to output ratio in a given year leads to 13% higher labour productivity, 2% higher total factor productivity, and 6% lower unit costs in the following year. Interestingly, these learning effects are most pronounced among established exporters. For new entrants to export markets, learning effects are insignificant and occasionally negative.

Although the superior economic performance of exporting firms relative to non-exporters has been extensively documented in a number of developed and developing countries,[1] the question of causality between exports and firm performance has only recently begun to receive attention. After all, the better average performance of exporters may simply be due to exporters self-selecting into export markets precisely because they are more efficient. On the other hand, it is also possible that firms might learn from exporting

* This chapter has been published in a special issue of Revue d'Economie du Développement, no. 1-2, 1999.

a I would like to thank David Dollar, William Easterly, Mary Hallward-Driemeier, Pascal Mazodier, Barry Naughton, Jakob Svensson, James Tybout, Colin Xu, and seminar participants at the World Bank and the Université d'Auvergne for helpful comments, and Jean Imbs for diligent research assistance. The opinions expressed herein are the author's, and do not necessarily reflect the views of the World Bank, its executive directors, or the countries they represent.

through a variety of channels. Somewhat informally, it is often argued that exposure to global markets elicits greater entrepreneurial effort on the part of managers, forcing them to become more 'competitive'. More concretely, there is evidence that developing-country exporters benefit from a range of trade-related linkages with their developed-country customers, such as production or managerial advice embedded in supplier specifications.[2]

Papers by Bernard and Jensen (1995, 1999a, 1999b) and Clerides et al. (1998) present attempts to disentangle the direction of causation between exports and firm performance, using panel data on samples of US firms and Colombian, Moroccan, and Mexican firms respectively. In contrast with the present chapter, both these papers find that there is little evidence that past exports are associated with improvements in future firm performance, casting doubt on the existence of learning effects. This chapter extends the work of these authors in two directions. First, I consider a different panel data set of 2105 large and medium-sized Chinese industrial enterprises between 1988 and 1992. The experience of these firms is of considerable independent interest given China's swift growth and the rapid expansion of its trade from a very low base during the 1980s. Although China's opening to world markets is often cited by many observers as one of the key factors responsible for China's growth, there is little evidence on the effects of trade on economic performance at the firm level.[3]

Second, I employ a somewhat different empirical methodology than these earlier papers. For a partial correlation between past exports and current performance to constitute evidence of learning from exporting, it is necessary to employ a methodology which rules out two alternative sources of this correlation: (i) unobserved firm-specific factors which are correlated with both exports and firm performance, and (ii) the confluence of persistence in firm performance and self selection of better firms into export markets. Accordingly, I employ a dynamic panel specification in which firm performance depends on lagged performance and lagged exports. I address the difficulty of unobserved firm-specific effects by working with a first-differenced specification, while the presence of lagged performance and an appropriate choice of instruments rules out the second explanation.[4] Finally, unlike these earlier papers, I allow the coefficient on lagged exports to vary with the export history of the firm, and so allow learning effects to depend on how long firms have been in export markets. I find that there are large differences in learning effects between recent entrants and established exporters. This raises the possibility that the failure of earlier studies to find learning effects may be simply because these studies pool information across firms with different export histories.

The chapter is organized as follows. The next section introduces the data and confirms the empirical regularity that exporting firms enjoy better performance than non-exporting firms in this sample of Chinese enterprises. The next section presents formal tests of learning from exporting. The final section offers concluding remarks.

2 ARE EXPORTERS AND NON-EXPORTERS DIFFERENT?

In this section, I first briefly discuss the data set and document the characteristics of the sample of firms. I then summarize some of the features of the exporting firms in the sample, and confirm that in China, as in other countries, exporters tend to be larger and more efficient than non-exporters. The question of causation between exports and firm performance is taken up in the following section.

Data and Sample Characteristics

This chapter exploits data from a rich panel data set of over 7000 large and medium-sized Chinese industrial enterprises between 1988 and 1992 compiled by China's State Statistical Bureau. The data set is a subsample of the annual Chinese industrial survey upon which published aggregate industrial statistics are based, and contains consistent time series for a large number of physical and financial indicators of enterprises, including exports. Unfortunately, there are many missing values in the data, especially for the exports variable, which forces consideration of a much smaller subsample of 2105 enterprises for which it is possible to construct a balanced panel of observations on all relevant variables. The details of how the variables used in the chapter were constructed from the underlying data are given in Appendix 1.

Tables 12.1 and 12.2 present an overview of key variables for the sample of 2105 firms. Although the sample represents only a tiny fraction of the hundreds of thousands of Chinese industrial enterprises, the large firms in the sample account for about 10% of industrial gross output value and employment, and 11% of exports in 1988. Although the share of the sample in total employment is roughly constant over the sample period, the share of the sample in gross output falls to 8.6% in 1992, and the share in exports falls precipitously to 6.8%. This is primarily due to biases in the composition of the sample of firms relative to the population of Chinese industrial enterprises, as documented in the first panel of Table 12.2. The sample of firms is heavily skewed towards state-owned enterprises, which have on average experienced slower output and export growth than the rest of the economy (World Bank, 1996; 1997). The sample is also somewhat skewed in its sectoral composition, with sectors such as textiles and ferrous metals over-represented, and many sectors entirely unrepresented. These compositional biases, as well as any additional selection biases caused by limiting the sample to a balanced panel, suggest that some caution is in order in extending the results of this chapter to all firms.

Table 12.1 Summary statistics for enterprise sample

	1988	1989	1990	1991	1992
Gross output value (billions yuan)					
Sample	185.06	220.37	232.94	263.48	320.34
Population[a]	1822.40	2201.71	2392.44	2824.80	3706.57
Sample/Population (%)	10.15	10.01	9.74	9.33	8.64
Employment (thousands)					
Sample	6502.64	6684.83	6724.11	6827.20	6978.28
Population[a]	61580.00	62280.00	63780.00	65510.00	66210.00
Sample/Population (%)	10.56	10.73	10.54	10.42	10.54
Exports (billions yuan)					
Sample	19.71	24.25	27.90	31.90	31.80
Population[b]	176.67	195.60	298.58	382.71	467.53
Sample/Population (%)	11.16	12.40	9.34	8.33	6.80

Notes:
a. Refers to industry only.
b. Refers to economy wide exports.

Characteristics of Exporting Firms

Table 12.3 presents summary statistics on the exporting firms in the sample. The first panel reveals that between 64 and 72% of all firms report positive exports over the sample period. Exporters account for a somewhat larger share of employment and gross output, reflecting the larger average size of exporters relative to non-exporters. The second panel shows that on average, exporting firms export between 12 and 15% of their gross output, but the large standard deviation indicates that there is substantial cross-sectional variation in this ratio across firms. Table 12.4 highlights the contribution to this variation of differences in export ratios across sectors and forms of ownership. In 1990, the state-owned enterprises which constitute the majority of the sample exported about 14% of their output, considerably less than collectively-owned enterprises who exported 25% of their output. Textiles, garments and pharmaceuticals are the most export-oriented sectors, exporting 30%, 21% and 19% of gross value of industrial output (GVIO) respectively, while automobiles and ferrous metals at 3 and 5% respectively are the least export-oriented sectors.

Table 12.2 Distribution of sample by ownership and sector, 1990 (%)

	Gross output value		Employment	
	Sample	Population	Sample	Population
By Ownership[a]				
State-owned units	95.92	54.60	96.07	68.42
Collectively-owned units	2.49	35.62	2.63	29.41
Others	1.59	9.77	1.30	2.16
By Sector[b]				
Textiles	25.69	14.55	29.29	14.05
Garments	1.20	2.63	0.92	3.11
Basic chemicals	5.59	9.47	4.11	7.20
Pharmaceuticals	5.14	2.26	3.56	1.53
Chemical fibres	3.77	1.73	2.08	0.64
Construction materials	1.36	n.a.	1.51	n.a.
Ferrous metals	32.11	8.25	27.15	5.66
Machinery	13.67	10.63	21.30	18.65
Automobiles	6.94	4.53	6.25	3.79
Electronics	4.52	3.71	3.84	2.96
Other[c]		42.24		42.42

Notes:
Sectoral distribution for population is approximate due to an imperfect concordance between documentation of dataset and published national totals.
a. Population refers to all of industry (including mining and utilities).
b. Population refers to manufacturing only.
c. Refers to sectors not represented in sample.

The large sectoral variation in the incidence of exporters documented in the second column of Table 12.4 suggests that the larger average size of exporters implied by Table 12.3 could simply be an artifact of the sectoral composition of exporting firms, with exporters being more prevalent in sectors populated by larger firms. However, Table 12.5, which reports average firm size controlling for the sectoral, regional and ownership composition of exporters, shows that this is not the case.[5] Even within these groups, exporters tend to be nearly twice as large as non-exporters, both in terms of gross output value and employment, and this difference is highly significant.

Table 12.3 Summary statistics on exporters

	1988	1989	1990	1991	1992
Number of exporting firms	1348	1410	1490	1509	1492
Exporters' percentage share of:					
Number of firms	64.04	66.98	70.78	71.69	70.88
Gross output value	73.24	77.14	81.32	83.57	82.14
Employment	72.09	76.52	80.38	82.22	81.27
Exports/gross output value					
Mean[a]	0.145	0.143	0.147	0.145	0.121
Standard deviation	0.218	0.217	0.217	0.225	0.216

Note: a. Weighted by gross output value.

Table 12.6 presents some indicators of the within-firm variation over time in exports between 1988 and 1992. The upper panel documents the fact that a firm's status as an exporter or non-exporter is highly persistent over time, by reporting the probabilities that an exporting (non-exporting) firm continues to export (not export) from one year to the next, averaging over all firms in all periods. Given that a firm exported in a particular year, the probability that a firm continues to export in the following year is 0.905. Similarly, the probability that a firm does not export in a given year, conditional on not having exported in the previous year, is 0.836, and the probability that a non-exporter breaks into export markets is only 0.164. This is not to say, however, that there is little time-series variation in the export ratio itself. The lower panel of Table 12.6 presents the mean and standard deviation of year-over-year changes in the export to gross output value ratio. The large standard deviations indicate that there is considerable variation around the average change in exports. For example, between 1990 and 1991, these figures indicate that fully half of the firms in the sample experienced a change in their export ratio larger than 7% in absolute value, and one quarter experienced changes greater than 12% in absolute value.

Table 12.4 Summary statistics on exporters by ownership and sector, 1990

		Exporter percentage share of:			Exports/gross output	
	Number of exporters	Number of firms	Gross output value	Employment	Mean	Standard deviation
By Ownership						
State-owned units	99	74.44	80.16	77.65	0.25	0.26
Collectively-owned units	1353	70.36	81.45	80.49	0.14	0.21
Others	38	77.55	75.10	77.86	0.16	0.19
By Sector						
Textiles	540	87.95	93.47	92.31	0.30	0.24
Garments	19	63.33	62.79	60.13	0.21	0.35
Basic chemicals	86	68.80	79.81	77.42	0.11	0.13
Pharmaceuticals	139	81.29	90.27	86.71	0.19	0.18
Chemical fibres	24	40.00	58.71	62.31	0.08	0.13
Construction materials	22	46.81	53.34	49.12	0.08	0.05
Ferrous metals	65	60.19	77.95	76.64	0.05	0.12
Machinery	414	62.73	76.27	75.41	0.11	0.17
Automobiles	58	45.67	78.01	72.51	0.03	0.08
Electronics	123	75.46	80.47	80.33	0.11	0.19

Table 12.5 Size of exporters and non-exporters (unweighted averages of selected variables [a])

		1988	1989	1990	1991	1992
Gross output value	Exporters	100545	120553	127133	145916	176370
(thousands yuan)	Non-exporters	65421	72497	70747	72643	93309
	P-value[b]	0.00	0.00	0.00	0.00	0.00
Employment	Exporters	3478	3628	3627	3720	3801
	Non-exporters	2397	2259	2145	2036	2133
	P-value[b]	0.00	0.00	0.00	0.00	0.00

Notes:
a. Controlling for ownership, sector and province effects.
b. P-value is for test of null hypothesis that the means for exporters and non-exporters are equal.

Table 12.6 Persistence and volatility of export status

Persistence: Transition matrix for export status				
	Export at time t + 1		Don't export at time t + 1	
Export at time *t*	0.905		0.095	
Don't export at time *t*	0.164		0.836	
Volatility: Change in exports/gross output value[a]				
	1988–89	1989–90	1990–91	1990–92
Mean	0.010	0.017	0.007	-0.020
Standard deviation	0.093	0.106	0.122	0.121

Note: a. Refers to firms with positive exports in both of the two years over which change is calculated.

Do Exporters Perform Better than Non-exporters?

In order to investigate differences in enterprise performance between exporters and non-exporters, I require indicators of economic performance over time for all firms. I consider three measures: labour productivity, total factor productivity and unit costs. I measure labour productivity as gross output per worker in constant 1990 prices, and unit costs as the current price ratio of cost of goods sold to sales revenue. Total factor productivity is constructed as the residual from a three-factor constant returns Cobb-Douglas gross output production function using capital, labour and materials as inputs. Capital is measured as the net value of fixed assets, labour input is measured as the annual average number of workers, and materials are measured in constant 1990 prices. The output elasticities are simply measured as the current-price shares of factor payments in gross output, and are allowed to vary across sectors and over time. In particular, the output elasticity of labour in each sector and year is estimated as the sectoral average of wage payments (including bonuses) to gross output, while the output elasticity of materials is measured as materials consumption divided by gross output. Given the assumption of constant returns to scale, the capital output elasticity is one minus the other two elasticities.[6]

It is worth noting in passing that considerable controversy surrounds various measures of enterprise productivity in China.[7] Much of this controversy results from efforts to reconcile the anomalous behaviour of various published price indexes for output and material inputs, and the consequences of different reconciliations for the relative productivity performance of state and non-state industry. Since I am not interested in comparisons between state and non-state industry, but rather between exporters and non-exporters in a sample consisting primarily of state-owned enterprises, I am able to sidestep much of the controversy surrounding the choice of appropriate deflators. Moreover, in the empirical work in the following sections, I enter the firm performance variables in logarithms and include ownership dummies interacted with period dummies, which has the effect of sweeping out any variation in deflators across ownership forms.

Table 12.7 summarizes the differences in firm performance between exporting and non-exporting firms. The first panel reports the simple averages of labour productivity, total factor productivity, and unit costs in exporting and non-exporting firms, pooling the data for all firms and years. Both measures of productivity are significantly higher in exporting firms, with exporters enjoying a productivity advantage of between 2 and 9% over non-exporters. In terms of unit costs, exporters appear to have slightly worse performance than non-exporters, but this is an artifact of the sectoral composition of exporters. The lower panel presents the same averages as the upper panel, but now controlling for the sectoral, regional and ownership distribution of exporters. The productivity advantage of exporters persists, and exporters now also enjoy slightly lower unit costs than non-exporters.

In summary, the empirical regularities observed in this sample of predominantly state-owned Chinese industrial enterprises are consistent with those documented in several other countries. Exporting firms tend to be larger than non-exporting firms, and enjoy higher productivity and lower unit costs. Although a firm's status as an exporter is very persistent over time, there is substantial time-series variation in the export to gross output ratio of exporting firms. This last feature of the data is important, because in the next section I will use the within-firm time-series variation in exports and performance measures to identify learning effects.

Table 12.7 Comparing performance of exporters and non-exporters

	Exporters	Non-exporters	p[a]
Unconditional			
Labour productivity	36.652	33.694	0.000
Total factor productivity	2.014	1.965	0.000
Unit costs	0.922	0.912	0.001
Conditional[b]			
Labour productivity	45.819	42.844	0.000
Total factor productivity	2.105	2.057	0.000
Unit costs	0.949	0.961	0.000

Notes:
a. P-value is for test of null hypothesis that the means for exporters and non-exporters are equal.
b. Conditioning on sector, ownership and regional effects.

3 DO EXPORTERS LEARN FROM EXPORTING?

In this section, I formally test whether the better average performance of exporting firms documented in the previous section can be attributed to exporters learning from exporting. In contrast to other work, I find a statistically and economically significant effect of lagged exports on current firm performance, suggesting the presence of learning from exporting.

Specification and Identification

The empirical strategy in this section is to test whether a firm's performance, as measured by labour productivity, total factor productivity, and unit costs, depends on its past export experience. For such a test to constitute evidence in favour of learning by exporting, it is necessary to rule out two alternative explanations for any observed correlation between past exports and current enterprise performance.

First, current enterprise performance may depend on past export experience due to unobserved enterprise characteristics that affect both performance and exports. For example, certain firms might have more energetic managers who run efficient operations with lower unit costs than their competitors, and also aggressively seek out foreign markets, while other firms might be run by more conservative managers who are unwilling to implement efficiency-enhancing reforms and also prefer to rely on traditional domestic markets. Such unobservable firm characteristics may give rise to spurious correlations between lagged exports and current enterprise performance. Second, firm performance is itself likely to be persistent over time, and is jointly determined with a firm's export performance. For example, if production is characterized by scale economies, an expansion of plant size today may result in lower unit costs for many periods in the future. If firms with better performance self-select into export markets, and if firm performance is correlated over time, then current performance will be correlated with past export behaviour even in the absence of learning effects.

To distinguish the learning hypothesis from these two alternative explanations, I estimate a series of regressions of firm performance on lagged exports and lagged firm performance. The estimation technique is selected so as to yield consistent estimates of the coefficient on lagged firm performance and lagged exports even in the presence of unobserved firm-specific time-invariant effects that are correlated with the explanatory variables.[8] To the extent that unobserved firm characteristics such as managerial ability do not vary over time, this rules out the first explanation for the correlation between lagged exports and current firm performance. The inclusion of lagged firm performance in the regression controls for serial dependence in this variable, and the appropriate choice of lagged variables as instruments addresses the problem that exports and firm performance are jointly determined. Hence, I can also distinguish the learning hypothesis from the second explanation mentioned above.

Specifically, I estimate variants on the following equation:

$$y_{ijt} = \beta \cdot y_{ij,t-1} + \gamma \cdot x_{ij,t-1} + \eta_i + \lambda_{jt} + \varepsilon_{ijt} \tag{12.1}$$

where y_{ijt} and x_{ijt} denote the logarithm of firm performance and the export to gross output value ratio of firm i of ownership form j at time t, η_i is an unobserved firm-specific effect, and λ_{jt} is an unobserved period-specific effect which may also vary across ownership forms. Finally, ε_{ijt} is a well-behaved zero-mean disturbance term.

To eliminate the individual and period-specific effects from equation (12.1), I take deviations of all variables from period- and ownership-specific means, and then difference these deviations to obtain:

$$\Delta\tilde{y}_{ijt} = \beta \cdot \Delta\tilde{y}_{ij,t-1} + \gamma \cdot \Delta\tilde{x}_{ij,t-1} + \Delta\tilde{\varepsilon}_{ijt} \tag{12.2}$$

where Δ is the first difference operator and $\tilde{y}_{ijt}$, $\tilde{x}_{ij,t\ 1}$, and $\tilde{\varepsilon}_{ijt}$ denote deviations from period – and ownership-specific averages.[9]

Two assumptions on the structure of the disturbances are required to identify the parameters of the model. First, I assume that there is no serial dependence in ε_{ijt}, that is, $E[\varepsilon_{ijt} \cdot \varepsilon_{ijs}] = 0$ for all $s \neq t$. Second, I assume that, although firm performance and exports are jointly determined, exports are predetermined with respect to ε_{ijt}, that is, $E[x_{ijt} \cdot \varepsilon_{ijs}] = 0$ for all $s > t$. Although the first-differencing introduces a correlation between the transformed residual and the first difference of lagged firm performance, the assumption of no serial dependence in the untransformed residual ensures that second and higher lags of firm performance are available as instruments for $\Delta\tilde{y}_{ij,\ t\ 1}$. The assumptions of no serial correlation and predeterminacy of exports imply that second and higher lags of exports are valid instruments for $\Delta\tilde{x}_{ij,\ t\ 1}$.

How valid are these identifying assumptions? If firm performance exhibits higher than first-order serial dependence, the residual term in equation (12.1) will also be serially correlated, invalidating the first identifying assumption. Since the short available time span of the data set makes it difficult to include several lags of the dependent variable, the only alternative is to test whether the estimated differenced residuals in equation (12.2) exhibit second-order serial dependence. It will turn out that they do not, providing some comfort for the first identifying assumption. The assumption that exports are predetermined with respect to ε_{ijt} would arise naturally in any model in which both exports and firm performance depend on their own and the other's lagged values (as well as other exogenous variables).[10]

Basic Results

The results of this basic specification are presented in Table 12.8. The model is estimated using one lag of firm performance and one lag of exports over the period from 1990 to 1992, since the differencing and choice of twice-lagged variables as instruments eliminates the first two years from the estimation period. As instruments, I use only the second lags of firm performance and exports. Results using the full set of all available second and higher lags as instruments are quite similar, and are not reported for brevity.[11]

The highly significant and positive coefficients on lagged firm performance in the first row of the table confirm that firm performance is persistent over time. More interestingly, there is statistically significant evidence of learning from exporting. Past exports are positively associated with current labour productivity and total factor productivity, and negatively associated with unit costs. The magnitude of these effects are also economically significant. Recalling that the performance measure is expressed in logarithms, the magnitudes of the coefficients on lagged exports imply that an increase of 0.1 in a firm's export ratio (roughly one sample standard deviation) causes a 13% increase in labour productivity, a 2% increase in total factor productivity, and a 6% reduction in unit costs in the following year.

Table 12.8 Basic model results

	Labour productivity	Total factor productivity	Unit costs
Lagged performance	1.037***	0.541***	0.221***
	(0.087)	(0.032)	(0.031)
Lagged exports	1.321***	0.233***	-0.647**
	(0.252)	(0.079)	(0.108)
P-value for no serial correlation test	0.003**	0.947	0.264

Notes:
Model estimated over the period 1990–1992, using second lags of firm performance and exports as instruments.
Standard errors in parentheses: (*) (**) (***) indicates significance at the (10%) (5%) (1%) level.

The last row of Table 12.8 reports the p-value associated with a test of the null hypothesis that there is no second-order serial correlation in the differenced residuals in equation (12.2). In the case of unit costs and total factor productivity, this null hypothesis is not rejected at a 5% level, suggesting that the identifying assumptions are indeed valid. In the case of labour productivity, the null is rejected at the 5% level. However, if I augment this specification with an additional lag of labour productivity, the null is no longer rejected, and the coefficient on lagged exports actually becomes much larger.

The rather large estimates of learning using these measures should be interpreted with some caution. Both exports and some measures of firm performance are quite persistent over time. As a result, lagged levels of these variables will not be very highly correlated with contemporaneous changes in these variables. This suggests that lagged levels may be weak instruments for the right-hand side variables in equation (12.2). In the case of weak instruments, it is well-known that in finite samples the instrumental variables estimates are biased towards the probability limits of the OLS estimates of equation (12.2). Therefore, the instrumental variables procedure I employ may only imperfectly address the endogeneity problems which motivate its use, and hence the learning effects may be somewhat overstated.[12]

Controlling for Export Histories

One shortcoming of the above regressions is that they do not control for the export history of a firm. The relationship between lagged exports and current firm performance may depend on the export history of a firm for a number of reasons. Suppose for example that learning from exporting is a one-shot affair in the sense that breaking into export markets is associated with a one-time improvement in firm performance. In this case, lagged exports should be positively correlated with firm performance only in the first few years after a firm enters the export market, but not if a firm has been exporting for many years.

If on the other hand learning is an on-going process, then lagged exports will be positively associated with current performance even in firms that have been exporting for many years. Moreover, if there are high entry costs which must be incurred before a firm can begin to export, then measured firm performance may initially deteriorate as it breaks into export markets. Only as the firm recoups these start-up costs will exports eventually be associated with better firm performance. Finally, it is even possible that firms choose to exit from export markets because they have exhausted all the learning benefits from exporting.

This raises the possibility that the basic regressions of the previous subsection are misspecified since they impose the same coefficient on lagged exports for all firms, regardless of their export history. I address this concern by re-estimating equation (12.1), allowing the coefficient on lagged exports to vary with the export history of the firm. Specifically, the export history of a firm may be thought of as a sequence of indicator variables for each firm in each year, which take on the value one if a firm exports in that year and zero if it does not. Even with only five years of data, a very large number of distinct export histories are represented in our sample of firms, which would result in a very large number of different coefficients on lagged exports to be estimated. In order to conserve on degrees of freedom and impose some structure on the problem, I instead consider five types of export histories: (i) firms that export over the entire sample period (established exporters); (ii) firms that initially do not export but at some point during the sample begin exporting and continue to export through the end of the sample period (entrants); (iii) firms that initially export but leave the export market for the duration of the sample period (exiters); (iv) firms that switch between exporting and not exporting more than once over the sample (switchers); and (v) firms that never export (non-exporters).[13] As shown in Table 12.9, slightly over half of the firms in the sample fall in the first category. Relatively few firms are classified as either entrants or exiters (252 and 113 respectively, representing 12 and 5% of the total sample), and the remainder are switchers (279) or never export at all (343).

Table 12.9 Export histories

	Number of firms	Share of total (%)
Always export	1 118	53.1
Entrants	252	12.0
Enter in 89	79	3.8
Enter in 90	67	3.2
Enter in 91	63	3.0
Enter in 92	43	2.0
Exiters	113	5.4
Exit in 89	26	1.2
Exit in 90	15	0.7
Exit in 91	36	1.7
Exit in 92	36	1.7
Switchers	279	13.3
Never export	343	16.3

Next, I specify a more general form of equation (12.1) in which the coefficients on lagged exports are allowed to vary with the export history of the firm. In particular, for $t = 1991$ and $t = 1992$, the following pair of equations relate performance to lagged performance and lagged exports:

$$y_{i91} = \beta \cdot y_{i90} + \begin{bmatrix} \gamma^{ENT} \cdot D_{i89}^{ENT} + \gamma^{EXT} \cdot \left(D_{i89}^{EXT} + D_{i90}^{EXT}\right) \\ +\gamma^{ALW} \cdot D_i^{ALW} + \gamma^{SWI} \cdot D_i^{SWI} \end{bmatrix} \cdot x_{i90} + \eta_i + \lambda_{91} + \varepsilon_{i91}$$

$$y_{i92} = \beta \cdot y_{i91} + \begin{bmatrix} \gamma^{ENT} \cdot \left(D_{i89}^{ENT} + D_{i90}^{ENT}\right) + \gamma^{EXT} \cdot D_{i91}^{EXT} \\ +\gamma^{ALW} \cdot D_i^{ALW} + \gamma^{SWI} \cdot D_i^{SWI} \end{bmatrix} \cdot x_{i91} + \eta_i + \lambda_{92} + \varepsilon_{i92} \tag{12.3}$$

where γ^j, $j = ENT, EXT, ALW, SWI$ is the coefficient on lagged exports for entrants, exiters, established exporters, and switchers, respectively; D_{it}^{ENT}

(D_{it}^{EXT}) is a dummy variable which takes on the value 1 if entrant (exiter) firm i enters (exits) the export market in year t; and D_i^{ALW} and D_i^{SWI} are dummy variables which take on the value 1 if the firm always exports or is a switcher. Firms that do not export are excluded.

Although equation (12.3) differs slightly from equation (12.2) in the sense that there are different right-hand-side variables in the two time periods, it can be estimated in the same manner as before. That is, I first take deviations of all variables from period – and ownership-specific means to eliminate period effects, and then take first-differences to eliminate firm-specific effects. Then, the assumptions that exports are predetermined and that there is no serial correlation in the residual again imply that second and higher lags of firm performance and exports interacted with the various indicator variables are available as instruments in each period. Note that there is no variation in twice-lagged exports of entrants for $t = 1990$ (since exports in 1988 are by definition zero for this group of firms). For this reason, I can only estimate this specification for $t = 1991$ and $t = 1992$.

The results of this more general specification are presented in Table 12.10 for the three measures of firm performance. For comparison purposes, the first panel presents the results of re-estimating the restricted model in equation (12.1) over the period 1991–1992, which are quite similar to those obtained for the full period. The lower panel allows the coefficient on lagged exports to vary with the export history of the firm. The most striking result which emerges is that learning effects are consistently positive and significant only for established exporters. Among entrants, there is weakly significant evidence that lagged exports are associated with lower current productivity, consistent with the view that entry into export markets is initially costly.

It is somewhat puzzling that learning effects seem to be most pronounced among established exporters – firms that report positive exports in all five years of the sample. This runs counter to the common intuition that new entrants to export markets should benefit most from exposure to the competitive pressures of global markets. One possible explanation for this relies on the structure of China's trade and foreign exchange institutions, which may have given the exporting firms in the sample preferential access to foreign exchange.[14] If this foreign exchange was used to purchase superior-quality imported capital goods and other inputs, it may account for the association between exports and enterprise performance documented above. However, this explanation is not entirely convincing during the sample period of the late 1980s and early 1990s, at which time a foreign exchange swap market was relatively well-established. Another explanation may simply be that the classification of 'established exporters' is misleading. If many of these firms began exporting shortly before the beginning of the sample period in 1988, and if learning from exporting occurs for several years after breaking into export markets, then the learning effects observed in the sample may be representative of those experienced by new entrants into export markets.

Table 12.10 Basic model controlling for export histories

	Labour productivity	Total factor productivity	Unit costs
Restricted model			
Lagged performance	0.811***	0.474***	0.195***
	(0.134)	(0.046)	(0.039)
Lagged exports	1.188***	0.227**	-0.687***
	(0.254)	(0.101)	(0.150)
Unrestricted model			
Lagged performance	0.778***	0.469***	0.196***
	(0.145)	(0.046)	(0.039)
Lagged exports in entrants	-5.428*	-1.082	-0.275
	(3.153)	(0.667)	(0.579)
Lagged exports in exiters	0.982	0.236	0.094
	(2.974)	(1.353)	(1.758)
Lagged exports in established exporters	1.477***	0.293***	-0.688***
	(0.295)	(0.110)	(0.164)
Lagged exports in switchers	0.735	0.151	-0.801*
	(0.743)	(0.309)	(0.414)

Notes:
Model estimated over the period 1991–1992, using second lags of firm performance and exports as instruments.
Standard errors in parentheses: (*) (**) (***) indicates significance at the (10%) (5%) (1%) level.

4 CONCLUSIONS

This chapter has examined whether firms learn from exporting, in the sense that past exports lead to improvements in current firm performance. In contrast to the findings of other authors for different countries, I find that in this sample of Chinese industrial enterprises, past exports are in fact significantly associated with higher labour productivity and total factor productivity, and with lower unit costs, suggesting that firms do in fact reap efficiency benefits from exporting. It is particularly interesting to note that these sizeable learning effects are present in a sample consisting primarily of state-owned enterprises, which have been widely viewed as being slow to respond to and benefit from China's move to a more market-oriented economy.

These results raise a number of questions for future research. Although the correlation between past exports and current firm performance provides interesting and suggestive evidence of learning from exporting, it is less clear what exactly firms are learning, from whom, and how. Do firms become better at producing their outputs (perhaps thanks to supplier specifications provided by their clients), or do firms simply learn to be better exporters (as they develop familiarity with export markets and distribution channels)? Do the benefits of learning accrue solely to the exporting firm, or are their external effects from one firm's exports to anothers' performance? How long does it take for the benefits of exporting to appear? Answers to these questions will require more detailed investigation and also better data with longer time-series coverage on the precise nature of exporting firms' relationships with their clients and with each other.

NOTES

1. See among others, Chen and Tang (1987) (Taiwan), Haddad (1993) (Morocco), Aw and Hwang (1995) (Taiwan), Bernard and Jensen (1995) (United States), Djankov and Hoekman (1997) (Bulgaria).
2. See Clerides et al. (1998) for examples and a theoretical model.
3. There is a vast literature on estimating the productivity performance of Chinese enterprises (see Jefferson et al. (1996) for an overview). This literature has primarily been concerned with the effects of China's incremental reforms on the productivity performance of state – and non-state-owned enterprises. Perkins (1996, 1997) are among the few papers in this literature which explicitly consider the role of exports at the firm level. They conclude that exporting firms enjoy higher productivity. Wei (1993) using city-level data finds that exports are associated with higher growth.
4. The model estimated by Clerides et al. (1998) allows for individual effects, but requires them to be independent of explanatory variables such as lagged exports. They address the problem of persistence and self-selection by jointly estimating a system which regresses firm performance on lagged performance and a sequence of lagged dummy variables indicating export market participation, and a probit equation to describe the decision to participate in export markets. Although the joint estimation of the performance and participation equations will yield more efficient estimates than the single-equation instrumental variables estimator employed here, it requires more restrictive distributional assumptions on the disturbances and individual effects. The evidence on causation from exports to firm performance in Bernard and Jensen (1995) consists of regressions of employment growth and wage growth on initial export status, controlling for observable

firm characteristics. Initial export status is a poor predictor of wage growth, but has some explanatory power for employment growth. This specification is subject to both of the concerns mentioned in the text.

5. Specifically, I report the coefficients on dummy variables for exporters and non-exporters in a cross-sectional regression of firm size on these variables and a set of industry, provincial and ownership dummies for each year in the sample.
6. It is well-known that measures of total factor productivity constructed in this simple manner will overstate productivity if there are increasing returns and/or firms have market power. Since I will be identifying learning effects from the within-firm variation in firm performance, these concerns are only relevant if there are changes in the extent of increasing returns and/or firms' market power varies over time, and moreover is correlated with export activity in the right way. It seems reasonable to think of the extent of increasing returns as a fairly stable feature of technology which is unlikely to vary much over time. It is however possible that firms' market power declines as firms break into export markets, as they are less able to charge markups over unit costs. As a result, export market participation may be associated with falls in measured total factor productivity. This will have the effect of obscuring, rather than exaggerating, any learning effects on this measure of firm performance.
7. See Jefferson et al. (1992, 1996) and Woo et al. (1993, 1994) for a review of these issues. In this chapter I use deflators for output and materials advocated by Jefferson et al. (1992, 1996), which are based on indexes of factory-gate prices of industrial products and material inputs, rather than the implicit gross output deflator.
8. I use a dynamic panel instrumental variables estimator proposed by Arellano and Bond (1991). For applications of this technique to cross-country growth regressions, see for example Caselli et al. (1996), and Easterly et al. (1996).
9. That is, I regress each variable on a set of time dummies interacted with a set of ownership dummies, and retrieve the residuals from this regression as deviations from period – and ownership-specific means.
10. Only if exports depend on future performance will this identifying assumption be invalid. In this case, only sufficiently-lagged exports will be valid instruments.
11. To allow for the possibility that exports depend on one-period ahead productivity, I also estimated the specification using thrice-lagged variables as instruments. This again yielded similar results, with even larger and more significant learning effects.
12. See Blundell and Bond (1998) for a further discussion of these issues, and possible remedies.
13. Clearly, since I do not have a full export history for every firm, but only five years of data, this categorization may misclassify some firms. For example, some firms which are identified as always having exported may have entered export markets in 1987, and hence should be classified as entrants.
14. During the 1980s, trade and foreign exchange continued to be subject to considerable regulation. Firms were subject to foreign exchange surrender requirements and had to rely on planned allocations of foreign exchange to finance imports. However, beginning in the early 1980s, firms were allowed to retain limited amounts of above-quota foreign exchange for their own use. See World Bank (1994) for details.

REFERENCES

Arellano, M. and S. Bond (1991), 'Some Tests of Specification for Panel Data: Monte Carlo Evidence and Application to Employment Equations', *Review of Economic Studies*, 58, pp. 277–97.

Aw, B.Y. and A.R. Hwang (1995), 'Productivity and the Export Market: A Firm-Level Analysis', *Journal of Development Economics*, 47, pp. 313–32.

Bernard, A. and J.B. Jensen (1995), 'Exporters, Jobs and Wages in U.S. Manufacturing: 1976–87', *Brookings Papers on Economic Activity Microeconomics*, pp. 67–119.

Bernard, A. and J.B. Jensen (1999a), 'Exceptional Exporter Performance: Cause, Effect or Both?', *Journal of International Economics*, 47(1), pp. 1–25.

Bernard, A. and J.B. Jensen (1999b), 'Exporting and Productivity', Manuscript, Yale University.

Blundell, R. and S. Bond (1998), 'Initial Conditions and Moment Restrictions in Dynamic Panel Data Models', *Journal of Econometrics*, 87, pp. 115–43.

Caselli, F., G. Esquivel and F. Lefort (1996), 'Reopening the Convergence Debate: A New Look at Cross-Country Growth Empirics', *Journal of Economic Growth*, 1, pp. 363–89.

Chen, T. and D. Tang (1987), 'Comparing Technical Efficiency Between Import-Substitution-Oriented and Export-Oriented Foreign Firms in a Developing Economy', *Journal of Development Economics*, 26, pp. 277–89.

Clerides, S., S. Lach and J. Tybout (1998), 'Is "Learning-by-Exporting" Important? Micro Dynamic Evidence from Colombia, Mexico and Morocco', *Quarterly Journal of Economics*, 103(3), pp. 903–48.

Djankov, S. and B. Hoekman (1997), 'Trade Reorientation and Productivity Growth in Bulgarian Enterprises', World Bank Policy Research Department, Working Paper No. 1707, http://econ.workdbank.org.

Easterly, W., N. Loayza and P. Montiel (1997), 'Has Latin America's Post-Reform Growth Been Disappointing?', *Journal of International Economics*, 43(3–4), November, pp. 287–311.

Haddad, M. (1993), 'How Trade Liberalization Affected Productivity in Morocco', World Bank Policy Research Department, Working Paper No. 109, http://econ.workdbank.org.

Jefferson, G., T. Rawski and Y. Zheng (1992), 'Growth, Efficiency and Convergence in China's State and Collective Industry', *Economic Development and Cultural Change*, 40(2), pp. 239–66.

Jefferson, G., T. Rawski and Y. Zheng (1996), 'Chinese Industrial Productivity: Trends, Measurement Issues and Recent Developments', *Journal of Comparative Economics*, 23, pp. 146–80.

Perkins, F.C. (1996), 'Productivity Performance and Priorities of the Reform of China's State-Owned Enterprises', *Journal of Development Studies*, 32(3), pp. 414–44.

Perkins, F.C. (1997), 'Export Performance and Enterprise Reform in China's Coastal Provinces', *Economic Development and Cultural Change*, 45(3), pp. 501–39.

Wei, S.J. (1993), 'Open Door Policy and China's Rapid Growth: Evidence from City-Level Data', NBER Working Paper No. 4602, www.nber.org.

Woo, W.T, W. Hai, Y. Jin and G. Fan (1994), 'How Successful Has Chinese Enterprises Reform Been? Pitfalls in Opposite Biases and Focus', *Journal of Comparative Economics*, 18(3), pp. 410–37.

Woo, W.T, W. Hai, Y. Jin and G. Fan (1993), 'The Efficiency and Macroeconomic Consequences of Chinese Enterprise Reform', *China Economic Review*, 4(2), pp. 153–68.

World Bank (1994), 'China: Foreign Trade Reform', Washington, DC, World Bank.

World Bank (1996), 'China: Fighting Inflation, Deepening Reforms', Washington, DC, World Bank.

World Bank (1997), 'China: Development Challenges in the New Century', Washington, DC, World Bank.

APPENDIX: DATA CONSTRUCTION

The variables used in the chapter were constructed as follows. Gross output value and materials consumption in current prices are taken directly from the original data set, and their constant 1990 values are obtained using the gross output and materials deflators for state industry reported in Table 3 of Jefferson et al. (1996). Employment is defined as the period-average workforce, and no attempt is made to adjust for non-production workers. Capital input is measured as the net value of fixed assets, as reported in the data set. This constitutes a very rough measure of capital, particularly because it is likely that firms simply cumulate undeflated annual investments to arrive at this stock.

Total factor productivity is constructed as

$$tfp_{ijt} = q_{ijt} \cdot \left(k_{ijt}^{\alpha_{kjt}} \cdot n_{ijt}^{\alpha_{njt}} \cdot m_{ijt}^{\alpha_{mjt}} \right)^{-1} \tag{12A.1}$$

where tfp_{ijt}, q_{ijt}, k_{ijt}, n_{ijt}, m_{ijt}, represent total factor productivity, gross output, capital input, labour input and materials input of firm i in sector j respectively. The output elasticities for labour and materials in sector j at time t, α_{njt} and α_{mjt}, are measured as the current price ratios of wages (including bonuses) and materials to gross output in that sector and year. The capital output elasticity is measured as one minus the other two elasticities. Unit costs are constructed as sales revenues divided by cost of goods sold, in current prices.

Constructing export to gross output ratios is complicated by the fact that the data reports exports in current prices for certain years, and in constant prices for other years. For 1988–1990, I take the ratio of exports to gross output at 1980 prices, while for 1991–1992 I use the current price ratio. While this splicing of two different measures is undesirable, it may not be too serious. For 1990, it is possible to construct both the current and constant 1980 price ratios, and the correlation across firms in this ratio is very high (0.97).

The original data set consists of 7252 firms. Restricting the sample to those firms with a complete time series on all variables of interest reduces the sample by about two-thirds. The sample of remaining firms was reduced to the final sample of 2105 firms by eliminating firms with obvious coding errors or other extreme outliers in the variables of interest.

13. Real exchange rate and income disparity between urban and rural areas in China: a theoretic and econometric analysis*

Sylvianne Guillaumont Jeanneney and Ping Hua[a]

1 INTRODUCTION

Studies on the effects of the exchange rate policy of developing countries principally focus on the general price level, the production or the balance of payments, or consider only a particular aspect of income distribution, such as the evolution of real wages or profit-wage sharing.[1] Only a few studies have investigated the issue of the relationship between the evolution of the exchange rate and the distribution of urban and rural incomes. This is due to the fact that the number of countries for which times series on income distribution between urban and rural areas are available, is very limited.[2] The lack of the studies is all the more cumbersome that it has often been argued that the overvaluation of developing countries' domestic currencies tends to penalize farmers, and that real depreciation should therefore be beneficial to the latter.[3]

Actually, annual series of urban and rural incomes for the whole country as well as by province are available in the case of China from 1978 onwards. During the 1978–1995 period, the disparity of incomes per capita between urban and rural areas accounted for 50% of income disparity between provinces (Lin et al., 1998). Since 1981, the exchange rate policy of the country has been very active, which has resulted in a substantial real

* This chapter has been published in a special issue of Revue d'Economie du Développement, no. 1-2, 1999.

[a] The authors would like to thank the participants in the international conference on the Chinese economy entitled Openness and Disparities in China, and especially A. Benassy-Quéré, for their valuable comments. Critics and suggestions from J.F. Brun, C. Daubrée, S. Démurger, P. Guillaumont and M.F. Renard, are also gratefully acknowledged. All remaining errors are ours.

depreciation of the Chinese currency (Guillaumont Jeanneney and Hua, 1996; Guillaumont and Guillaumont Jeanneney, 1997). The case of China is thus especially relevant for assessing the relationship between the real exchange rate and the geographical distribution of incomes.

The chapter comprises three sections. The first section examines the evolution of the ratio of incomes per capita in urban areas to incomes per capita in rural areas during the various phases of the exchange rate policy. Income disparity between urban and rural areas is also analysed in relation to the disparity between geographical zones (coastal versus inland areas) as well as to the individual income disparity. In the second section, we develop a model of the relationship between the real effective exchange rate and the ratio of urban to rural incomes. The model leads to the prediction that the real depreciation of the Chinese currency might have raised the urban bias during the 1978–1996 period. However, the prediction may be opposite for coastal areas whose activities are typically more outward-oriented. The last section presents econometric results.

2 EVOLUTION OF THE DISPARITY BETWEEN URBAN AND RURAL INCOMES PER CAPITA DURING THE VARIOUS PHASES OF CHINA'S EXCHANGE RATE POLICY

The exchange rate policy pursued by China since the beginning of the liberalization programme has been quite complex, since, from 1981 to 1993, it involved a double exchange rate regime, whose nature has moreover changed over time. Since 1979, planned imports have been supported by priority foreign exchange allowances while some non-planned imports have been financed either by foreign capital or through a system of foreign exchange retention. The latter, which has been progressively expanded, allows enterprises to use part of foreign exchange earnings derived from exports to finance their own imports. Previously, foreign exchange earnings had to be entirely remitted to the central government. The retention system, which mainly aims at promoting exports of manufactured products, involves a high rate of foreign exchange retention for these exports, which should *a priori* be of greater benefit to urban areas. Since 1981, Chinese enterprises have been allowed to sell part of their export receipts at a rate, which remains fixed by the government but exceeds the commercial rate applied to planned imports. In 1985, the commercial rate was replaced by the official rate before exclusively applied to non commercial operations, whereas in late 1986 the second commercial rate, which was more favourable to enterprises, became a market price. Until their unification in January 1994, the differential between the two commercial rates have fluctuated between 10% and 70%. Both rates have markedly depreciated. In contrast, the unified exchange rate, now subject to a controlled floating regime, only slightly depreciated (compared to the dollar) in 1994 and then slightly appreciated in 1995 and 1996. These various changes explain the highly contrasted evolution of China's exchange rate policy over time.

The size of the variation in the nominal and real value of the Chinese currency (the Renminbi)[4] can be inferred from the evolution of a nominal effective exchange rate and of a real effective exchange rate respectively, with both rates being calculated allowing for the relative importance of commercial transactions (made with either one rate or the other) as well as for the geographic structure of trade[5] (see Table 13A.1). It appears that, from 1978 to 1985, the nominal and real effective exchange rates rose (which here corresponds to a depreciation) by 75% and 38% respectively. The depreciation accelerated from 1985 to 1993 since the nominal and the real effective exchange rates increased by 237% and 127% respectively. From 1993 to 1996, the nominal effective exchange rate depreciated by 1.4% while the real effective exchange rate appreciated by 29%.

Urban and rural incomes per capita were deflated by the consumer price index of each area. According to the definition of the State Statistical Bureau of China, urban income refers here to the disposable income of urban households which can be used for daily expenses, that is, total income minus income tax, property tax and other current transfers. Rural income, defined as the net income of rural households, refers to the total income of the rural households net of expenses for productive operations, the taxes and payments to collective units. The measure of these incomes is however not straightforward. In particular, the relative evolution of urban and rural incomes does not reflect the relative evolution of living standards, since the calculation of incomes does not include the indirect (in kind) incomes derived from public services (education, health and housing), which actually benefit urban households much more than rural households. When including the monetary value of these services in the calculation of incomes, the ratio of urban to rural per capita incomes is estimated to increase from 2.27 to 3.13 in 1995 (in 1990 prices) (Cai, 1998). In contrast, 16% of the incomes of rural households consists self-consumption of cereals, which, until 1990, were valued according to administered prices. Since the official price of cereals represented, on average, 72% of the market price in 1985 compared to 48% in 1990, this resulted in an increasing underestimation of agricultural incomes.

The evolution of the ratio of urban to rural incomes differs depending on whether it refers to nominal or real incomes (that is, incomes deflated by the consumer price index of each area). Indeed, over the whole period analysed here (1978–1996), and except for the years 1989 and 1990, consumer prices rose faster in urban areas than in rural areas. Indeed, between the beginning and the end of the period, the ratio of consumer prices in urban areas to consumer prices in rural areas increased by 24% (see Table 13A.1). This continuing divergence of prices has contributed to reduce the disparity between real incomes in urban and rural areas.

If we now compare the evolution of the real effective exchange rate with the evolution of the ratio of urban to rural real per capita incomes. It appears that during the first phase of reforms from 1978 to 1985, when prices of goods were still largely administered and the real exchange rate registered only a slight depreciation (except in 1981 when the depreciated commercial rate was introduced), the discrepancy between urban and rural incomes, both expressed in 1990 prices, sharply declined: the urban income, which was 2.86 times higher than the rural income in 1978, was only 1.73 times higher in 1985 (see Table 13A.1). In contrast with the previous period, this reduction in income disparity between urban and rural areas occurred in a period of rapid growth of real incomes – 15% per year in rural areas and 7% per year in urban areas. In contrast, from 1985 to 1993, while the Chinese economy shifted towards a market economy and the real effective exchange rate strongly depreciated, the disparity between urban and rural incomes widened again, as a result of a drastic slowdown in the growth rate of rural income, with the latter falling to 1.8% per year whereas the growth rate of urban income remained stable (5.7% per year). Hence, the ratio of urban to rural incomes, as before measured at constant prices,[6] reached 2.36 in 1994. This evolution should be related to the fact that the retention rate of foreign exchange is higher for industrial goods compared to agricultural goods, which implies that the exchange rate depreciation pertaining to exports of industrial products (which, precisely, are mainly produced in urban areas) has been stronger. After 1993, in a context of exchange rate unification, the real effective exchange rate appreciated, and income disparity again started to lessen, subsequent to the high growth rate of rural incomes (10.1% compared to 5.6% in urban areas). However, rural and urban income inequality in China remains one of the highest in the world. In fact, the ratio of urban to rural income in nominal terms is 2.27 for China in 1996, whereas it is generally below 1.52 in developing countries (Yang and Zhou, 1996). In the country, the persistant strong discrepancy between urban and rural income can largely be imputed to the regulation of migration from rural to urban areas, which involves low levels of urbanization and lower urban poverty levels.

The disparity between urban and rural areas constitutes the main source of income inequality in China. According to World Bank estimates (World Bank, 1997, p. 3), the disparity between urban and rural areas would account for one-third of total income disparity as measured by the Theil index in 1995, and for half of the rise in the Theil index between 1985 and 1995. At the same time, income disparity between coastal and inland provinces (in favour of coastal provinces) explains one-fourth of total income inequality in 1995 and one-third of the rise in income inequality since 1985 (World Bank, 1997, p. 3). The higher growth of GDP per capita in coastal provinces compared to inland provinces is easy to explain. Coastal provinces enjoy natural advantages due to the proximity of foreign markets as well to communication infrastructures. The impact of such advantages on growth has been strengthened by the opening-up policy, with the latter being itself supported by the depreciation of the real exchange rate. In addition, coastal areas have benefited from preferential measures with respect to credit policy as well as to pilot reforms in the field of economic and trade liberalization (Tsui, 1996).

However, the phenomenon of higher growth of per capital income in coastal areas compared to inland areas since 1985, appears to be more pronounced for rural areas than for urban areas (World Bank, 1997, p. 21). This means that income disparity between urban and rural areas has increased more rapidly in inland provinces than in coastal provinces. Indeed, if considering the evolution of the ratio of urban to rural real per capita incomes, no longer for the whole country, but for each of the 28 Chinese provinces,[7] it appears that there are some differences in urban–rural income disparity between inland and coastal provinces.[8] The rise in the ratio of urban to rural incomes over the period 1985–1993 is indeed more pronounced for inland provinces than for coastal provinces. This result could not be expected *a priori*. Indeed, the share of foreign direct investments in total investment is higher in coastal provinces compared to inland provinces, and these investments are also more concentrated in industry, which should *a priori* be of benefit to urban areas. This result suggests that the specialization differential between coastal and inland provinces, with the activities of the former being more largely outward oriented, is more salient in rural areas than in urban areas. In fact, rural industrial activities have considerably developed since 1985 in coastal areas, contributing thereby to the rise in coastal rural incomes (Kao, 1995).

At first sight, it seems that, contrary to the effect usually expected, the relative income of rural households might have been adversely affected by the real depreciation of the Renmimbi, at least since 1985. However, there may have been an opposite effect in coastal areas.

3 MODELLING OF THE RELATIONSHIP BETWEEN THE REAL EFFECTIVE EXCHANGE RATE AND URBAN–RURAL INCOME DISPARITY

The economy is divided into two zones: the urban zone, which produces industrial goods and services, and the rural zone, whose production primarily consists of agricultural goods but also of industrial goods. In each zone, a rise in the relative price of (internationally) tradable goods, which is usually defined as the 'real exchange rate' in the literature relating to developing countries, exerts an effect on per capita income which is all the more favourable as agents produce a larger share and consume a smaller share of tradable goods. The rise in the relative price of tradable goods will therefore be translated into a change in urban–rural income disparity since urban and rural households do not produce and consume the same proportion of tradable goods.

However, the evolution of the relative price of internationally tradable goods to non-tradable goods differs with respect to the goods which are produced and to the goods which are consumed. Consequently, there are theoretically two different real exchange rates, with one applying to production and the other to consumption, which actually cannot be directly inferred from available price indexes. The real effective exchange rate, as calculated in the previous section, is only an approximation. It is therefore important to specify the relationship between the real effective exchange rate and the relative price of tradable goods, with respect both to production and consumption, and to assess the way the variations in these relative prices affect incomes in each zone.

3.1 The Relationship between the Real Effective Exchange Rate and the Relative Price of Tradable Goods (Consumed or Produced)

The real effective exchange rate, called ρ, can be defined as follows :

$$\rho = n\,\frac{P_C^*}{P_C} = n\,\frac{P_{CT}^{*\delta^*}\cdot P_{CNT}^{*(1-\delta^*)}}{P_{CT}^{\delta}\cdot P_{CNT}^{(1-\delta)}} \tag{13.1}$$

where,

n Nominal effective exchange rate

P_c and P_c^* Consumer price indexes of China and of its main trading partners

P_{CT} and P_{CNT} Price indexes of tradable and non-tradable consumption goods in China

P^*_{CT} and P^*_{CNT} Average price indexes of tradable and non-tradable consumption goods in China's main trading partners

δ and δ^* Weighting coefficients of tradable goods in the consumer price index of China and of country's main trading partners.

The price of tradable consumption goods vis-à-vis non-tradable goods in China (ψ) is equal to P_{CT} / P_{CNT}. Assume that China is a price taker on international markets and that consumed tradable goods in China are similar to those consumed in country's main trading partners.[9] Denote by θc, the coefficient of protection of consumption goods in China, so $P_{CT} = n\ P^*_{CT}\ \theta$. And suppose besides that the prices of non-tradable goods move in a parallel way in rural and urban zones, reacting similarly to macroeconomic policy,[10] so

$$P_{CNTi} = P_{CNT} \text{ and } \psi = n\ \frac{P^*_{CT}\ \theta_c}{P_{CNT}} \tag{13.2}$$

which implies,[11]

$$\psi = \rho^{\frac{1}{1-\delta}}\ \psi^{*\frac{(1-\delta^*)}{(1-\delta)}}\ \theta_c^{\frac{1}{(1-\delta)}} \tag{13.3}$$

where ψ^* is the relative price of tradable consumption goods abroad, ψ is an increasing function of ρ, with the elasticity of ψ relative to ρ equal to $1/(1\text{-}\delta) > 1$. Variations in ψ are therefore amplified compared to variations in ρ (Edwards, 1989).[12]

The relationship between the real effective exchange rate and the relative price of tradable goods to non-tradable goods produced in a given zone is more difficult to assess than for the consumption goods since produced tradable goods are different for each zone and cannot be equated to the tradable goods consumed abroad.

Denote by P_{Ti}, the price of tradable goods produced in zone *i*. Denote by P^*_{Ti} the international prices of these goods expressed in foreign currency and by θ_i, the protection coefficient of these goods. Assuming here again that China is a price taker on international markets, one can write:[13]

$$P_{Ti} = P^*_{Ti}\ .\ n\ .\ \theta_i \tag{13.4}$$

As the real effective exchange rate, ρ, is equal to $n\, P^*_C / P_C$, it flows that the relative price of tradable goods produced in zone i (γ_i) can be specified as (Guillaumont and Guillaumont Jeanneney, 1991, 1996):

$$\gamma_i = \frac{P_{Ti}}{P_{NTi}} = \frac{P^*_{Ti}}{P^*_C} \cdot \rho \cdot \theta_i \cdot \frac{P_C}{P_{NTi}} \tag{13.5}$$

If we make the simplifying assumption that non-tradable goods produced in both zones consist of consumer goods, the last term of the equation, that is, P_C / P_{NTi}, can be considered as equivalent to ψ^δ.[14] We thus obtain:

$$\gamma_i = \frac{P^*_{Ti}}{P^*_C} \cdot \rho^{\frac{1}{1-\delta}} \cdot \theta_i \cdot \left[\psi^{*\frac{(1-\delta^*)}{(1-\delta)}} \cdot \theta_c^{\frac{1}{1-\delta}} \right]^\delta \tag{13.6}$$

Like ψ, γ_i is an increasing function of ρ, with the elasticity of γ_i relative to ρ (1/1-δ) superior to 1. The relative price of tradable goods produced in zone i depends not only on the real effective exchange rate but also on the real international price of tradable goods which are specifically produced in the zone as well as of their related protection coefficient. Thus, assessing the effect of the variation in the real effective exchange rate on the disparity of incomes per capita between urban and rural areas requires the introduction of some variables to control for the evolution of the international price of goods which are specifically produced in each zone as well as for the protection policy pertaining to these goods. The expression in square brackets, which is common to urban and rural zones, may be neglected in the rest of the analysis.

When θ_i is smaller than 1, its evolution depends on the levy on producers, which results from the disconnection between the more or less regulated domestic prices and international prices. This was the case for most agricultural products until 1994 in China. Prior to reforms, the prices of agricultural products were artificially fixed at a low level by the government in order to finance industrialization. The level of levy was so high that agricultural production stagnated. Although the purchasing price of agricultural products rose sharply in the 1980s, the rate of levy on agricultural products still ranged between 16% and 50% in 1988 depending on products. The discrepancy between domestic and international prices declined rapidly in 1989, so that various agricultural products received some protection in 1989 and 1990 (Guo et al., 1993). This trend sharpened in the following years. In 1994, domestic prices for most agricultural products were very close to, or even exceeding, international prices. With respect to industrial products, China has rather resorted to a subsidy policy, which implies that θ_i is superior to unity.

3.2 Relative Price of Tradable Goods and Urban–Rural Income Disparity

In each zone i, the income (Y_i) is equal to production (Q_i) multiplied by price (P_i):

$$Y_i = Q_i \,.\, P_i \tag{13.7}$$

Production is a function of the working population (L_i) as well as of physical and human capital of each zone (K_i):

$$Q_i = A_i \, L_i^{\alpha} \, K_i^{\beta} \tag{13.8}$$

In a market economy, the use of production factors depends on the evolution of relative prices. In the case of China, it will be assumed that, over the period covered by the study, production factors are, to a large extent, exogenous. Indeed, we have in mind that migration from rural to urban areas is subject to regulations and that investments in both physical and human capital (health, education) remain largely controlled by the government. It will be assumed however that total factor productivity, denoted by $A_{i,}$ may be sensitive to variations in relative prices.

First, in assessing the impact of the relative price of tradable goods, it is important to distinguish, for each zone, between the production sector of tradable goods and the production sector of non-tradable goods:

$$Y_i = (Q_{Ti} \,.\, P_{Ti}) + (Q_{NTi} \,.\, P_{NTi}) \tag{13.9}$$

Let us divide the income of each zone i by its total population (N_i) and deflate it by the consumer price index of the zone (P_{ci}) in order to obtain the real per capital income (y_i). Denote by a_i, the share of tradable goods in total production of zone i: $a_i = Q_{Ti}/Q_i$. It implies that:

$$y_i = \frac{Y_i}{N_i \, P_{Ci}} = a_i \, \frac{A_i \, K_i^{\beta} \, L_i^{\alpha}}{N_i} \, \frac{P_{Ti}}{P_{Ci}} + (1 - a_i) \, \frac{A_i \, K_i^{\beta} \, L_i^{\alpha}}{N_i} \, \frac{P_{NTi}}{P_{Ci}} \tag{13.10}$$

Given the real exchange rate of zone i, $\gamma_i = P_{Ti}/P_{NTi}$ (which is specific to each zone since goods which are produced in the rural zone differ from goods produced in the urban zone), it flows that:[15]

$$y_i = \frac{A_i\, K_i^{\beta}\, L_i^{\alpha}}{N_i}\, \frac{P_{NTi}}{P_{Ci}}\, [a_i\, \gamma_i + (1 - a_i)] \tag{13.11}$$

Second, assessing the impact of the real exchange rate requires allowing for the variation in the relative price of consumed tradable goods. Indeed, if households in rural zones consume a larger proportion of non-tradable goods (partly because of self-consumption) compared to urban households, the depreciation of the real exchange rate will entail a smaller rise in consumer prices in the rural zone compared to consumer prices in the urban zone. This assumption seems relevant in the case of China in view of the evolution of the ratio of prices in the two zones (see Table 13A.1).

As we have assumed that prices of tradable goods consumed in urban and rural zones, as well as non-tradable ones, move in a parallel way, and that only the shares of these goods in household consumption are variable, it can be written that:

$$P_{Ci} = P_{CT}^{\delta_i} \,.\, P_{CNT}^{(1-\delta_i)}$$

where δ_i denotes the weighting coefficient of tradable goods in the consumer price index of zone i.

Given that $\psi = P_{CT}/P_{CNT}$, it flows that:

$$P_{Ci} = \psi^{\delta i} \,.\, P_{CNT}$$

and

$$y_i = \frac{A_i K_i^{\beta} L_i^{\alpha}}{N_i} \cdot \frac{P_{NTi}}{P_{CNT}\, \psi^{\delta i}} \left[a_i \gamma_i + (1 - a_i)\right] \tag{13.12}$$

Suppose again that non-tradable goods consist of consumption goods and so that $P_{Nti} = P_{CNT}$, this implies that:

$$y_i = \frac{A_i\, K_i^{\beta}\, L_i^{\alpha}}{N_i} \cdot \frac{1}{\psi^{\delta i}}\, [a_i\, \gamma_i + (1 - a_i)] \tag{13.13}$$

If denoting the urban zone and the rural zone by u and r, respectively, the ratio of real per capita incomes of the two zones (I) can be expressed as follows:

$$I = \frac{y_u}{y_r} = \frac{A_u}{A_r} \cdot \frac{K_u^{\beta}}{K_r^{\beta}} \cdot \frac{\dfrac{L_u^{\alpha}}{N_u}}{\dfrac{L_r^{\alpha}}{N_r}} \cdot \psi^{(\delta_r - \delta_u)} \cdot \left[\frac{a_u \gamma_u + (1 - a_u)}{a_r \gamma_r + (1 - a_r)}\right] \qquad (13.14)$$

Since γ_u et γ_r are increasing functions of the real effective exchange rate (see equation 13.6), it flows from the expression between square brackets that income disparity between urban and rural zones increases (that is, Y_u / Y_r increases) as the real exchange rate depreciates, if the urban zone produces a higher proportion of tradable goods compared to the rural zone ($a_u > a_r$). This assumption seems reasonable in the case of China. Of course, urban areas produce more services (which are essentially non-tradable) compared to rural areas; however, due to the self-sufficiency policy pursued by the Chinese authorities, the major part of agricultural production is devoted to self-consumption and to the protected domestic market. The share of self-consumption in the daily consumption expenditure was 59% in 1978 and was still 34% in 1995.[16] Agricultural products bought by the government are mainly for the consumption of urban zones. Farmers have been progressively allowed to sell the residual production (that is, the production after compulsory deliveries and self-consumption) on the domestic market. Exports and imports of agricultural products are still largely controlled by the government. Industrial activities in rural zones appear also mainly oriented towards the domestic market. The assumption relative to the ratio of tradable to non-tradable goods in rural and urban zones may however be opposite for coastal provinces where, agricultural production, and especially industrial operations in rural areas, are more largely export-oriented.

Moreover, the nature of the relationship between urban–rural income disparity and the real effective exchange rate is not altered when assuming that a_u and a_r are increasing functions of γ.

The adverse effect of the depreciation of the real effective exchange rate on urban–rural income disparity may however be mitigated (or even reversed) if rural households consume a lower share of tradable goods compared to urban households ($\delta_r < \delta_u$) as ψ is also an increasing function of the real effective exchange rate (see equations 13.3 and 13.14).

In order to assess the direction of the relationship between the real effective exchange rate and urban–rural income disparity, it is moreover important to discern the policy measures, which have specifically affected urban and rural incomes. As regards urban incomes, we think of the wage policy in the public sector. Prior to reforms, the Chinese government pursued a low wage policy in the public sector. It has since then tried to introduce a wage system linking wage levels to productivity. Thus bonuses and complementary wages have been introduced; fixed wages were replaced by floating wages. However, this bonus system has actually worked as a means to compensate for inflation and poor labour standards rather than as an effective means to reward individual performance. The pressure to allocate bonuses on an equal basis has strongly contributed to raising wages in the public sector. Moreover, urban agents may benefit from increased incomes due to the strong development of the parallel economy, which is itself favoured by the premium on the parallel market for foreign exchange (Yin and Stoever, 1994; Ding, 1998).

With respect to rural incomes, we think of the gradual implementation of the household responsibility system, which has notably improved the productivity of farmers. The agricultural household responsibility system was initiated in 1978 by farmers in the Anhui province. The system directly linked agricultural household compensation to production. Previously, farmers were compensated on an equitable basis, depending on the time spent on the farm. Owing to the strong incentives provided by the responsibility system, farmers have experienced very good performances. The system has been rapidly adopted in many other provinces, though it was acknowledged by the government as a national policy only in 1983.

The following control variables should thus be incorporated in the above model (equation 13.14) in order to estimate the relationship between the real effective exchange rate (ρ) and the ratio of urban to rural real per capita incomes (I):

- the relative evolution of the international terms of trade of industrial and agricultural goods (z), with the former being considered as equivalent to tradable goods produced in urban areas and the latter as equivalent to tradable goods produced in rural areas;
- the ratio of protection coefficients of industrial and agricultural goods (p);
- the ratio of urban to rural employment rates (relative to total population) (l);
- the relative levels of physical capital (k) and education per capita (e) in urban areas compared to rural areas;
- economic policy factors which specifically affect incomes in each zone, as the wage policy in the public sector (s), the foreign exchange

premium (ϕ) and the percentage of agricultural households resorting to the responsibility system (f).

Thus, the estimated function, with expected signs indicated below each variable, is as follows:

$$\begin{array}{c} I = f(\rho, z, p, l, k, e, s, \phi, f) \\ ?, +, +, +, +, +, -, +, + \end{array} \qquad (13.15)$$

According to the above model (see equation 13.14), the sign of the coefficient of ρ is *a priori* ambiguous.

4 ECONOMETRIC ANALYSIS

The econometric analysis comprises two stages. In the first stage, the analysis applies to the whole country for the period 1978–1996. Results exhibit a positive impact of the real effective exchange rate on the ratio of urban to rural incomes per capita, which means that the depreciation contributed to raise urban–rural income disparity. In the second stage, we shed light on the cross-incidence of the location (coastal or inland) of provinces with respect to the impact of the real effective exchange rate on urban–rural income disparity, using a panel analysis, in which the real exchange rate is multiplied by a dummy which controls for the coastal location of the various provinces. Results show that the positive effect of the real depreciation on the urban bias is mitigated (or even reversed) for coastal provinces.

4.1 Econometric Analysis for the Whole Country

Three econometric models were estimated. The first refers to equation 13.15 and aims at testing for the positive influence of the real effective exchange rate on the ratio of urban to rural real incomes. The two other models are designed to identify the channels through which the real exchange rate influences income disparity. More specifically, the second model, which excludes the variables relating to the use of production factors (l and k), allows for testing the assumption that the use of production factors does not depend on prices, and thus on the real exchange rate. In the third model, the dependent variable is the ratio of urban to rural nominal income per capita; based on the shift in the coefficient of the real exchange rate, the regression allows for testing whether the effect of the exchange rate occurs through consumer prices. Estimations are performed using annual series over the period 1978–1996. All variables are expressed in logarithms and their definitions are detailed in Annex 13A.3. Regression results are displayed in Table 13.1.

Due to data limitations, one of the variables included in the theoretic model could not be introduced in the regressions, namely, the relative education level in urban and rural areas. In China, there is a strong disparity of average education levels between urban and rural areas, which certainly contributes to the explanation of the disparity of per capita incomes between the two areas. However, according to the World Bank (1997 p. 33), the disparity has not significantly changed over time. Physical capital, for which there is no statistical information, was approximated by the real gross investment per capita.

We first performed stationarity tests on variables (see Table 13.2). Four variables (urban–rural income disparity, the ratio of urban to rural per capita investment, the real effective exchange rate of Renminbi and the real wage in the public sector) turned out to be stationary in level while all other variables appeared to be stationary in first difference. To assess whether our model is balanced, we also performed a test on the residuals of the regression, which appeared to be stationary. Therefore, following Granger (1995), we can infer that trends in variables, which are non-stationary in level, cancel out and that the model is balanced. According to Granger, in such a case, most of the dependent variable characteristics can be explained by the independent variables. However, this result only provides a necessary condition for a consistent specification, it does not constitute a sufficient condition. Therefore, the usual tests were also performed.

Control variables, some of which are proxies for theoretical variables, appeared to have the expected signs. The ratio of international prices (in dollars) of industrial and agricultural goods and the ratio of related protection coefficients have positive signs and thereby contribute to the increase in urban–rural income disparity. Ratios of urban to rural employment rates and urban to rural per capita investments both tend to broaden urban–rural per capita real income disparity. A positive variation in public sector wages appears to have the same impact. Moreover, it appears that the exchange premium tends to favour urban incomes. On the other hand, the agricultural household responsibility system exerts a favourable effect on rural incomes, as previously evidenced by Lin (1988), McMillan and Zhu (1989) and Johnson (1996), who estimated that the shift in the incentive structure induced by the system has entailed a rise in agricultural productivity ranging from 30% to 50%.

The real depreciation of the Renminbi contributed to the rise in urban–rural income disparity (through a positive effect on the ratio of urban

Table 13.1 Regression results, 1978–1996

Ratio of urban/rural per capita income	Real disparity 4.1	Real disparity 4.2	Nominal disparity 4.3
Explanatory variables			
Constant (*c*)	8.28***	6.18***	8.77***
	(6.24)	(23.1)	(5.78)
Real effective exchange rate of Renminbi (ρ)	0.12**	0.16***	0.16***
	(2.53)	(3.20)	(3.02)
International terms of trade industry/agriculture (*z*)	0.25**	0.32**	0.16
	(2.43)	(2.88)	(1.36)
Ratio of protection industry/agriculture (*p*)	0.24**	0.36***	0.10
	(2.12)	(3.14)	(0.80)
Ratio of urban/rural employment rates (*l*)	0.53**		0.44*
	(2.23)		(1.68)
Ratio of urban to rural real per capita investment (*k*)	0.08**		0.09**
	(1.95)		(2.53)
Real wage in the public sector (*s*)	0.24**	0.19**	0.48***
	(2.40)	(2.58)	(4.17)
Exchange premium on parallel markets (φ)	0.11***	0.36***	0.09**
	(3.44)	(3.14)	(2.53)
Share of agricultural households resorting to the responsibility system (*f*)	-0.44**	-0.45***	-0.48***
	(-8.13)	(-7.52)	(-7.77)

Adjusted R^2	0.95	0.93	0.93
F- statistics	45	44	32
DW test	2.32	1.97	2.48
LM test	0.46	0.10	0.82
BP test	0.15	1.00	0.56
Chow test	0.48	1.71	0.26

Note: *** = significant at the 1% level; ** = significant at the 5% level; * = significant at the 10% level.

to rural real per capita income). A 10% increase in the real effective exchange rate induces a 1.2% increase in the income disparity ratio (see regression 4.1, Table 1). This implies that the 127% increase in the exchange rate between 1985 and 1993 entailed a 15.2% increase in the ratio of urban to rural real income per capita.

In regression 4.2, Table 1, in which ratios of employment rates and per capita investments have been excluded from explanatory variables, as well as in regression 4.3, Table 1, in which the dependent variable is the ratio of urban to rural nominal per capita incomes, the coefficient of the real effective exchange rate amounts to 0.16 compared to 0.12 in regression 4.1, Table 1. The Wald test however indicates that these coefficients range in the same confidence interval, which suggests that the effect of the real exchange rate on urban–rural income disparity does not significantly arise from a change in the use of production factors (however, an increase in volumes may result from a rise in factor productivity). Moreover, the adverse effect of the real exchange rate on urban–rural income disparity which results from the relative variation in producer prices does not appear to be significantly mitigated by its effect on the relative variation in consumer prices in urban and rural zones.

4.2 Panel Data Analysis

To isolate the specificity of provinces with respect to their location (coastal or inland), an econometric analysis was conducted on panel data. The procedure allows the model to be tested using both the regional and temporal dimensions. The real effective exchange rate was thus multiplied by a dummy variable (μ) which takes the value 1 for coastal provinces and 0 for inland provinces. This enabled us to shed light on the differential impact of the real exchange rate with respect to province location. The expected sign of the dummy (μ) is negative. The panel specification can be described as follows:

$$I_{it} = f(\rho_t, l_{it}, k_{it}, f_{it}, s_{it}, z_t, \phi_t, p_{it}, \mu_* \rho_t, u_i, \varepsilon_{it})$$
u_i = individual effect
ε_{it} = error term

Since statistical data on investment by province divided into urban and rural areas are not available for the whole period, but only from 1985 to 1996, we estimated the model on two periods, namely, 1978–1996 without investment, and 1985–1996 with investment (see regressions 4.5 and 4.6, Table 13.3).[17]

Panel data are not balanced. We first tested whether our model entailed specific effects with respect to the individual dimension (within individual effects). The LM-test statistic of Breusch-Pagan is highly significant at the 1% level for all regressions. The LR-test, which enables us to test the OLS specification (without specific effects) against the specification with individual effects, also turns out significant. The results suggest the presence of specific effects, which leads to the rejection of the OLS specification without specific effects. Finally, the results of the Hausman-test do not allow rejection of a specification with random effects.

Table 13.2 Stationarity tests results

	Level	First difference
Ratio of urban/rural per capita real income (*I*)	-3.58**	
Real effective exchange rate of Renminbi (ρ)	-3.38**	
International industry/agriculture terms of trade (*z*)	-0.4	-4.41**
Ratio of industry/agriculture protection (*p*)	-0.17	-4.33**
Ratio of urban/rural employment rates (*l*)	-1.68	-3.74**
Ratio of urban/rural per capita investment (*k*)	-3.81**	
Real wage in the public sector (*s*)	-3.88**	
Exchange premium on parallel markets (ϕ)	-0.52	-3.40**
Residual of regression 4.1, Table 13.1	-5.17**	
Residual of regression 4.2, Table 13.1	-4.15**	
Residual of regression 4.3, Table 13.1	-5.21**	

Notes:
Critical values of MacKinnon are originated from MacKinnon (1991).
** = significant at the 5% level.

With respect to control variables, estimation results are on the whole similar to those obtained on time series. However, the ratio of employment rates (*l*) turns out insignificant over the 1978–1996 period though significant at the 10% level over the 1985–1996 period. This certainly reflects the poor quality of population data relative to provinces. We also controlled the quality of education, using the ratio of the number of students per teacher in urban areas to the number of students per teacher in rural areas. The variable did not turn out significant. Related regression results are not displayed in Table 13.3.

Let us first compare the results of the panel analysis over the 1978–1996 period (regression 4.5, Table 13.3) with the results of the analysis for the whole country (which excludes production factors) (see regression 4.2,

Table 13.1). Results of panel regressions exhibit a positive effect of the real effective exchange rate on the ratio of urban to rural per capita income, which appears slightly strengthened for inland provinces: the coefficient of the real effective exchange rate increases from 0.16 in the general model to 0.22 in the panel model. The coefficient of the dummy indicates that the effect of the real exchange rate in coastal provinces is only slightly positive (0.05). For the 1985–1996 period (regression 4.6, Table 13.3), the effect of the real effective exchange rate on inland provinces increases (0.24). As expected, the

Table 13.3 Regression results on panel data

	1978–1996	1978–1996	1985–1996
Ratio of urban/rural per capita income	4.4	4.5	4.6
Explanatory variables			
Real effective exchange rate of the Renminbi (ρ)	0.17***	0.22*** (8.70)	0.24*** (7.28)
International industry/agriculture terms of trade (*z*)	0.14*** (4.36)	0.12*** (4.15)	0.13*** (3.43)
Ratio of industry/agriculture protection (*p*)	0.17*** (5.11)	0.13*** (4.17)	0.15*** (3.48)
Ratio of urban/rural employment rates (*l*)	0.08 (1.52)	0.03 (0.54)	0.14* (1.68)
Ratio of urban/rural per capita investment (*k*)			0.04** (2.14)
Real wage in the public sector (*s*)	0.48*** (9.97)	0.46*** (10.7)	0.50*** (5.73)
Exchange premium on parallel markets (ϕ)	0.11*** (7.10)	0.10*** (6.40)	0.05*** (3.67)
Percentage of agricultural households adopting the responsibility system (*f*)	-0.42*** (-16.4)	-0.42*** (-17.6)	
Dummy variable (μ*ρ)		-0.17*** (6.72)	-0.29*** (6.30)
Number of observations	482	482	303
Adjusted R^2	0.64	0.67	0.65
F Statistics	23	27	17
LR test	207	242	197
LM test	310	299	148
Hausman test	15.1	14.2	8.7

Notes:
Critical values of MacKinnon are originated from MacKinnon (1991).
** = significant at the 5% level.

effect becomes slightly negative for coastal provinces (-0.05). Actually, in coastal provinces, rural agents produce and consume roughly the same proportion of internationally tradable goods as urban agents. Due to the proximity of foreign markets, a larger part of agricultural production is probably for export. In particular, since 1985, rural producers have engaged to a greater extent in the production of industrial goods, with the latter also being exported more often. At the same time, the share of services (non-tradable goods) provided in urban zones is larger in coastal provinces than in inland provinces.

5 CONCLUSION

The real depreciation of the Chinese currency before 1993 played a crucial role in the opening-up policy, but it also contributed to the raising of income inequality between urban and rural areas as it appears from the econometric analysis for the whole country. However, the panel analysis has shown that this phenomenon is only very significant in the inland provinces. Instead, in the coastal provinces, rural and urban agents seem to produce and consume the same proportion of tradable goods, chiefly because of rural industrialization. Inversely, in inland provinces the rural agents produce principally agricultural products for the domestic market, so that a real depreciation of the exchange rate did not favour them. This effect is not compensated in a significant manner by consumption of a greater share of non-tradable goods. So long as income disparity can be considered as prejudicial to growth (notably because disparity generates social frustrations), the appreciation of the exchange rate since 1994 can be seen as a favourable factor.

NOTES

1. See for instance Alejandro (1963), Twomey (1983), Edwards (1989), Agenor and Montiel (1996). See also the contributions of Knight (1976) and Morrisson (1991) which are closer to our analysis.
2. There are similar limitations with respect to the analysis of the relationship between the evolution of the exchange rate and the individual disparity of incomes.
3. See for instance the World Bank analysis study on the reasons for agricultural stagnation in Africa in the early 1980s (Berg, 1981), and more generally the contributions of Morrisson (1991), Bourguignon and Morrisson (1992), Guillaumont (1993) and Minot (1998).
4. The renminbinis the name of the Chinese currency while the yuan is the account unit.
5. As is usually done in the case of developing countries, the real effective exchange rate is calculated using the consumer price indexes of China and the country's major trading partners.

6. The ratio of nominal incomes was 2.63 in 1994.
7. Chinese provinces are officially classified in three zones according to their location. The coastal zone comprises three independent municipalities (Beijing, Tianjin and Shanghai), eight provinces (Hebei, Liaoning, Jiangsu, Zhejiang, Fujian, Shangdong, Guangdong and Hainan) and an independent region (Guangxi). The central zone includes eight provinces (Shanxi, Jilin, Heilongjiang, Henan, Anhui, Hubei, Hunan and Jiangxi) and an independent region (Inner Mongolia). The west zone comprises six provinces (Gansu, Shaanxi, Sichuan, Guizhou, Yunan and Qinghai), three independent regions (Ningxia, Xingjiang and Tibet) and one independent municipality (Chongqin, established in 1997). Inland provinces therefore consist of all non-coastal provinces, that is, the provinces of both the central and west zone. In our study, the independent region of Tibet and Hainan province (formed in 1988), are excluded due to statistical limitations. Data pertaining to Guangdong were corrected by excluding the data relative to Hainan before 1988.
8. Sources: *Quanguo Gesheng Zizhiqu Zhixiashi Lishi Tongji Ziliao Huibian 1949–1989 (China's Provincial Statistics, 1949–1989)* and *China Regional Economy, A Profile of 17 years of Reform and Opening Up*
9. This is a common hypothesis in the literature, which equates the real effective exchange rate to the relative price of tradable goods.
10. This implies that regional markets are integrated, which is certainly questionable in the case of China.
11. See Annex 2 for the derivation.
12. ψ^* tends to decrease over time, as a result of economic growth in the rest of the world, which may reduce ψ. We neglect this issue in our analysis.
13. Here, we neglect the fact that prior to the unification of exchange rates in 1994, the nominal exchange rate applying to the various exported goods might be different, due to different retention rates (see section 2).
14. Given that $\psi = P_{CT}/P_{CNT}$ and $P_C = P_{CT}^{\delta} \cdot P_{CNT}^{(1-\delta)}$, if $P_{CNT} = P_{NTi}$, it follows that $P_C/P_{NTi} = \psi^{\delta}$.
15. The assumption that a_i depends positively on γ_i would not alter the predictions of the model.
16. *China Economic Systems Reform Yearbook 1996*, p. 260.
17. Regression 4.4, Table 13.3, does not include dummy variables.

REFERENCES

Agenor, P.R. and P.J. Montiel (1996), *Macroeconomics Development*, Princeton, NJ: Princeton University Press.

Alejandro, C.F.D. (1963), 'A note on the impact of devaluation and the redistributional effect', *Journal of Political Economy*, 73, pp. 577–80.

Berg, E. (1981), *Accelerated development in Sub Saharan Africa. An Agenda for Action*, the World Bank, Washington, DC.

Bourguignon, F. and C. Morrisson (1992), *Adjustment and Equity in Developing Countries, A New Approach,* OCDE, series adjustment and equity in developing countries, Paris.

Cai, J.M. (1998), 'The differences of comparative productive forces and relative income between town and countryside in China, *Jingji Yanjiu* (*Economic Research Journal*), Monthly, No. 1, pp. 11–9.

Ding, J.P. (1998), 'China's foreign exchange black market and exchange flight: analysis of exchange rate policy', *Developing Economics*, XXXVI, 1, March, pp. 24–44.

Edwards, S. (1989), *Real Exchange Rates, Devaluation, and Adjustment, Exchange Rate Policy in Developing Countries*, Cambridge, MA, and London: MIT Press.

Granger, C.W.J. (1995), 'Modeling non linear relationships between extended-memory variables', *Econometrica*, 63(2), March, pp. 265–79.

Guillaumont, P. (1993), 'Politique d'ajustement et développement agricole', *Economie Rurale*, 216, July–August, pp. 20–9.

Guillaumont, P. and S. Guillaumont Jeanneney (1991), 'Exchange rate policies and the social consequences of adjustment in Africa', in A. Chhibber and S. Fischer (eds), *Economic Reform in Sub-Saharan Africa, A World Bank Symposium*, World Bank, Washington, DC, pp. 12–24.

Guillaumont, P. and S. Guillaumont Jeanneney (1996), 'Does devaluation lead to higher real producer prices to export crops in developing countries?', in M. Benoit-Cattin, M. griffon and P. Guillaumont (eds), *Economics of Agricultural Policies in Developing Countries*, Edition de la Revue Française d'Economie, Paris, pp. 125–54.

Guillaumont, P. and S. Guillaumont Jeanneney (1997), 'Politique de change et transition vers l'économie de marchés: expériences comparées de la Chine et du Vietnam', *Développement et transition vers l'économie de marché*, Actes des 3èmes Journées Scientifiques du Réseau Analyse économique et développement, AUPELF-UREF, Montréal, pp. 100–14.

Guillaumont Jeanneney, S. and P. Hua (1996), 'Politique de change et développement des exportations manufacturées en Chine', *Revue Economique*, May, 47(3) pp. 851–60.

Guo, S.T., X.H. Ma, F. Cai. and F.N. Zhong (1993), 'An Analysis of the current situation of China's agricultural protection, Zhongguo nongcun jingji (*China's Rural Economy*), No. 3, pp. 11–4.

Johnson, D.G. (1996), 'China's rural and agricultural reforms: successes and failures', *Working Paper*, No. 96/12, February, Chinese Economies Research Center, The University of Adelaide.

Kao, C. (1995), 'The impact of the development of township enterprises on population migration and rural–urban disparity', *Working Paper*, Chung-Hua Institution for Economic Research, NSC 83-0301-H-170-002, July, p. 138.

Knight, J.B. (1976), 'Devaluation and income distribution in less-developed economies', *Oxford Economic Papers*, 28(2), July, pp. 208–27.

Lin, J.Y.F. (1988), 'The household responsibility system in China's agricultural reform: a theoretical and empirical study', *Economic Development and Cultural Change*, 36(3), supplement, S199–S224.

Lin, J.Y.F., F. Cai and Z. Li (1998), 'Social consequences of economic reform in China: an analysis of regional disparity in the transition period', International Conference on Chinese Economy entitled Openness and Disparities in China, 22–23 October, IDREC/CERDI.

MacKinnon, J.G. (1991), 'Critical values for cointegration test', in R.F. Engle and C.W.J. Granger (eds), *Long-Run Economic Relationships: Readings in Cointegration*, Oxford: Oxford University Press, pp. 267–76.

McMillan, W.J. and L.J. Zhu (1989), 'The impact of China's economic reforms on agricultural productivity growth', *Journal of Political Economy*, 97(4) pp. 781–807.

Minot, N.W. (1998), 'Distributional and nutritional impact of devaluation in Rwanda', *Economic Development and Cultural Change*, 46(2), January, pp. 379–402.

Morrisson, C. (1991), 'Adjustment with growth and equity', *World Development*, Special Issue, November, pp. 1633–51.

Tsui, K.Y. (1996), 'Economic reform and interprovincial inequalities in China', *Journal of Development Economics*, 50, pp. 353–68.

Twomey, M.J. (1983), 'Devaluations and income distribution in Latin America', *Southern Economic Journal*, 49(3), pp. 804–21.

World Bank (1997), 'Sharing rising incomes disparities in China', in *China 2020*, Washington, DC: The World Bank.

Yin, J.Z. and W.A. Stoever (1994), 'Testing the causes of discontinuities in the black market exchange rate in China', *World Development*, 22(9), pp. 1413–24.

Yang, D.T., and H. Zhou (1996), 'Rural–urban disparity and sectoral labor allocation in China', paper presented at the annual meeting of the association for Asian Studies, April, Honolulu.

ANNEX 1

Table 13A.1 Evolutions of real incomes per capita, consumer prices in rural and urban areas, real and nominal effective exchange rates of Renminbi

	Real incomes per capita (yuans, 1990)					Consumer prices (indexes)			Effective exchange rates (indexes)	
	Rural 1	Urban 2	% (2)/(1)	Coastal 3	Inland 4	Rural 5	Urban 6	% (6)/(5)	Nominal 7	Real 8
1957	135	527								
1965	214	548								
1978	245	702	2.86	2.35	3.19	54.5	45.1	82.6	32.4	35.1
1979	294	813	2.77	2.24	2.90	54.6	45.9	84.1	28.6	33.4
1980	348	891	2.56	2.03	2.43	55.0	49.3	89.7	26.9	33.3
1981	402	906	2.25	1.83	2.09	55.6	50.5	91.0	51.3	68.7
1982	479	960	2.00	1.70	1.92	56.4	51.5	91.3	47.0	66.1
1983	544	1001	1.84	1.52	1.73	57.0	52.6	92.3	45.0	64.5
1984	605	1125	1.86	1.53	1.77	58.7	54.0	92.0	43.4	64.1
1985	656	1134	1.73	1.62	1.87	60.6	60.5	99.8	44.7	61.3
1986	659	1280	1.94	1.75	2.11	64.3	64.7	100.7	70.5	89.5
1987	678	1302	1.92	1.68	2.08	68.3	70.4	103.1	91.4	109.8
1988	679	1318	1.94	1.67	2.02	80.2	84.9	105.9	110.1	114.3
1989	629	1277	2.03	1.79	2.19	95.6	98.7	103.2	109.9	104.2
1990	686	1387	2.02	1.80	2.12	100.0	100.0	100.0	100.0	100.0
1991	693	1470	2.12	1.79	2.28	102.3	105.1	102.7	101.8	106.3
1992	732	1600	2.19	1.88	2.37	107.1	114.1	106.6	116.2	121.1
1993	757	1763	2.33	1.98	2.57	121.7	132.5	108.9	150.7	139.1

Table 13A.1 *(continued)*

	Real incomes per capita (yuans, 1990)					Consumer prices (indexes)			Effective exchange rates (indexes)	
	Rural	Urban	%	Coastal	Inland	Rural	Urban	%	Nominal	Real
	1	2	(2)/(1)	3	4	5	6	(6)/(5)	7	8
1994	813	1919	2.36	2.07	2.59	150.2	165.7	110.3	158.0	122.9
1995	894	2012	2.25	1.93	2.53	176.5	193.5	109.6	159.3	109.5
1996	1011	2079	2.06	1.79	2.32	190.4	210.5	110.6	153.3	99.3

Average annual growth rate of real per capita incomes (%)

	Rural	Urban
1957–78	2.88	1.37
1978–96	8.19	6.22
1978–85	15.12	7.10
1985–93	1.80	5.70
1993–96	10.10	5.60
1980–95	6.50	5.58
1980–85	13.55	4.94

Notes:
The Chinese currency is the Renminbi, but the monetary unit is the yuan.
Rural incomes are deflated by the rural consumer price index for the period 1985–1996; prior to 1985, retail prices are used because consumer prices are not available. Urban incomes are deflated by the urban consumer price index. The calculation of the real effective exchange rate of the Renminbi is detailed in Annex 3.

Sources: *China Statistical Yearbook 1997*, p. 293; *Quanguo Gesheng Zizhiqu Zhixiashi Lishi Tongji Ziliao Huibian 1949–1989* (China's Provincial Statistics, 1949–1989), p. 35.

ANNEX 2

Relationship between the Real Effective Exchange Rate (ρ) and the Relative Consumer Price of Internationally Tradable Goods (ψ)

As the real effective exchange rate (ρ) is defined as follows,

$$\rho = n \frac{P_{CT}^{*\delta *} \cdot P_{CNT}^{*(1-\delta *)}}{P_{CT}^{\ \delta} \cdot P_{CNT}^{\ (1-\delta)}}$$

We obtain,

$$\log \rho = \log n + \delta^* \log P_{CT}^* + (1-\delta^*) \log P_{CNT}^* - \delta \log P_{CT} - (1-\delta) P_{CNT}$$

As the relative consumer price of tradable consumption goods (ψ) is equal to:

$$\psi = \frac{P_{CT}}{P_{CNT}} = n \frac{P_{CT}^*}{P_{CNY}} \theta_c$$

Thus, $\log \psi = \log n + \log P_{CT}^* - \log P_{CNT} + \log \theta_c$

We therefore obtain

$$\log \psi - \log \rho = (1-\delta^*)\left[\log P_{CT}^* - \log P_{CNT}^*\right] + \delta\left[\log P_{CT} - \log P_{CNT}\right] + \log \theta_c$$

$$\log \psi - \log \rho = (1-\delta^*) \log \frac{P_{CT}^*}{P_{CNT}^*} + \delta \log \frac{P_{CT}}{P_{CNT}} + \log \theta_c$$

$$\log \psi - \log \rho = (1-\delta^*) \log \psi^* + \delta \log \psi + \log \theta_c$$

$$\log \psi = \frac{\log \rho}{1-\delta} + \frac{1-\delta^*}{1-\delta} \log \psi^* + \frac{\log \theta_c}{1-\delta}$$

Consequently, $\psi = \rho^{\frac{1}{1-\delta}} \cdot \psi *^{\frac{(1-\delta *)}{(1-\delta)}} \cdot \theta_c^{\frac{1}{(1-\delta)}}$.

ANNEX 3 STATISTICAL SOURCES AND DEFINITION OF VARIABLES

All Chinese annual statistics at the national level are from the *Statistical Yearbook of China*, various editions, whilst province level data are from *Quanguo Gesheng Zizhiqu Zhixiashi Lishi Tongji Ziliao Huibian 1949–1989 (China's Provincial Statistics, 1949–1989)* and *China Regional Economy, A Profile of 17 Years of Reform and Opening Up*. The exchange rate and the importance of trade between China and its main trade partners were provided by the IMF *International Financial Statistics*, and *Direction of Trade* respectively. The unit value of manufactured products for developing countries was obtained from the *International Trade Statistics Yearbook* and *Monthly Bulletin of Statistics of the United Nations*. The unit export value of agricultural products in China was provided by the UN Food and Agriculture Organization (FAO). The exchange rate on the parallel market is given in *World Currency Yearbook*, various editions, but for 1995 and 1996 data are from World Bank, *World Development Indicators*. All variables were converted in indexes (100 = 1990) and expressed in logarithms.

I = Ratio of urban/rural per capita real income. Deflators were consumer prices in urban areas and rural areas respectively. Retail prices for rural areas are used for the period 1978–1984, since consumer price indexes were not available for this period.

ρ = Real effective exchange rate of the Renminbi. It was constructed as the weighted geometric average of exchange rate indexes of the Renminbi, relative to the currencies of China's main export trading partners, multiplied by the ratio of the average of the consumer price indexes of trading partners to the consumer price index of China. Weights were modified each year (Paasche index) so as to allow for the rapid change in the geographical structure of Chinese trade over the period. Exchange rates were computed as the weighted average of the official rate (commercial rate from 1981 to 1984 and official rate for other years) applied to commercial transactions and of the rate (fixed until 1986 and free thereafter) applied on foreign exchange markets. The weighting of the two rates is defined based on the retention rate of exports. An increase in the effective exchange rate index corresponds to a depreciation.

z = International terms of trade (in dollars) of industrial and agricultural goods. Prices of industrial goods correspond to the unit export value of manufactured products (in dollars) for developing countries; prices of agricultural goods are given by the unit export value of China's agricultural products.

p = Relative ratio of protection of industrial and agricultural goods. The protection rate of industrial goods is measured by the ratio of the price of China's industrial products (expressed in yuans) to the unit export value of manufactured products for developing countries, converted in yuans. The protection rate of agricultural products is measured by the ratio of the purchasing price of agricultural products in yuans to the unit export value of China's agricultural products, expressed in dollars and converted into Chinese currency.

l = Ratio of urban to rural employment rate (relative to total population of each zone).

k = Relative level of gross investment in urban areas compared to rural areas, divided by the number of employed people.

s = Real wages in the public sector, defined as nominal wages deflated by urban consumer price indexes.

ϕ = Exchange rate premium on the parallel market. It is equal to the ratio of the price of foreign currencies on the parallel market compared to their price on authorized markets for foreign exchange.

f = Percentage of agricultural households resorting to the responsibility system. Related data were provided by Lin (1988) for the period 1978–1987. Percentages for the period 1988–1996 are supposed to be the same as those for 1987.

Index